Paul Lebowitz's 2011 Baseball Guide

A Complete Guide to the 2011 Baseball Season

Paul Lebowitz

iUniverse, Inc.
Bloomington

Paul Lebowitz's 2011 Baseball Guide
A Complete Guide to the 2011 Baseball Season

iUniverse books may be ordered through booksellers or by contacting:

iUniverse
1663 Liberty Drive
Bloomington, IN 47403
www.iuniverse.com
1-800-Authors (1-800-288-4677)

ISBN: 978-1-4620-0231-3 (sc)
ISBN: 978-1-4620-0232-0 (ebk)

Printed in the United States of America

iUniverse rev. date: 3/4/2011

Contents

American League East Predicted Standings

		Wins	Losses	GB
1.	Boston Red Sox	100	62	---
2.	New York Yankees	89	73	11
3.	Tampa Bay Rays	86	76	14
4.	Toronto Blue Jays	83	79	17
5.	Baltimore Orioles	66	96	34

Boston Red Sox

2010 Record: 89-73; 3rd place, American League East.

2010 Recap:

The Red Sox had built their 2010 club based on pitching and defense and eschewed the usual purchasing and/or trading of big-ticket free agents and stars to try a stat zombie tenet of run prevention. Early in the season, the pitching was injury-riddled and struggled; and the defense wasn't as good as it was supposed to be.

Injuries to Mike Cameron, Josh Beckett, Jacoby Ellsbury, Dustin Pedroia and Kevin Youkilis would've been a convenient excuse for the Red Sox to finish as a .500 team. Instead, spurred by above-and-beyond performances from Adrian Beltre, Clay Buchholz and Jon Lester; a renaissance from David Ortiz; and with unsung youngsters and fill-ins Ryan Kalish, Daniel Nava, Darnell McDonald and Bill Hall, they finished close to a playoff spot.

Only the presence of two superior (and healthier) teams, the Yankees and Rays, kept the Red Sox from what would've been a heroic berth in the playoffs.

2011 ADDITIONS:

1B Adrian Gonzalez was acquired from the San Diego Padres.
LF Carl Crawford was signed to a 7-year, $142 million contract.
RHP Bobby Jenks was signed to a 2-year, $12 million contract.

RHP Dan Wheeler was signed to a 1-year, $3 million contract with 2012 club option.
RHP Matt Albers was signed to a 1-year, $875,000 contract.
RHP Jason Bergmann signed a minor league contract.
LHP Andrew Miller was acquired from the Florida Marlins, was non-tendered and signed a minor league contract.
RHP Alfredo Aceves signed a 1-year, split contract for $650,000 in the big leagues; $200,000 in the minors.
INF Drew Sutton signed a minor league contract.
LHP Dennys Reyes signed a minor league contract.
Pitching coach Curt Young was hired.

2011 SUBTRACTIONS:

3B Adrian Beltre was not re-signed.
C/1B Victor Martinez was not re-signed.
INF/OF Bill Hall was not re-signed.
3B/1B Mike Lowell retired.
2B/OF Eric Patterson was traded to the San Diego Padres.
1B Anthiny Rizzo was traded to the San Diego Padres.
RHP Casey Kelly was traded to the San Diego Padres.
OF Reymond Fuentes was traded to the San Diego Padres.
LHP Scott Schoeneweis was released.
INF Felipe Lopez's option was declined.
LHP Dustin Richardson was traded to the Florida Marlins.
C Dusty Brown was not re-signed.
RHP Taylor Buchholz was non-tendered.
RHP Fernando Cabrera was not re-signed.
3B Jack Hannahan was not re-signed.
OF Jonathan Van Every was not re-signed.
Pitching coach John Farrell was hired to manage the Toronto Blue Jays.

2011 PROJECTED STARTNG ROTATION: Josh Beckett; Jon Lester; John Lackey; Clay Buchholz; Daisuke Matsuzaka; Tim Wakefield.

2011 PROJECTED BULLPEN: Jonathan Papelbon; Bobby Jenks; Daniel Bard; Dan Wheeler; Hideki Okajima; Matt Albers; Scott Atchison; Michael Bowden; Felix Doubront.

2011 PROJECTED LINEUP: C-Jarrod Saltalamacchia/Jason Varitek; 1B- Adrian Gonzalez; 2B-Dustin Pedroia; 3B-Kevin Youkilis; SS-Marco Scutaro; LF-Carl Crawford; CF-Mike Cameron; RF-J.D. Drew; DH-David Ortiz.

2011 BENCH: OF-Jacoby Ellsbury; INF-Jed Lowrie; OF-Darnell McDonald; OF-Ryan Kalish; OF-Daniel Nava; OF-Josh Reddick.

2011 POSSIBLE CONTRIBUTORS: 1B-Lars Anderson; INF-Yamaico Navarro; RHP-Junichi Tazawa; RHP Robert Coello; RHP-Alfredo Aceves; LHP-Dennys Reyes.

ASSESSMENTS MANAGEMENT:

There are always the relentless defenders of everything GM Theo Epstein does as if it's part of some master scheme to conquer the baseball world.

Few see it for what it is as the Red Sox and Epstein occasionally and conveniently forget what they said in the past to repair holes that their reliance and experimentation with stat zombie tenets like "run prevention" have created.

Much like the winter of the 2006-2007 season when a missed playoff spot caused the Red Sox to toss money at each and every one of their problems and were rewarded with a World Series win, the strategy of pitching and defense was put aside as was the attempt to sign affordable and pluggable players like Adrian Beltre and Mike Cameron.

In the winter of 2010-2011 the Red Sox went to the checkbook and got the best that money could buy.

By signing Carl Crawford and trading for Adrian Gonzalez, the Red Sox got the best of both worlds. They acquired excellent defenders and MVP-caliber bats to bolster a lineup that was productive despite the injuries, but needed to replace Adrian Beltre and Victor Martinez;

they also needed to make the lineup more intimidating. As much as it's said that the Red Sox "still had the second best offense in the American League in 2010", there was something missing and it was *not* due to injuries.

They were streaky; they were able to be pitched to.

Despite the aforementioned above-and-beyond the call work of the youngsters and journeymen bench players, the Red Sox were smart enough to strike when they had the opportunity. Epstein jumped in on Gonzalez and gave up youngsters who weren't going to contribute to the current Red Sox club. Because they've been so smart with their draft picks, they were able to surrender top prospects like Casey Kelly to get Gonzalez.

Epstein is one of the best GMs in baseball, but it's not due to any evil, long-range plan to rule the world. In fact, when the Red Sox have gotten into trouble it was when they relied on shaky ideas like the "closer-by-committee"; held fast to the storyline that they didn't have the money to make major mid-season acquisitions as they claimed in 2006; or went with "run prevention".

There's nothing wrong with covering up one's mistakes with money. In fact, that's what *has* to be done. It's the height of selfishness and arrogance to cling to that which isn't working. Epstein addressed every need—the lineup and bullpen—the Red Sox had. He did it by spending on Crawford, Bobby Jenks and Dan Wheeler; and by trading young players for Gonzalez.

No one's going to notice how they did it if they play up to their potential and Epstein and his staff will get the credit. It's not exactly a stat zombie how-to manual.

Who cares?

For a manager with two World Series wins to his credit, Terry Francona probably did the best job of his career in 2010.

There was every excuse in the book for the team to fall apart as the injuries mounted and the blueprint of the front office was decimated. But rather than make excuses, the Red Sox continued to win and a major part of that was the way Francona handles his clubhouse.

Contrary to the popular notion that he's the "best" manager in baseball, he does have flaws. Francona is still enacting the edicts of the front office; it's one of the main reasons (along with the World Series wins and handling the Boston media) that he's survived as long as he has. He's entrenched now, but he's not in a strategic class with a Tony La Russa who can win with less talent because of his strategic acumen and the work of his pitching coach, Dave Duncan.

That said, there's probably not a better manager *for the Red Sox* than Francona. He knows his place and generally makes the correct moves. In the hierarchy of the Red Sox, Francona is what he is. When he got the job, it was because he was willing to take short money for the opportunity; he'd do as he was told by the front office; and he was an agreeable choice for Curt Schilling to okay a trade to Boston. Now he's a major part of their success.

Much like Epstein, what difference does it make that he's not La Russa? He's Terry Francona and he's got two championship rings and players throughout baseball respect him, like him and want to play for him.

STARTING PITCHING:

Josh Beckett and John Lackey were supposed to be the veteran anchors of the starting rotation with terrific post-season pedigrees. Both were disappointing.

Beckett started only 21 games in 2010 due to a back injury and when he pitched, he was terrible for long stretches. His numbers were across-the-board awful. He allowed 151 hits in 127 innings; gave up 20 homers; and he walked 45 in those 127 innings a year after walking 55 in 212 innings.

Having signed a $68 million contract extension to forgo his pending free agency, the Red Sox need Beckett to rebound into the pitcher he was from 2007-2009.

If he's healthy, he's young enough (31 in May) that he can regain his form; I'd be concerned about the injury issues he's had in recent years. If it was an elbow or shoulder, that would be one thing; but he's had issues with his oblique and his back. This is not something to dismiss.

I'd expect Beckett to rebound and have at least an 170-190 inning year and 13-16 wins. It helps that the Red Sox have an excellent offense, defense and bullpen to support him when he runs into trouble. Mere competence will get him 15 wins if things go as they should in other areas.

At the very least, after he missed time in his final two seasons with the Angels with shoulder problems, Lackey was durable for the Red Sox pitching 215 innings. For the most part, he was good enough in 2010. His numbers were blown up by a few starts (mostly early in the season) in which he got shelled. He's always allowed around a hit-per-inning and the bad starts made that look far worse than normal as he allowed 233 in 215 innings. His strikeout numbers and control were in line with what he usually delivers as well.

Lackey's about guts more than stuff; the transition from laid back Anaheim to crisis-a-day Boston couldn't have been easy despite his history of handling pressure. Lackey will have a bounce back year and win 15-18 games.

The true emerging stars of the Red Sox starting rotation are their homegrown lefty-righty duo of Jon Lester and Clay Buchholz.

Lester just turned 27 and has emerged as one of the top-tier pitchers in all of baseball. In 2010 he pitched over 200 innings for the third year in a row; he won 19 games; he struck out 225; his hits/innings-pitched ratio improved to 167/208; he only allowed 14 homers and finished fourth in the AL Cy Young Award voting.

He's improved every single full year he's been in the big leagues and is prepared to step forward as the ace in name and not simply the "ace of the future". He'll contend for the Cy Young Award and win 20 games for the first time.

Buchholz justified the Red Sox faith and their reluctance to include him in any trade (especially for Adrian Gonzalez who they got anyway).

Buchholz developed more slowly than Lester—partially because the Red Sox didn't have room for him in the rotation; partially because they were babying him. Now, at age 26, he too is blossoming into a top-of-the rotation starter. The beauty of the Red Sox depth is that he won't be required to throw 200 innings this season if they want to continue to incrementally increase his workload.

He went 17-7 with a sparkling 2.33 ERA and 142 hits allowed in 173 innings. He missed time in 2010 with a hamstring problem, but that should be of little concern going into 2011. There could be something of a sophomore slump since Buchholz just completed his first full season in the big leagues; a 2.33 ERA is hard to match for a young pitcher, but he doesn't *have* to repeat that work to be a successful starter with the Red Sox lineup and defense.

A columnist for NESN suggested that Daisuke Matsuzaka might be the "best no. 5 starter ever".

Yah.

That would make sense if he'd never seen Daisuke Matsuzaka pitch. Or if he even knew what he was talking about.

Considering the hype (stifling and absurd); the posting money ($51 million); the contract ($52 million); and his performance (mediocre), he's been a bust.

The problem with Matsuzaka isn't simply that the expectations were too high or that he cost too much money; the problem with Matsuzaka is that he's the type of pitcher who teases with a brush at greatness and then reverts back to what he is: a pitcher who can't throw consistent strikes, can't pitch deeply into games, nor be trusted to stay healthy.

This is before getting into his complaints over the training regimen in North America in comparison to those in Japan.

On the surface, he doesn't look that bad. His 2008 season of 18-3 was misleading because he was the beneficiary of an excellent team with a deep bullpen playing behind him; he was injured for chunks of 2009; and through August of 2010, he'd pitch 5-6 innings (with 100 or so pitches), give up 3 runs here, 4 runs there, 7 runs in this game; 0 runs in that game—and end up with a winning record.

But he can't be trusted. What's most aggravating about him is that lack of definition in his game. I'd rather have a pitcher who I at least know is going to go out there, give me 7 innings, give up 4 runs, gut his way through and do that every single time. With Matsuzaka, he almost no-hits the Phillies, then slowly degenerates back into the 3-4 runs in 5 innings pitcher he is.

He'll win 12 or more games on this team because they're so good, but don't think anyone's comfortable with him as the starting pitcher that day and I'm sure the Red Sox would love to be rid of him.

"The best no. 5 starter ever"?

Please.

With Matsuzaka's faults in mind and the injury histories of the other starters, it's nice to have Tim Wakefield still around just in case. Yes, he's 44. No, he can't pitch as often nor as well as he did when he was younger; but he's still able to start or relieve and is willing to do anything to help the team win. Wakefield's body has broken down in recent years, but he'll still be there when they need him and, given the club's history, they *will* need him at some point. And he'll deliver.

BULLPEN:

Jonathan Papelbon and the Red Sox are entering their final season together. He's sick of them not respecting the work he's done with a long-term contract extension; they're sick of him being Jonathan Papelbon.

The Red Sox aren't going to sign him to a big contract and he's going to go elsewhere to get paid. I had thought (and said repeatedly) that the Red Sox were going to trade Papelbon this winter. I almost guaranteed it. In fact, I might have guaranteed it. But now, I think they'll keep him for the year to try and win another championship with the proven post-season closer on their side, then let him leave and take the draft pick compensation when he signs elsewhere.

On the field, Papelbon was inconsistent in 2010; but he was reliable for the most part. In truth, his ancillary numbers were consistent from 2009 (when he had a 1.85 ERA and 38 saves) to 2010 (when he had a 3.90 ERA and 37 saves). Papelbon's stats were nearly identical from one year to the next. His strikeouts, homers, hits per inning and walks were right in line with what he's always done. There were a few games in 2010 in which he got blasted and saw his ERA skyrocket.

Papelbon is a top-tier closer and he'll want to have a superb year to ensure a long-term deal with someone for a lot of money.

Erstwhile White Sox closer Bobby Jenks—another reliever with a post-season pedigree and a championship ring—signed with the Red Sox to be their set-up man. Jenks's fastball isn't the easy 100 it was earlier in his career as he effortlessly hit the triple digits with regularity and he's gotten progressively worse after emerging as a force in the White Sox championship run during the 2005 season. That said, he still throws very hard and perhaps the change-of-scenery will help him regain his form.

Jenks's strikeouts per innings pitched had declined precipitously from 2006 onward, but he was back over one-per-inning in 2010. Jenks throws strikes and doesn't usually allow many homers (3 in 52 innings last season); his ERA is bloated for a closer, but that stems more from his gacks. When he's off, he's *off* and gets ripped all over the place. But for the most part, he was reliable for the White Sox in his time there. He'll do fine as a set-up man with the Red Sox.

Had Papelbon been traded, Daniel Bard was seen as the heir apparent and new closer; he had some trouble in his save opportunities last season and that may have given the Red Sox pause before handing him the job especially if they had it in mind to craft the juggernaut they constructed this winter. A bad or unprepared closer can wreck any team's season as the Braves showed year-after-year in the 1990s and early-to-mid 2000s.

Bard's fastball is also up around the 100-mph range and he struck out 76 in 74 innings in 2010. He can be a bit wild with 30 walks in those 76 innings and he allowed 6 homers. With the presence of Jenks, there will be less pressure on Bard and the 25-year-old will learn how to be a big game reliever without the eyes of Boston upon him wondering if he can handle it.

Veteran Dan Wheeler signed a 1-year contract to further bolster the Red Sox bullpen. Wheeler also has closing experience and has pitched in many playoff games with the Rays and Astros. He's an intense competitor who throws strikes. He gives up too many homers and his slider is the key to his success.

Lefty Hideki Okajima was non-tendered by the Red Sox and then re-signed. The normally reliable Okajima had a bad year in 2010. His WHIP rose from 1.262 to 1.717; his normally solid numbers against both lefties and righties took a nosedive. Okajima regained his form over the last month of the season. With the fluctuating performances prevalent in the careers of veteran relievers, I'd expect a return to form from Okajima in 2011. Even with that, I'd probably like to have another veteran lefty in the bullpen to help him along.

Former Oriole and Astro Matt Albers signed a 1-year contract. I've always liked his fastball, but his results are what they are. Aside from 2008 when he had some success, Albers has always been inconsistent at best. He's wild; gives up too many hits and homers; and doesn't strike out batters with any great frequency. As an extra arm, he'll be fine with the Red Sox as long as they don't ask—or expect—too much.

Journeyman Scott Atchison was an unsung hero for the Red Sox in 2010. Atchison had brief shots with the Mariners and Giants before going to Japan. He returned to North America and pitched serviceably for the Red Sox. He's a veteran long reliever who probably won't have much work to do with the Red Sox starting rotation being as solid as it is, but he's good to have around as he'll do anything asked and give length in a game to rest the other relievers.

Michael Bowden is another of the Red Sox homegrown arms. The 24-year-old righty has been a starter in the minors and pitched quite well. There's not much room in the Red Sox current starting rotation for him unless Matsuzaka pitches so terribly that he gets pulled and Wakefield can't handle the full time job as a starter at this point in his career. Bowden can also be a long reliever with much more upside than Atchison.

Felix Doubront could be the second lefty (or first lefty) out of Francona's bullpen. He's lean and deceptive and dominated lefty bats in 2010. He's been a starter in the minors, but as said earlier, there's little room in the Red Sox starting rotation. Doubront is a sleeper as a lefty specialist.

The Red Sox signed veterans Dennys Reyes and Alfredo Aceves to contracts and invited them to spring training. Reyes's is a minor league deal; Aceves's is a split contract. Reyes is a solid veteran lefty specialist; Aceves is returning from injury.

LINEUP:

I tore into the Red Sox when they re-signed Jason Varitek.

In fairness, this was prior to their acquisitions of Adrian Gonzalez and Carl Crawford, but there was a basis for my ire. The Red Sox, more than any other club, eschew sentiment in their treatment of former stars. Varitek can't hit anymore; he can't really throw anymore; he's injury-prone; and he was living off his reputation as the "captain and leader" of the Red Sox as they continually brought him back for diminishing returns. Had the lineup stayed the same as it was last season with Jacoby Ellsbury and Mike Cameron both playing regularly and in need of a new third baseman, then it would have been a disastrous and mistaken decision to bring Varitek back.

That was before they supercharged the offense.

The prior lineup had black spots that were evident and exploitable; Varitek was one of those black spots. Now, they can carry him in the lineup in a platoon role. With the reputations of Beckett, Lackey, Papelbon and Jenks, they need a conduit to the manager to run the clubhouse and Varitek—despite the tiresome nature of his "intangibles"—is the man to do it.

Jarrod Saltalamacchia has yet to fulfill the potential that made him a first round pick of the Braves in 2003 and a centerpiece of the Mark Teixeira trade from the Rangers to Atlanta.

Saltalamacchia has been injury-prone with back injuries, leg injuries, hand injuries; he hasn't hit when he's gotten the chance to play, but the potential is still there; it's put up or shut up time for him. He *should* be the Red Sox everyday catcher, but will he be able to stay healthy? He's got the quirky personality to handle Boston. He doesn't throw well from behind the plate and the Red Sox pitchers aren't going to be happy if there's a dispute on pitch selection; one would assume they'd be more comfortable with Varitek catching them.

It's a bad sign that Saltalamacchia didn't hit in the hitter's heaven of Arlington while he was with the Rangers.

Only about to turn 26, there's time for Saltalamacchia to re-start his career. This may be his last shot with a contending team and I'm dubious as to whether he'll come through. The Red Sox may be on the lookout for a veteran catcher at mid-season the likes of Ronny Paulino from the Mets or someone of his ilk.

Epstein finally got his power bat when he traded for Adrian Gonzalez.

It's long been assumed that the Red Sox were going to be at the front of the line if and when Gonzalez became a free agent at the end of the 2010 season; they were trying to get him in a trade going back at least a year. The Padres were facing the certainty of knowing Gonzalez was going to leave amid the hope that they'd again receive the great pitching they got in 2010 that allowed them to contend with a weak offense. Had they waited until mid-season, there was the chance that not only would Gonzalez be on the market, but so too would Albert Pujols and Prince Fielder.

The best choice for them was to trade Gonzalez and the Red Sox were waiting.

Gonzalez is one of the best all-around players in baseball. He'll be 29 in May, so he's just entering his prime; he's put up massive numbers playing his home games in a cavernous home park; he's a terrific fielder; and he's the type of person who'll thrive in the pressure of Boston.

Gonzalez has yet to sign a contract extension to preclude his free agency, but there are persistent rumors that the contract is in place and is only being held up by the Red Sox desire to avoid complications with the luxury tax. He's not going anywhere.

Adrian Gonzalez is going to contend for the MVP and those who didn't know who he was because he was playing in a moderate baseball town like San Diego will realize how good he is. He's going to have a huge year.

Star second baseman Dustin Pedroia missed almost the entire second half of the 2010 season with a broken left foot. He's an excellent all-around player and a feisty mouth on the field who isn't afraid to do whatever he has to do to win.

Foot problems are no joke and it's something to watch once spring training starts; apart from that, Pedroia will put up the numbers as he's done since his big league arrival.

Kevin Youkilis's versatility was what allowed the club to go after Gonzalez in the first place. That he doesn't complain and is willing to do anything he's asked—including shifting from his Gold Glove position of first base to third—is indicative of why the Red Sox have been so consistently good over the past decade.

Youkilis is a perennial MVP candidate who missed the last two months of the season after a thumb injury. The Red Sox might miss Adrian Beltre's defense at third slightly, but Youkilis is *not* a defensive liability at third. Just as he worked his way into becoming one of the most dangerous hitters in baseball, he worked his way into being a Gold Glove first baseman. This isn't to say he'll win a Gold Glove at third, but don't put it past him.

Marco Scutaro had the usual Scutaro-type year in 2010. He hit his 11 homers; had 38 doubles; got on base a fair amount; played okay defense; and provided a big hit here and there. In the Red Sox lineup, he's not a focal point, but is a bit dangerous if the pitcher makes a mistake. What's lost in all the free agent shortstops and attempted acquisitions the Red Sox have made in recent years like Julio Lugo and Edgar Renteria is that neither lived up to their billing; Scutaro, at the very least, did that. The billing wasn't in bright lights and too much wasn't expected of him, but he delivered as he was supposed to and will again in 2011.

Not expected to be major factors in the race for Carl Crawford (they were supposedly more interested in Jayson Werth), the Red Sox struck like lightning and nabbed the star left fielder with a deal worth $142 million.

Much has been suggested about Crawford being a speed player who's going to be failing by the time the contract is five years old.

It's silly.

Crawford is 29; he hits the ball to all fields and hits it with authority; he's a great athlete who'll learn to handle the nuance of the Green Monster; he'll steal bases and, although he occasionally lapses on the basepaths, is still fast enough to overcome any mistakes.

I could see if Crawford were a Willie Wilson or Vince Coleman who couldn't do much of anything without his speed, but even if (I don't say when because players like Rickey Henderson and Lou Brock were still able to maintain their speed and basestealing acumen late into their careers) he does lose a step or three, he's still going to hit. Crawford is going to bash that wall in left field and have a ton of extra base hits.

He's going to have a tremendous year and compete with Gonzalez for the MVP. This was a great signing for the Red Sox.

The consensus belief is that Jacoby Ellsbury will be the regular center fielder for the Red Sox, but I think when all is said and done Mike Cameron will get a bulk of the playing time. Ellsbury has been injury prone and, bottom line, Cameron is more productive at the plate. Ellsbury may be trade bait.

Cameron and Ellsbury both missed significant time with injuries in 2010 and will probably both receive playing time in center early in the season. Cameron has a history of, like Scutaro, doing what it is Cameron does. He hits his 20 homers; is *very* streaky; plays good defense; and strikes out a lot.

J.D. Drew had a subpar year in 2010. His usually high on base percentage was down to .341 (his career mark is .387); he hit 22 homers and had 24 doubles. This is likely Drew's last year in Boston as he's a free agent at the end of the season. He'll want to cash in one more time in his career at age 35, so he should have a good comeback season. The Red Sox lineup is so strong that Drew won't have to do too much which will allow him to relax and return to form.

David Ortiz complained openly about not receiving a contract extension from the Red Sox; about the club exercising his $12.5 million option for 2011; that he was disrespected as he got off to another slow start and began hitting in mid-May when he was again thought to be finished.

Epstein and his staff basically shrugged at Ortiz's complaints which, much like those of Varitek's, were meaningless. What was he going to do about it? Not come to spring training?

Unless he has a tremendous year or takes a short term deal to stay (both viable possibilities), this could be the last year in Boston for Ortiz. I'm going to cease writing Big Papi off. I defended him in 2009 when he wasn't hitting because his problems looked more mechanical than due to losing his skills. In 2010, he looked lost and proved me and a lot of people wrong. In this lineup, he won't be the focal point and he'll put up his 30 homers and usual good on base numbers.

BENCH:

Jed Lowrie had a fine year as a utility infielder after injuries and slumps sabotaged him in 2009. Batting .287 with a .381 OBP and 9 homers, Lowrie was a major part of the Red Sox staying in contention through all their injuries. It's a benefit to have a switch-hitting utility player on the bench.

Jacoby Ellsbury missed almost the entire season with a persistent rib injury from a collision with Beltre. I'm admittedly not a fan of Ellsbury. He's never going to hit with enough power to justify playing every day with the Red Sox. He's got a sweet lefty swing and steals lots of bases, but to me they're better off with Cameron playing center field regularly over Ellsbury. I'd try to re-establish Ellsbury's value and trade him.

Darnell McDonald was an afterthought before the injuries mounted. He'd pinballed from the Orioles to the Twins to the Rays to the Indians before landing in Boston. With Cameron, Ellsbury and Drew in and out of the lineup, McDonald had a lot of big hits playing all three outfield positions.

Ryan Kalish is a young outfield prospect who was pressed into duty amid all the injuries. The 22-year-old acquitted himself well and could see some time in center field depending on what happens with Cameron/Ellsbury. He's shown some pop, good baserunning skills and the ability to get on base in the minors.

Daniel Nava's story was everywhere in 2010. A former independent league player, the then-27-year-old's lone homer last season was a grand slam against the Phillies on the Fox Game of the Week. The switch-hitter has murdered the ball in the minors and will be a useful fifth outfielder in 2011.

Josh Reddick is another outfield prospect who's struggled in the high minors and in brief shots with the big club. He'll probably be at Triple A Pawtuckett.

PREDICTION:

Ridiculous comparisons of the 2011 Red Sox to the 1927 Yankees or any of the greatest teams in history aside, this is the best team in the American League. By a lot.

The have power; they have speed; they have good defense; they have deep starting pitching; and a very good, battle-tested bullpen. Contrary to popular belief, there are holes. Drew is injury-prone; Ortiz will eventually hit a wall; the catching situation is unsettled.

These are negligible issues. Like the winter of 2006-2007, the Red Sox threw money at their problems. Unlike the winter of 2006-2007, they signed quality in Carl Crawford and by trading for Adrian Gonzalez.

Winning the Hot Stove championship is meaningless—the Mets have proven that repeatedly—but the Red Sox are primed to make a wire-to-wire run to the playoffs and go deeply into the playoffs when they get there.

Don't forget that they also have the prospects and aggressive GM to make bold mid-season acquisitions if they feel the need to do so. Jose Reyes or Carlos Beltran of the Mets come to mind as possible mid-season lineup boosts.

Crawford and Gonzalez will compete for the MVP; Lester for the Cy Young Award. Papelbon will have a wonderful year in his free agent audition.

This Red Sox team is the class of the American League; they're far better than any of their competitors including the Yankees and will run away with the American League East and, like that 2007 team, will advance to the World Series.

PREDICTED RECORD: 100-62

New York Yankees

2010 Record: 95-67; 2nd Place, American League East; Won Wild Card.
Defeated Minnesota Twins in ALDS 3 games to 0.
Lost to Texas Rangers in ALCS 4 games to 2.

2010 Recap:

For almost any other team, 95 wins and a loss in the ALCS would be an acceptable result.

For the Yankees? Not so much.

Success or failure in a given season isn't based on what happens in the regular season, but whether the Yankees win the World Series. This is a byproduct of their success in recent years and the "win or else" edicts from the late George Steinbrenner.

Expectations and fan reactions aside, 2010 was a successful season for the Yankees as a team by any reasonable metric. They overcame a short, shaky and injured starting rotation; an inconsistent bullpen; subpar years from Derek Jeter, Curtis Granderson and Jorge Posada; and turmoil on the coaching staff and won 95 games.

Is that a "bad" season?

Under the criteria of "World Series or bust", then yes, they failed and had a "bad" season; but the idea that any team can win a championship every year regardless of strength, money and competition is absurd.

It's the perception that's the problem; not the result.

2011 ADDITIONS:

RHP Rafael Soriano signed a 3-year, $35 million contract with opt-outs after 2011 and 2012.
C Russell Martin signed a 1-year, $4 million contract.
LHP Pedro Feliciano signed a 2-year, $8 million contract.
Pitching coach Larry Rothschild was hired.
OF Andruw Jones signed a 1-year, $2 million contract.
OF Justin Maxwell was acquired from the Washington Nationals.
RHP Mark Prior signed a minor league contract.
RHP Bartolo Colon signed a minor league contract.
RHP Freddy Garcia signed a minor league contract.
INF Ronnie Belliard signed a minor league contract.
3B/1B Eric Chavez signed a minor league contract.
RHP Luis Ayala signed a minor league contract.
RHP Brian Anderson signed a minor league contract.
RHP Buddy Carlyle signed a minor league contract.
LHP Andrew Sisco signed a minor league contract.
LHP Neal Cotts signed a minor league contract.
C Gustavo Molina signed a minor league contract.

2011 SUBTRACTIONS:

Pitching coach Dave Eiland was fired.
LHP Andy Pettitte retired.
RHP Kerry Wood was not re-signed.
RHP Javier Vazquez was not re-signed.
OF/DH Marcus Thames was not re-signed.
DH/1B Nick Johnson's option was declined.
RHP Alfredo Aceves was non-tendered.
RHP Chad Gaudin was not re-signed.
DH Lance Berkman was not re-signed.
OF Austin Kearns was not re-signed.
C Chad Moeller was not re-signed.
RHP Dustin Moseley was not re-signed.
LHP Royce Ring was not re-signed.

2011 PROJECTED STARTING ROTATION: C.C. Sabathia; Phil Hughes; A.J. Burnett; Ivan Nova; Freddy Garcia; Bartolo Colon.

2011 PROJECTED BULLPEN: Mariano Rivera; Rafael Soriano; Joba Chamberlain; David Robertson; Pedro Feliciano; Boone Logan; Sergio Mitre; Damaso Marte; Buddy Carlyle.

2011 PROJECTED LINEUP: C-Russell Martin; 1B-Mark Teixeira; 2B-Robinson Cano; 3B-Alex Rodriguez; SS-Derek Jeter; LF-Brett Gardner; CF-Curtis Granderson; RF-Nick Swisher; DH-Jorge Posada.

2011 BENCH: INF-Ramiro Pena; C-Francisco Cervelli; OF-Andruw Jones; INF-Eduardo Nunez; OF-Justin Maxwell; OF-Colin Curtis; OF-Greg Golson; OF-Kevin Russo.

2011 POSSIBLE CONTRIBUTORS: C-Jesus Montero; RHP-Dellin Betances; RHP-Romulo Sanchez; 3B-Brandon Laird; OF-Jordan Parraz; LHP-Neal Cotts; RHP-Mark Prior; RHP-Andrew Brackman; INF-Ronnie Belliard; RHP-Luis Ayala; 3B/1B-Eric Chavez.

ASSESSMENTS

MANAGEMENT:

I find the idea that GM Brian Cashman is to blame for the failure to sign Cliff Lee to be ludicrous.

What more was he supposed to do aside from offer the most money and a winning club for whom to play?

That said, had George Steinbrenner been around, Lee would be a Yankee; there's no doubt in my mind about that; but the days of the Yankees blowing their competition out of the water with their financial might are over. Rightly or wrongly, Steinbrenner would've offered an amount of money that Lee could not possibly refuse even if he was going to be elected King of Philadelphia along with their guaranteed money.

Bottom line, they didn't get him. The market for other starting pitchers—a Yankees off-season priority—was so weak that the next "biggest" name in the free agent market was Carl Pavano.

Yes. *That* Carl Pavano. And they inexplicably made him an offer!!!

The trade market? It wasn't good either; nor were they helped by the questions surrounding Zack Greinke's emotional capacity to deal with New York.

Is this Cashman's fault? Is he to be held responsible for not spending a metric ton of money for the one big starting pitcher available? One whose heart was clearly back in Philadelphia?

No.

The reluctance to overspend for immediate gratification left the Yankees in an unusual and untenable situation.

Cashman doesn't want to mortgage the future to get a veteran starter now; nor was he willing to sacrifice first round draft choices for "whatever was left" like Rafael Soriano.

But Cashman's bosses were.

And they—Randy Levine, Hank and Hal Steinbrenner—overruled the GM who had previously been thought to have full autonomy and final say in personnel matters.

Is it a rift? Or a reality check that no GM has full autonomy?

The Cashman blueprint has been to hoard the draft picks; adhere to stats above all else; and build through signings that reflect the new age tenets which Cashman has pledged allegiance to.

This led to the difficult Derek Jeter negotiations; the ridiculous attempt to bring back Pavano (which would've been, at best, unexplainable to the veterans who were there during Pavano's first tenure with the club; apparently Cashman learned nothing from the second go-round with Javier Vazquez); and the battle over Soriano which Cashman lost.

After Soriano, they've had to move forward with the questionable decision to sign Russell Martin to take over as the primary catcher; shift Jorge Posada to DH; sign Pedro Feliciano from the Mets; take fliers on Bartolo Colon, Freddy Garcia and Mark Prior among other cheap gambles.

Cashman is aggressive in-season as he showed with his trades for Kerry Wood and Lance Berkman at mid-season 2010; and with how close he came to getting Lee from the Mariners.

While he's not a great GM—his decisions on pitchers like Javier Vazquez and stat zombie-type players like Nick Johnson failed miserably—but he knows how to navigate perhaps the toughest GM job in sports and is able to maintain his composure without panicking as others might.

At mid-season 2011, there may be some big name pitchers available such as Chris Carpenter, Ervin Santana or possibly even Ubaldo Jimenez. And Cashman will be in on all of them as he tries to improve on the fly in the summer since he couldn't do it in the winter—through no fault of his own.

Following the 2010 season, Cashman fired pitching coach Dave Eiland and hired respected veteran pitching coach and former Rays manager Larry Rothschild. The reason for Eiland's dismissal was not disclosed and the Yankees did him a favor by not sullying his reputation and keeping quiet whatever the real reason was for Eiland's monthlong leave-of-absence in the summer. Cashman had every right to make a change and Eiland would be well-served to keep his mouth shut (a suggestion he was *not* adhering to during interviews) about the Yankees.

In addition to the failed pursuit of Lee, there was the contentious negotiation with Derek Jeter in which Cashman made the Yankees' offer and, when it was met with borderline aghast by Jeter's representatives, he rightfully told Jeter to shop it around and see if he could do better. He kept Mariano Rivera as well.

The Yankees GM is in a very tough spot. He's trying to keep the payroll under control and reward his veteran stars for time served, but he also wants to preserve the club's future. In the past, Steinbrenner would've gone all out to get Lee in the interests of winning again while Jeter, Rivera, Alex Rodriguez and Jorge Posada could still contribute. Now, those days are over and Cashman has to walk the tightrope. It just so happened that the tightrope prevented them from overpaying to get Lee.

He's doing the best he can under the circumstances.

Much like the criticism levied at Cashman for his "failures" in the winter, there were actually calls for Joe Girardi's job after the Yankees ALCS loss to the Rangers.

No, he's not a great strategic manager yet, but Girardi's job is even tougher than Cashman's. Having replaced a legendary figure on and off the field in Joe Torre; weathered the storm of taking over a club which still housed a large number of contemporaries and former teammates; working his way through the media/fan firestorms that pop up on a daily basis; surviving a missed playoff year in his first season and winning the World Series in 2009, Girardi has done a good job.

He still overmanages; he's still following commands from the front office (and from his ever-present blue binder) that he'd be better-served to toss into the circular file and manage like one of his mentors Don Zimmer—from the gut; but the players seem to like him and the team has won with him and will continue to do so. Players are not avoiding the Yankees because of Joe Girardi.

As he gains experience and with the security of the 3-year contract extension he signed, perhaps he'll learn to be a little looser and stop being so obsessed with matchups and the paranoia that comes from being in New York and trying to placate everyone. Sometimes a manager has to make the right move that he *knows* is the right move and is against the so-called "book" (or binder).

It's that nuance that makes a great manager and Girardi isn't there yet. He has the potential though. I'd like to see him relax. It would help him and his clubhouse.

STARTING PITCHING:

C.C. Sabathia finished third in the AL Cy Young Award voting and cemented his reputation as one of baseball's great horses. He threw 237 innings; went 21-7 and struck out 197. His numbers from 2009 were nearly identical in 2010. He's a big, tough, durable linchpin who will do whatever his manager asks him to do without complaint.

Sabathia reported to spring camp having lost 30 pounds which would concern me; sometimes there are pitchers and players who are better carrying extra bulk.

He's still one of the top five pitchers in baseball and will remain so for the foreseeable future.

Will necessity force the Yankees to remove the training wheels from Phil Hughes in 2011?

They were still babying him with his own "Hughes Rules" that, in my mind, hindered his development. He was rolling along, getting his groove and learning to pitch in the big leagues when the deranged method of developing young pitchers—an amalgam of doctor's orders, historical studies, Tom Verducci and "The Verducci Effect" (please), and fear of someone getting hurt while performing the unnatural act of throwing a baseball overhand—was put into action and they gave Hughes extra rest in June.

Naturally when he was allowed to pitch again he was rusty.

It also appeared to be a paramilitary style disciplinary act of "we're the bosses here" as Hughes, from Southern California, had his start against the Dodgers at Dodger Stadium bumped due to the regulations. To me, it was bullying; like most acts of bullying, it was unnecessary.

So what now?

Without the acquisition of Lee; with A.J. Burnett still...A.J. Burnett, will the Yankees push Hughes to try and win if they have to? Or are they going to adhere to the failures therein and move forward, possibly costing themselves a playoff spot in the process?

Hughes pitched consistently well he has top-of-the-rotation potential. The problem the Yankees have is that they're not as good as they were in 2010 when Hughes rode the wave of a great lineup and good bullpen to 18 wins. He has to pitch a bit better in 2011; they have to let him grow up; and he has to cut down on the home run ball.

He can do it.

If they let him.

And I don't know if they will.

In fact, history has shown that they won't.

A.J. Burnett.

A.....J.....Burnett.

A...........J..............Bur.....nett.....

Now we're hearing that Burnett's marital problems were a large cause of his mostly horrible 2010 season.

Maybe they were.

But that doesn't diminish the fact that Burnett is not, nor has he ever been anything more than, at best, a pitcher who's going to win 15 games (if he's healthy), lose 12 games and be maddeningly inconsistent for someone who's got a mid-90s fastball with movement, a wicked curveball and is mean enough to brush hitters off the plate.

Part of the reason Eiland may have been dismissed was that Burnett fell off a cliff without Eiland there and the club was unable to piece him back together afterwards.

The problem with an enigmatic pitcher is that the questions that lead to him *being* an enigma also elicit enigmatic and undefinable answers.

We can't say "this" is what's wrong with Burnett because no one knows what's "wrong" with Burnett. Is he tipping his pitches? Is his location off? Is it confidence? Is it the catcher's fault? The pitching coach? Off-field distractions? All of the above?

Burnett is 34-years-old now.

For all that potential, *this* is what he is. Over and over we've heard that all he needs is the right pitching coach; the right situation; one year in which he's healthy; a great bullpen—whatever excuse there is for someone not fulfilling the expectations of others—and every year Burnett disappoints those who believe he can be more than what he is.

He is what he is.

He'll be better than he was in 2010 because he can hardly be any worse; but to think that Larry Rothschild will succeed where the vast array of other pitching coaches who've been unable to get through to Burnett have failed is fantasy. He's going to pitch brilliantly in some games, maybe with a near no-hitter or two; he'll walk the ballpark in others and stand on the mound wiping sweat off his brow with a bewildered countenance; he'll give up towering homers to successive batters; and he'll gut his way through a few games to accumulate wins.

This is if he's healthy and his injury history is not something to discount because he's been durable in his two years with the Yankees; he's due an injury.

The Yankees signed A.J. Burnett.

And they got A.J. Burnett.

Don't expect anything other than that because he is who he is. For better or worse.

Or both.

The Yankees failure to secure a veteran starter may force them to rely somewhat heavily on young Ivan Nova.

The most impressive thing about Nova in his brief stay in the majors in 2010 wasn't his fastball and presence, but that he refused to be intimidated when, in his first big league start against the Blue Jays, he threw a pitch that wasn't all that close to Jose Bautista's head but stood his ground when Bautista acted as if it was in an attempt to scare the rookie. Nova didn't back down; nor did he hang his head when Bautista homered off him and took about a half hour running around the bases. This, more than anything else, is a good sign for a productive big league career; especially in New York.

I can't see the Yankees pushing Nova too hard. There will be rules for him and they'd be remiss in their duties to go crazy trying to force feed a 24-year-old too much too soon. He threw over 180 innings between the minors and majors last season and they're not going to ask him to give much more than that in 2011.

Veterans Freddy Garcia and Bartolo Colon were signed to minor league contracts.

Garcia has no velocity left on his fastball and he's nowhere close to the big, durable winner he was earlier in his career, but he did pitch serviceably for the White Sox last season despite a hits/innings pitched ratio of 157/171.

Colon hasn't pitched in the big leagues since 2009 (also for the White Sox), but didn't pitch poorly. He's 38-years-old.

In both cases, they're "why not?" pitchers. Why not have a look?

BULLPEN:

Mariano Rivera had his usual year.

That his "usual year" includes a 1.80 ERA; 39 hits allowed in 60 innings; 33 saves; and only 2 homers allowed is a testament to Rivera's greatness.

Rivera is 41-years-old and eventually even he will start to slow down, but I doubt it's going to be in 2011. After an odd flirtation with the Red Sox as a free agent and an offer from the Angels, Rivera signed a 2-year, $30 million contract to remain with the Yankees. His negotiation was under-the-radar and there was no way he was ever going to leave.

He's still the best closer in baseball.

Rafael Soriano spent 2010 with the Rays and had a good statistical year on the surface, but there are lingering questions about his capacity for dealing with the pressure of New York and whether his attitude will play well in the no-nonsense Yankees clubhouse still run by Jeter.

Soriano threw tantrums when Rays manager Joe Maddon wanted him to pitch more than one inning at a time; his strikeouts were down with 57 in 62 innings; and he's always been prone to the home run ball in a big spot and was so again in the ALDS as he allowed a game-breaking homer to Ian Kinsler in the ninth inning of game 5 essentially putting the game out of reach for the Rays.

He's getting paid closer money and has opt-outs in his contract after this year and next.

I wouldn't worry about him in the regular season in a relatively meaningless game in July, but in September in Boston? Will he be able to handle the pressure? Or will he grip the ball too tightly; try to throw it too hard; have his fastball flatten and get taken deep.

I don't trust him in a big game, but he'll pitch well most of the time. Whether the Yankees are getting that shut-down bullpen they're expecting is a question in my mind.

The Yankees traded for Kerry Wood at mid-season in 2010 because they didn't trust either Dave Robertson or Joba Chamberlain to get the big outs in the playoffs.

With good reason.

Chamberlain's star has fallen to the point where the debate as to whether he should be a starter or reliever has become moot. No one cares anymore. He's a name that could be bandied about in a trade and with another bad year, it wouldn't be inconceivable—were he "just another guy" and not "Joba"—that he could be non-tendered.

Adding to his poor reputation, he arrived in spring camp far overweight.

It's not solely Chamberlain's fault that his star has fallen so precipitously. The club has stagnated his development with the ridiculous Joba Rules and jerking him back-and-forth between the starting rotation and bullpen. He got a little too impressed with himself as most young people who are subjected to that kind of attention and special treatment will be and has looked to be out of shape and arrogant.

Many people are to blame for the fall of Joba.

So what do the Yankees do about it?

Chamberlain still has the stuff that made comparisons to a young Roger Clemens commonplace. Does he have the work ethic? The intensity? The determination? Or does he expect everything to be handed to him as it was when he burst onto the scene in 2007?

Chamberlain is salvageable and the Yankees can salvage him and their reputations for nurturing young pitchers if they let the still-young man pitch.

Like the questions surrounding Hughes, I don't know if they will.

Don't be surprised to see Chamberlain's name bandied about in getting a veteran starter via trade if they don't replenish him while in a Yankee uniform. Someone else might unlock his talent; that may be what has to happen for him to succeed.

David Robertson got off to a bad start and he, like Chamberlain, was unable to grab hold of the set-up man's role despite terrific strikeout stuff. Robertson settled in and pitched well for most of the season. His mechanics are atrocious and his stiff landing leg and bullwhipping arm still causes me pain every time I watch him pitch.

Veteran workhorse lefty specialist Pedro Feliciano was signed to a 2-year, $8 million contract to join the Yankees from the Mets. Feliciano was miscast in the Mets attempts to use him against both lefties and righties and I have to wonder when the overwork due to the frequent bullpen changes by Mets managers Willie Randolph and Jerry Manuel will eventually catch up to the sidearming Feliciano.

He's reliable; he throws strikes; he doesn't allow many homers and he's still very tough on lefties. I doubt Girardi is going to abuse him as the Mets did and he'll be a solid lefty specialist who'll do his job well.

Hard throwing lefty Boone Logan had a solid year as the Yankees primary lefty reliever in 2010. He struck out 38 in 40 innings and allowed 34 hits. He also held lefty hitters to a .190 batting average and a .501 OPS. He and Feliciano are going to get a lot of work against the Red Sox newly acquired duo of Carl Crawford and Adrian Gonzalez to go along with returning bats David Ortiz and J.D. Drew.

For all the laughter and ridicule he engenders in part due to his failures; in part due to manager Joe Girardi's clear affinity for him, Sergio Mitre isn't all that bad as a long reliever. If they have to use him as a starter over the long term, then the Yankees have far bigger problems than anything Mitre caused. He's not good more than one time through the lineup, but he throws strikes out of the bullpen and can pitch 3 innings if the starter gets knocked out of the box early.

Contrary to popular belief, Damaso Marte pitched serviceably for the most part in 2010 before he got hurt. The Yankees made the mistake of keeping only Marte as the lefty in the bullpen and he was overworked and over-warmed up. Eventually his shoulder gave out. He did allow 10 hits, 8 runs and 11 walks in 17 innings, but the numbers look worse because of a couple of bad outings. He usually did his job.

If Marte's able to pitch, he'll be useful against the aforementioned Red Sox bats and the presence of Feliciano to go along with Logan should preclude any abuse heaped on Marte.

Veteran swingman Buddy Carlyle was signed to a minor league contract after spending the 2010 season in Japan. Carlyle has good breaking stuff and was very useful to the Braves as a long reliever/spot starter in 2008; he had a bad year in 2009. He strikes out around a hitter per inning and can pitch multiple innings; I think he'll stick with the Yankees and be a help to them.

LINEUP:

Russell Martin was signed to a 1-year, $4 million contract to take over as the primary catcher for Jorge Posada. Posada is shifting to DH.

Martin was a blossoming star as recently as 2008 when he could hit, hit for power, run and throw. He can still throw, but he missed the last two months of the season with a torn hip labrum and the Dodgers non-tendered him. His across-the-board numbers declined from 2008 until 2010. He's not going to be as much of a focal point in the Yankees star-studded lineup and this should benefit him. How he handles the pitching staff—specifically Burnett and Chamberlain—are the keys to success for himself and the club.

Posada was unfairly blamed for the struggles of the starters and the issues should've been addressed before they spiraled out of control. Perhaps Martin and a fresh face will be a better fit defensively and calling the game.

I don't believe Martin will regain the reputation as a hitter he'd cultivated in 2007-2008, but in the Yankees lineup I believe he'll hit 15 homers and be an important, unsung cog in the batting order.

Mark Teixeira was seen to be having an "off" year in 2010, but he recovered from his atrocious first half and still hit 33 homers, drove in 108 and had 69 extra base hits and a .365 on base percentage. He also won a Gold Glove and his ALDS homer against the Twins in the first game was the key to the Yankees sweep. Teixeira will be back to a realistic MVP candidate in 2011.

Robinson Cano had a massive year with a .319 batting average, 29 homers and 73 extra base hits. Unlike past years when he's gotten off to a slow start, Cano started hitting immediately and didn't stop. He won his first Gold Glove, finished 3rd in the MVP voting and, at age 28, is rivaling Chase Utley as the best second baseman in baseball.

Alex Rodriguez had something of an "off" year for him considering the ridiculous standards he set for himself early in his career. A-Rod's batting average was down to .270; his on base to .341; he hit 30 homers and drove in 125, but it's a legitimate question as to whether this slide is going to continue. He's not young anymore at age 35 and injuries have slowed him.

The problem the Yankees have is that A-Rod, as his game declines, is still being paid as if he's 25 and getting better. He's due to make $31 million this year and at least $20 million annually through 2017. It's a safe bet that the Yankees won't be getting good value on that deal for A-Rod. He's still dangerous, but nowhere near what he was. Not even close.

Derek Jeter's contentious contract negotiation sullied his image of being above the fray in messy off-field team-player relations. Jeter wanted to be paid based on his past; the Yankees didn't want to be held hostage by the Captain's popularity and legacy.

This created a rift that was embarrassing more for the Jeter camp than the organization. It was a switch and it was unattractive for someone of Jeter's sterling reputation to have to endure the media firestorm that accompanied the very idea that he was being greedy.

Eventually it was worked out as he was guaranteed $51 million through 2013 to stay.

On the field, Jeter had a subpar year. He batted .270 with a .340 on base; he still managed 46 extra base hits and won a Gold Glove based on reputation more than achievement.

Jeter will be 37 in June, but I won't write off a big comeback year from him. He's been criticized before and made it his life's mission to shove it to those who doubted him. He can still play. He's not what he was, but there's no one more trustworthy in a clutch situation both offensively and defensively and his baseball acumen is still nonpareil.

Brett Gardner rewarded Girardi's faith in him with a terrific year. Gardner can fly on the bases and in the outfield and plays with reckless abandon. He stole 47 bases and I still believe that he's going to hit for more power as he gets accustomed to being a big league regular. Gardner was far better against righties than lefties, but I'd give him a shot to play every single day. He can hit lefties well enough and his speed makes up for a multitude of sins.

Curtis Granderson took some time to get accustomed to New York, but his numbers wound up being respectable after a rotten first half. Granderson hit 17 of his 24 homers in the second half and while he may never regain what he had in 2007 as he batted .302 with 38 doubles, 23 triples and 23 homers, he can still be a very good producer for the Yankees. His defense was respectable as well.

Nick Swisher played in pain for much of the year with aches to much of his entire body. He still batted .288 with 29 homers. His on base percentage dropped from its usual heights of .370 and above to .359, but he played good defense in right field. Swisher's a consistent and productive unsung player.

How will Jorge Posada respond to being a primary DH?

My guess is not well.

But....but.....*but!!!*

The Yankees have a chance to get a quiet and productive year out of Posada for one reason and one reason only: his impending free agency.

Posada can't really throw well enough to catch regularly anymore, but the bickering between him and a large chunk of the pitching staff should've been squashed in Girardi's first year as manager. It wasn't. Posada was able to deal with Roger Clemens, David Wells and Orlando Hernandez, but he can't come to a consensus with A.J. Burnett and Joba Chamberlain?

I think *that* might have been one of the big sticking points. Posada may have listened to what the Yankees pitchers in years gone by had to say and taken their feelings into account while still being the hardheaded Posada; with Burnett and Chamberlain, I wouldn't blame the veteran catcher for reacting indignantly and asking, "Who the hell are *you* to be questioning my pitch selection? What credentials do you have?"

It's irrelevant now. Martin's going to catch. Posada's going to DH.

Posada can still hit. He's not the force he once was, but the incentive of a new contract somewhere, perhaps to catch again, may allow him to experience a renaissance.

If, by some strange occurrence, the Yankees find themselves out of contention late in the season, Posada might be trade bait and, unlike in past years when he would've invoked his no-trade clause, this time he might accept to bolster his post-season pedigree further as he heads to free agency once more if he still wants to play.

BENCH:

Andruw Jones isn't the star he was with the Braves and his defense is nowhere near the state-of-the-art thing of beauty it once was; he hit 19 homers for the White Sox last season; batted .230 with a .341 on base in 328 plate appearances. As a fourth outfielder, he's adequate.

Ramiro Pena is a utility infielder who batted .227 in 154 at bats with 2 extra base hits. He can run a bit.

Francisco Cervelli was being called a potential starting catcher early in the season until the pitchers figured him out. He wound up with a .271 average, 11 doubles and 3 triples in 317 plate appearances. Cervelli gets on base at a good clip and isn't very good at throwing out baserunners nor did he play well defensively the more time he saw in the lineup.

Eduardo Nunez is a righty-swinging infielder who batted .280 in a brief big league stay. He's shown speed in the minors.

Justin Maxwell was acquired in a trade with the Washington Nationals. Maxwell's had 30 stolen base speed, pop and some on base ability in the minors and has yet to do much in the big leagues.

Veteran infielder Ronnie Belliard signed a minor league contract. Belliard had some pop in his bat in the past and a flair for the dramatic. The 36-year-old batted .216 for the Dodgers last season.

Colin Curtis imprressed everyone in spring training and wound up back in Triple A where the 26-year-old outfielder batted .289 in 269 plate appearances.

Greg Golson has had 30 at bats in the big leagues and not walked once. In the minors, the former first round pick of the Phillies has shown speed and occasional pop; but he's a journeyman defensive replacement and pinch runner more than anything else. If that.

Kevin Russo is a 26-year-old outfielder who batted .184 in 54 plate appearances in 2010. The West Babylon, New York native hasn't been particularly impressive in the minors either.

PREDICTION:

The Yankees are a team in flux.

They don't want to overspend to bolster the declining veterans they currently have and they don't have many young players slated to slide into regular duty right now. Jesus Montero may or may not be ready to contribute to the team at some point in 2011, but can he save the pitching staff which is woefully short?

Cashman had a choice: overpay for Lee or gut the system trying to find a pitcher to assuage concerns that the team hadn't done anything to improve in the winter; or wait it out and see what comes available at mid-season.

What are the Yankees going to do if A-Rod, Jeter and Posada continue their slide and the rest of the offense can't account for the runs the compromised pitching staff is going to need to win?

Will they stay the course and take the beating they're surely going to get from an expectant media and spoiled rotten fan base? Or will Cashman panic and do something stupid to try and save the season, possibly making things worse in upcoming years?

The Yankees had the worst off-season I remember them having since Greg Maddux spurned them to take less money from the Braves; when few were willing to join the still-rebuilding and long-suffering franchise unless they overpaid. The division they're playing in is very, very tough and no one is going to be standing in line to help them if things spiral downward.

Every team has lulls. The Yankees have avoided them; but they're old, fading and, most importantly, the pitching is very, very short even with that bullpen.

Will manager Joe Girardi, with a clear edict that the bullpen is the key to the club's fortunes, go so far over-the-top in his micro-managing and tax his bullpen early in the season?

Bullpens are a key *in* the playoffs, but will they help a team make the playoffs in a very rough division?

The Red Sox are a better team on paper and in practice; the other contending clubs in the American League are going to have an easier road to accumulate wins than the Yankees in the AL East.

Their age, shortness in starting pitching, Soriano's shakiness in big games and the chasm in the front office will all contribute to the Yankees missing the playoffs in 2011.

PREDICTED RECORD: 89-73

Tampa Bay Rays

2010 Record: 96-66; 1st place, American League East.
Lost to Texas Rangers in ALDS 3 games to 2.

2010 Recap:

The young Rays rebounded from what amounted to a hangover in 2009 as they fell from the American League champions to a dysfunctional and immature club that barely finished above .500.

Winning the AL East, they were carried by their young pitching led by David Price and Matt Garza; a superlative bullpen with Rafael Soriano; and an offense that was more than the sum of its parts. The Rays were third in the American League in runs scored despite not having one hitter with 30 homers and while carrying such feast or famine spots in the lineup like the .196 hitting Carlos Pena; the mercurial B.J. Upton; and a rotating DH with the likes of Pat Burrell (released early in the season) and Willy Aybar.

In the playoffs, they were bested by Cliff Lee and the Rangers in five games as the one big bugaboo of Soriano reared its head and he allowed a backbreaking homer to Ian Kinsler in the ninth inning of game 5.

2011 ADDITIONS:

OF Johnny Damon signed a 1-year, $5.25 million contract.
DH Manny Ramirez signed a 1-year, $2 million contract.
RHP Kyle Farnsworth signed a 1-year, $3.25 million contract with 2012 club option.

RHP Joel Peralta signed a 1-year, $950,000 contract.
RHP Adam Russell was acquired from the San Diego Padres.
RHP Brandon Gomes was acquired from the San Diego Padres.
LHP Cesar Ramos was acquired from the San Diego Padres.
RHP Cole Figueroa was acquired from the San Diego Padres.
RHP Chris Archer was acquired from the Chicago Cubs.
OF Brandon Guyer was acquired from the Chicago Cubs.
C/INF Robinson Chirinos was acquired from the Chicago Cubs.
SS Hak-Ju Lee was acquired from the Chicago Cubs.
OF Sam Fuld was acquired from the Chicago Cubs.
RHP Juan Cruz signed a minor league contract.
1B Casey Kotchman signed a minor league contract.
OF/1B Chris Carter was signed to a minor league contract.

2011 SUBTRACTIONS:

LF Carl Crawford was not re-signed.
1B Carlos Pena was not re-signed.
RHP Matt Garza was traded to the Chicago Cubs.
OF Fernando Perez was traded to the Chicago Cubs.
DH Willy Aybar was non-tendered.
SS Jason Bartlett was traded to the San Diego Padres.
OF Rocco Baldelli was not re-signed.
RHP Rafael Soriano was not re-signed.
RHP Grant Balfour was not re-signed.
RHP Lance Cormier was non-tendered.
LHP Randy Choate was not re-signed.
RHP Joaquin Benoit was not re-signed.
3B/1B Hank Blalock was released.
OF Brad Hawpe was not re-signed.
OF Gabe Kapler was not re-signed.
C Dioner Navarro was non-tendered.
RHP Dan Wheeler was not re-signed.
RHP Chad Qualls was not re-signed.
RHP Dale Thayer was not re-signed.

2011 PROJECTED STARTING ROTATION: David Price, James Shields, Jeff Niemann, Wade Davis, Jeremy Hellickson.

2011 PROJECTED BULLPEN: J.P. Howell; Joel Peralta; Adam Russell; Andy Sonnanstine; Kyle Farnsworth; Mike Ekstrom; Jake McGee; Matt Bush; Cesar Ramos; Chris Archer.

2011 PROJECTED LINEUP: C-John Jaso; 1B-Dan Johnson; 2B-Sean Rodriguez; 3B-Evan Longoria; SS-Reid Brignac; LF-Johnny Damon; CF-B.J. Upton; RF-Ben Zobrist; DH-Manny Ramirez.

2011 BENCH: C-Kelly Shoppach; INF-Elliott Johnson; OF-Desmond Jennings; OF-Sam Fuld; OF-Matt Joyce; OF/1B-Chris Carter.

2011 POSSIBLE CONTRIBUTORS: LHP Cesar Cabral; RHP Alex Cobb; RHP Dane De La Rosa; RHP Brandon Gomes; RHP Albert Suarez; RHP Alexander Torres; RHP Cory Wade; LHP-R.J. Swindle; C Jose Lobaton.

ASSESSMENTS MANAGEMENT:

I'll admit it. I'm developing a man-crush on GM Andrew Friedman.

Having abandoned Jeff Francoeur as the prior object to my non-sexual affections in the baseball world, Friedman has won me over. Just as I was beginning to write this section on the Rays, the news broke that they'd traded Matt Garza to the Cubs for a large package of prospects.

Then, late in the winter, they struck with a shocking ferocity that shook the baseball world when they signed both Johnny Damon and Manny Ramirez to 1-year contract.

This is nothing new in the world of the Rays.

After a rocky start in which they initially didn't appear to have the faintest clue as to what they were doing when they took command, they've evolved into one of the best and most fearless front offices in all of baseball.

The Rays do it right. Of course they're helped along by the absence of passion in the average fan in Florida. I'm curious as to whether the Rays would be so preemptively aggressive in their dealings if they had a fan base that scrutinized every decision they made to the point of nausea.

It's hard to know the answer to that question.

But it doesn't really matter, does it? Much like the way they run their baseball operations, the Rays look at their circumsstances and react accordingly. They'd gotten everything they could reasonably have expected from Jason Bartlett and traded him to a desperate Padres team for four pitchers; Carlos Pena was a reclamation project who hit for power and little else, so they let him leave as a free agent without a fight; Garza was due a big raise in arbitration, they have a replacement for his spot in the rotation in Jeremy Hellickson, so they traded Garza to another desperate team, the Cubs; the way to properly build a bullpen is to find bargains and plug them in, trying to squeeze every ounce of value from them before discarding and they did this with Grant Balfour, Rafael Soriano, Joaquin Benoit and Randy Choate.

The Rays do it right.

Friedman has packed the organization with prospects, they're scouring the globe—literally—for talent; they've got a wealth of compensatory picks coming to them for the lost free agents; and if they were allowed to trade the draft picks, I have no doubt they'd move up and down the board to get the players they want like an MLB version of former football coach/draft guru Jimmy Johnson.

They're smart; they're fearless; and they do what needs to be done within a budget.

It's a man-crush.

Sue me.

No, I don't like the way Joe Maddon manages.

Yes, I've repeatedly said that the Rays may need to bring in a more disciplined voice to handle the likes of B.J. Upton and give him a good, swift kick in the ass—perhaps literally—to get him to hustle.

But the Rays are evolving from the team they were with the dipatching of the aforementioned veterans and going with a bunch of new/young faces. With that in mind, Maddon *is* the right man for the job to steer this ship.

Unlike others, my criticism of Maddon had more to do with disciplinary issues and his new age style. For example, the silliness that he encourages with road trips dedicated to wearing various jerseys from hockey teams sabotages discipline. If it were me, they're wearing a suit and tie on the road and that's it. It was suggested that the issues with Upton were a byproduct of the lax atmosphere and I'm not on board with that. Upton would be a nuisance no matter what manager he's playing for. That's on him.

Maddon's the manager of this team and he's not going anywhere. It's the front office that makes or breaks the Rays's success or failure anyway, not the manager.

STARTING PITCHING:

Young David Price exploded into the big time as a starter in 2010.

The big lefty finished 2nd in the AL Cy Young Award voting behind Felix Hernandez. He won 19 games; allowed 170 hits in 208 innings; struck out 188; walked 79; and only allowed 15 homers. He also pitched well enough to have won six more games.

Price showed his maturity and courage when he was pressed into service as a closer in the 2008 post-season and saved Game 7 of the ALCS against the Red Sox. The Rays have been cautious in his use and, at age 25, he's a burgeoning superstar.

Much like the other pitchers in the Rays stable present and past, it's a question as to whether they'll lock him up contractually for the long term. The Rays have tended to push their young starters, use them until they grow too expensive, then move them. They did this with Scott Kazmir in 2009 and now with Matt Garza. They won't have to worry about that with Price for a couple of years; years in which he'll be the ace of the young Rays pitching staff.

James Shields's overall numbers have gotten progressively worse after his rise in 2007-2008. He pitched poorly in 2009 and was worse in 2010. He gave up a deranged 246 hits and 34 homers in 203 innings; led the league in runs allowed with 117 and had a 5.18 ERA.

To be fair, much of the damage was done on days in which he got rocked and was left in games to take a beating. For the most part, he was serviceable much of the time. With the departure of Garza and the reliance on young pitchers Jeff Niemann and Jeremy Hellickson, the Rays are going to need Shields to step back up into the top of the rotation starter he was becoming in 2007-2008.

Maddon was criticized for starting Shields in game 2 of the ALDS, but Shields pitched well enough for four innings before a hit by pitch, bunt force out and ground ball base hit chased him; Chad Qualls entered the game and allowed a homer to Michael Young for which two of the runs were charged to Shields. Had it been a regular season game, he never would've been pulled in that situation.

I think Shields is going to have a good bounceback year.

With the trade of Garza, former first round draft pick Jeff Niemann has to step into the breach. Niemann's been a late-bloomer and has gone 25-14 in the past two seasons, but his pitching has been inconsistent. Mostly a six inning pitcher, Niemann gives up too many baserunners and homers (25 in 174 innings) and has benefited from being on a very good team that scores a lot of runs and plays solid defense. His stuff is relatively pedestrian; he's missed time due to shoulder problems as well.

It's safe to say that unless Wade Davis and Jeremy Hellickson mature in a hurry or Shields becomes an 18 game winner, Niemann is a key to the Rays hopes for contention in 2011. He's in his third full season; the caution with a young pitcher will be gone and, at age 28, it's time for him to step up.

I tend to believe that Niemann is what he is, what his numbers in 2009-2010 say he is and that's an okay mid-back rotation starter and he'll repeat his work in 2011.

Righty Wade Davis has the talent to eclipse Niemann in the rotation hierarchy. Aside from a bad game here and there, Davis regularly allowed only 2-3 runs in his 6 innings of work. Davis is a contact pitcher who throws strikes and should benefit from the Rays defensive speed. He could emerge into the 15 game winner that Garza was in 2010.

Soon to be 24-year-old righty Jeremy Hellickson was compared to Greg Maddux when he arrived in the majors in August.

This is, of course, insanity.

But Hellickson's control is Maddux-like as he only walked 8 in 36 innings and looked fantastic in five August starts. He's a strikeout pitcher who's dominated at every level. One would assume that the Rays are going to be careful with him as they've been with their other young pitchers. If Niemann and Davis step forward and Shields is able to rejuvenate his game, the pressure on Hellickson won't be as great. Either way, the Rays aren't going to push him; he could be a force at the top of the starting rotation in years to come. They won't expect him to throw more than 150-170 innings this year.

BULLPEN:

J.P. Howell saved 17 games in 2009 but missed the entire 2010 season after having shoulder surgery. Howell has a quirky and deceptive left-handed motion, good control and a wide array of pitches. He strikes out a lot of hitters and allows a few too many homers for a closer. More than any other club, the Rays have the personnel and guts to go with a closer-by-committee.

In the past, they've gone with the "one closer" in the cases of Troy Percival and Rafael Soriano, but they've also used what they've had and made risky decisions out of necessity like the post-season in 2008 when they used Price. If Howell is healthy, he'll be a big part of their bullpen.

Has anyone come up with a reasonable explanation as to why the Nationals non-tendered Joel Peralta after the veteran journeyman had his best season at age 34 for them?

Peralta struck out 49 in 49 innings, walked 9 and allowed 30 hits. He was good against both lefties and righties as well. Naturally, there's the chance that he was one of those relievers who has one solid season in a well-traveled career, but considering the Nationals spending on Jayson Werth, why would they pinch pennies with Peralta?

The Rays have a habit of finding pitchers like Peralta (Joaquin Benoit, Grant Balfour) and getting great use out of them.

6'8", 255 pound right Adam Russell was acquired from the Padres in the Jason Bartlett trade. Russell will be 28 in April and has never gotten a full shot in the big leagues despite great strikeout numbers. He was a closer in Triple A in 2010 but gave up a lot of hits and walks (1.742 WHIP in 51 minor league innings).

Andy Sonnanstine is a soft-tossing righty with a barely mediocre fastball and floating breaking pitches. His quirky slingshot motion may be better suited to going through the lineup once. Sonnanstine doesn't have the stuff to get big league hitters out consistently, but perhaps as a long reliever in between the hard throwing starters and late inning relievers, the change can confuse the batters and let Sonnanstine be effective for spurts.

The Rays are the latest team to roll the dice on the talent of Kyle Farnsworth. I suppose it's possible that they signed Farnsworth for his fighting skills so he can scare the lackadaisical play out of B.J. Upton; if he can do *that*, he's worth the money if he doesn't even pitch. Rays pitching coach Jim Hickey has been quite good at rehabilitating reclamation projects who'd had no success anywhere else like Grant Balfour; if he can do the same with Farnsworth, get him to harness and consistently deploy that natural ability, he'll start to enter the Dave Duncan realm of pitching gurus.

No, I don't expect it to happen either; but Farnsworth is the epitome of the "hey, why not?" guy. So? Hey, why not?

Mike Ekstrom showed promise in 15 relief appearances for the Rays in 2010. He's small for a pitcher (5'11"), but has shown strikeout ability. His control isn't particularly good as he walked 9 in 16 innings last season. A reliever who can't throw strikes doesn't do anyone any good.

Jake McGee is a lefty who was a mediocre starter in the minors and could get a shot out of the Rays bullpen in 2011. His strikeout numbers in the minors have been brilliant and he doesn't give up many homers.

Matt Bush is a fascinating case and epitomizes what the Rays do in seeking out players.

Bush was the first pick in the 2004 draft for his hometown San Diego Padres in 2004 as a shortstop and was a historic bust. He had off-field legal issues and didn't hit. Converted into a pitcher, he's shown a power fastball and good control. It's unlikely that he'll stick with the big club this year, but if he behaves himself and does well in the minors, perhaps he can be a late season call up.

Cesar Ramos was acquired from the Padres in the Bartlett trade. The lefty's numbers were blown out of proportion by one game on May 21st when he allowed seven earned runs in one inning; aside from that, he was effective with 9 strikeouts in 8 innings. He's been a starter and reliever in the minors and may be best suited to be a lefty specialist.

Righty Chris Archer is a top right-handed pitching prospect who was acquired from the Cubs in the Garza trade. The Cubs may rue the day they traded him. He's put up big strikeout numbers as a starter in the minors and was dominating at two levels for the Cubs in 2010 with a 15-3 record, 2.34 ERA; he also had 149 strikeouts in 142 innings and allowed 102 hits and only 6 homers. Could Archer pull a David Price and contribute to the Rays out of the bullpen late in the season? Maybe.

LINEUP:

Lefty swinging catcher John Jaso was a revelation in 2010. Jaso had been in the Rays' system since 2003 and always put up good on base numbers and showed extra base pop. Given his shot to play regularly in the big leagues, Jaso posted a .750 OPS in 404 plate appearances. His defense was serviceable and he was a far cry better at the plate than the former starter Dioner Navarro.

Carlos Pena was allowed to leave as a free agent and the Rays are again hoping to find someone in the same way they found Pena—through luck.

Pena was a journeyman with some power and on base skills when the Rays invited him to spring training in 2007. The Rays were prepared to release him, but had a change-of-heart and kept him around. He responded by hitting 46 homers and putting up MVP-caliber numbers. Pena declined in subsequent years and, even though he showed power, his batting average declined into the low .200s and below.

Now they may be preparing to move forward with another journeyman, Dan Johnson, at first base. Johnson was a top prospect for the Athletics and has had some big hits for the Rays during their playoff runs. Johnson has extra base power and on base skills, but I wouldn't expect anything from him.

Sean Rodriguez was a former Angels top prospect who was acquired in 2009 in the trade of Scott Kazmir. Rodriguez batted .251 with a .308 on base, 19 doubles and 9 homers in part-time duty. His numbers are far superior against lefties so he may wind up as a platoon player.

Evan Longoria is the leader of the Rays on and off the field. It was Longoria's leg injury that compromised the Rays' offense as much as the Rangers pitching in the ALDS. An MVP candidate, Longoria is a basher with high on base skills; he hits in the clutch and is a fine fielder. He'll contend for the MVP award if the Rays are in contention.

Reid Brignac replaces the traded Jason Bartlett at shortstop. Bartlett had his career year at the plate in 2009 and predictably reverted to the mediocre hitter he always was. The lefty batting Brignac is an average fielder who's shown power in the minors and hit 8 homers in 326 plate appearances in 2010.

Johnny Damon signed a 1-year contract to return to the American League East. Damon had a solid year with the Tigers in 2010 with 36 doubles, 5 triples and 8 homers. He batted .271, had a .355 on base and stole 11 bases. I get the impression that Damon will see time at first base for the Rays and need frequent rest days because he's not going to be able to withstand the pounding his 27-year-old body will take on the Rays artificial turf, but Damon can still hit and his presence will limit the expectations on rookie Desmond Jennings.

Ah, B.J. Upton.

So talented and so moody.

Someone has to get it through Upton's head that he's never going to get the lucrative contract extension he desires unless two things happen: 1) he has to act like he wants to play baseball on an everyday basis and cares about what he's doing; and 2) he has to hit better than .237 with 18 homers and a .322 on base.

2010 was the second year in a row that Upton's numbers declined from his excellent 2008 season and there was the incident in which he failed to hustle for a ball hit into the gap against the Diamondbacks and was confronted in the dugout by Longoria resulting in a near fistfight. The one thing I found laughable was the idea that this was the first time Upton was challenged by a teammate for his lackadaisical play.

This was, more than likely, the first time it was done publicly. You can bet teammates have gotten into his face before; it was just kept from the media.

Upton has MVP talent, but his attitude is atrocious. He can be a Gold Glove fielder and steal 50 bases with 25 homers if he sets his mind to it.

Will he?

Who knows? The Rays were very willing to deal Upton, but with all the roster upheaval, I'd expect them to keep him for the time being to see if he grows up. I don't blame Maddon for Upton's behavior at all. He's benched him and spoken to him; presumably he's yelled at him and fined him. What else is he supposed to do? Besides, if Upton were playing for Tony La Russa, Bobby Cox or Joe Torre I can't see him behaving any differently.

Versatile Ben Zobrist is may see most of his playing time in right field to start the season. Zobrist was an All Star in 2009 and fell back in every department in 2010. His homers fell from 27 to 10; his batting average from .297 to .238; his on base from .405 to .346.

Did the pitchers learn to pitch to Zobrist or was it an off-year? He put up similar numbers every season in the minors, but it's hard to imagine the switch-hitter repeating his 2009 season. I do expect him to rebound and hit 20 homers with better across-the-board production.

Manny Ramirez may have a terrible reputation and his power has declined drastically, but he still gets on base at a .400 clip and as long as he's Manny, the threat and caution will still be there. You can't take a chance that he's going to get into a hot streak and hurt you. He did bat .298 last season with a .409 on base and 9 homers in 320 plate appearances. He's a bargain at $2 million no matter what he does for his still looming presence in the lineup.

BENCH:

Desmond Jennings will get a chance to play substantially in 2011 without the pressure of replacing Carl Crawford; that's the positive affect of the twin signings of Damon and Manny.

Jennings is one of baseball's hottest prospects and has been compared to...Carl Crawford in his game. He'll have to learn to hit for more power if he's truly going to be compared to Crawford, but he did hit 11 homers in 2009 with Double and Triple A. Jennings can do it all and is going to be a Rookie of the Year candidate.

Veteran catcher Kelly Shoppach split time with Jason and batted .196. He doesn't hit for a high average, but he's not under .200 bad. He's shown power in the past and handles the pitchers well. Depending on Jaso and whether there's a fallback in his production from last year, Shoppach may see some substantial playing time.

Elliot Johnson is more famous for his spring training collision with Yankees backup catcher Francisco Cervelli in in 2008 than for his play.

It was a clean hit, for the record.

Johnson's a 27-year-old, switch-hitting utility player who batted .319 with a .375 on base and 11 homers in 481 plate appearances at Triple A Durham in 2010. He may get a chance in the big leagues in 2011.

Outfielder Sam Fuld was acquired in the Garza trade. Fuld showed promise in 2009 in 65 games with the Cubs batting .299 with a .409 on base. He slumped in 2010 and wound up back in the minors. He's

29 and has hit for a high average with good speed in his minor league career.

Matt Joyce was a disaster in his first, injury-plagued year with the Rays in 2009 after being acquired from the Tigers for Edwin Jackson. In 2010, he hit 10 homers and had a .360 on base percentage in 261 plate appearances. He's shown power, some speed, on base skills and a high batting average in the minors.

Intense Chris Carter was signed to a minor league contract with an invitation to spring training. He showed some power with the Mets and plays the game all out, all the time. He's highly intelligent and I'd like to see him stick in the big leagues because he's fun to watch.

PREDICTION:

The Rays have turned their playoff roster over to a remarkable degree. The whole bullpen is gone; they traded their number 2 starter; their first baseman, shortstop and left fielder—all former All Stars—are gone as well.

But the Rays front office has proven that they're smart and resilient. With the starting pitching that remains and organizational depth, they can make a bold trade at mid-season if they're in contention or they can move forward with what they have and wait for the cache of youngsters they've accumulated to be big league ready.

The mix of veterans and kids; the young pitching and the way they seem to score runs regardless of low batting average and mixing and matching, the Rays will hang around contention for the Wild Card. They don't have the personnel to compete with the Red Sox, but a win total in the 80s might be enough to garner a playoff spot in the parity-laden American League, especially considering the weakness exhibited by the Yankees.

Manny and Damon can't be expected to be centerpieces of the offense anymore, but they don't need them to be; their veteran savvy will assist the younger players to a remarkable degree.

I don't see them making the playoffs; they won't win 96 games again, but they'll contend and build for a very bright future with all that young talent and an increasingly impressive front office.

PREDICTED RECORD: 86-76

Toronto Blue Jays

2010 Record: 85-77; 4th Place, American League East.

2010 Recap:

The Blue Jays had a strategy when they went up to the plate in 2010. It basically went like this: look for the first fastball you see and try to hit it into space.

It was brutal; it was softball leagueish; it was primordial.

And it worked.

To a point.

The Blue Jays led the major leagues in home runs with 257 including an amazing 54 from Jose Bautista. Despite that, they were only 6th in the American League in runs scored as their power display was counteracted by the fact that they were 12th in the league in on base percentage.

I don't think OBP is the end-all/be-all of existence, but there has to be a medium somewhere and the absence of walks that came from the aggressiveness affected the team's ability to put all those homers to their best possible use.

In addition to the power, the Blue Jays had a very young, impressive array of pitchers arrive on the scene. Ricky Romero, Brandon Morrow, Brett Cecil, Kyle Drabek, Mark Rzepczynski and Shaun Marcum were part of a solid starting rotation; their bullpen was serviceable as well.

Had the Blue Jays not endured horrendous fallback years from Aaron Hill and Adam Lind and had Travis Snider been a bit better as a rookie, this team could very well have contended. As it was, they wound up with an 85-77 record and a bright future.

2011 ADDITIONS:

Manager John Farrell was hired.
OF Juan Rivera was acquired from the Los Angeles Angels.
C Mike Napoli was acquired from the Los Angeles Angels
RHP Frank Francisco was acquired from the Texas Rangeers.
RHP Octavio Dotel signed a 1-year, $3.5 million contract with 2012 club option.
RHP Jon Rauch signed a 1-year, $3.75 million contract with 2012 club option.
OF Rajai Davis was acquired from the Oakland Athletics.
3B Edwin Encarnacion signed a 1-year, $2.5 million contract with 2012 club option.
LHP Wil Ledezma was claimed off waivers from the Pittsburgh Pirates.
OF Corey Patterson signed a minor league contract.
RHP Brian Stokes signed a minor league contract.
2B Brett Lawrie was acquired from the Milwaukee Brewers.
RHP Carlos Villanueva was acquired from the Milwaukee Brewers.
C Ryan Budde signed a minor league contract.

2011 SUBTRACTIONS:

Manager Cito Gaston was not re-signed.
OF Vernon Wells was traded to the Los Angeles Angels.
C Mike Napoli was traded to the Texas Rangers.
RHP Shaun Marcum was traded to the Milwaukee Brewers.
1B Lyle Overbay was not re-signed.
RHP Jeremy Accardo was non-tendered.
C John Buck was not re-signed.
LHP Scott Downs was not re-signed.
RHP Kevin Gregg was not re-signed.
RHP Shawn Hill was released.
OF Fred Lewis was non-tendered.
LHP Brian Tallet was not re-signed.
OF DeWayne Wise was not re-signed.
1B Mike Jacobs was not re-signed.

2011 PROJECTED STARTING ROTATION: Ricky Romero; Brett Cecil; Brandon Morrow; Kyle Drabek; Marc Rzepczynski; Jesse Litsch.

2011 PROJECTED BULLPEN: Octavio Dotel; Jon Rauch; Frank Francisco; Jason Frasor; Shawn Camp; Casey Janssen; Jesse Carlson; David Purcey; Wil Ledezma; Josh Roenicke; Scott Richmond; Carlos Villanueva.

2011 PROJECTED LINEUP: C-Jose Molina; 1B-Adam Lind; 2B-Aaron Hill; 3B-Jose Bautista; SS-Yunel Escobar; LF-Juan Rivera; CF-Rajai Davis; RF-Travis Snider; DH-Edwin Encarnacion.

2011 BENCH: INF-John McDonald; C-J.P. Arencibia; INF-Mike McCoy; OF-Darin Mastroianni; C-Brian Jeroloman.

2011 POSSIBLE CONTRIBUTORS: RHP-Brian Stokes; 2B-Brett Lawrie; LHP-Rommie Lewis; RHP-Dustin McGowan; LHP Jo-Jo Reyes.

ASSESSMENTS MANAGEMENT:

GM Alex Anthopoulos already deserves executive of the year for finding someoene to take almost the whole Vernon Wells contract off his hands.

When he got the job following the long overdue firing of J.P. Ricciardi, the absence of an interview process and his simple anointing made me wonder whether the Blue Jays knew what they were doing. It didn't matter because Anthopoulos continually shows he himself knows what he's doing.

He's gutsy and makes unique moves to assist his organization such as when he traded for Miguel Olivo with no intention of picking up the catcher's option because he wanted to get his team an extra draft pick. This is outside-the-box thinking and I like it.

After the way his team overachieved in 2010, the easiest thing to do would've been to keep Cito Gaston as manager (I don't think Gaston wanted to quit managing); to go over-the-top in trying to run before the club could walk by doing something stupid.

Instead, he allowed negligible and replaceable talents like John Buck and Kevin Gregg walk; he traded Shaun Marcum; and he made what I see as a risky hire in John Farrell to take over as manager.

In the American League East, the unheralded teams like the Blue Jays and Orioles have to go for the deep strike—one of my favorite strategies—to compete with the Yankees and Red Sox. In this case, the deep strike wasn't going after a big free agent name or pulling off a blockbuster trade, but it was continuing on the current road and hiring a manager like Farrell with a wealth of experience with pitchers, but no managing experience.

Even though they hit all those homers last year, the Blue Jays' future is tied to how their pitchers develop; while I'm not a fan of hiring pitching coaches as managers, it does make some sense here.

The way this team is being constructed is positive. They may not seriously contend unless things go perfectly, but the foundation is in place for a viable playoff run as soon as 2012 and the GM deserves the credit for it. He's doing a fine job.

John Farrell's resume is very, very impressive. He was a journeyman pitcher in the big leagues and was pretty good; he was the Director of Player Development for the Indians; he was a college coach and recruiter; and he was a respected pitching coach for the Red Sox. For me, the two blots on his resume are that he never managed before and he's a former pitcher.

The rarity with which pitchers become successful managers is striking and it's not due to a lack of opportunity. For every Tommy Lasorda and George Bamberger, there are five Ray Millers and Larry Rothschilds who didn't make it as managers in making the jump from pitching coach. Even the current manager/former pitcher and pitching coach Bud Black of the Padres, who's had success, isn't a good strategic manager when handling the lineup and hitters.

I wouldn't hire a former pitcher as a manager unless he's the rare exception of someone who I speak to and wows me in the interview with his grasp of how to run a game. Orel Hershiser is one pitching name I'd hire as a manager.

Farrell? I can't say one way or the other until he's managing the team. As I said earlier, the easiest part of his job will be doing what he knows and handling the pitchers. He has a good bench coach, former Mariners manager Don Wakamatsu to help him, so I'd expect him to learn as he goes. He also sat next to Terry Francona and the pressure-packed arena of Boston.

I *think* he'll be fine. Then again, I also thought Trey Hillman was a terrific hire for the Royals and he was a disaster in every facet.

With Farrell, we won't know until we know.

STARTING PITCHING:

Lefty Ricky Romero has been compared to a young Johan Santana; it's a bit of a stretch, but Romero has a quirky motion and wide array of pitches including a good change-up, so the comparison has some validity.

He threw 210 innings last year, allowed 189 hits and only 15 homers. He walked 82 and threw 18 wild pitches which are two areas upon which he has to improve; he struck out 174. Romero could blossom into a top-of-the-rotation starter or be a mid-rotation cog once the other pitchers develop. Last August, he signed a 5-year, $30.1 million extension with a large option for $13.1 million in 2016.

Lefty Brett Cecil struggled in his first shot in the majors in 2009, but went 15-7 in 28 starts in 2010. He's a contact pitcher who allowed 175 hits and a respectable 18 homers in 172 innings, walking 54 and striking out 117. He's much more effective against lefties, but he isn't afraid to come inside to righties and can handle them. For the most part, he was durable and pitched 6-7 innings with a few excellent games sprinkled in. Of course there were games in which he got blasted. Once the younger Blue Jays pitchers gain more experience and learn to pitch in the big leagues, Cecil will be a mid-back of the rotation starter and a pretty good one.

Here's what I wrote (in part) in last year's book about Brandon Morrow:

Morrow has 18-win stuff and needs to be a starter. Period. It may take some work and time for the Blue Jays to unravel and rebuild Morrow, but that time will be worth it for the 25-year-old to fulfill that potential. I think he will. By late in the 2010 season, Morrow will look like the pitcher the Mariners expected him to be, only he'll be doing it in a Blue Jays uniform.

Freed from the looming shadow of Tim Lincecum, in a more nurturing atmosphere where he wasn't jerked between the starting rotation and bullpen, Morrow showed everyone why he was drafted *before* Lincecum.

Yes, he only went 10-7; yes, he had a 4.46 ERA and got knocked around a few times; but it was all part of the re-tooling process to start his career over and get him on the right path. What Morrow *could* do—and what he never would've been able to accomplish in Seattle—was exemplfied by his virtuoso performance against the Rays on August 8th and almost pitched a no-hitter.

The no-no was broken up with 2 outs in the ninth inning by Evan Longoria, but Morrow finished the 1-hit shutout after throwing 137 pitches, walking one and striking out 17.

The stuff is there for him to be a star.

The stuff was *always* there for him to be a star.

After that performance, his name became known and the talk of his brilliant arsenal of pitches was commonplace. He may not even become a star this year, but he's on his way.

He's on his way.

In years to come, even though they surrendered one of the best and guttiest pitchers of his generation Roy Halladay, that trade will be looked upon as a stroke of genius for Anthopoulos and the Blue Jays because the various maneuverings netted Morrow and Kyle Drabek.

Drabek, the son of former Cy Young Award winner Doug Drabek, has a motion and stuff almost identical to that of his dad. He uses a simplified motion, has powerful leg drive, control of a good sinking fastball along with a curve and slider. And he's mean.

He's 23, has dominated the minors; will win the AL Rookie of the Year in 2011; and is eventually going to be a frontline starter and superstar.

Marc Rzepczynski reminds me of a young Mark Mulder in stuff and motion; he missed time with an injured finger in 2010 and that hindered his development. His overall big league numbers were mediocre as he allowed 72 hits in 63 innings; walked 30 and gave up 8 homers; but he also struck out 57 and had flashes of brilliance. I like Rzepczynski a lot and think he'll eventually be a 15-game winner.

In 2008, righty Jesse Litsch went 13-9 and looked to be on the way to being a very good starting pitcher. He had Tommy John surgery in 2009 and a torn labrum in his hip in 2010. If he can come back from those injuries, he could be a contributor as a starter or long reliever in 2011; I'd hesitate to give up on him.

BULLPEN:

The Blue Jays are repeating their strategy from 2009 and signed a mediocre, veteran closer to a cheap, short-term contract. Last year it was Kevin Gregg; this year, Octavio Dotel.

Dotel is 37, saved 22 games with the Pirates and Dodgers and struck out 75 in 64 innings; as is customary with Dotel, he also allowed 9 homers. People forget that Dotel spent the last few weeks of the 2010 season with the Rockies after the Dodgers traded him for a player to be named later.

In the same category as Kevin Gregg, Dotel is a cheap stopgap; he'll convert most of his save opportunities if he's healthy and he'll be trade bait down the stretch if the Blue Jays are out of contention. If I were a GM, I wouldn't want Dotel as my closer, but there are worse out there.

Veteran set-up man and occasional closer Jon Rauch signed a 1-year, $3.75 million contract. Rauch doesn't have the dangerous fastball he once did, but the 6'11" righty was a key to the Twins bullpen early last season when he closed in place of the injured Joe Nathan. He can close if needed; doesn't allow many homers and throws strikes.

Frank Francisco was acquired from the Rangers when they spun the newly acquired Mike Napoli to Texas. Francisco was the Rangers closer prior to Neftali Feliz's rise. He's shaky in big games and missed the post-season with arm problems. Francisco is a power pitcher with a great fastball and racks up the strikeouts. He gives up a few too many homers (usually about 5 per year) and has a temper. Francisco throws strikes and is a good set-up man.

Righty Jason Frasor has been a part-time closer in the past. He's proven to be a durable and consistent reliever who strikes out more than a batter per inning and only allowed 4 homers in 63 innings in 2010. He has a good fastball and curve and handles righties and lefties well. I'd take a chance on Frasor as my closer before signing a Dotel.

Veteran Shawn Camp has gotten better on an annual basis with the Blue Jays after having some rough years with the Devil Rays. The 35-year-old righty with a slingshot motion appeared in 70 games, allowed 71 hits in 72 innings and 8 homers. He's a contact pitcher who throws strikes. Camp's ERA in his final year with the Devil Rays was 7.20; in his three years with the Blue Jays—with an incrementally increasing workload (40 games; 59 games; 70 games), it's been 4.12; 3.50 and 2.99 last season.

Versatile righty Casey Janssen appeared in 56 games, threw 68 innings, allowed 74 hits and 8 homers. His strikeout numbers took a jump for what was customary for him in prior years. In his best season, 2007, he struck out 39 in 70 games; last season he struck out 63. He's best suited for the bullpen, but he can start if necessary and he throws strikes.

Lefty Jesse Carlson was up and down between the majors and minors last season. He's a lefty specialist and their performances tend to fluctuate good and bad. He's best suited for that role.

David Purcey is a big lefty who could be useful as a long reliever/ spot starter. Purcey held lefties to a .163 average last season and found a home in the Blue Jays bullpen. He struck out 32 in 34 innings.

Another lefty, veteran journeyman Wil Ledezma, was claimed off waivers from the Pirates. Aside from intermittent and very moderate success with the Tigers and Padres, Ledezma has never gotten good results. His hits-to-innings pitched ratios are poor and he doesn't strike anyone out. I suspect he's still around only because he's lefty and is breathing. For his career, he's actually been much better against righties than against lefties so that detonates any reason to keep him around other than the breathing part.

I'm still holding out hope that one day Josh Roenicke will put it all together. He's got a sneaky, power fastball and has always struck out a lot of hitters. Best case scenario, he'll be a Grant Balfour type and have it kick in at some point. He doesn't allow many homers, but he has trouble throwing strikes.

Independent league foundling Scott Richmond missed almost the entire 2010 season with a shoulder injury. He showed some poise and potential as a starter/long man in 2009 and perhaps he can return to provide that again.

Righty Carlos Villanueva was acquired from the Brewers. Villanueva strikes out a lot of hitters and is durable. He's homer-prone and has started in the minors, but he throws strikes. I'd keep him in the bullpen and try him in important situations to see if he blossoms.

LINEUP:

John Buck priced himself out of Toronto; they traded for Miguel Olivo from the Rockies and declined his option so they could get the draft pick. Now they're facing the prospect of having Jose Molina at the top of their depth chart.

Molina handles the pitchers well and he's a great thrower, but he can't hit. Can the Blue Jays lineup carry Molina?

Yes, if Aaron Hill and Adam Lind return to form and Yunel Escobar hits as he did in 2009 with the Braves. Otherwise, it's tough to have an automatic out in an American League lineup that's weakened from last year.

Adam Lind is making the move to first base. Adam Lind had a horrific year after his 35 homer, 114 RBI, .305 batting average; .370 OBP and .932 OPS from 2009.

Along with Aaron Hill, Lind fell off the planet with a woeful 23 homer, .712 OPS season. He also struck out 144 times after k'ing 110 times in 2009. He was horrendous. I have to ask the question as to whether that which worked with the likes of Bautista and Wells hindered the development of Hill and Lind. No one could've expected them to repeat their 2009 seasons, but the way they hit in 2010 was borderling embarrassing.

It was a catch-22. The hitters the flourished under the go-for-broke style in 2010 may not have hit as well had they been more patient. It turned out that it didn't work for Hill and Lind. They need both to regain form especially with the subtractions mentioned earlier.

Aaron Hill busted out in 2009 and fell apart in 2010. After a 36 homer, 108 RBI, .829 OPS season in '09, Hill wound up with 26 homers and a .665 OPS with a woeful .205 batting average last season. Hill is locked up financially through 2014 and a second baseman who hits 20+ homers is valuable, but those numbers aren't going to cut it. Plus the Blue Jays need him to hit to counteract the loss of Buck and flightiness of Escobar and Edwin Encarnacion along with the possibility of a statistical correction by Bautista.

Bautista had a year that was, um, suspicious in the Luis Gonzalez-way and Bautista was never as good a hitter as Gonzalez was before their respective power-surges.

Bautista defenders say that the main problem he had was that he never got the chance to play regularly, his detractors call him a testament to PEDs.

I can understand both sides of the argument and I'm not going to accuse him of using anything to assist his newfound power. I will say this: someone who has never hit more than 24 homers at any professional level suddenly busting out with 54 is dubious to say the least. The skepticism can stem from the possibility of PED use or it could be of the "he's never going to do that again" variety. The Blue Jays hitting style of swinging for the fences was a factor. There's no question about that. But 54 homers at 29-years-old?

Let's see how Bautista does when the season starts. He got off to a bad start last year and hit 12 homers in May. Scrutiny will surround him to see if it was a fluke or it was achieved by some other means. Who's to say, though, that he's still not going to be doing whatever it was that assisted him in his explosion? There's not a testing procedure to be able to stop it if he was using HGH.

I believe he's going to hit for power again; probably not 50 homer power, but 35 homer power.

Before spring training, Bautista signed a 5-year, $65 million contract extension to remain with the Blue Jays in the long term. It's a worthwhile gamble for both sides, but the Blue Jays had better hope it was no fluke.

Yunel Escobar's attitude was what forced the Braves to deal him to the Blue Jays for veteran Alex Gonzalez. Escobar has MVP talent, but does....not.....listen. He's got Gold Glove fielding potential; a howitzer of an arm; power and some speed. But he's moody and throws tantrums that drew the ire of the business-minded Braves clubhouse and was loathed by Bobby Cox.

The Braves clubhouse erupted in applause when Gonzalez entered the room. Literally.

Escobar's no kid; he's 28. I love his ability and he played better after getting to Toronto. Perhaps Bautista and Molina can be good influences on him to play at his best and fulfill his potential. Like with Encarnacion, who knows?

Juan Rivera was acquired from the Angels in the Wells trade. He's a free agent at the end of the season and the Blue Jays have been listening to offers for him in a trade, but they may be stuck with him for the start of the season. Rivera is a cog. He'll hit 15-20 homers; doesn't walk much; doesn't strike out much; doesn't get on base; and plays serviceable defense in left field.

Rajai Davis had the best year of his career with the Athletics and was traded to the Blue Jays for two minor leaguers. Davis stole 50 bases and adds much-needed speed to the Blue Jays lineup. He'll move to center field to replace the traded Wells.

Top prospect Travis Snider wound up back in the minors after getting a chance to play regularly in the majors early in the season. He slumped badly and was sent down in May; he returned at midsummer and played better. Snider ended up with 14 homers in 319 plate appearances. He strikes out a lot and needs to work on his pitch selection, but he's only 23. The Blue Jays should throw him out there every day and let him play.

Edwin Encarnacion was with the Blue Jays last season; was claimed on waivers by the Athletics after the season; he was non-tendered by the Athletics and re-signed by the Blue Jays.

Encarnacion has the ability to be a great fielder.

He isn't and sometimes looks like he's watching birds fly overhead rather than paying attention to what's going on on the field.

Encarnacion has the ability to hit 25 homers and drive in 100 runs with a .280 batting average.

He hit 21 last season including 3 in one game in May and 5 over the final four games of the season.

Encarnacion is 28. It's time to put it together already. Or not.

BENCH:

John McDonald's claim to fame will always be his near fistfight with Alex Rodriguez after the "HA" incident a couple of years ago. McDonald can't really hit, but he's a valuable utility player in the field.

J.P. Arencibia could conceivably get a chance to catch semi-regularly if he can handle the pitching staff. The 25-year-old has shown good power in the minors and thrown well. The Blue Jays have to be careful with their young pitchers and, to start the season, may be better off with Molina catching regularly; they can work Arencibia into the lineup if they need his bat.

Mike McCoy is a journeyman utility player who batted .195 in 90 plate appearances for the Blue Jays last season. He's shown impressive speed and on base ability in the minors, but he's going to be 30-years-old. Expecting too much is a mistake.

Darin Mastroianni is a speedy, 25-year-old outfielder who could stick as a bench player. He's shown on base ability in the minors and can play all three outfield positions.

Brian Jeroloman is a 26-year-old catcher who throws well and has a good eye at the plate. He bats lefty and has been a part-timer in the minors.

PREDICTION:

The Blue Jays played far better than the expectations in 2010. Some thought they were going to lose 100 games. This was absurd. They had enough pitching that they were not going to lose 100 games. I certainly didn't expect them to play as well as they did, nor hit with the power to accumulate 257 homers.

Can they repeat this in 2011? And will the pitching mature fast?

This Blue Jays team, with a little luck, could make a Wild Card run. If Bautista comes anywhere close to his 2010 season; if Drabek and Morrow develop; if Encarnacion and Escobar learn to play baseball and pay attention, who knows?

The keys to the season are the pitching and Hill/Lind. If Hill/Lind return to 2009 form, the Blue Jays will make a run. Whether they can rediscover their swings from 2009 is the question and might mean the difference between under .500 and a win total in the high-80s and playoff contention.

I have questions about the new manager Farrell. His resume's great, but that means nothing once the games start.

The Blue Jays are still building and they're doing it on the fly. Their future is bright, but I can't see them being viable contenders this year. With the depth of pitching in the organization, they're close to taking the next step; it just won't be this year.

PREDICTED RECORD: 83-79

Baltimore Orioles

2010 Record: 66-96; 5th Place, American League East.

2010 Recap:

The Orioles had two different seasons. Before Buck and After Buck.

Buck Showalter arrived in August to show the Orioles the "way". The way to play baseball; the way to behave; the way to respect the game and do things correctly.

It's amazing how a team with limited talent can turn things around with the simple act of respecting themselves and doing the right things at the right times; by playing as a team.

The Orioles had some talent to start the season but unlike previous years under manager Dave Trembley, they didn't get off to a good start only to come apart in the summer.

No.

This time they got off to an atrocious start and played terribly for the whole season until Trembley was fired and replaced by Juan Samuel. They didn't play much better under him. The numbers are what they are. Under Trembley, the Orioles were 15-39; under Samuel, 17-34; and under Showalter, 34-23.

Was this somthing of an anomaly? Slightly. But Showalter's mere presence invigorated the organization that was once the blueprint of how to do it right and has become a dysfunctional laughingstock.

I'll always believe that had Orioles closer Mike Gonzalez not blown 2 of the first 3 games of the season in dramatic fashion that the season could've gotten off to a better start than it did. In the AL East, the teams ahead of the Orioles wouldn't have allowed them to escape the cellar, but they could've been respectable.

In the long run, they were better off that the season unraveled. Had they treaded water and looked to be on the way up with the young talent and bargain basement pickups by Andy MacPhail, they may not have hired Showalter and created an atmosphere of hope where there was little of that before he arrived.

2011 ADDITIONS:

3B Mark Reynolds was acquired from the Arizona Diamondbacks.
DH Vladimir Guerrero signed a 1-year, $8 million contract.
SS J.J. Hardy was acquired from the Minnesota Twins.
1B Derrek Lee was signed to a 1-year, $7.25 million contract.
RHP Kevin Gregg signed a 2-year, $10 million contract with club option.
INF Brendan Harris was acquired from the Minnesota Twins.
RHP Jeremy Accardo signed a 1-year, $1.08 million contract.
RHP Justin Duchscherer signed a minor league contract.
RHP David Riske signed a minor league contract.
RHP Josh Rupe signed a minor league contract.

2011 SUBTRACTIONS:

INF Ty Wigginton was not re-signed.
RHP David Hernandez was traded to the Arizona Diamondbacks.
RHP Kam Mickolio was traded to the Arizona Diamondbacks.
RHP Matt Albers was non-tendered.
1B Michael Aubrey was not re-signed.
LHP Alberto Castillo was not re-signed.
LHP Mark Hendrickson's option was declined.
INF Julio Lugo was not re-signed.
RHP Cla Meredith was not re-signed.
RHP Kevin Millwood was not re-signed.
INF Scott Moore was not re-signed.
OF Corey Patterson was not re-signed.

2011 PROJECTED STARTING ROTATION: Jeremy Guthrie; Brian Matusz; Brad Bergesen; Jake Arrieta; Chris Tillman; Justin Duchscherer.

2011 PROJECTED BULLPEN: Kevin Gregg; Mike Gonzalez; Koji Uehara; Jim Johnson; Jason Berken; Jeremy Accardo; Rick Vanden Hurk; Troy Patton; Josh Rupe.

2011 PROJECTED LINEUP: C-Matt Wieters; 1B-Derrek Lee; 2B-Brian Roberts; 3B-Mark Reynolds; SS-J.J. Hardy; LF-Luke Scott; CF-Adam Jones; RF-Nick Markakis; DH-Vladimir Guerrero.

2011 BENCH: OF-Nolan Reimold; OF-Felix Pie; INF-Robert Andino; INF-Cesar Izturis; C-Jake Fox; C-Craig Tatum; 3B-Josh Bell.

2011 POSSIBLE CONTRIBUTORS: LHP-Zach Britton; RHP-Brandon Erbe; RHP-Alfredo Simon; LHP-Pedro Viola; INF-Pedro Florimon; INF-Brandon Snyder; OF-Matt Angle; RHP-David Riske.

ASSESSMENTS MANAGEMENT:

As respected a baseball man as Andy MacPhail is, he's along for the ride now.

The Buck Showalter ride and, given the way Showalter's mere presence lit up the franchise, MacPhail has a choice: get on the bus or be under it.

Despite last winter's acquisitions having failed, MacPhail brought credibility to the Orioles again. It may not have shown up on the field, but the organization was developing prospects and eschewing owner Peter Angelos's impatient overspending on veteran free agents to long-term contracts that were either too expensive or doled out to players for performances they'd achieved elsewhere and were looking for that one final payday in their careers—if they had to go to Baltimore for the money and lose nearly 100 games in embarrassing fashion, so be it.

Be that as it may, there's always been a disconnect between the Angelos way and the MacPhail way. Even when there's money available to spend, MacPhail prefers to save it. Going back to the building of two World Series champions with the Twins under a tight budget; and his time with the Cubs when he almost brought them to the World Series, rarely has there been a big ticket free agent signed under MacPhail's watch.

His most impressive accomplishment as Orioles GM has been to convince Angelos that his way wasn't working and the club had to clear out the ambivalent veterans for youth and rebuild the right way; the way the Orioles under Earl Weaver did. Unfortunately, when he signed cogs like Mike Gonzalez and Garret Atkins and traded for Kevin Millwood, all turned out to be disasters. His reluctance to hire a strong-handed manager also contributed to the chaotic atmosphere and on-field mistakes.

After keeping former manager Dave Trembley far too long, the negotiations with Showalter took a long time. It was said that MacPhail preferred Eric Wedge to manage the team. Presumably that would be because if Wedge were hired, MacPhail would still have the final say. With Showalter? Put it this way: what Buck wants, Buck gets, especially after the way the team played over the last two months when he took over.

MacPhail's power has been mitigated and I wouldn't be surprised to see 2011 be his last with the Orioles. He's not going to win a power struggle, so it might be best for him to move on.

Speaking of Eric Wedge, he's a good manager and will do well in Seattle handling the Mariners. But as far as being a difference-maker? No, Wedge is not a difference-maker. Buck Showalter is.

The managers who either have the startegic acumen, reputation and organizational support to keep the players in line are few and far between. Joe Torre didn't have that all-encompassing power while he was at his height with the Yankees dynasty. Bobby Cox didn't have it either. Tony La Russa has it; Lou Piniella had it; Mike Scioscia has it; and Buck Showalter has it.

Showalter is the boss now. What he says goes. There's not going to be any turf wars with a player because if the player crosses the line, Showalter's smart enough to either get rid of a player he didn't really want anyway to send a message, or he'll coax the player to fall into line. I'm curious as to what would've happened had Showalter been managing the Orioles when center fielder Adam Jones was asked to play shallower and Jones responded that he'd think about it. Would Showalter have butted heads with the talented Jones by saying he can think about it in Norfolk playing at Triple A? Or would he have made it appear that he was disciplining Jones with the selfish knowledge that he needed the center fielder to succeed, using gentle nuance and fatherly persuasion rather than the disciplinary hammer?

Showalter is calculating, smart and ruthless; his attention to detail and anal retentive nature has worn on each and every one of his prior clubs. The Orioles situation could be different because he doesn't have that one star he has to handle and befriend. They're a collection of pieces to a puzzle and that's the way Showalter likes it.

He'll succeed with the Orioles—eventually, the odds are he'll wear out his welcome, but they know he's in charge; he's not a no-name like Trembley who had no professional playing resume and little chance of success due to circumstances both in and out of his control. Showalter is the man in Baltimore and the most important thing is that the players know it.

STARTING PITCHING:

Jeremy Guthrie happens to be a good pitcher that few realize is any good because he plays for the Orioles. Guthrie's not young (he's 32); and it took him awhile to even make the big leagues and longer to stick. As he's established himself in the majors, he's gotten better and better.

He went 11-14 in 2010, but his other numbers were very good. In 209 innings, he allowed 193 hits. He's a contact pitcher who neither strikes out many, nor walks many and he gives up too many homers. With a good fastball and secondary pitches, along with a meanness on the mound, Guthrie may not be the prototypical ace, but he's the veteran on the Orioles staff and has been consistently good even if outsiders don't know it.

Brian Matusz is one of the young Orioles starters who will lead to a renaissance in Baltimore if he continues to develop. The 24-year-old lefty was the Orioles 1st round draft pick in 2008 and had his first full year in the majors in 2010. After going 10-12 and allowing 173 hits in 175 innings, Matusz will be a key to the Orioles turnaround if he becomes the ace that such a high draft pick is expected to be. If he was on a better team, Matusz pitched well enough to have won 17 games last season. He may not become a star in 2011, but he'll take the next step in learning his craft.

Brad Bergesen is a 24-year-old righty who pitched well in his first season in the bigs in 2009 and struggled in 2010. His ERA was a bloated 4.98, but that was a byproduct of some terrible starts; he pitched very well over the last month of the season under Showalter. He gives up a lot of homers like the other Orioles pitchers; I don't think that will bother the manager all that much as long as he throws strikes and the homers don't create a crooked number. More than any other pitcher on the Orioles staff, Bergesen should benefit from the improved infield defense. He might break out and be a 15-game winner this year.

Righty Jake Arrieta went 6-6 as a rookie in 2010. Another contact pitcher, he gives up too many walks. He's been terrific in the minors across the board, including with his control. For a contact pitcher, Arrieta only allowed 9 homers. He too should benefit from the infield defense. Arrieta's wildness makes it easy to run his pitch count up. A contact pitcher with bad control is a lethal combination, but the fact that he doesn't allow many homers is a saving grace. The Orioles have to convince him to trust his stuff.

Chris Tillman is a 6'5" righty who was, along with Adam Jones, one of the keys to the trade of Erik Bedard to the Mariners after the 2007 season. Tillman, 23, has been inconsistent at best in his 23 big league starts spaced over 2009-2010. But he's shown flashes of brilliance and he struck out a lot of hitters in the minors. He gives up a too many homers and his control has been lacking, but these are growing pains. Tillman is going to be a top-of-the-rotation force. It probably won't be this year, but this year is more of a nascent, innocent climb for the Showalter-led Orioles and these young pitchers are a major part of that process.

Two-time All Star (as a starter and reliever) Justin Duchscherer signed a minor league contract after most of the past two seasons with various injuries. He's had problems with both hips, his elbow and battled depression. He's got a good fastball, slow curve and control when he's healthy, but to think he's suddenly going to be able to pitch is delusional.

BULLPEN:

Showalter doesn't believe in the "one closer" to save the games just because he's the closer. This strategy can only work when the manager is in complete command and doesn't have the ego-fueled short man who wants the glory of the save stat.

With Kevin Gregg and Mike Gonzalez, both are sufficiently mediocre that neither is going to complain when they're not automatically inserted in the ninth inning regardless of the game situation. It won't be a closer-by-committe; nor will it be "it's Gregg's time" or "it's Gonzalez's time".

The righty Gregg is wild and allows too many homers. That said, he was mostly reliable for the Blue Jays in 2010 and the Orioles aren't contending this season, so Gregg is an affordable stopgap who could be traded as his 2-year contract expires in 2012 and the Orioles move nearer to relevance.

Mike Gonzalez was signed to be the new closer last season, blew two games in the first week and it was later revealed was trying to pitch through shoulder pain to justify his contract. Gonzalez, when healthy, has dominating stuff—a power fastball and wicked slider. He pitched well after Showalter took over.

Both Gonzalez and Gregg will be solid as the Orioles late-inning relievers.

Koji Uehara was tried as the Orioles closer last season; he was solid enough, but allows too many homers to be a closer. His numbers wound up looking respectable; numbers don't tell the whole story. Uehara saved 13 games and had 55 strikeouts in 44 innings; he only allowed 37 hits and 5 walks. Uehara's control may have been too good; so good in fact that the hitters weren't concerned that he was going to brush them back. He won't be closing, but he's a strikeout set-up man.

Jim Johnson is a right-handed long reliever who throws strikes, gives up a fair amount of hits and too many homers. He missed a chunk of last season with an elbow issue.

Righty Jason Berken was awful as a starter in 2009, but found his niche as a reliever in 2010. Berken posted a 3.03 ERA in 41 games in relief; allowed 64 hits in 63 innings and 5 homers. He struck out 45 and walked 19. Not great, but not bad either. Certainly not as bad as 164 hits in 119 innings, which is what he allowed in 2009.

Jeremy Accardo was signed after the Blue Jays non-tendered him. Accardo was on the way to becoming a good closer after saving 30 games and posting excellent across-the-board numbers in 2007; former Blue Jays GM J.P. Ricciardi had pulled off a heist getting Accardo from the Giants for the clubhouse poison Shea Hillenbrand. Since then, Accardo's been mostly terrible. He spent much of 2010 in the minors. If the Orioles are getting the pitcher from 2007, they've got themselves a bargain; if not, he was worth a shot.

6'8" righty Rick Vanden Hurk was acquired from the Marlins for Will Ohman last season. Vanden Hurk has terrific stuff but has never put it all together. I always pictured him as a starter if he was able to cut down on his wildness and the number of pitches he threw, but perhaps he's better suited to be a reliever as he can strike people out.

Troy Patton has had injury problems and been good as a starter in the minors, but his role in the big leagues may be a long man/lefty specialist.

Josh Rupe is a veteran journeyman righty who signed a minor league contract. Rupe can be wild and gives up a few homers, but he may stick as a reliever for the Orioles.

LINEUP:

While the other hot, young catching prospect—Buster Posey—was winning the Rookie of the Year and a championship ring with the Giants, Matt Wieters was learning that being anointed as a future star doesn't necessarily mean it's going to come easily.

Wieters did well defensively, but struggled at the plate with 11 homers, 55 RBI and 94 strikeouts in 502 plate appearances. The 25-year-old murdered all pitching in the minors, but the switch-hitter had problems from the right side of the plate. Wieters is too talented to continue having these issues, but he's proving that it's not as easy as it looks from the outside; nor can minor league success immediately translate to the big leagues.

That said, I think he'll have a breakout year in 2011.

Respected veteran Derrek Lee signed a 1-year contract to take over at first base. Lee is good defensively and as recently as 2009 finished in the top 10 in the MVP voting. He's 35 and has lost a step defensively, but can still hit. The friendly confines of Camden Yards will let Lee return to 30 homer production.

Along with the bullpen issues, Brian Roberts's abdominal strain and resulting stay on the disabled list contributed mightily to the Orioles poor start. Roberts is a fine all-around player with pop when he's healthy and the Orioles need his veteran leadership and stability to take the next step.

I've long said I'm not a fan of Mark Reynolds. Stat zombies point to his big home run numbers and that he plays third base; since it's difficult to find a productive third baseman, Reynolds's flaws—striking out 220 times; a batting average under .200; mediocre fielding with a spectacular play here and there to make him look better than he is defensively—are glossed over.

Two things about the Orioles acquisition of Reynolds: 1) he's way better than what they had; and 2) he'll hit a lot of homers in Camden Yards.

They could've done worse.

J.J. Hardy's star has fallen like a plummeting meteorite. Hardy hit 50 homers in 2007-2008 for the Brewers; was an All Star and looked to be a big time player. Then he fell off the planet and even wound up back in the minors in 2009. Traded to the Twins, Hardy was a little better at the plate, but not much. His power has disappeared. Maybe the pitchers have discovered a flaw and Hardy hasn't been able to adjust in turn.

Considering he's replacing the no-hit Cesar Izturis as the regular shortstop, the Orioles have taken another step up on the left side of the infield; and Hardy's a very good fielder.

Like Reynolds, the improvement with Hardy is attributable to that which he is replacing than what Hardy can do at this point. He's only 28 and has time to rediscover his game.

His idiotic political rants aside (in case you missed it, Luke Scott doesn't think that President Obama was born in the United States), he's a very good hitter.

One question: why does anyone care what *Luke Scott* thinks about politics enough to ask him about it and then take interest in what he says after the fact? Aside from his controversial (and idiotic) rant, it's not something to take seriously.

On the field, Scott's a pro. He's got power and hits 55 or so extra base hits a year. He gets on base a fair amount and, while not great against lefties, he's not clueless either. As long as he keeps his mouth shut about politics, I'd love to have Scott in my lineup.

He'll play left field with the addition of Guerrero.

Suffice it to say that under Showalter there won't be the "I'll think about it" attitude from Adam Jones when asked to do something to help the team. Jones was an All Star and Gold Glove winner in 2009 and regressed in 2010, partially because of that attitude. His hitting numbers wound up close to what they were in 2009 (19 homers, 69 RBI), but he played in 30 more games in 2010 than he did in 2009.

The 25-year-old Jones has star talent and will fulfill it under the new manager.

Nick Markakis is a star-caliber player. His home run numbers have declined from 20 in 2008 to 12 in 2010. His other numbers have been the same. He's good for 45 doubles; a high on base percentage; pretty good defense; and the right attitude on the field. He won't be alone on an island as the only power bat the Orioles have with Reynolds, Hardy and Lee; this bodes well for a return to a 20+ homer year for Markakis.

Veteran Vladimir Guerrero signed a 1-year, $8 million contract to be the Orioles DH. Guerrero had a rejuvenating year on and off the field for the Rangers and played a big part in the maturation of the young players in Texas. He wasn't a product of Arlington's friendly confines either. Overall he batted .300 with a .345 on base, 29 homers and 115 RBI.

The 36-year-old Guerrero will be a conduit for Showalter to teach the young Orioles how to behave on and off the field and he's always been great with the younger players as a mentor. His contribution won't be indicative with the Orioles record, but in the future, Guerrero will be a large reason why they improve.

BENCH:

Nolan Reimold will get substantial at bats if he's healthy. Reimold burst onto the scene in 2009 with 15 homers in 411 plate appearances, but wound up back in the minors in 2010. He has power and gets on base and plays a pretty good left field.

Felix Pie showed star potential in the minors with the Cubs, but when he didn't perform immediately in the big leagues, Cubs manager Lou Piniella benched and dispatched him. With the Orioles, Pie has shown flashes and has yet to put it all together.

Robert Andino is a utility infielder who batted .295 in 66 big league plate appearances in 2010. He played regularly in Triple A last season and has speed.

Cesar Izturis is more suited to be a backup and defensive replacement than the everyday shortstop and with the acquisition of Hardy, that's what he's going to be.

Jake Fox is a journeyman backup catcher, corner infielder and outfielder who's shown power, but never gotten a chance to play regularly in the big leagues. Showalter will find a way to use him and perhaps he can be a versatile Jim Leyritz-type bat.

Craig Tatum is a backup catcher who batted .281 in 126 plate appearances in 2010. He throws well and has never hit in the minors.

Josh Bell is a top third base prospect who was acquired from the Dodgers when the Orioles traded George Sherrill. Bell's a switch hitter who batted .214 with 3 homers in 161 big league plate appearances, but that's not important. He's 24 and the implication that his way to playing regularly is blocked by the acquisition of Reynolds is silly. If he hits, they'll find a place for him to play. His numbers stagnated in the minors last year, but he's still a top hitting prospect who might get a chance to play regularly in the big leagues sometime this season.

PREDICTION:

The Orioles burst under Showalter is not unimportant; it's a great sign; but it has to be taken in full context. The team had been so atrocious that the credibility of having a manager who knew what he was doing and wasn't going to tolerate crap gave the club confidence. They're on the right track and are going to get better; eventually they'll contend.

That said, don't make the mistake of thinking that it's an indicator of a fast turnaround.

It isn't.

That division is a torture chamber and the Orioles pitching is very, very young.

Guerrero will be a leader on the club and he can still hit.

They have plenty of talent and Showalter's teams generally don't leap into contention until his second full year on the job; the free agent crop was weak this past winter and the Orioles made most of their improvements via addition by subtraction and through trades.

The players that are there will help the team be better simply by playing the game in a fundamentally correct fashion. Occasionally, it's not the participants themselves that are important, but how they're utilized; Showalter is the master at inserting players into the proper situations based on his constant and intense scrutiny of everything from the wind currents to the umpire to his gut.

But I keep going back to the division and the young pitching. It's hard to win with those two factors staring you in the face.

The Orioles have direction now. They have talent and a proven manager.

In 2011 they'll be better, but it won't show in their won/lost results.

Sometimes other things are more important. Things like credibility. With Showalter they have that.

One small step at a time.

PREDICTED RECORD: 66-96

American League Central Predicted Standings

		Wins	Losses	GB
1.	Chicago White Sox	92	70	---
2.	Detroit Tigers *	90	72	2
3.	Minnesota Twins	76	86	16
4.	Kansas City Royals	72	90	20
5.	Cleveland Indians	67	95	25

*Denotes predicted Wild Card winner.

Chicago White Sox

2010 Record: 88-74; 2nd place, American League Central.

2010 Recap:

The White Sox got off to a terrible start and had a blazing hot streak that curtailed talk that they were going to clean house of veterans Paul Konerko, A.J. Pierzynski and possibly some younger players like Gordon Beckham.

Having made the mistake of going with a rotating DH rather than a consistent producer, the White Sox offense was lacking. Injuries to Jake Peavy and inconsistency in the rest of the pitching staff—Gavin Floyd and Bobby Jenks specifically—along with in-fighting between mangaer Ozzie Guillen and GM Kenny Williams, made the White Sox look dysfunctional.

That said, they always looked dysfunctional even when they were winning the World Series and making the playoffs.

88-74 looks better than the way they played. Their streakiness culminated in an 8 game losing streak in September against the Tigers and Twins. Since they were chasing the Twins, this cost them a chance to win the AL Central and let the Twins walk away with the division. On September 6th, the White Sox were 3 ½ games out of first place; two weeks later, they were 11 games out of first place and finished.

2011 ADDITIONS:

DH/1B/OF Adam Dunn signed a 4-year, $56 million contract.

RHP Jesse Crain signed a 3-year, $13 million contract.
LHP Will Ohman signed a 2-year, $4 million contract.
RHP Jeff Gray signed a minor league contract.
RHP Kyle Cofield was acquired from the Atlanta Braves.

2011 SUBTRACTIONS:

OF/DH Manny Ramirez was not re-signed.
RHP Bobby Jenks was non-tendered.
RHP J.J. Putz was not re-signed.
RHP Freddy Garcia was not re-signed.
OF Andruw Jones was not re-signed.
OF/1B Mark Kotsay was not re-signed.
RHP Scott Linebrink was traded to the Atlanta Braves.
LHP Erick Threets was non-tendered.
RHP Carlos Torres was released.
LHP Randy Williams was not re-signed.

2011 PROJECTED STARTING ROTATION: Jake Peavy; Mark Buehrle; John Danks; Gavin Floyd; Edwin Jackson.

2011 PROJECTED BULLPEN: Matt Thornton; Chris Sale; Jesse Crain; Sergio Santos; Will Ohman; Tony Pena; Freddy Dolsi.

2011 PROJECTED LINEUP: C-A.J. Pierzynski; 1B-Paul Konerko; 2B-Gordon Beckham; 3B-Mark Teahen; SS-Alexei Ramirez; LF-Juan Pierre; CF-Alexis Rios; RF-Carlos Quentin; DH-Adam Dunn.

2011 BENCH: INF-Omar Vizquel; INF-Dayan Viciedo; C-Ramon Castro; 3B/SS-Brent Morel; INF/OF-Brent Lillibridge; C-Tyler Flowers.

2011 POSSIBLE CONTRIBUTORS: OF-Alejandro De Aza; RHP-Kyle Cofield; RHP-Lucas Harrell; RHP-Jeffrey Marquez; RHP-Jhonny Nunez; INF-Eduardo Escobar; OF-Stefan Gartrell; RHP-Anthony Carter.

ASSESSMENTS
MANAGEMENT:

GM Kenny Williams knew his club needed a bat.

He signed Adam Dunn.

They needed to make a change at closer.

He non-tendered Bobby Jenks.

He wanted to improve the bullpen.

He signed Jesse Crain and Will Ohman.

He'd grown tired of the constant battles with manager Ozzie Guillen and the growing rift in their once close relationship and was willing to listen to the Marlins when they came with a trade offer to acquire Guillen; it never came to pass; in fact, it didn't go very far; but that he would even consider such a thing as trading his manager is a window into the mind of baseball's James Bond Villain, Kenny Williams.

He doesn't care what you say; what you think; how you feel about his decisions. He does what he thinks is right for his club; he acts aggressively to fill the holes his club has and he does it in quick strike fashion.

The White Sox are again a contender because of Williams's fearlessness and intelligence and he's going to be ready to move at mid-season as well.

Williams was willing to let Guillen leave and the continued vitriol over Ozzie's son Oney's revelations of sensitive clubhouse information, there's still a problem there. The White Sox, under Williams have been able to overcome these distractions—indeed, at times they've seemed to encourage them—but there comes a point where it's too much and is harming the team.

I've speculated on Ozzie Guillen's time with the White Sox ending before because of the lunacy he covets and crafts. But before there wasn't the constant tension between Williams and Guillen; the tension was infesting the clubhouse to where a split appeared inevitable, but the White Sox exercised Guillen's contract option for 2012 so he looks like he's staying.

Guillen's a terrific game manager; he's interesting and fun to watch, but that explosiveness comes with a price and he's been reluctant to tell his son to stop with the Twitter stuff; to keep from letting the world in on things that must be kept inside the clubhouse.

It's not good.

And Ozzie's starting a website.

The team has gone through this before and weathered the storm of Ozzie.

STARTING PITCHING:

Every year I've waited for Jake Peavy's all-out, all the time, bullwhipping, arm shredding motion to lead to his arm going flying off at the shoulder when he unleashed one of his fastballs.

Last year, I gave in to Peavy's continued ability to pitch and stay reasonably healthy with those atrocious mechanics by picking him to win the AL Cy Young Award.

Naturally, Peavy got off to a terrible start and, guess what, his entire latissimus dorsi detached and he was lost for the season.

My timing is sometimes not....good.

Peavy might not be ready to start the 2011 season after surgery to repair the injury and no one can tell what the White Sox will be getting when he returns. Will he be able to put such an injury out of his mind and pitch the same way? Will he have the capacity to generate the same force as he did in his heyday?

Does anyone know?

I have questions about it. Serious questions.

If the White Sox have 75% of the dominating Peavy from his Padres days by June, they should be happy with that.

Mark Buehrle was mentioned as a possible trade target for teams like the Yankees after they missed out on Cliff Lee, but it's hard to see the White Sox giving up on their longtime innings-gobbling, pseudo-ace. Buehrle's a free agent at the end of the season, but the White Sox have made it a habit of not trading their impending free agents even when they're having a bad season. This past winter alone, they kept A.J. Pierzynski and Paul Konerko when it was a legitimate question as to whether either were going to return.

Buehrle went 13-13 in 2010 with a 4.28 ERA; he gave up a lot of hits (246 in 210 innings) but he *always* give up a lot of hits. Buehrle actually gave up far fewer homers (17) than he normally does. He doesn't walk many; doesn't strike out many; he guts his way through even when he doesn't have his good stuff or gives up a crooked number in the first inning. And when he's on his game, he's got the habit of throwing a no-hitter or a perfect game. Buehrle is what he is and what that is is a lefty horse for the White Sox. He's not going anywhere and will put up his usual numbers.

That's what he does.

Lefty John Danks is similar to Buehrle in his consistency, but he has better stuff and results. For the last three seasons, Danks has had an ERA ranging between 3.2 and 3.7; he's thrown around 200 innings; he's had a very good hits/innings pitched ratio (last season it was 189/210); he gives up a homer here and there, but he throws strikes. Danks went 15-11 in 2010 and may be ready to take the next step into becoming an 18 game winner. Williams stole Danks from the Rangers for Brandon McCarthy after the 2006 season.

In addition to the suggestion that the White Sox might listen to offers on Buehrle, it was also said that they might listen to offers for Gavin Floyd. Floyd has slumped since his breakout year in 2008 in which he went 17-5. His numbers were better than his 11-11 record in 2009, but in 2010, he got off to a terrible start and his ERA was over 6 into June. Apart from a few bad games, Floyd regained his form and pitched well for the rest of the season. I'd expect a good season from the start for Floyd.

Williams needed a starting pitcher at mid-season, so he traded his top pitching prospect Daniel Hudson to get Edwin Jackson from the Diamondbacks. It was suggested that Jackson was only stopping over in Chicago and was possibly a part of the package to get Adam Dunn from the Nationals. It didn't happen and Jackson stayed with the White Sox.

Jackson pitched a 149 pitch no-hitter for the Diamondbacks against the Rays in June. That no-hitter and my subsequent blog posting defending the Diamondbacks then-manager A.J. Hinch for leaving the big, tough and durable Jackson in the game to complete the no-no was discussed on the Diamondbacks broadcast the next week by Daron Sutton and Mark Grace.

Jackson is a horse at the top of the rotation who is willing and able to throw 120-140 pitches in a game. He's a free agent at the end of the season and is represented by Scott Boras, so you can pretty much forget a contract extension mid-season. People don't realize how young Jackson is because he was in the big leagues for the Dodgers at 19, but he's going to be a free agent at 28. He's primed to have a big year and make himself a lot of money.

BULLPEN:

With the departure of Bobby Jenks, the White Sox will be in need of a new primary closer. Veteran lefty Matt Thornton was used occasionally in the role last season after Jenks was demoted. He throws very, very hard; handles both lefties and righties; doesn't allow many homers; and throws strikes. I'd give him the job and let him run with it.

Another option is rookie Chris Sale. Sale, another lefty, was taken in the first round of last year's draft with the 13th pick. The White Sox brought him to the big leagues and he posted a 1.93 ERA in 21 games with 3 saves and 32 strikeouts in 21 innings. There's a possibility that he might be used as a starter and one would assume that's contingent on Peavy's progress and how Thornton handles full-time closing.

Sale is a Rookie of the Year candidate.

Jesse Crain's signing does two things for the White Sox: 1) it brings in a proven veteran reliever with experience and strikeout ability; 2) it weakens the Twins bullpen considerably.

Crain is a longtime member of the deep and versatile Twins bullpen. He throws strikes and struck out 62 in 68 innings last season. Williams was criticized for paying $13 million over 3-years for a set-up man. Know what? He doesn't care! He needed bullpen help, targeted Crain and got him.

Righty Sergio Santos was a 26-year-old rookie in 2010 and appeared in 56 games, threw 51 innings, struck out 56 and allowed only 2 homers. He's a former infielder and throws very hard. Santos is an interesting case because he was a first round pick of the Diamondbacks as an infielder, bounced to the Blue Jays and Twins before the White Sox converted him into a pitcher. He was in the majors a year later.

Veteran lefty Will Ohman signed 2-year, $4 million contract as a free agent. Ohman is durable, throws strikes and been historically consistent as a lefty specialist, but he can get righties out as well.

For a pitcher who throws so hard, Tony Pena doesn't strike anyone out. In 2010, he walked 45 and struck out 56 in 100 innings; he also gave up 10 homers. With his fastball, he might be able to close; with those results? No.

Pena's been durable and is a useful secondary bullpen arm.

Righty Freddy Dolsi was picked up off waivers from the Tigers after the 2009 season and spent 2010 in Triple A for the White Sox. He's wild, gives up too many homers and doesn't strike out enough hitters to be a factor over a full season for a contending club.

LINEUP:

A.J. Pierzynski got off to a horrible start at the plate in 2010 and had the White Sox been able to find someone they felt comfortable with replacing him, it's hard to imagine them bringing him back; but the market for catchers was weak and they know Pierzynski (for better or worse considering his reputation), he handles the pitchers well and he hit well enough after a rancid start (he was hitting under .200 into May) to end the season respectably. He's on the downside, but still has attributes to offer and is signed through 2012 at $8 million.

Paul Konerko was a free agent but unlike Pierzynski, he had a terrific year. The leader of the White Sox on and off the field had an MVP-caliber 39 homer; 111 RBI; .312 average; .393 on base, with 70 extra base hits. Konerko signed a 3-year, $37.5 million contract that was criticized because of Konerko's age (35); but he's proven to be consistent and durable; I think he'll hit for the entirety of the contract.

Gordon Beckham had a terrible sophomore season when many had labeled him a future star. Mentioned in trade talks (I think it was more that teams were asking for him than that the White Sox were shopping him), Beckham was hovering around the Mendoza-line into July, but raised his average 50 points over the final two months. He struck out too much and his selectivity was poor, but he'll improve as he gains experience. It helps that he won't be relied on as much with the improved offense supplied by Adam Dunn.

Mark Teahen was all-around terrible both offensively and defensively. He batted .258 in 262 plate appearances and had 19 extra base hits. That's not going to cut it. Teahen missed a large chunk of the season with a finger injury, but he wasn't hitting when he was playing. Teahen looked like he was going to evolve into a solid everyday player for a couple of years with the Royals, but he's been a liability over the past two years.

Alexei Ramirez improved markedly at shortstop in 2010. The 29-year-old Cuban is still raw as a baseball player; his improved defense shows he still has some upside at the plate and shouldn't simply be seen for what his stats say he is. He steals some bases, but gets caught often; he hits for some power, but doesn't get on base. Like many of the Cuban players, he has a flair for the dramatic. Much like he figured it out defensively, there's a chance he could do the same offensively and become a productive force rather than an occasional comet. This winter he signed a 4-year contract extension through 2015 worth a guaranteed $32.5 million.

Juan Pierre was acquired from the Dodgers before the season and, given the chance to play regularly again, did what Pierre does.

It's interesting how many players the White Sox have who "do what it is they do". Could it be part of Kenny Williams's master plan?

Pierre stole 68 bases and played good defense in left field.

Alexis Rios had a fine first full-year with the White Sox after he was acquired on waivers from the Blue Jays late in the 2009 season. Rios was terrible for the White Sox upon his arrival (.199 average, 3 homers); but he was back to the player he was with the Blue Jays; the player who earned a long-term contract that the Blue Jays regretted to the point of dumping him for nothing.

Rios had 21 homers, 88 RBI and 34 stolen bases. He also played respectable defense in center field.

Like many of the White Sox players, Carlos Quentin got off to a rotten start in 2010. He'd been inconsistent and injury-prone since his 36 homer, near-MVP season in 2008 and was unable to handle the role of being the club's main power threat...until he got hot at mid-season and started crushing the ball. Quentin is streaky and his blazing hot streak coincided with the White Sox getting back into playoff contention.

Quentin was approached about a contract extension, but he declined. He's a free agent after 2012 and might be trade bait at some point before then; he's not going to be DHing which will increase the risk of injury.

Adam Dunn is the epitome of the "I know what I'm getting". He's going to hit his 35-40 homers; he's going to walk a lot; he's going to strike out a lot; and he's going to play every day. He signed a 4-year, $56 million contract and, as a DH, is a huge step up from last year's primary DH, Mark Kotsay.

BENCH:

Omar Vizquel returns for another year and, if Teahen doesn't hit, he might find himself playing semi-regularly again. While he shouldn't be playing regularly for a team with playoff aspirations, Vizquel still does little things like stealing a base with canniness, bunting, takin the extra base and playing good, smart defense—these are things that help a club win games.

Dayan Viciedo could also get a chance to win the third base job. Viciedo is from Cuba and is listed(?) as about to turn 22, but who knows?

He batted .308 in 106 plate appearances last season with 5 homers; he's shown 20 homer pop and no plate discipline at all in the minors, but if Teahen doesn't look good in the spring, don't be surprised to see Viciedo take over at third base.

Veteran catcher Ramon Castro has power at the plate, handles the pitchers well and can throw.

Infielder Brent Morel is another potential third base replacement. Morel's 24 and batted .231 in a brief big league stay last season. He's shown some power and on base ability in the minors.

Brent Lillibridge is a utility infielder with a .194 career batting average in the majors, no power and little speed. He'll be lucky to make the big league club.

Tyler Flowers looked like he was going to be a good young hitter while he was in the Braves system, but he's fallen on hard times with the White Sox. Flowers batted .220 in Triple A last year and he doesn't have a spot open to get a chance to play. He's a catcher, but Pierzynski's signed for two years; he doesn't hit enough to be a DH and Dunn is blocking his way. If he replenishes his image, he could be fodder for a trade.

PREDICTION:

Based on their pitching and that I felt they had enough hitting despite the obvious holes, I picked the White Sox to win the World Series last year.

Early in the season, it looked like an awful pick, but Williams stuck with his club and they stormed back into contention. It was the last month of the season and their poor play against the Twins that ruined any chance they had.

This year, they've filled all the holes apart from closer and Thornton is going to do a fine job in that role if it's given to him. Dunn brings a basher to the DH spot; Beckham can't possibly be as bad as he was in 2010; Quentin is going to start thinking about a large contract and will want to play well because of it. Ramirez has star potential.

The Twins have been compromised due to their free agent losses that have gutted their bullpen and middle infield; the Tigers are good, but have question marks. The most complete team in the AL Central is the White Sox and they're going to win the division.

PREDICTED RECORD: 92-70

Detroit Tigers

2010 Record: 81-81; 3rd place, American League Central.

2010 Recap:

The Tigers got off to a good start and were in playoff contention into the early part of the summer. Tied for first place with the Twins into July, injuries, a lack of pitching and faltering performances did them in.

Joel Zumaya fractured his arm throwing a pitch; Rick Porcello was terrible; Brennan Boesch came out of nowhere and ignited, only to disappear; Scott Sizemore was a disaster; and the club faltered in the second half.

If anything exemplified the "just missed" nature of the Tigers season, it was the perfect/imperfect game pitched by Armando Galarraga.

On the positive side, Miguel Cabrera nearly won the triple crown; Austin Jackson showed All Star potential; Max Scherzer overcame a demotion to the minors; and Porcello found his groove late in the season.

2011 ADDITIONS:

C/1B/DH Victor Martinez signed a 4-year, $50 million contract.
RHP Joaquin Benoit signed a 3-year, $16.5 million contract.
RHP Brad Penny signed a 1-year, $3 million contract.
SS Argenis Diaz signed a minor league contract.
RHP Kevin Eichhorn was acquired from the Arizona Diamondbacks.
LHP Ryan Robowski was acquired from the Arizona Diamondbacks.

2011 SUBTRACTIONS:

OF Johnny Damon was not re-signed.
RHP Jeremy Bonderman was not re-signed.
C Gerald Laird was not re-signed.
RHP Armando Galarraga was traded to the Arizona Diamondbacks.
LHP Bobby Seay was not re-signed.
LHP Eddie Bonine was not re-signed.
OF Jeff Frazier was not re-signed.

2011 PROJECTED STARTING ROTATION: Justin Verlander; Max Scherzer; Rick Porcello; Brad Penny; Phil Coke.

2011 PROJECTED BULLPEN: Jose Valverde; Joaquin Benoit; Ryan Perry; Brad Thomas; Enrique Gonzalez; Daniel Schlereth; Joel Zumaya.

2011 PROJECTED LINEUP: C-Victor Martinez; 1B-Miguel Cabrera; 2B-Carlos Guillen; 3B-Brandon Inge; SS-Jhonny Peralta; LF-Ryan Raburn; CF-Austin Jackson; RF-Magglio Ordonez; DH-Brennan Boesch.

2011 BENCH: INF-Will Rhymes; INF/OF-Don Kelly; C-Alex Avila; SS-Ramon Santiago; INF-Danny Worth; INF-Scott Sizemore.

2011 POSSIBLE CONTRIBUTORS: LHP-John Bale; LHP-Fu-Te Ni; INF-Argenis Diaz; RHP-Robbie Weinhardt; OF-Clete Thomas; RHP-Al Alburquerque; LHP-Duane Below; OF-Casper Wells.

ASSESSMENTS
MANAGEMENT:

It's hard to pigeonhole Tigers GM Dave Dombrowski as a good GM or a mediocre one.

He's won a championship with the Marlins; he's won a pennant with the Tigers; he played a large part in the building of the very good Expos teams of the 1980s. He's made some great moves and some terrible moves. He was criticized for his part in the three-way the trade he made a year ago in which he traded Curtis Granderson and Edwin Jackson, but it turned out that the Yankees got the worst of the deal. Max Scherzer and Austin Jackson look like they're going to be winning acquisitions for the Tigers.

For the most part, he's not going to embarrass anyone as an executive; he's aggressive sometimes to the point of appearing desperate; and he works well with manager Jim Leyland.

Dombrowski had money to spend this winter and he spent it. You can debate the long-term merits of the contracts he gave to Victor Martinez and Joaquin Benoit, but in the short-term, they filled two giant holes for the club.

His teams are generally competitive and he's very, very active in-season; true his and Leyland's Tigers teams have tended to collapse late in seasons or fade out completely; there's been something of a dysfunction at times as well. Dombrowski's penchant for overpaying for and extending the contracts of players when he probably shouldn't is a frailty, but he's a competent, veteran executive.

Both Dombrowski and manager Jim Leyland's contracts are up at the end of the 2011 season, but owner Mike Ilich has defied convention in running all of his sports teams. He's very, very loyal and that says to me that, barring an absolute collapse both Dombrowski and Leyland will be running the Tigers in the front office and on the field for as long as they want.

Leyland is one of the most respected managers in baseball, but he can't escape the perception that his jittery nature and constant tweaking has contributed to his teams faltering late in seasons. His Pirates clubs never could get past the championship series after winning three straight division titles; he had the excuse of a lack of funds to protect him as the Pirates were a bad team for the rest of his tenure. He won his title with the Marlins; watched as the club was dismantled and lost over 100 games; then he went to the Rockies, appeared burned out and resigned after one awful year.

He resurfaced with the Tigers and won the pennant in his first year, 2006. Since then, the Tigers have underachieved. Because he's such a good game manager with a breadth of experience and gruff demeanor that intimidates the sportswriters, has he gotten away with more failure than manager of less repute?

Maybe.

It's also forgotten, in the afterglow of the pennant, that the 2006 Tigers collapsed down the stretch and righted themselve in the playoffs. The 2007 team was expensive and star-studded and ran out of gas at the end of the season amid in-fighting, injuries and underachievement; the 2008 team was 74-88 with Leyland making panicky lineup and position changes; the 2009 team should've had a playoff spot locked up, but the Twins blazing hot streak and another Tigers late season stumble cost them a playoff spot. And you know what happened in 2010.

Leyland's a good manager and the players respect him. He's played a part in a highly paid club's failures in recent years. I doubt he's going to leave yet, but he's also 66-years-old. I wonder how much longer he's going to want to manage, especially if he has another heart-wrenching season as the Tigers have had for his entire tenure.

STARTING PITCHING:

Justin Verlander is a true ace and horse at the top of the Tigers rotation. He takes the ball every fifth day (or more if asked); he gobbles innings; he throws strikes; he's hard to hit with a fastball in the mid-to-upper 90s and a power curve; he strikes out a lot of batters and doesn't allow homers (14 in 224 innings).

Verlander is still only 28 and with the way he uses his legs to generate force, he's going to remain durable at least into his early 30s. This is the bust-out year for Verlander and he's going to win the Cy Young Award and 20 games for the first time.

I may have been wrong about Max Scherzer.

Yes.

You read that right.

I.

May.

Have.

Been.

Wrong.

With his stuff—a power fastball and wicked slider—I felt he'd be better as a closer. His motion is somewhat stressful and while I'm not as concerned about his "head jerk" at the end of his motion (who cares?), it's a Jason Isringhausen-type, all-out delivery that lends itself to breaking down.

But he's been durable in his first two seasons as a starter and his innings are building up to the point where he can be counted on for close to 200 this season.

Scherzer was pitching poorly and found himself back in the minors for a couple "get straightened out" starts; he pitched well in Triple A, came back to the big leagues and was terrific from July onward. He's a strikeout pitcher and his ball is hard to pick up coming out of his hand because of that wild, herky jerky motion.

Scherzer could breakout and win 15 games this season as a legitimate #2 starter behind Verlander.

Rick Porcello's name was bounced around in trade talks as he slumped in his second full big league season. It's hard to know how serious the talks were; perhaps it was more of teams calling and asking and the Tigers listening; but the Tigers have been notoriously sharp and made terrible misjudgments in personnel in the past (trading Jair Jurrjens for Edgar Renteria for example), so it's not out of the realm of possible that they were considering moving Porcello.

Porcello's overall 2010 numbers look terrible. 188 hits in 162 innings; 18 homers; a 4.92 ERA; he was very, very hittable. Like Scherzer, Porcello wound up back in the minors and pitched better after his return.

I'd hesitate to think Porcello is going to develop as quickly as I think Scherzer will. In fact, I'm concerned about how many hits he gives up. I see him as a .500 pitcher at this point.

Veteran Brad Penny was signed to a 1-year contract.

Penny was expected to be the latest in the long line of repair jobs by Cardinals pitching coach Dave Duncan, but he got hurt with a pulled muscle in his back. In his nine starts for the Cardinals, he appeared to be taking to the Duncan perscription well and was going to have a solid season.

Penny has been a National League pitcher his whole career and he didn't pitch particularly well for the Red Sox in 2009. Tigers pitching coach Rick Knapp stresses throwing strikes and using the defense; perhaps that strategy will benefit Penny. He's 33 and still has something left if he can stay healthy, but I wonder if he can.

Lefty Phil Coke is being tried as a starter. He was a pretty good one in the minors and has the stuff to be decent in the role. He's been a reliever for the past two years and the transition isn't easy, but he's done it before. His control is up-and-down and he gives up too many homers, but his results are essentially the same against lefties and righties. He's not a dominant lefty against lefties and the other issues indicate that he profiles better as a starter.

BULLPEN:

Jose Valvede and his potbelly were great in the first half of last season. I watch Valverde and wonder how he's able to generate the force and throw a fastball in the upper 90s. He must have gigantic hands to leverage his way past a lack of arm speed.

It was the faltering of the Tigers bullpen in 2010 that cost them as much as anything and Valverde was a big part of that. He was unhittable in the first half; poor at best in the second half. He strikes out a batter per inning and has had some truly wonderful years in his career as a closer. In a weird twist, they've been in alternating seasons; based on that, he'd due for a great year. And I think he'll have one.

Joaquin Benoit was a reclamation project for the Rays, had a brilliant season and cashed in. The Tigers aren't afraid to spend money on relievers even though it's become less and less prevalent. Benoit has had shoulder problems and injuries have sabotaged him; there's never been a question about his stuff. He racks up the strikeouts with a power fastball and slider; he throws strikes; he gives up the occasional homer.

Benoit's contract is big—3 years, $16.5 million—and the long term ramifications for the Tigers are something to think about; I can't see him being 100% healthy for all three years given his history. But they needed a set-up man for 2011 and Benoit will be good for this year at least.

Young Ryan Perry has become Leyland's go-to guy out of the bullpen. It's understandable. He throws strikes; takes the ball without complaint; and has strikeout stuff with a power fastball. The 24-year-old righty will be an important part of the Tigers bullpen in 2011.

33-year-old, Australian lefty Brad Thomas was a solid arm out of the Tigers bullpen last season. He got knocked around early in the season, but got better as the season went along. Thomas was used against both lefties and righties, but righties hit him hard; he could be used as both a long man and a lefty specialist.

Righty Enrique Gonzalez has a great fastball, can be wild and gives up too many homers. He was serviceable for the Tigers in 26 games and could stick as an extra arm.

Daniel Schlereth is a former first round pick of the Diamondbacks who was acquired in the Granderson/Jackson trade last year. The 25-year-old lefty walks too many hitters and was actually far better pitching to righties than lefties. His numbers in the minors last year were quite good, but those walks are a big problem and Leyland does *not* use pitchers who can't throw strikes. They drive him to smoke. Unless he solves that control problem, he's not going to be on the big league roster.

Will Joel Zumaya be able to pitch?

I hated being right about this, but I've consistently said that Zumaya and his 102 mph fastball will be the stuff of barstool legend as he pops in and out, comes back and disappears to the disabled list. Zumaya was back to the dominating and mean fastballer who exploded onto the national scene in the 2006 playoffs as he made the likes of Alex Rodriguez look inert.

In 2010, he'd struck out 34 in 38 innings; walked only 11 and allowed 1 homer—then he blew out his arm against the Twins.

I was watching the game on June 28th when Zumaya unleashed a fastball. The announcer said something to the tune of, "Oh boy, Zumaya's hurt," as the pitcher's face turned ashen, he flung his glove off and collapsed to a knee behind the mound in agony and tears.

It was horrifying.

Will he be back? Pitchers who've broken their arms pitching have tended to continue breaking them when they come back. Tony Saunders and John Smiley come to mind as having dealt with this issue; Tom Browning couldn't regain his effectiveness.

I hope Zumaya can come back, but I have a hard time believing he will.

LINEUP:

Victor Martinez was signed to a 4-year, $50 million contract to fill the Tigers lineup hole and take over at catcher, in that order.

I'm not the biggest fan of Victor Martinez, but he's got power; he gets on base; he's serviceable behind the plate; and he probably won't be catching regularly for the duration of the contract. He'll always be able to hit as a DH/part-time first baseman. He was one of the better bats on the market and played a position where the Tigers had a need. I don't see this as a bad deal as others have speculated. The switch-hitting Martinez will boost the Tigers lineup.

Miguel Cabrera finished second in the MVP voting after having a massive year. He hit 38 homers; drove in 126; had 45 doubles; batted .328, and had a .420 on base. Cabrera also redeemed himself off the field after his embarrassing episode late in the 2009 season in which he was arrested after a drunken altercation with his wife on the last weekend of the regular season.

Cabrera put up those numbers essentially alone in the Tigers weak lineup. With the addition of Martinez, he'll see more pitches to hit and have more baserunners to knock in. He's going to contend for the MVP again.

Cabrera was arrested for DUI and resisting arrest after arriving at spring training. He's receiving outpatient treatment.

Carlos Guillen is listed as the Tigers intended second baseman. Guillen has been a shortstop; a third baseman; a left fielder; a first baseman and a DH. He hasn't been able ot stay healthy at any of those positions since 2006. He's been a walking disabled list stay since 2007. His contract is up after 2011, so maybe that will spur him to get out on the field. His injuries have been of the muscle-pulling/joint variety which makes them a greater concern. He's had calf, hamstring and shoulder problems.

I can't imagine Guillen, at age 35, being able to play more than 120 games. He can still hit, but you can't count on him to be in the lineup and his lack of range at second base combined with the immobility of Cabrera at first is going to be a problem for the Tigers pitchers who pitch to contact.

Brandon Inge is what he is. A fine defensive third baseman, he has pop, strikes out way too much and doesn't get on base. In the Tigers improved lineup, he won't be relied on as much and will be a useful contributor.

Jhonny Peralta really can't play shortstop all that well anymore and this, like the defense on the right side of the infield, could be a problem with the Tigers contact pitchers. He can still hit for some power and did well in the post-season when he was with the Indians in 2007.

Career backup Ryan Raburn had a coming out year in 2010. Finally given a chance to play, the 29-year-old had 15 homers and 41 extra base hits in 410 plate appearances; a .280 batting average and a .340 on base. It's not star level, but it's a contribution. He's also a good outfielder and can play pretty much anywhere. Raburn spent parts of five years in Triple A; his production in 2011 was in line with what he posted in the minors, so it's unlikely that it's a fluke.

Austin Jackson is still raw. He struck out 170 times and needs to learn his way in center field, but he has speed, hit 34 doubles and 10 triples in 2010 and has shown some pop in the minors; he may hit 10-15 homers in the majors once he's acclimated. He's learning how to play in the bigs, but he's only 24 and has All Star potential.

His long-term, pricey contract expired, Magglio Ordonez returns to the Tigers for another season. He's been in and out of the lineup with injuries, but his production at the plate has been consistent. He's hit over .300 in each of the past four years; gets on base; has some pop left and doesn't strike out. Considering their options, the Tigers were smart to bring Ordonez back for another year at $10 million.

Brennan Boesch burst onto the scene and led everyone to believe he was the next hot thing until the pitchers figured him out. He's a hacker and chases breaking pitches which leads to strikeouts. He's got power and, if he's playing regularly, should hit his 18-20 homers; he strikes out a lot and doesn't walk.

BENCH:

Like Boesch, Will Rhymes was a longtime minor leaguer who took advantage of a shot in the bigs due to failed prospects and injuries and took advantage of it. Rhymes has shown speed and good on base ability in the minors; he's a good defensive second baseman. With Guillen penciled in at second base and the Tigers not having a prototypical DH, Rhymes will get a chance to play second when Guillen is DH-ing.

Don Kelly is a journeyman corner infielder/outfielder who batted .244 with a .272 on base in 251 plate appearances. He's a defensive replacement who's shown the ability to hit and get on base in the minors. He's 31-years-old.

Alex Avila will get his share of time behind the plate when Martinez is the DH or playing first base. The Tigers are strangely versatile with a weak defense, if that's an attribute. Avila is solid defensively and has hit for power in the minors. He only batted .228 in 333 plate appearances in 2010, but the 24-year-old should be better than that as he gains big league experience.

Ramon Santiago lost his shortstop job with the acquisition of Peralta. Santiago is a veteran, switch-hitting utility player who can hit a bit.

Danny Worth is a 25-year-old backup infielder with no power, speed and little on base ability.

Let's get the embarrassment out of the way: I picked Scott Sizemore to win the AL Rookie of the Year last season based on the fact that the Tigers needed a second baseman and Sizemore was getting the job out of spring training; his numbers in the minors were good, but last season was a disaster offensively and defensively.

We won't discuss this again.

PREDICTION:

The Tigers signed a few more risky contracts with Benoit and, to a point, Martinez; in the long-term, they may be paying big money for a drastically declining performance. But, for the 2011 season, the Tigers filled their holes in the lineup and bullpen. Both Martinez and Benoit will help the Tigers greatly this season; Penny is a worthwhile signing as well.

Cabrera is a basher in the middle of the lineup and they'll score runs; the starting rotation is solid enough and will be very good if Scherzer develops as I think he will. Leyland and Dombrowski have had their heads in the noose before and the team has repsonded on the field.

They're somewhat strangely constructed and could straddle the line between a playoff team or an also ran. With the improving Jackson in center field, Martinez and another MVP-caliber year from Cabrera, the Tigers are a contender. Dombrowski's been aggressive on the trade market in the past and the team has money to spend to make in-season improvements.

With Verlander fronting the rotation, they're always going to have that ace every fifth day.

Despite those question marks, this is a good team that has the advantage in their division of beating up on the weak Royals and Indians and compromised Twins. They're going to make a run at—and get—a playoff spot as they take the Wild Card in the American League.

PREDICTED RECORD: 90-72

Minnesota Twins

2010 Record: 94-68; 1st place, American League Central.
Lost to New York Yankees 3 games to 0 in ALDS.

2010 Recap:

2010 was supposed to be the Twins year.

They were supposed to finally get over the hump and beat the Yankees.

Even though they lost Joe Nathan to Tommy John surgery in spring training and Justin Morneau to a concussion at mid-season, they still had enough firepower; a competent, strike-throwing starting rotation; and a deep, diverse bullpen—which they augmented heavily during the season getting Matt Capps and Brian Fuentes.

They won the AL Central going away and were never truly threatened by the White Sox or Tigers.

2010 was supposed to be their year.

And for five innings in ALDS game 1 vs the Yankees, their blueprint was coming to life.

They led 3-0 and Francisco Liriano was rolling along with a 2-hit shutout. He struck out Nick Swisher to start the sixth inning.

Then the wheels came off.

In what seemed like a lightning strike without one cloud visible in the sky, the Yankees exploded for four runs to take a 4-3 lead. The Twins showed the last bit of fight they would in the entire series as they came back to tie the score on a C.C. Sabathia walk with the bases loaded; but Mark Teixeira homered off Jesse Crain in the seventh and the Yankees never looked back as they blew the Twins away—again—in three straight.

2011 ADDITIONS:

SS Tsuyoshi Nishioka signed a 3-year, $9.25 million contract with club option.
RHP Jim Hoey was a acquired from the Baltimore Orioles.
RHP Brett Jacobson was acquired from the Baltimore Orioles.

2011 SUBTRACTIONS:

2B Orlando Hudson was not re-signed.
SS J.J. Hardy was traded to the Baltimore Orioles.
LHP Brian Fuentes was not re-signed.
RHP Matt Guerrier was not re-signed.
RHP Jesse Crain was not re-signed.
RHP Clay Condrey was not re-signed.
LHP Randy Flores was not re-signed.
LHP Ron Mahay was not re-signed.
INF Nick Punto's option was declined.
RHP Jon Rauch was not re-signed.
INF Brendan Harris was traded to the Baltimore Orioles.

2011 PROJECTED STARTING ROTATION: Francisco Liriano; Carl Pavano; Scott Baker; Nick Blackburn; Kevin Slowey; Brian Duensing.

2011 PROJECTED BULLPEN: Joe Nathan; Matt Capps; Pat Neshek; Jose Mijares; Alex Burnett; Jeff Manship; Glen Perkins.

2011 PROJECTED LINEUP: C-Joe Mauer; 1B-Justin Morneau; 2B-Alexi Casilla; 3B-Danny Valencia; SS-Tsuyoshi Nishioka; LF-Delmon Young; CF-Denard Span; RF-Michael Cuddyer; DH-Jason Kubel.

2011 BENCH: DH-Jim Thome; INF-Matt Tolbert; C-Drew Butera; INF-Trevor Plouffe; OF-Jason Repko; OF-Ben Revere.

2011 POSSIBLE CONTRIBUTORS: 1B/OF-Chris Parmalee; INF-Luke Hughes; RHP-Deolis Guerra; RHP-David Bromberg; RHP-Rob Delaney; RHP-Jim Hoey; RHP-Anthony Slama; RHP-Anthony Swarzak; RHP-Eric Hacker; RHP-Yorman Bazardo; LHP-Phil Dumatrait.

ASSESSMENTS MANAGEMENT:

GM Bill Smith is aggressive. Give him that.

He makes some smart moves; he makes some strange moves; he makes some bad moves.

The Twins take some risks that pay off and some that miss the mark. They went for it all last season with team-friendly contracts given to Jim Thome and Orlando Hudson; they made major mid-season upgrades to their bullpen with Matt Capps and Brian Fuentes; and the minor league system was productive with young players like Danny Valencia and the bulk of the starting rotation having come from within.

Because they missed out after the "go for it" mentality of 2010, they've made some changes to the roster and it's not necessarily for the better.

It's understandable that the Twins didn't want to get into a bidding war for Jesse Crain and Matt Guerrier; that they let Hudson and Jon Rauch leave; that they traded the disappointing J.J. Hardy. But the replacements for these important cogs are giant question marks.

The Twins have their own unique way of doing business and they don't apologize for it. Smith has redeemed himself—to a point—after the disastrously botched Johan Santana trade before the 2008 season; but the Twins have a lot of patched together holes that will need serious repair during the season. Sometimes the aggressiveness and worrying about later, later pays dividends; sometimes it doesn't. Last year, for the Twins, it didn't.

Manager Ron Gardenhire finally received recognition for all his success over the years when he was named Manager of the Year.

Gardenhire's been the Twins manager for nine years, has had one losing season and made the playoffs in six of those years. His teams know he's in charge; they play the game correctly or they don't play; he uses his whole roster; is skillful at handling his pitchers in the starting rotation and bullpen and is widely respected and liked throughout baseball.

There have been accusations that Gardenhire's reliance on players who shouldn't be playing regularly like Nick Punto have cost the team games; that another manager who is more immersed in statistics and not his eyes and his gut would have more success than Gardenhire. I don't see how that's possible. The losses in the playoffs have not been the fault of the manager and his steady, guiding hand along with the way he steers the ship have been a major reason that the Twins have been one of the most successful organizations in baseball during his tenure.

He's one of the best managers in baseball because of his attention to fundamentals and that his players buy into the system. It also helps that they know if they *don't* buy into the system, they'll be gone. In order for that to work, a manager has to have the support of the front office and Gardenhire does. Deservedly so.

STARTING PITCHING:

Francisco Liriano is the psuedo-ace of the Twins staff. With his stuff, he's got the potential to dominate. But there's still an underlying sense of foreboding around the lefty as if the Twins and Liriano don't know if he's going to unravel or get hurt again.

He has the fastball, slider and change-up to dominate; he was masterful for much of 2010; the only thing preventing him from being a top-of-the-line starter with C.C. Sabathia and Justin Verlander is his durability. Liriano threw 191 innings last season; allowed 184 hits; struck out 201; and only gave up 9 homers. His control was terrific, walking 58.

Will Liriano, at age 27, take the next step into being a 220 inning-eating ace? He's getting to the point in his career where he's going to want a long-term contract, but will the Twins give it to him?

I'm still iffy about Liriano staying healthy and the Twins apparently are as well because they've indicated a willingness to listen to offers for him in a trade. My guess is they'll wait a few months to see where they are in the standings before making a decision either way. He might be available in the summer.

Carl Pavano continued a remarkable comeback after his embarrassing tenure with the Yankees. Pavano pitched well for the Indians and Twins in 2009, then was the horse of the Twins workmanlike starting rotation in 2010. He went 17-11; led the American League in complete games with 7; pitched 221 innings and was a leader on the club.

After a free agent foray that included a bizarre flirtation to return to the Yankees, Pavano signed a 2-year $16.5 million contract to stay in Minnesota.

Pavano is a pure contact pitcher who benefited from the Twins attention to fundamentals. He epitomizes what the Twins preach to their pitchers: throw strikes and let the fielders do the work. With his poor strikeout rate and security of another multi-year contract, will Pavano revert back to the disinterested and injury-prone butt of jokes he was with the Yankees? I doubt it, but after the ludicrous spate of injuries and mishaps that befell him in the Bronx, I don't rule anything out. He's not going to win 17 games again.

Scott Baker missed time with a shoulder problem, returned to almost pitch a no-hitter (in which manager Ron Gardenhire was booed for removing the pitcher even though he was 100% right in doing so); and ended the season with a record of 12-9 in 29 starts.

Baker allowed 186 hits in 170 innings, but that number was skewered by a few games in which he allowed 10+ hits. Baker's a typical Twins homegrown pitcher. He throws strikes; keeps the ball down; gives up a few homers and some hits; but gives them what they need with 6-7 innings. It may not show in his record this season because the bullpen is slightly downgraded, but Baker is consistent in his performance.

Like Baker, Nick Blackburn is consistent, but I'm not sure that's necessarily a good thing. In his first two big league seasons in 2008-2009, Blackburn went 11-11 in both; he gave up a lot of hits per innings-pitched and a lot of homers. Blackburn was sent to the minors at mid-season, but his numbers were in line with what he's done his whole career. He allowed 194 hits in 161 innings and 25 homers. A soft-tossing righty with mediorce stuff, Blackburn is a .500 pitcher at best who's benefited from the Twins bullpen. I wouldn't be surprised to see him have a 10-17 type year if things go badly for the Twins in 2011.

Kevin Slowey? Another righty with similar results as Baker and Blackburn. He gives up a lot of hits (172 in 155 innings); homers (21); throws strikes and is a contact pitcher. He went 13-6 by hanging around in games and waiting for the Twins solid offense and bullpen to get him a better record than his ancillary numbers indicate he should have. This is what he's been his whole career.

Brian Duensing was selected to start the make-or-break game 3 of the ALDS against the Yankees, danced through the raindrops for a couple of innings, then got knocked around. The lefty Duensing was a reliever until being moved into the starting rotation in August. He pitched very well as a starter with a 7-2 record and had overall good numbers across the board. He's a contact pitcher who's been up-and-down as a starter in the minors. He's not as good as his numbers were as a starter in 2010 and once he gets around the league, I think he'll have some trouble getting through lineups twice in a game.

BULLPEN:

Joe Nathan has been one of the top closers in baseball since 2004. The only thing separating him from the more recognizable "star" closer names like Mariano Rivera and Jonathan Papelbon have been his post-season gacks of which there have been many. He missed the entire 2010 season after undergoing Tommy John surgery and is expected back this season. One would assume, with the way the Twins value loyalty and "doing right" that Nathan will be given back his job as closer until he proves he can no longer do it. He'll want to have a big year because the Twins hold a $12.5 million option for 2012 (with a $2 million buyout). Pitchers have come back regularly and with few hitches from Tommy John, so I expect Nathan to be back to his hard-throwing and reliable (in the regular season anyway) best.

Matt Capps was acquired from the Washington Nationals at mid-season for top catching prospect Wilson Ramos. It was curious that, despite the presence of Joe Mauer blocking his way, the Twins still traded a hot prospect catcher for a relief pitcher; one would assume that Ramos could've been packaged for a starting pitcher or middle infielder.

Be that as it may, Capps is a gutty reliever who never gives in. He was very good for the Twins and Nats and can set-up or close. If Nathan can't go on back-to-back days returning from surgery, it's good to have someone like Capps who has no fear of the job.

If he can get lefties out, sidearming Pat Neshek could have a more prominent role in the Twins bullpen with the departures of Jon Rauch, Jesse Crain and the workhorse Matt Guerrier. Neshek missed time in 2010 with a finger injury and spent much of the season in Triple A where he pitched serviceably. Because of his sidearm delivery, he's not a viable candidate to replace Crain or Guerrier. He's a situational righty who hasn't pitched in the big leagues regularly or stayed healthy since 2008.

Jose Mijares is a lefty who was mostly used situationally, but pitched to righties as well. The platoon splits are almost identical with a .268 average against both and too-close-for-comfort on base and slugging percentages. He throws strikes and strikes out around a batter per inning. He's not going to be able to replace Rauch's Crain's or Guerrier's innings either.

Alex Burnett is a 23-year-old righty who pitched in 41 games in relief in 2010. He walked 23 and struck out 37 in 47 innings, gave up 52 hits and 6 homers. He throws hard, has a good curveball, has closed in the minors and put up excellent across the board numbers. Burnett might be asked to pick up some of the innings lost with the free agent departures.

Jeff Manship is a 26-year-old righty who's spent parts of the past two seasons with the Twins. In the minors, he's been a serviceable starting pitcher, but his role in the majors will likely be as a long man out of the bullpen. He strikes hitters out, so he could fill one of the holes.

Glen Perkins is a 28-year-old lefty who's been a starter and went 12-4 with a predictable "Twins pitcher" cavalcade of hits allowed. He throws strikes and if he stays in the majors, it will likely be as a reliever.

LINEUP:

After winning the MVP in 2009 with a .365 average; .444 on base; 28 homers; 69 extra base hits and a Gold Glove Award, Joe Mauer came back down to earth with a .328 average; a .402 on base; and 9 homers. Mauer missed 25 games with various injuries to his knee and heel. The Twins spacious new ballpark contributed to his diminished power output.

Mauer is still one of the best hitters in baseball and a terrific catcher who's always an MVP candidate. Given his lack of power last season, it's unrealistic to expect anything more than 15 or so homers, but the average, doubles and on base skills, plus his defense will always be there.

Justin Morneau was on his way to the MVP award before a concussion ended his season after 81 games. He had 18 homers, a .345 batting average; a .437 on base and was on his way to a massive season before Blue Jays second baseman John McDonald accidentally kicked him in the head while completing a double play in Toronto. Post-concussion symptoms kept him out of the lineup. He's expected to be ready to start the season, but concussions are tricky. Morneau is one of the most dangerous hitters in baseball and I believe he'll come back and have a normal, big power/on base year that we've come to expect from the 2006 AL MVP.

Alexi Casilla gets his old second base job back after losing it with a terrible season in 2009. Orlando Hudson was signed to play second in 2010, so Casilla was a utility man. He batted .276 with a .331 on base and he seemed humbled by his demotion and that a starting job in the majors isn't automatically assumed. It's more pronounced with a team like the Twins that doesn't put up with garbage. Casilla has no power; little stolen base speed; and isn't a particularly good defensive second baseman. I wouldn't expect much more than a .270 average and .330 on base.

Danny Valencia took over at third base and wound up third in the Rookie of the Year voting. Valencia, 26, was a decent minor leaguer who'd spent 2009 and half of 2010 in Triple A Rochester before getting the call. He batted .311 with a .351 on base; hit 7 homers and 18 doubles. He's good defensively and doesn't strike out much.

Tsuyoshi Nishioka comes to North America (Middle America) from Japan and was signed to a 3-year contract. The 26-year-old switch-hitter won the Japanese League batting title with a .346 average and hit 11 homers. It's impossible to know what he'll do in the big leagues. The Japanese imports have run the gamut from being MVP/Cy Young Award candidates—Ichiro Suzuki, Hideki Matsui, Hideo Nomo; to overhyped and mediocre semi-useful cogs—Daisuke Matsuzaka; Akinori Iwamura; to overpriced disasters—Kaz Matsui; Hideki Irabu; Kenji Johjima.

Which is Nishioka going to be? I have no idea, but I wonder about middle-infielders making the transition from shortstop in Japan with artificial surface and the grass fields of North America; Kaz Matsui was a gold glove winner in Japan and horrific playing shortstop for the Mets.

I have no clue what to expect, but I'm not expecting much.

Delmon Young had a breakout year in 2010. Finally behaving himself and harnassing both his emotions and talent, Young hit 21 homers, drove in 112 and batted .298. He's still remarkably impatient with only 28 walks, but the Twins don't worry about on base percentage. He only struck out 81 times. Young's defense in left field is mediocre. If he learns a little bit more patience, he could become an MVP candidate. It took some time for him to calm down with his behavior, so I wouldn't rule him out as eventually learning to be more selective.

Denard Span was supposed to be the one to have a breakout season in 2010, but took a step back. Span's average dipped from .311 in 2009 to .264 in 2010 and his other numbers took a dive as well. Span stole 26 bases and his range in center field is lacking. Even with that, he's only 27 and is closer to the player he was in 2009 than what he produced in 2010. I expect a bounce back year from Span.

Michael Cuddyer's power numbers took a dive just as Mauer's did. Presumably because of the new ballpark. Aside from that, Cuddyer is consistent. He'll get his 160 or so hits; 35 doubles; double-digits in homers, a few of the clutch variety; and take a few walks. He's versatile and can play first base or even third base if necessary, though he's best suited for the outfield. Cuddyer's a solid, all-around righty bat.

Jason Kubel and Jim Thome will share time at DH with Kubel playing the outfield some of the time. The lefty batting Kubel has 20-homer power and has shown a decent skill at getting on base.

Thome is a slugging veteran whose presence helped save the Twins season after Morneau got hurt. In part-time duty (340 plate appearances), Thome did what he does best: hit homers and walk. He had 25 homers and a .412 on base percentage. Always a threat to go deep, he'll get a similar number of at bats this season. He stayed with the Twins despite the Rangers offering a substantially larger deal.

BENCH:

Matt Tolbert is a veteran utility infielder who can play second, third or shortstop; he has no power, no speed and doesn't do much of anything worthwhile at the plate. He is a switch hitter.

Drew Butera has the job as "backup to the star quarterback"; he may as well sit on the bench with his hat backwards holding a clipboard. Barring a catastrophic injury to Mauer, he's not going to play more than 20 games at most. He batted .197 in 155 plate appearance in 2010. It's interesting to note that Drew Butera is former big league backup Sal

Butera's son. Judging from Sal Butera's hitting numbers, he taught his son everything he knows about hitting.

Trevor Plouffe is a 24-year-old middle infielder who's shown some pop in the minors with a low batting average and on base percentage.

Jason Repko is a journeyman backup outfielder and defensive replacement with a very strong arm. Repko's shown some pop in the minors, but he's the 25th man on a roster.

Ben Revere is a 23-year-old former 1st round pick of the Twins. He's had a high average and on base percentage and stolen plenty of bases in the minors.

PREDICTION:

How long can the Twins continue to lose players and find fill-ins to pick up the slack? To keep plugging in interchangeable pieces and using fundamentals and the "Twins way" to keep winning?

And what happens when they're losing important, but lesser-known soldiers like Crain, Rauch and Guerrier? Do they have replacements at the ready for those bullpen arms? I don't see it.

Guerrier was imperative to what the Twins do. He always took the ball and most of the time got the job done. With the starting pitchers trained to give 6-7 innings, who's going to take the ball now? Burnett? Neshek? Manship?

I have deep concerns about the Twins bullpen and deployment of the bullpen has been one of the keys to keeping them in contention for so long. The starting pitching behind Liriano—who has questions of his own surrounding him—is mediocre. Without the deep, reliable bullpen, how can they win those close games?

Yes, with Capps and Nathan in the eighth and ninth innings, they're in good hands with a lead after seven, but what about *getting* there?

The lineup is also a concern. The new combination at second base and shortstop has, in my mind, more of a chance to fail than succeed. Valencia is in his second year and the pitchers will adjust; Morneau is expected back, but a concussion problem could linger.

There's also the lingering disappointment from the whitewashing at the hands of the Yankees. The Twins put everything into last season; they spent money; they made big upgrades to the bullpen during the season; they looked ready to finally take the Yankees...until the Yankees hit them back. They folded completely. This type of disappointment has the potential to have a carryover effect into the 2011 season.

I don't like what the Twins have done this winter. They've proven to be a resilient group that wins in spite of everything, but the Tigers have improved; the White Sox are very good. The Twins have downgraded.

This is going to be one of those transition years for the Twins and they're going to fall into also-ran status relatively quickly.

PREDICTED RECORD: 76-86

Kansas City Royals

2010 Record: 67-95; 5th place, American League Central.

2010 Recap:

2010 was the seventh losing season in a row for the Royals; it was their 16th losing season in 17 years; and 6th time in 7 years that they didn't win 70 games.

Their ace, Zack Greinke, after winning the AL Cy Young Award in 2009, wound up at 10-14 with an ERA over 4.00; their former first picks in the draft, Alex Gordon and Luke Hochevar have been slow to develop. The expensive free agent signings did little-to-nothing to help the team. Gil Meche (injured and shifted to the bullpen); Kyle Farnsworth and Jose Guillen (traded); and the extra free agents on short-term deals (Rick Ankiel, Willie Bloomquist, Scott Podsednik) weren't much use either.

On the positive, Billy Butler is becoming an excellent all-around hitter; and Joakim Soria is a top-notch closer; the bullpen was overall pretty good.

Manager Trey Hillman was horribly overmatched from the time he took the job until he was fired in May. Former Brewers manager Ned Yost took over for the rest of the season and the Royals ended up, predictably, in last place in the AL Central.

2011 ADDITIONS:

RF Jeff Francoeur signed a 1-year, $2.5 million contranct with 2012 mutual option.
OF Melky Cabrera signed a 1-year, $1.25 million contract.
LHP Jeff Francis signed a 1-year, $2 million contract.
RHP Vin Mazzaro was acquired from the Oakland Athletics.
SS Alcides Escobar was acquired from the Milwaukee Brewers.
OF Lorenzo Cain was acquired from the Milwaukee Brewers.
RHP Jeremy Jeffress was acquired from the Milwaukee Brewers.
RHP Jake Odorizzi was acquired from the Milwaukee Brewers.
OF Brett Carroll signed a minor league contract.

2011 SUBTRACTIONS:

RHP Zack Greinke was traded to the Milwaukee Brewers.
SS Yuniesky Betancourt was traded to the Milwaukee Brewers.
OF David DeJesus was traded to the Oakland Athletics.
RHP Gil Meche retired.
RHP Brian Bannister was not re-signed.

2011 PROJECTED STARTING ROTATION: Kyle Davies, Luke Hochevar; Vin Mazzaro; Jeff Francis; Bruce Chen.

2011 PROJECTED BULLPEN: Joakim Soria; Robinson Tejeda; Dusty Hughes; Jesse Chavez; Blake Wood; Kanekoa Texeira; Sean O'Sullivan; Jeremy Jeffress.

2011 PROJECTED LINEUP: C-Jason Kendall; 1B-Kila Ka'aihue; 2B-Chris Getz; 3B-Mike Aviles; SS-Alcides Escobar; LF-Alex Gordon; CF-Melky Cabrera; RF-Jeff Francoeur; DH-Billy Butler.

2011 BENCH: C-Brayan Pena; INF-Wilson Betemit; OF-Gregor Blanco; OF-Mitch Maier; OF-Lorenzo Cain.

2011 POSSIBLE CONTRIBUTORS: RHP-Henry Barrera; RHP-Aaron Crow; RHP-Greg Holland; RHP-Kevin Pucetas; 1B-Clint Robinson; OF-Jarrod Dyson; OF-Derrick Robinson.

ASSESSMENTS
MANAGEMENT:

GM Dayton Moore has built what's being called the best minor league system in baseball; all the while he's making strange trades he didn't have to make; signing the same tired old free agents who have nothing much to offer; and running a club that has almost no chance whatsoever until someday...someday...someday the dream prospects will come.

The Royals are a terrible big league team. Moore has made one awful signing after another and he continues to do so. Finally getting out from under the contracts of Jose Guillen and dumping Yuniesky Betancourt; having already moved Kyle Farnsworth and Rick Ankiel, what does he do? Does he find some young, cheap players who have upside? Does he look for veterans who deserve a chance to play everyday in a venue where there's little chance to win so he can see what they can do?

No.

He signs Melky Cabrera and Jeff Francoeur.

It's ludicrous.

The Royals may have a terrific foundation on the way, but the end result must be attended to competently and I question whether Moore has the capacity to do that. There are plenty of baseball executives who were not meant to be the top dog in an organizational hierarchy. People have nothing but nice things to say about Paul DePodesta as an assistant and as a person, but he was a disaster as a GM; Dave Littlefield? The same thing. Jack Zduriencik of the Mariners is crafting his own train wreck on and off the field for the Mariners. And Moore has done a terrible job with the big league club.

Failing is nothing to be ashamed of, but the Royals are running the risk of letting Moore be the man who ruins these terrific prospect they supposedly have. He's signed through 2014 which, coincidentally, is when the hot young prospects that permeate the organization are slated to be ready to help the Royals contend.

We'll see.

And we're going to have to wait another three years to see it.

Ned Yost was hired to replace Trey Hillman after the Royals got off to a 12-23 start. Hillman plainly and simply didn't work. He couldn't handle the media; his strategies were haphazard; he abused his closer Joakim Soria; and his impressive resume turned out to be a false hope for big league managerial success.

Yost was the manager of the Brewers for six seasons and led the on-field rebuilding effort in Milwaukee. He handled the young Brewers players well enough, but just as Moore may be better as an assistant, Yost might be better as the "guy before the guy"; the manager who taught the players to play the game properly and then was moved out for someone to take the team to the next level.

Yost's intensity and distracting explosiveness was in danger of sabotaging the Brewers playoff hopes in September of 2008 when he was fired with 12 games left in the season. Had the Brewers not made the move, I don't think they would've made the playoffs that season.

The Royals played better under Yost and there are worse managers to have shepherding youngsters into the big leagues. He's strategically competent as well. There's also a possiblity that he learned his lesson from the Brewers experience and will be the man to lead his club into respectability and beyond. I'm willing to give him that chance; a chance he deserves after the work he's done with the Brewers, Royals and in baseball in general.

STARTING PITCHING:

For reasons I can't quite understand, the Royals rushed to trade Zack Greinke. He was signed through 2012. What was the big hurry?

Because they traded Greinke, the Royals have to hope that either Kyle Davies or Luke Hochevar steps into the role of number 1 starter.

Davies has been one of those pitchers who you look at, watch pitch, examine his stuff, then look at his record and say, "how is this possible?" It reminds me of when I was a freshman in college and a counselor looked at my record and said, "Okay, before anything else, how does someone with *this* reading level have *these* grades?"

I didn't have an answer then; I don't have an answer now.

I suspect it's the same thing with Davies.

He has a good fastball with control; a good curve and changeup.

He can hit too.

Then you look at his record and every year it's the same thing. Under .500; an ERA above 5.00 and usually over 6.00; an embarrassing hits/innings pitched ratio; and a lot of home runs allowed. And he can't blame it on playing for the Royals either. He'll pitch well for a string of starts, then he'll get blasted; he'll pitch well, then get blasted.

It happens again and again.

Davies is 27 and it's getting to the point where he may need a pitching coach guru to try and get through to him. But the pitching coach guru is on the other side of Missouri with the Cardinals. It's 2011 or bust for Davies. Given his history, he's not going to put it together; at least not in a Royals uniform; but he'll continually get chances elsewhere when they dump him because he's that talented. It's a vicious circle that can only be broken by one person—Kyle Davies.

Luke Hochevar reminds me of Roy Halladay with the way he moves; the way he throws; and because of his imposing size.

After that, he's nothing like Roy Halladay.

Hochevar was about as bad as Davies for awhile; but under Yost he pitched better. He missed time with an elbow injury last season and spent time in the minors, but there was a spurt in late May-early June that he looked like he could fulfill all that potential that made him a first round draft pick of the Dodgers in 2005 (he didn't sign) and with the Royals as the first overall pick in 2006. He's not a strikeout pitcher, but he can be a winner if he throws strikes and locates his pitches.

Vin Mazzaro was acquired from the Athletics for David DeJesus. Mazzaro was up and down between the big leagues and the minors for the A's last season, but he was impressive for much of the season in the majors.

Mazzaro allowed 127 hits in 122 innings and 19 homers; but he pitched much better than that. From mid-June to late-August, he pitched into the sixth inning in 12 of his 14 starts; he's a contact pitcher who can get slightly wild, but he has a knack and know-how for what he's doing on the mound. He's 24 and has been borderline dominant in the minors. Moore got himself a useful piece in Mazzaro.

Former Rockies ace Jeff Francis was signed to a 1-year, $2 million contract. Francis is still trying to come back from shoulder surgery and is a low-cost flier for the Royals. His shoulder wasn't 100% last season, but when he pitched he was about as effective as he was before the injury. He's always given up a lot of hits and homers and had good control. I'd hesitate to expect too much, but the Royals needed pitching and Francis has been successful before. Shoulders tend to be hard to rebuild to full strength, but Francis was never a power pitcher anyway. He may have to learn to pitch differently, but lefties have had more success doing that than righties; he can have a second career after an injury as Frank Tanana did. It may not happen for a couple of years though.

Veteran journeyman Bruce Chen was re-signed by the Royals to a 1-year contract worth $2 million with incentive bonuses. Chen doesn't throw hard, but he has a changeup and the ability to hang around in the big leagues without good stuff. His numbers in 2010 are pretty good. A 12-7 record; 140 innings; 136 hits; 57 walks and 98 strikeouts. He was particularly good over the last month of the season. Chen is a competent, back-of-the-rotation starter for a bad team.

BULLPEN:

After the Royals traded Greinke, teams—the Yankees specifically—began calling about closer Joakim Soria and were flatly rejected.

This makes no sense.

Why trade the ace starter who's signed to through 2012 and keep the closer (who's had arm trouble and been overused) who's signed through 2014?

Unless they think Soria's going to be the closer for the club when the youngsters arrive and the team takes the next step into respectability and contention, it's better to deal him now, isn't it? The Royals have no chance of competing this season and probably next season; what do they need Soria for?

Soria was an absolute steal by Moore in the Rule 5 draft of 2006. Last year, Soria saved 43 games; allowed 53 hits and struck out 71 in 65 innings; only gave up 4 homers and walked 16. He has a good fastball and a great curve. Moore could get a lot for him in a trade and he should explore it before Soria gets hurt.

Righty Robinson Tejeda had a shaky start to his career with the Phillies and Rangers, but has become a very reliable reliever with the Royals. He throws very hard and racks up the strikeouts; his control is improving markedly and he's durable. Tejada is only 29 and could be a valuable trade chip.

Dusty Hughes is an undersized lefty (listed at 5'10") who was utilized against both righties and lefties last season and pitched well. He doesn't strike out many hitters and allowed 59 hits in 56 innings. He was knocked around when he was asked to pitch multiple innings, so he may be better served to be a one-inning arm.

Jesse Chavez is with his fourth organization in two years. The Pirates traded him to the Rays for Akinori Iwamura; the Rays traded him to the Braves for Rafael Soriano; the Braves traded him to the Royals in the deal to get Rick Ankiel and Kyle Farnsworth.

Chavez has a good fastball but doesn't strike anyone out. He throws strikes and gives up too many hits and homers, but I think there's something salvageable there. He's only 27 and could be a Grant Balfour-type reliever who figures it all out one year.

Blake Wood is a 25-year-old righty who appeared in 51 games for the Royals in 2010. He doesn't strike out many hitters and allowed 54 hits in 49 innings; he can pitch multiple innings and is streaky, but can be a decent middle-reliever.

Kanekoa Texeira was picked up off waivers from the Mariners in June and may have found a home in Kansas City. He doesn't strike out many hitters, but has a sinker that could be used to induce ground balls to wriggle out of trouble. He throws strikes and allowed 3 homers in 42 innings.

Sean O'Sullivan was acquired from the Angels in the trade of Alberto Callaspo. His results have been mediocre, but he's been a starter in the minors and might be a durable innings-eater out of the bullpen in the majors. He doesn't strike out many hitters and gave up a ridiculous 14 homers in 14 games (13 starts) for the Royals.

Jeremy Jeffress was acquired from the Brewers in the Greinke trade. Jeffress, a 23-year-old righty taken in the 1st round of the 2006 draft, has racked up the strikeouts in the minors as a reliever. He has closer potential, but has been in trouble off the field and been suspended twice for drug violations. I don't like players with character issues and I wouldn't have touched Jeffress; I don't care how talented he is.

LINEUP:

Jason Kendall's defense is declining and he can't hit a lick. Plus, judging from the struggles of the Royals pitchers, he wasn't doing them much good behind the plate. I'd dump Kendall and play Brayan Pena and see what I've got, but Yost is a former catcher and will probably be more comfortable with the veteran Kendall.

Kila Ka'aihue has put up massive on base numbers in the minors and never really gotten a chance to play in the big leagues. Last season, he played semi-regularly over the last two months and didn't hit batting .217 with a .306 on base (close to 100 points higher than a weak batting average is pretty good); Ka'aihue will be 27 and this is probably his one and only shot to grab hold of the Royals first base job. He has a magical ability to get on base and he doesn't strike out. He's also hit for power in the minors. The Royals have to give him a legitimate shot and not dump him if he's slumping in April.

I'd give him until at least late June before abandoning ship. This is a case where the numbers are too stark to disbelieve them.

Chris Getz will get a chance to win the everyday second base job. He's 26 and has never had the opportunity to play every day in the big leagues either. He's got some speed and is an adequate defensive second baseman. He's hit for some pop in the minors so perhaps, like Ka'aihue, all he needs is a chance.

Mike Aviles came from nowhere to win the shortstop job in 2008 and batted .325 with excellent across-the-board stats; then he got hurt and lost his job; returned in 2010...and batted .304 with good across-the-board stats. He's hit every year in the minors too. Aviles is a good player who should play every day at third or second base.

Alcides Escobar was acquired from the Brewers in the Greinke deal. Escobar is a 24-year-old shortstop who was handed the Brewers starting job after their trade of J.J. Hardy and flopped. He batted .235 with an embarrassing .288 on base percentage and 28 extra base hits. Also going to the Brewers in the trade was Yuniesky Betancourt; Betancourt's numbers at the plate are strikingly similar to Escobar's save one thing: Betancourt hits for some power. Escobar is a better defensive shortstop and is 4 years younger.

Escobar was an impressive hitter in the minors and stole a lot of bases. He has the talent and it's up to the Royals to unlock it.

Former 1st round pick Alex Gordon has been a bust so far. He's been injured with a torn hip labrum and other nagging problems. He's 27 and it's time to embark on a successful big league career. He batted .215 last season with 8 homers in 281 plate appearances. He's been shifted from third base to left field and I'm getting a Phil Nevin-vibe from him in that he's a top pick as a third baseman who's getting his position changed and is taking a long time to find his legs in the majors. I question whether he's going to make it in Kansas City; he may need a change of scenery.

Moore signed Melky Cabrera and Jeff Francoeur to short-term deals to play everyday in center and right field.

Cabrera was horrendous and disinterested for the Braves in 2010 after playing solidly and providing clutch hits for the World Series champion Yankees in 2009. He was out of shape for the Braves and Bobby Cox appeared to want to strangle him as did half of his teammates. If he's looking for outside motivation, I don't know how he's going to find it in Kansas City. He's behaved this way in two of the past three seasons and he was playing for contending teams. I can see Cabrera lollygagging his way out of the lineup by May; then out of Kansas City entirely by mid-season. This signing made no sense.

I've always been enamored of Jeff Francoeur's talent. He *does* have the talent to win an MVP; but I've come to the conclusion that he's never going to listen to anyone other than his enablers that tell him his way is best and as long as he's true to himself, his abilities will help him achieve the star status he clearly seeks.

Francoeur has shown spurts of trying to be patient; mostly it was when he was told he wasn't going to play unless he altered his approach. He hit the ball to the opposite field; waited for a pitch to hit and would have a hot streak that would make people like me—who believe in him—say maybe, *maybe* he's getting it.

Then he'd lapse back into what he knows—hacking.

I've said before I would tell Francoeur to approach each at bat—until he has 2 strikes on him—as if it's a 3-0 count and he's got the take sign unless the pitch is in his zone. In essence, he should zone on the first pitch and if it's not where he wants it, take it.

Clearly he doesn't listen. It's not easy to change that which one has done forever; what's been allowed to go on through much of his professional career. I'm a believer in personal responsibility, but it's not all Francoeur's fault. Now, the Phillies were interested in him. He'd have been a part-time player, but would have had a hitting guru who worked wonders with Manny Ramirez, Phillies manager Charlie Manuel, trying to fix his swing and approach. Instead he chose to go to the Royals where the GM doesn't understand the concept of players who are patient.

Francoeur's not changing. It's time to accept this and move on without wondering what might have been.

Billy Butler is evolving into an All Star player. For the second season in a row, he surpassed 180 hits; batted over .300; had a rapidly improving on base percentage (.388); hit for some power (15 homers and 45 doubles); and played in nearly every single game. He's only 24 and will make his first All Star team this year. People will learn the name of Billy Butler sooner rather than later.

BENCH:

I mentioned Brayan Pena earlier as probably having more upside to catch every day than Kendall. Pena's not young at 29; has never played regularly in the majors; doesn't hit for much power, but he can throw and he's better than Kendall at this point as an all-around player.

Wilson Betemit disappears; is the butt of jokes; bounces around and then returns to hit a little bit. Betemit hit 13 homers in 315 plate appearances; batted .297 and had a .378 on base percentage. If Getz doesn't hit, I can absolutely see Aviles shifted to second and Betemit given the third base job.

Gregor Blanco was acquired in the Farnsworth/Ankiel trade. Blanco can play all three outfield positions, can run and is a good bunter. He should be playing instead of Cabrera.

Mitch Maier played regularly last season and in 421 plate appearances batted .263 with 5 homers and 26 extra base hits. He can run a little bit and is a fifth outfielder.

Lorenzo Cain might get a chance to play regularly this season. Acquired in the Greinke trade, the 25-year-old Cain batted .306 in 158 plate appearances for the Brewers last season. He's put up big average/ on base numbers in the minors and can steal bases. He's also a good center fielder.

PREDICTION:

This is a dangerous time for the Royals. GM Moore is getting a lot of anticipatory credit for what's on the horizon. Young players like Eric Hosmer and Mike Moustakas among others have been lauded as part of the future Royals contenders. This contender is supposed to be ready to do some damage by 2013-2014.

But what about 2011-2012? The Royals have some young players on their roster now that they're struggling to develop; the excuse that Moore didn't draft Gordon, to me, is hollow. One thing has little to do with the other. Gordon, Hochevar, Davies, Ka'iahue—all have yet to improve dramatically while with the Royals.

This is a bad sign and I don't think it's healthy for the organization to expect talent to win out and shine through while basically throwing this season and next into the heap of "we're rebuilding, be patient".

Why was there this desperation to trade Greinke and a reluctance to even listen to offers on Soria?

Is there a plan?

2011 will open a window into the Royals future not because of the young players on the way up, but because they have Cain and Escobar in the mix to go along with those mentioned above. If they play well or at least look like they're fundamentally sound and hustling, then the Royals future will likely be as bright as has been suggested; but it's far from a guarantee. Considering the mostly horrible decisions Moore has made as GM, I'm wondering why he's being given such leeway based on players who are still in the minors?

As for this season, the Royals are again going to be among the worst teams in the American League; but apparently, that's not the point. They're looking toward 2013-2014.

Why fans would pay to see a team that has made this acknowledgment is beyond me because I wouldn't.

PREDICTED RECORD: 72-90

Cleveland Indians

2010 Record: 69-93; 4th place, American League Central

2010 Recap:

Put it this way: their best player, Grady Sizemore, missed most of the season with micro-fracture surgery on his knee and the surgery doesn't always work; they don't know if Sizemore will make it back and how compromised the five tool player will be if and when he does.

Travis Hafner, still owed $28.75 million through 2012, had another injury-shortened year in which he only played in 118 games; if Hafner's healthy, he can hit and the Indians would be able to move if not for that contract. But, in both cases, he is and isn't going anywhere.

Fausto Carmona had a solid year; Mitch Talbot was a cheap pickup who showed some potential; Chris Perez was serviceable as the closer. But the Indians have gotten nothing from the players they acquired in the salary dump trades of Cliff Lee and C.C. Sabathia and haven't had any money to make improvements at all.

The only winning month they had all season was in September at 15-12 and it was that which allowed them to finish ahead of the Royals and out of last place.

2011 ADDITIONS:

OF Austin Kearns signed a 1-year, $1.3 million contract.
INF Orlando Cabrera signed a 1-year contract.
INF Jack Hannahan signed a minor league contract.

OF Travis Buck signed a minor league contract.
SS Adam Everett signed a minor league contract.
RHP Doug Mathis signed a minor league contract.
C Paul Phillips signed a minor league contract.
RHP Chad Durbin signed a 1-year, $800,000 contract.

2011 SUBTRACTIONS:

INF Andy Marte was not re-signed.
INF Mark Grudzielanek was not re-signed.
RHP Saul Rivera was not re-signed.
INF Drew Sutton was not re-signed.
LHP Aaron Laffey was traded to the Seattle Mariners.

2011 PROJECTED STARTING ROTATION: Fausto Carmona; Mitch Talbot; Justin Masterson; Carlos Carrasco; Josh Tomlin; David Huff.

2011 PROJECTED BULLPEN: Chris Perez; Tony Sipp; Rafael Perez; Joe Smith; Frank Herrmann; Jensen Lewis; Joe Martinez.

2011 PROJECTED LINEUP: C-Carlos Santana; 1B-Matt LaPorta; 2B-Jason Donald; 3B-Jayson Nix; SS-Asdrubal Cabrera; LF-Michael Brantley; CF-Grady Sizemore; RF-Shin-Soo Choo; DH-Travis Hafner.

2011 BENCH: INF-Luis Valbuena; C-Lou Marson; OF-Austin Kearns; OF-Trevor Crowe; DH/1B-Shelley Duncan; 3B-Jack Hannahan; INF-Orlando Cabrera.

2011 POSSIBLE CONTRIBUTORS: OF-Ezequiel Carrera; RHP-Jeanmar Gomez; LHP-Nick Hagadone; RHP-Zack McAllister; RHP-Vinny Pestano; RHP-Hector Rondon; RHP-Jess Todd.

ASSESSMENTS MANAGEMENT:

Chris Antonetti takes over for Mark Shapiro as the new GM. Shapiro has been moved upstairs as the president of the club and one would assume he'll still have significant say in player moves.

Antonetti has been with the Indians since 1999 and is left with a difficult task in rebuilding a club with mediocre talent and little money to spend. Shapiro has long been respected as one of the savviest and fearless executives in baseball. It was Shapiro's decision to move forward from the team that John Hart had built into a powerhouse and rebuild. He acquired such underrated players as Casey Blake and Travis Hafner; and made the franchise making trade of Bartolo Colon for Cliff Lee and Grady Sizemore.

The Indians have degenerated fast from the team that was one win from the World Series in 2007; manager Eric Wedge is gone; most of the players who comprised that club are gone; and Shapiro is no longer the GM.

Antonetti has his work cut out for him. They're stuck with Hafner's contract and decisions have to be made on Fausto Carmona and a rising star like Shin-Soo Choo who the club might be better served to trade for volume.

It's hard to win when the biggest acquisition you've made in a winter is to bring back a player—Austin Kearns—that you traded the previous summer; and to sign veteran journeyman Orlando Cabrera.

You have to feel for manager Manny Acta.

He's a solid game manager who's respected by players and peers; he makes mostly the right moves and runs the clubhouse well. But he's been saddled with bad teams his entire managerial career—first with the Washington Nationals and now with the Indians.

This team has literally no chance to compete.

But there are two ways to look at these circumstances for Acta.

One, he's not going to get the blame for the team when they lose close to 100 games because they're atrocious; Tony La Russa, Billy Martin and Earl Weaver combined wouldn't win more than 70 games;

because of that, he's able to do the best he can and be absolved due to lack of talent.

Two, the Indians aren't going to fire him. His job is safe because he's got a contract through 2012 and they're not going to pay him to sit around so another manager can lose all those games.

It's a certain freedom that Acta has because of this.

No one is suggesting that Acta doesn't want to win, but he knows what he's got; he knows the difficulty a team that lost 93 games the prior year will have if they don't make any substantial acquisitions; in a way, he can be comfortable with the losing and try to develop the youngsters since there would be a borderline ticker-tape parade if this team somehow managed to keep from losing 100 games.

Comparatively, it's not a terrible situation because of diminished (or non-existent) expectations. It's similar to any manager who was fired by Peter Angelos or, in the NFL, Al Davis of the Raiders—there's a legitimate case for the phrase, "What could I do in that situation?"

That's reality.

STARTING PITCHING:

Fausto Carmona's performance ebbs and flows. From his heinous and short-lived stint as the Indians closer in 2006; to a 19-game winner and Cy Young Award contender in 2007; to two dreadful and rapidly degenerating years in 2008-2009 where he wound up back in the minor leagues and seemingly lost all command of the strike zone; to another comeback year in 2010 in which he had a very good all-around season. If he Carmona had been on a better team with a good bullpen, he'd have come close to equaling or surpassing his 19-8 record in 2007.

Carmona regained his control and only walked 72 in 210 innings; he allowed 203 hits and 17 homers and pitched 4 complete games.

He's mentally tough enough to get past these adversities and fight his way back into being a competent starter; when he's at his best, he's an All Star.

With the Indians in their current financial and practical circumstances, they may be well-served to trade Carmona for a package of prospects. Perhaps, if he's pitching well they can also insist that the trading team take Travis Hafner. That's a bit of a tall order.

Carmona is signed 2011 at $6.1 million with club options in 2012 ($7 million) and 2013 ($9 million).

Righty Mitch Talbot was acquired from the Rays for Kelly Shoppach and pitched very well for the Indians in 2010. The 27-year-old Talbot had never gotten a full shot in the big leagues until last season and he took advantage of it.

Talbot started 28 games and, before he missed time late in the season with a back strain and shoulder inflammation, opened plenty of eyes with his aggressiveness and stuff. His control sometimes eludes him and he racks up large pitch counts by the fifth or sixth innings, but he showed enough to be a useful starter. He only allowed 13 homers in 159 innings. He's been a durable and consistent starter in the minors.

Justin Masterson pitched better than his 6-13 record in 2010. There have been calls to move him back to the bullpen where he started his career with the Red Sox and his slingshot right-handed motion may be better suited to relieving. He did well at it while with the Red Sox. For right now, his home is in the starting rotation. In 180 innings he allowed 197 hits and 14 homers, but the hit total is skewered by games in which he allowed 10, 10, 13 and 11 hits. Apart from that, he was mostly effective. Masterson has strikeout stuff and his control sometimes eludes him. He's only 26 and deserves another year to try and make it as a starter before a full shift to the bullpen.

Carlos Carrasco is one of the prospects the Indians acquired in 2009 when they traded Cliff Lee to the Phillies. None of the others have worked out as planned yet, but Carrasco, 24, was impressive in a brief big league trial in 2010. He's been a strikeout pitcher in the minors and he throws strikes. Carrasco could be a top rotation starter and Rookie of the Year candidate.

Did the Indians keep Carrasco's innings below 45 so he'd qualify as a rookie in 2011? He threw 44 2/3 innings, so it's not a difficult assumption to make that they did.

Josh Tomlin went 6-4 in 12 starts as a rookie in 2010. Tomlin allowed 72 hits in 73 innings and 10 homers; he's a contact pitcher who isn't afraid to throw strikes. He's been a good starter in the minors and is a darkhorse to make it as a useful mid-rotation starter.

Lefty David Huff had a rotten year in 2010 at 2-11 with a 6.21 ERA. In a clear indication of how won/lost record should be put into context, Huff went 11-8 in 2009 with essentially the same (or worse!) ancillary numbers. His hits-to-innings pitched ratio; walks and strikeouts were unchanged; in 2010 he lost the games he won in 2009.

Huff is a better pitcher than his numbers indicate, but he's a replaceable part.

BULLPEN:

Righty Chris Perez has the stuff to be a good closer. Last season, after Kerry Wood was hurt and traded, Perez took over the closer's job and saved 23 games. He allowed 40 hits in 63 innings and struck out 61. He's a good bet for an All Star berth this season.

Tony Sipp is a lefty who could be more than a lefty specialist. His numbers against lefties and righties were nearly identical. Lefties batted .212 against him; righties .223—and he pitched regularly against both. He allowed too many homers with 12. His control is a little scattershot as well with 39 walks in 63 innings, but he struck out 69. If he could cut down on the home run ball, he'd be a solid set-up man.

Rafael Perez continued the bizarre trend of being a lefty reliever... who gets blasted by left-handed batters. He allowed a .306 average vs lefties; .295 against righties. Perez gives up a lot of hits but, for the most part, wriggles out of self-crafted trouble. He's been good and awful in alternating seasons in his career and since he was serviceable last year, that would mean that he'll be awful this year.

Joe Smith is a side-arming righty who was up-and-down between the majors and minors in 2010. Smith is a righty specialist, pure and simple. Letting him pitch to lefties in a game-breaking situation will not happen; nor should it.

Frank Herrmann is a righty who appeared in 40 games in relief in 2010. Herrmann allowed 48 hits in 44 innings and 6 homers; but he only walked 9. He's not a strikeout pitcher, but he throws strikes and has pitched well out of the bullpen in the minors.

Righty Jensen Lewis throws hard and has set-up man potential. In 36 innings in 2010, Lewis allowed 28 hits and struck out 29. He only allowed 1 homer and his control was suspect with 19 walks.

Joe Martinez was acquired from the Pirates after the new year. He's tough (anyone coming back from a line drive to the head is tough); and has shown potential as a starter in the minors. Perhaps he can be a right-handed long man for the Indians.

LINEUP:

Carlos Santana was lucky last season. Lucky that Ryan Kalish didn't tear his knee to shreds when he slid into him on a play at home against the Red Sox last August.

Santana missed the rest of the season, but the injury wasn't serious. One of the top prospects in baseball, Santana was acquired from the Dodgers for Casey Blake in 2008. He's reminded some of the former Indians catcher Victor Marinez in that both are switch-hitters with pop. Santana doesn't strike out and walks a lot. At the age of 25, he's ready to bust out as a potential superstar player.

Matt LaPorta was one of the main components of the trade that sent C.C. Sabathia to the Brewers in 2008 and has yet to live up to the billing. LaPorta is 26 and it's time to make a move. He hit 12 homers last year, but his on base percentage was awful at .308 and he batted .221. He's posted good power/on base numbers in the minors and he's going to get another shot to play regularly in the big leagues in 2011. So far he seems overmatched.

Jason Donald was acquired from the Phillies in the Lee trade and, more famously, was the baserunner who was called safe by umpire Jim Joyce in Armando Galarraga's imperfect-perfect game. Donald is 26 and hasn't hit much in the minors or majors. He's better defensively at second base than shortstop and can steal a base here and there.

Donald looks like more of a utility player than anything else.

Jayson Nix is the last man standing at third base for the Indians. The journeyman utility player hit 13 homers in 306 plate appearances last season. He's shown mid-teens power and some on base skills in the minors, but he's 28 and is what he is at this point.

Switch hitter Asdrubal Cabrera shifted to shortstop from second base last season and played the position well enough defensively. He missed time with forearm and wrist injuries in 2010 and had a terrific year at the plate in 2009. Cabrera has no power, but hit 42 doubles in 2009 while batting .308. He can steal a few bases too. Cabrera is a good, underrated player.

Michael Brantley is a 24-year-old outfielder and son of former big leaguer Mickey Brantley. Michael batted .246 with a .296 on base percentage in 325 plate appearances in 2010. He too was acquired in the Sabathia trade. He's had a high average/on base in the minors and stolen plenty of bases. He could be a good player in the majors as a catalyst at the top of the lineup.

Grady Sizemore could do it all.

He could hit for power; stole bases; played excellent defense and is a good guy. Now, after micro-fracture surgery, no one knows whether he'll be back and what they're getting when and if he returns. Micro-fracture surgery involves creating new fractures in the bone to grow cartilage and repair the pain-making problem.

No, I don't understand it either.

Athletes, specifically in the NBA, have had the surgery and returned to play at a high level; it doesn't always work.

Sizemore is owed $8 million through this season with an option for 2012. The best thing for the Indians now would be for him to return and play well enough for them to trade him and get some value.

I wouldn't expect him to come back as the Grady Sizemore he was before; it's a shame because he's only 28.

Shin-Soo Choo had an all-world year with a .300 average, .401 on base; 22 homers; 31 doubles; 90 RBI; and 22 stolen bases. He also reduced his strikeout from 151 in 2009 to 118 in 2010. At age 28, he's a star. Choo is a very good defensive right fielder and, after winning the Gold Medal in the Asian Games last November allowed him to avoid his mandatory two-year South Korean military commitment.

The Indians should either think about locking him up in a long term contract or trading him for a giant package of prospects.

Travis Hafner was one of the most dangerous and productive hitters in baseball, but injuries have left him a shell of his former self. He can still crush a fastball as he proved by taking Stephen Strasburg deep (pulling him no less), but he's got recurring shoulder problems and his contract is an albatross.

BENCH:

Veteran infielder Orlando Cabrera signed a 1-year contract to compete for playing time at either second base or shortstop. Cabrera's range at shortstop has declined drastically and after being a consistent .280+ hitter, he fell to .263 last season with the Reds. He's 36-years-old.

Luis Valbuena is a utility player who batted .193 in 310 plate appearances mostly appearing at second base. Valbuena showed some power in 2009 with 10 homers, but didn't hit at all in 2010.

Catcher Lou Marson was acquired from the Phillies in the Lee trade and isn't going to play much behind Santana. Marson is excellent defensively, especially throwing; but he hasn't hit yet in the big leagues despite showing some ability to hit for average and on base in the minors. He's only 24, so there's hope for him to develop as a big league hitter.

Veteran Austin Kearns was traded by the Indians at mid-season to the Yankees for pitching prospect Zach McAllister and returned to

Cleveland as a free agent. Kearns has some power as a fourth outfielder and a moderate on base skill.

Trevor Crowe is a switch-hitting, 27-year-old outfielder. He batted .251 with 20 stolen bases in 479 plate appearances. In the minors he's stolen some bases and shown a skill at getting on base. He's a fourth outfielder in the big leagues, if that.

Shelley Duncan is a slugger off the bench and part-time DH. Duncan hit 11 homers in 259 plate apperances and is known more for his wild enthusiasm for playing hard and fighting than any actual success on the field. Duncan can hit the ball out of the park and that's a useful thing to have on the bench.

Veteran journeyman Jack Hannahan was signed to a minor league contract and might supplant Nix as the regular third baseman. That's more of an indictment of the Indians current circumstances than any credit doled out to Hannahan.

PREDICTION:

The Indians do have some talent, but it's hard to improve on 69-93 when the big off-season acquisitions are Austin Kearns and Orlando Cabrera.

Will Sizemore be back? Can they get anything out of the young players they got in the big trades of Lee and Sabathia? That's the key for the Indians and it's underreported when clubs perpetrate a housecleaning how many times the prospects they get—all of them—are busts.

It happens. People remember the big trades teams like the Twins made in 1989 of Frank Viola and got Rick Aguilera, Kevin Tapani and David West forming the foundation of their championship team two years later. For every deal of that magnitude you see teams like the Indians who got the right names in the trades; have the intelligent personnel in their scouting department to make the right recommendations, and sit by helplessly as the prospects fail.

Santana has star potential; Carrasco can be good; but the other players haven't done anything to get excited about. With their lack of money to spend, it's hard for the Indians to compete.

And they won't.

The best thing for them to do is field offers for Carmona; hope that Sizemore comes back healthy and trade him; and listen to offers for Choo.

This team is terrible.

PREDICTED RECORD: 67-95

American League West Predicted Standings

		Wins	Losses	GB
1.	Los Angeles Angels	87	75	---
2.	Texas Rangers	86	76	1
3.	Oakland Athletics	84	78	3
4.	Seattle Mariners	65	97	22

Los Angeles Angels

2010 Record: 80-82; 3rd place, Amercian League West

2010 Recap:

Year-after-year the Angels are at the top of the American League West no matter what. Be it tragedy; injury; player defections; opposing clubs who are worshiped by the media and make flashy moves—it always came down to the Angels.

It was that way until 2010.

The Angels had a bad year at 80-82 and were never really in any kind of contention for a playoff spot.

They had essentially the same cast of characters led by respected manager Mike Scioscia. With solid citizens and leaders, a deep starting rotation and diverse bullpen, they had the personnel to contend and win the division again. But it didn't work. Not even their annual aggressive trade for a star player (in 2010 it was Dan Haren) failed to jump start them.

All year long they were short offensively and shaky in the bullpen. The ludicrous season became fodder for lampooning when budding star first baseman Kendry Morales, celebrating a game winning homer, leapt onto home plate...and broke his ankle.

Morales was out for the season and required surgery.

It was a microcosm for the entire 2010 campaign for the Los Angeles Angels.

2011 ADDITIONS:

OF Vernon Wells was acquired from the Toronto Blue Jays.
LHP Scott Downs signed a 3-year, $15 million contract.
LHP Hisanori Takahashi signed a 2-year, $8 million contract.

2011 SUBTRACTIONS:

C/1B Mike Napoli was traded to the Toronto Blue Jays.
OF Juan Rivera was traded to the Toronto Blue Jays.
DH Hideki Matsui was not re-signed.
OF Robb Quinlan was not re-signed.
INF Kevin Frandsen was not re-signed.
OF Cory Aldridge was not re-signed.
C Ryan Budde was not re-signed.
RHP Brian Stokes was released.
RHP Scot Shields was not re-signed.
OF Michael Ryan was not re-signed.

2011 PROJECTED STARTING ROTATION: Jered Weaver; Dan Haren; Ervin Santana; Joel Pineiro; Scott Kazmir.

2011 PROJECTED BULLPEN: Fernando Rodney; Scott Downs; Hisanori Takahashi; Kevin Jepsen; Jason Bulger; Francisco Rodriguez; Rich Thompson; Michael Kohn; Jordan Walden.

2011 PROJECTED LINEUP: C-Hank Conger; 1B-Kendry Morales; 2B-Howie Kendrick; 3B-Alberto Callaspo; SS-Erick Aybar; LF-Vernon Wells; CF-Peter Bourjos; RF-Torii Hunter; DH-Bobby Abreu.

2011 BENCH: C-Jeff Mathis; INF-Maicer Izturis; INF-Brandon Wood; OF-Reggie Willits; C-Bobby Wilson.

2011 POSSIBLE CONTRIBUTORS: RHP-Bobby Cassevah; RHP-Trevor Bell; RHP-Anthony Ortega; RHP-Matt Palmer; INF-Andrew Romine; INF-Freddy Sandoval; INF-Mark Trumbo; OF-Chris Pettit; OF-Jeremy Moore.

ASSESSMENTS MANAGEMENT:

The Angels front office is known as one of the most aggressive and respected in all of baseball.

Owner Arte Moreno and GM Tony Reagins had the intention of spending money to fill all their holes. Those holes were in the lineup and bullpen. They had their sites set on Carl Crawford going back forever and when they thought they had a competitive offer of over $100 million prepared for the Rays free agent outfielder, they were stunned to see the Red Sox do what the Angels usually do—make a rapid and unexpected lightning strike with little telegraphing or warning. Instead of the Angels coming from nowhere to make the prototypical "offer he can't refuse", it was the Red Sox with their $142 million that snagged Crawford.

There were other players the Angels pursued. They were in on Cliff Lee; Rafael Soriano; Adrian Beltre; Adrian Gonzalez. They got none of them.

In their desperation, they were even prepared to go back on their vow—stemming from the contentious and perceived dishonest negotiation the club and Scott Boras engaged in for Mark Teixeira—and make a move on Jayson Werth.

That didn't work either as the Nationals gave Werth $126 million.

The Angels were left out in the cold.

The only maneuvers Reagins made were to sign two left-handed relief pitchers, Hisanori Takahashi and Scott Downs; and to let Hideki Matsui leave as a free agent.

Until they made the decried and expensive move to get Vernon Wells from the Blue Jays.

Not only did they give up a productive part-time hitter in Mike Napoli and the somehwat useful Juan Rivera, but they took $81 million of the $86 million Wells is owed for the rest of his contract.

As criticized as the deal was, it's not as bad as all that.

Wells isn't worth that money, it's true; but he's a pretty good player and that's pretty good. The Angels needed a bat and Wells will hit his 25 homers and drive in 100; he's shifting to left field for Peter Bourjos to get a shot in center and Wells can always move back to center if Bourjos isn't ready. They needed to do something drastic and they did.

In the past, Reagins and Moreno have been the ones who set the market by marking their target, making a competitive and occasionally over-the-top offer, telling him he has a set timeframe to accept it, waiting for an answer and reacting accordingly. If the offer was rejected, they went to the next man on their list; if it was accepted, they went down the line to other holes that needed filling.

The Red Sox and Phillies beat them at their own game in the free agent market.

Manager Mike Scioscia has been above reproach for the majority of his days as Angels manager. While he had his own way of doing things—a way from which he never deviated as it cost his club dearly in the post-season—and it was accepted as part of the Scioscia package of having a manager who was in complete command of his clubhouse and a large part of the organization. In 2010 however, it was in the wind that all wasn't as rosy as it's been in the past for Scioscia.

Questions about his strategies which cost the Angels badly in the 2009 ALCS, which Joe Girardi and *his* mistakes placed on a platter for an Angels team that, by all rights should've gotten swept, carried into the 2010 season. The Angels had a bit of a controversy at closer as Brian Fuentes struggled and Fernando Rodney was dominant; but Scioscia followed one of his own rules by maintaining loyalty to his troops despite it being a detriment to the club.

Who can know which way is better? Is it more advantageous to make a switch when things aren't working? Or is it better to read the back of the bubble gum card for a veteran player with confidence that, if left alone, he'll figure it out and return to form?

Scioscia's patience is one of the reasons the Angels have been a perennial contender; but his adherence to small ball regardless of personnel and situation has been a negative, especially in the playoffs.

He's one of the most respected managers in baseball; players love to play for him; and if a free agent doesn't want to come to the Angels, it will not be because of the manager. His teams play the game correctly and they behave themselves off the field. Changing managers is not the answer and the Angels are not going to replace Scioscia.

STARTING PITCHING:

Although his record doesn't show it, Jered Weaver had a great year. He went 13-12, but deserved to win over 20 games on the season. At the age of 28, Weaver is a star pitcher few are aware of. He's durable, he throws strikes, doesn't allow many hits and has a sneaky motion and control of all his pitches. Leading the league in strikeouts with 233, Weaver's hits/innings pitched ratio was a terrific 224/187. He's one of the best pitchers in baseball and an All Star.

Dan Haren was acquired from the Diamondbacks at mid-season for Joe Saunders and a package of minor leaguers. Haren was pitching poorly for the Diamondbacks, but it looked as if he was waiting to be traded and had been bogged down by being the last man standing for a club that as recently as 2009 was a playoff contender. Regaining his form after joining the Angels, Haren again was a workhorse who throws strikes. The change-of-scenery did wonders for him and he was back to the top tier starter he's been for several years. He and Weaver are a fine 1-2 punch; Haren is an All Star and Cy Young Award contender, just like Weaver.

Having a pitcher who won 17 games and logged 222 innings as your third starter is a pretty good deal and that's what the Angels have in Ervin Santana. Santana is a contact pitcher and gives up his share of home runs, but he battles through with a power fastball and hard slider and, like Weaver and Haren, throws strikes.

Joel Pineiro was on his way to having the exact year I predicted he'd have when critics were suggesting that the reinvention of Pineiro was a St. Louis/Dave Duncan incarnation and would disappear as soon as he went elsewhere.

It didn't.

On the surface, Pineiro's numbers appear serviceable, but he pitched much better than his 10-7 won/loss and 3.84 ERA. He successfully brought the lessons he learned from Duncan in St. Louis to the Angels and would have won 16-18 games had he not injured an oblique and missed most of the second half of the season. There were games in which Pineiro was masterful; and games in which he got blasted and his ERA and ancillary numbers (hits to innings pitched) were blown out of proportion. Pineiro gave up over 6 earned runs in a game five times. Apart from that, he was exactly what the Angels expected. He's a free agent at the end of the year and if he's healthy, he'll pitch in a similar way. For a back-of-the-rotation starter, that's very good.

Scott Kazmir is also a free agent at the end of the season.

Well, technically he has a $13.5 million option, but I have as much chance of getting that option picked up as Kazmir does. For all his talent and all the savagery former Mets pitching coach Rick Peterson engendered for his suggestion that Kazmir was too small and his motion too stressful to make it as a consistent big league starter, he was right.

Like Dan Duquette was right about Roger Clemens when he allowed the Red Sox icon to leave Boston after the 1996 season and said that Clemens was in the twilight of his great career, Peterson, in retrospect, was right. Clemens of course regained his greatness through illicit (though prevalent) means which were winked and nodded at by baseball itself, but that doesn't eliminate the fact that Duquette was right.

Peterson was right.

Unless he cuts down on the number of pitches he throws, Kazmir doesn't have the stamina to be a full time starter in the big leagues.

I've said for years he should be a closer, but the Angels aren't going to do that. They'll start him and leave him in games to get the desired number of innings out of him. He'll pitch well in some; get blasted in others and will move on after the season. Maybe someone, somewhere will have the guts and presence of mind to explain to Kazmir that, like Billy Wagner, he could be a dominant left-handed strikeout artist out of the bullpen.

But since he's starting this season, he'll be a starter on the free agent market next season. And not a particularly good or reliable one.

Peterson was right.

BULLPEN:

Fernando Rodney takes over as the closer from the start of the season after Brian Fuentes was traded to the Twins last summer.

Rodney is gutsy as he proved in logging inning after inning when he was clearly exhausted in the Tigers ill-fated division title push in 2009. He's not the most reliable closer. Rodney is wild (35 walks in 68 innings); for a pitcher who can touch 97-98 on the radar gun, he doesn't strike out many hitters (53); gives up a few homers (4 last season; 8 in 2009). Rodney's streaky, but reliable for the most part. He'll have a week in which he'll blow a bunch of games, he'll give his manager, pitching coach and teammates a collective heart attack with walks, but as a free agent after the season I think he'll be at least as consistent as Fuentes was. For what that's worth.

Scott Downs is one of the two "big" free agent signings the Angels made this winter. The veteran lefty Downs signed a 3-year, $15 million contract to leave the Blue Jays. Downs is 35 and has been a consistent durable innings-eater out of the bullpen. He can get out both righties and lefties and has closed in the past. I don't know if I'd have gone to 3 years for Downs, but he's a solid and versatile bullpen arm.

Hisanori Takahashi arrived from the heavens for the Mets last season. Takahashi started, pitched long relief and closed after Francisco Rodriguez's suspension. He performed all duties professionally and fearlessly. The value of having a pitcher like Takahashi who can and will do anything witout complaint is immeasurable. In games where the starting pitcher got knocked out early, Takahashi repeatedly came into games and quieted them down giving the Mets a chance to fight back and win. As a closer, he threw strikes and wasn't intimidated by the unfamiliar role. He's a terrific pick-up for the Angels and they'll love him in Anaheim.

Kevin Jepsen is a flamethrowing righty with closer potential. He strikes out nearly a batter per inning with a dominating fastball. He throws strikes and doesn't allow many homers.

32-year-old righty Jason Bulger is a journeyman minor leaguer who'd made it to the big leagues to stay in 2009 and appeared in 64 games. He missed a chunk of last season with a shoulder problem. He's a good strikeout pitcher, has some trouble with his command, but handles both righties and lefties.

Francisco (Not K-Rod) Rodriguez is a 28-year-old righty who appeared in 43 games as a rookie in 2010. He struck out 36 in 47 innings. He's hittable and can be wild, but is a useful middle reliever.

Australian Rich Thompson is a 26-year-old righty who posted a 1.37 ERA in 13 appearances for the Angels in 2010. He struck of 15 in 19 innings, walked 4 and allowed 12 hits. He's shown closing potential in the minors and can dominate.

Michael Kohn is a 24-year-old righty with big strikeout numbers throughout his professional career. Unfortunately, he also has big walk numbers as well. He doesn't allow homers and if he can get the ball over the plate, he can be a weapon out of the bullpen.

Jordan Walden is another strikeout machine. The 23-year-old righty struck out 23 in 15 innings for the Angels last season while issuing only 7 walks. He's been both a starter and a reliever in the minors and been good at both; it's hard to gauge his role in the big leagues for the future, but for 2010, presumably he'll be in the bullpen.

LINEUP:

The Angels traded Napoli and have the no-hit veteran Jeff Mathis on the roster, but prospect Hank Conger is the best bet to get offensive producting and decent defense behind the plate. The 23-year-old Conger has a career .297 average in the minors with a .360 on base; he has 10-15 homer pop and throws well. Mathis and Bobby Wilson might share time with Conger early in the year, but he's going to be the regular not long into the season.

Kendry Morales returns and it's a safe bet that he's not going to be leaping into the pile after a game-winning hit ever again in his career.

That injury was something that, in previous years, I could only see happening to the Mets. It was that ludicrous.

Be that as it may, the switch-hitting Morales is back and before the injury was developing into one of the American League's top overall power threats. He's a better hitter left-handed, but can hit for power from both sides of the plate and had 79 extra base hits in 2009 with 34 homers and batted .306. At the age of 27, Morales could become a star as long as he doesn't go jumping into any piles and breaking his bones in an ill-thought-out celebratory scrum.

Howie Kendrick has star potential if he can be a little bit more patient and consistent at the plate. Kendrick had 10 homers, 41 doubles and 75 RBI in 2010; he batted .271 and had a .313. on base. He's a potential .300 hitter and can steal bases. Kendrick is an average defensive second baseman.

Alberto Callaspo was acquired from the Royals at mid-season and it's about time people realized that Callaspo is a pretty good hitter. He fell back in 2010 after a terrific 2009, but he's got some pop and has the ability to get on base. Third base is probably his best defensive position. The Angels were interested in Adrian Beltre, but lost him to the Rangers.

Switch-hitting Erick Aybar took a major step back at the plate in 2010 after a fine 2009. His average fell from .312 to .253 and his strikeouts rose from 54 to 81. He's good defensively and steals 20+ bases.

Vernon Wells was acquired from the Blue Jays to bolster the Angels lineup. Forget his contract; it's over and done with; they're paying it and that's that. Wells is a decent outfielder and will be better in left than he was in center; he hit 31 homers last sesason and had 44 doubles; he doesn't get on base with a great frequency, but he's a power bat in the middle of the lineup for the Angels and he'll have a solid year freed from the expectations in Toronto that came with the contract.

Peter Bourjos was recalled at mid-season 2010 and Torii Hunter was moved to right field in a concession to the future. The 24-year-old Bourjos is one of the Angels top prospects. He batted .204 in 193 plate appearances, but this was just a "get used to the big leagues" situation. Bourjos has been a five tool player at every level in the minors. He has 10-15 homer pop and speed to get double figures in doubles and triples. He can really go get the ball in center field as well. He might need some more minor league seasoning, but he could be a Rookie of the Year candidate.

Torii Hunter didn't complain about moving out of the glamour position of center field and this tells you what type of person and teammate Hunter is. Not every player is so agreeable and willing to help a young player push him off to the side, but Hunter did it. It's indicative of the type of team the Angels put together that this was done so smoothly.

Hunter had a solid year at the plate with 23 homers and 90 RBI. He batted .281 with a .354 on base and 36 doubles. He adjusted well to right field defensively.

Bobby Abreu will see his share of time in the outfield, but he'll be DH'ing a significant amount of the time as well. Abreu had a down year and at age 37, he may be on the decline. Abreu's customary .300 average fell to .255; his on base to .352. He hit 20 homers and 41 doubles; he's still a threat, but not what he once was. He's got a contract option at the end of the season worth $9 million for 2012 with a $1 million buyout.

BENCH:

Jeff Mathis made a name for himself by almost singlehandedly destroying the Yankees in the ALCS of 2009, but he reverted back to what he is at the plate in 2010. Mathis batted .195 in 218 plate appearances and his defense behind the plate wasn't particularly good either.

Maicer Izturis missed a chunk of the 2010 season with injuries to his forearm and shoulder. He's a useful utility player who will get playing time at all infield positions. He's a switch-hitter with speed and surprising, occasional pop.

Brandon Wood is 26, has gotten chance after chance to win a job as a regular in the big leagues and responded by hitting under .200 consistently. In 81 games and 243 plate appearances, Wood batted .146. He'll probably no longer be with the Angels by the time you read this.

Reggie Willits is a defensively-minded backup outfielder who batted .258 in 182 plate appearances last season. He's a fifth outfielder.

PREDICTION:

The Angels have one of the best starting rotations in all of baseball and if Kazmir pitches well, they have a case for it being the best; and that includes the Phillies.

With the criticized acquisition of Wells and the under-the-radar signings of Downs and Takahashi, the lineup and bullpen have been strengthened enough to support that rotation. With Morales back at full strength, better seasons from Kendrick, Aybar and Abreu, the Angels will score enough to win.

This is the second year in a row that the expectations for one of the best run organizations in baseball have been muted to the degree of near laughter.

I don't think the Wells acquisition is as ludircous as others do; it will work in the short term at least and the other contenders in the division have flaws of their own.

I've seen it too many times. The Angels find a way to win.

And they're going to do it again as they shut up the naysayers by taking the AL West title.

PREDICTED RECORD: 87-75

Texas Rangers

2010 Record: 90-72; 1st place, American League West.
Defeated Tampa Bay Rays 3 games to 2 in the ALDS.
Defeated New York Yankees 4 games to 2 in the ALCS.
Lost to San Francisco Giants 4 games to 1 in World Series.

2010 Recap:

The Ranagers finally broke their hex.

After so many years as a franchise in both Washington and Texas, the Rangers—who've had more good teams than bad in the past decade-and-a-half—not only won the first playoff series in franchise history, but they beat their old nemesis, the Yankees, in the ALCS to advance to the World Series.

The Rangers of the late 1990s were a good team; one of the best in the American League; the problem they had was that they continually ran into the Yankees and got bounced. In 1996, 1998 and 1999 the Rangers faced the Yankees in the ALDS. They won one game in the three series.

That all changed in 2010 and it came in dramatic fashion. Following a dramatic 5 game win over the Rays in the division series, the Yankees again stood in their way.

After the game 1 meltdown in which the Rangers bullpen gacked up a 5-0 lead, no greater authority than Yankees broadcaster *Michael Kay* declared the series over; that the Rangers had no chance of coming back after such a heartbreaking loss.

Of course I'm being sarcastic when I call Michael Kay an authority in anything but outright buffoonery.

The Rangers won game 2 in decisive fashion, then Cliff Lee dominated the Yankees in game 3 and the Rangers biggest weak spot—the strategic gaffes of manager Ron Washington—paled in comparison to the mistakes Yankees manager Joe Girardi made by not using Mariano Rivera to keep game 3 close and staying too long with A.J. Burnett in game 4.

After taking the Yankees out in six games, the Rangers moved onto the World Series where they ran into a team with magic of their own. The Giants, led by such unsung heroes as Juan Uribe, Edgar Renteria and closer Brian Wilson, ended the Rangers dream season by beating them in 5 games.

2011 ADDITIONS:

3B Adrian Beltre signed a 5-year, $80 million contract with option for 2016.
LHP Arthur Rhodes signed a 1-year, $3.9 million contract with 2012 option.
RHP Brandon Webb signed a 1-year, $3 million contract.
C Yorvit Torrealba signed a 2-year, $6.25 million contract.
C/1B/DH Mike Napoli was acquired from the Toronto Blue Jays.
INF Brian Barden signed a minor league contract.

2011 SUBTRACTIONS:

LHP Cliff Lee was not re-signed.
DH/OF Vladimir Guerrero was not re-signed.
RHP Frank Francisco was traded to the Toronto Blue Jays.
C Bengie Molina was not re-signed.
OF Jeff Francoeur was not re-signed.
OF Brandon Boggs was not re-signed.
1B Ryan Garko was not re-signed.
1B/3B Jorge Cantu was not re-signed.
RHP Brandon McCarthy was not re-signed.
RHP Dustin Nippert was non-tendered.

INF Alex Cora was released.
INF Cristian Guzman was not re-signed.
RHP Rich Harden was not re-signed.
RHP Doug Mathis was not re-signed.

2011 PROJECTED STARTING ROTATION: C.J. Wilson; Colby Lewis; Tommy Hunter; Derek Holland; Brandon Webb; Scott Feldman.

2011 PROJECTED BULLPEN: Neftali Feliz; Darren Oliver; Arthur Rhodes; Alexi Ogando; Darren O'Day; Matt Harrison; Yoshinori Tateyama.

2011 PROJECTED LINEUP: C-Yorvit Torrealba; 1B-Mitch Moreland; 2B-Ian Kinsler; 3B-Adrian Beltre; SS-Elvis Andrus; LF-David Murphy; CF-Josh Hamilton; RF-Nelson Cruz; DH-Michael Young[1]*.

2011 BENCH: C/1B/DH-Mike Napoli; OF-Julio Borbon; C-Matt Treanor; C-Taylor Teagarden; INF-Andres Blanco; 1B-Chris Davis.

2011 POSSIBLE CONTRIBUTORS: LHP-Michael Kirkman; RHP-Pedro Strop; RHP-Mark Lowe; RHP-Eric Hurley; OF-Engel Beltre; OF-Craig Gentry.

ASSESSMENTS
MANAGEMENT:

Nolan Ryan's old-school manner melded neatly with the deliberate yet aggressive GM Jon Daniels. I wasn't sure it would, but it did. When Ryan took over, I was dubious as to how the relationship was going to evolve. Was Ryan, a bit of an intentional intimidator and outright bully while he was playing, going to allow his young GM to do his job? Was he going to listen to him and, if they disagreed, consider the case of Daniels before a final determination was made?

1 Michael Young, fed up with being shuttled all over the field and finally to the DH slot with the acquisition of Adrian Beltre; and sure to see his at bats diminished with the addition of Mike Napoli, has formally requested a trade. As of this writing, the Rangers are discussing deals to get Young out of Texas.

It worked.

Daniels has become one of the best and most respected GMs in baseball and Ryan is Ryan. Players want to play for a team that's run by the great Ryan; Daniels brings the right players into the mix.

We've come a long way from when Daniels made what might possibly be the worst trade ever made in the history of baseball—Adrian Gonzalez and Chris Young to the Padres for Adam Eaton and Akinori Otsuka. It was five years ago now and the Rangers have a packed farm system and an American League pennant all because of the smart drafting and trading of Daniels and the old-school Texas swagger of Nolan Ryan.

Ron Washington failed a drug test in 2009, testing positive for cocaine.

But he wins.

Ron Washington came up with one of the most absurd and unbelievable assertions imaginable *after* failing the drug test—it was the first time he'd ever used the drug.

But he wins.

Ron Washington is one of the worst game managers I've ever seen in baseball.

But he wins.

Ron Washington handles a bullpen about as horribly as a manager can.

But he wins.

Ron Washington, had I been running the Rangers when he failed the drug test, would've been fired immediately.

But he wins.

In fact, I'd have fired Washington long before the failed drug test for cause; the cause being that he doesn't know what he's doing.

But he wins.

The Rangers players play for Ron Washington. They never quit; they stand behind him; they support him; and they carried him all the way to the World Series. I can't defend his tactics in the dugout, but something about the relationship works and when something's working, it's stupid to mess with it. The Rangers could function without a manager and the games would be run with more competence than when Washington's running it.

But he wins.

STARTING PITCHING:

C.J. Wilson proved me wrong. I had thought that it was a crazy idea to take a team that needed the left-handed arm in the bullpen to move him to the starting rotation. Wilson had been a starter in the minors and not a particularly good one; he had strikeout stuff in the bullpen and could get out both lefties and righties. Most importantly, he didn't give up a lot of home runs and pitching in a hitter's haven ballpark like Rangers Ballpark in Arlington, that's important.

But the Rangers made Wilson into a starter and he was terrific. Wilson threw 204 innings, allowed 161 hits and 10 homers. He can be a bit wild as he led the league in walks with 93; this leads to high pitch counts in the early innings and diminishes the depth he can provide; but he struck out 170 and went 15-8. He throws hard and has a very good curve. Whether or not he's ready to step in and be the prototypical ace of a contending staff is in question, but Wilson is for real and he's for real as a starting pitcher.

Colby Lewis returned to the big leagues from Japan and had a far better year than his 12-13 record indicates. Lewis allowed 174 hits in 201 innings; walked 65 and struck out 196. He also pitched the most important game of the Rangers season in game 2 of the ALCS. With his team reeling after the shocking loss in game 1, Lewis pitched into the sixth inning and only allowed 2 runs, getting the win. He then pitched 8 innings of 3 hit, 1 run ball in the decisive game 6. Oh, and he allowed 2 runs in 7 2/3 innings in the Rangers only win of the World Series. It took him a long time to fulfill his potential, but he's doing it now.

24-year-old right Tommy Hunter went 13-4 in his first full season in the big leagues. Hunter is big and throws hard. He's a contact pitcher who throws strikes. He allowed 21 homers in 128 innings. Hunter struggled a bit in the post-season, but the Rangers were only using him for 4 innings a start and then got him out of the game at the first sign of trouble. Hunter showed flashes of brilliance during the regular season and should be a solid, mid-rotation starter.

Derek Holland is a 24-year-old lefty who has dominated the minor leagues at every level. He's a strikeout pitcher with great control and, once he matures, could be a top-of-the-rotation starter. He was used as a starter and reliever in the big leagues in 2010, but his future is in the rotation.

Former National League Cy Young Award winner (and two time runner-up) Brandon Webb signed a 1-year, $3 million, incentive-laden contract to join the Rangers and rebuild his injury-ravaged career.

Webb was quite possibly the best pitcher in baseball for four straight seasons. He was durable; he was tough; he pitched deeply into games; and he racked up shutouts with his naturally sinking fastball. Shoulder woes and eventual surgery robbed him of 2009 and 2010 and the Diamondbacks let him walk.

In his auditions for clubs last summer, his fastball was said to be puttering in at around 82 mph. That's not going to cut it unless he becomes a radically different pitcher and such a transformation takes a long time to complete. There's a major disparity between a bowling ball sinker that travels 90 mph in comparison to 82 mph. Perhaps Webb needs time to regain his strength and spring training will provide that.

I'm dubious.

Pitchers have come back from shoulder surgeries before, but in general, they lose a great deal of their stuff. An elbow injury has been more predictable when it comes to a pitcher's success when returning. The Rangers lost out on trying to re-sign Cliff Lee and Webb was a relatively inexpensive gamble. He's no risk/massive reward.

That said, I'd expect nothing out of Brandon Webb and be thrilled if he was able to give 140 innings and some competence at the back of the rotation. He was heading for the Hall of Fame before he got hurt; now he's just trying to salvage his career. It's a shame.

Scott Feldman came back to earth after his imitation of Roy Halladay's motion yielded 17 wins in 2009. He missed a chunk of the

2010 season with a knee injury and perhaps that contributed to his fall-off. A contact pitcher, Feldman gave up 181 hits in 141 innings as he fell to 7-11. He wasn't as good as his record in 2009; he's not as bad as his record in 2010.

Feldman's a competent back-of-the-rotation starter who throws strikes and needs his defense for success.

BULLPEN:

Neftali Feliz was the closer on a pennant-winning team and won the Rookie of the Year. The flamethrowing righty has lights out stuff with a fastball hovering around 100 mph. He's been a starter in the minors and Feliz, at 23, may eventually return to the starting rotation for the Rangers. Feliz will get a chance to start in the spring and may be a starter or reliever this season.

Veteran Darren Oliver's teams somehow find their way into the playoffs. Oliver is a durable lefty and respected clubhouse presence who is calm in any situation. He throws strikes; never complains about his role; strikes out around a batter per inning and, even though he's been up-and-down in the post-season, he's an important piece to his club *getting* to the post-season.

Arthur Rhodes has rejuvenated his career after looking finished a few years ago. Rhodes was terrific for the NL Central champion Reds last season and the 41-year-old still throws hard. He signed a 1-year, $3.9 million contract with the Rangers. Rhodes handles both lefties and righties, throws strikes and k's around a batter per inning.

Alexi Ogando is a tall, gangly righty who also throws very, very hard. Ogando struck out 39 in 41 innings as a rookie and allowed 31 hits and 2 homers. He's got a power fastball and could be used as a set-up man or eventual replacement for Feliz if Feliz is made back into a starter.

Darren O'Day is a submarine-style right-hander who's been great since joining the Rangers early in the 2009 season. Used predominately against righties, O'Day can get lefties out as well, but with Rhodes and Oliver, there's no reason to let him pitch to a lefty in an important situation. O'Day's a durable contact pitcher and throws strikes.

Matt Harrison is a 25-year-old lefty who appeared in 37 games in 2010, 31 in relief. He allowed 80 hits and 10 homers in 78 innings and his control isn't great with 39 walks, so he may not be suited for the bullpen. He's been up-and-down as a starter in the minors, but that may be the role he's best suited for. He pitched far better against lefties in 2010 than he did against righties, but his lack of control is a problem.

Yoshinori Tateyama is a diminutive (5'10", 165 lbs) righty coming over from Japan. He's 35 and is a veteran reliever who's struck out a batter an inning and closed occasionally for the Nippon Ham Fighters. He posted a 1.80 ERA in 58 games last season, but as with most players coming over from Japan, who knows what he'll do in North America?

LINEUP:

Veteran catcher Yorvit Torrealba signed a 2-year contract to replace Bengie Molina as the starting catcher. Torrealba had a solid year at the plate with the Padres in 2010; he also did a terrific job handling the Padres impressive pitching staff; and he threw out 37% of the runners trying to steal against him. Torrealba's a better hitter than he's given credit for and, as a part-timer with the Rangers, perhaps the Rangers hitter-friendly park will help him achieve new heights at the plate.

Mitch Moreland received a chance to play first base regularly when Chris Davis bottomed out and Justin Smoak was traded to the Mariners in the Cliff Lee deal. Moreland contributed 9 homers to the Rangers division winning effort and had a fantastic post-season. I'm sure the Rangers would prefer Davis to stop striking out so much and hit for power consistently, taking the job, but I expect Moreland to be the opening day first baseman.

Ian Kinsler has been hobbled by numerous injuries over the past couple of seasons. In 103 games in 2010, Kinsler hit 9 homers, batted

.286 and had a .382 on base. He stole 15 bases and is a fine defensive second baseman. The one problem he has is staying healthy. Like many Rangers hitters, he hammers the ball at home and is barely average on the road.

Adrian Beltre was signed away from the Boston Red Sox to take over at third base. Beltre had an MVP-caliber year at the plate and in the field for the Red Sox and it's not the first time he's had a superior season prior to free agency. He finished second in the MVP voting in 2004, got a huge contract from the Mariners and his offensive numbers took a nosedive. That could be attributed to the Mariners spacious home park and won't be an issue in Texas as he's hit .306 in his career there.

His on base numbers in general have never been as high as they were in 2010 at .365 and it's doubtful he'll hit 49 doubles again, but Rangers Ballpark may allow him to repeat his 28 homer output from last season. He's a Gold Glove-caliber fielder who, combined with shortstop Elvis Andrus, will give the Rangers pitchers comfort to throw the ball over the plate and let the fielders handle their job.

Elvis Andrus is only 22 and has star potential. He's a superior defensive player and can steal bases. He's a contact hitter and is learning to be more patient; eventually he'll use his speed to hit more doubles and triples; but for right now, he's a singles hitter.

David Murphy is an all-around good player. He has 10-15 homer pop; batted .291 last season with 26 doubles and 14 stolen bases in 16 attempts last season. The left-handed hitting Murphy doesn't strike out much and can handle left-handed pitchers.

Josh Hamilton's career came full circle in 2010 as he won the MVP of the American League and made it to the playoffs for the first time. Hamilton missed much of September with fractured ribs and only played in 133 games. It was enough for him to win the MVP with 32 homers, 100 RBI, a league-leading .359 average and a .411 on base. He also had 40 doubles and 3 triples.

There's nothing Hamilton can't do on the field, but his injury history is a concern as is his off-field drug and alcohol problems. Regardless of his success, I would not give him a long-term deal before he becomes a free agent and that won't be until 2013. Whether the Rangers are thinking the same way as I do remains to be seen, but I'm reluctant to hand a person who's had those issues $100+ million. The Rangers and Hamilton avoided arbitration for 2011-2012 by agreeing to a $24 million extension.

When he's healthy, he's one of the best hitters in baseball, but even the winter hasn't been free of illness as Hamilton was stricken with pneumonia that forced him to be hospitalized.

Nelson Cruz, after so many starts and stops, is fulfilling his potential. Cruz missed a chunk of time with hamstring problems, but if he'd been healthy all season he might have challenged Hamilton for the MVP. Cruz batted .318 in 445 plate appearances with 22 homers and 78 RBI. He also stole 17 bases and had 31 doubles. Cruz is 30-years-old now and won't be a free agent until 2014. He's a player I'd look to lock up in a long term contract.

Michael Young was asked to make another position shift and has apparently had enough. The Rangers want him to DH and he officially asked to be traded..

He can still play all the infield positions.

Young is highly paid ($16 million annually through 2013), but he's a good hitter with pop and is a leader in the clubhouse. Respected throughout the league for his professionalism, Young will deliver his 60 extra base hits like clockwork. I could never figure out why stat zombies dislike him so much because he's a good player.

How they're going to go about moving him is an open question. A guaranteed $48 million, a no-trade clause to all but 8 teams and his pending 10 and 5 status in May makes it a priority to get rid of him quickly.

It's going to take some creativity, eating of money or a contract exchange to get it done.

BENCH:

Veteran catcher/first baseman Mike Napoli was acquired from the Blue Jays after they got him from the Angels in the Wells trade. Napoli proved to be a good defensive first baseman last season when he was pressed into duty after the injury to Kendry Morales; but he was exposed as a part-timer when the Angels were forced to play him full-time.

He can hit the ball out of the park and will get significant at bats this season.

Julio Borbon played almost every day for the Rangers in 2010 because of the injuries to Hamilton and Cruz. He's a good defensive outfielder with speed and has shown high average/on base skills in the minors. He batted .276 in 409 plate appearances last season.

Matt Treanor is a veteran backup catcher who's solid defensively and handles a pitching staff well. He's not much of a hitter, but had a good ALCS against the Yankees with a homer.

Taylor Teagarden was supposed to combine with Jarrod Saltalamacchia for a young catching tandem. Saltalamacchia was dumped on the Red Sox and Teagarden is a backup. He missed time with the big league club due to food poisoning and was sent all the way back down to Double A where he hit .242. He's a good defensive catcher, but is littler more than filler right now.

Andres Blanco is a veteran utility infielder who had his best big league season at the plate in 2010. Blanco had bounced from the Royals to the Cubs before getting to the Rangers and batted .277 in 185 plate appearances. He can play every infield position and is a switch hitter.

Chris Davis is the odd man out going into the season. He has massive power, but strikes out a ridiculous number of times to play every day. At least in 2008-2009, Davis's home run output provided something to the team; but in 2010, Davis started the season as the everyday first baseman, didn't hit and was sent to the minors; Smoak didn't hit either, so Davis was recalled and he still didn't hit. Smoak was traded to the Mariners for Lee, but the Rangers traded for Jorge Cantu and gave Moreland a chance. Davis was a pinch-hitter in September. It was in September when Davis hit his sole home run for the year. A .192 average and 40 strikeout in 136 big league plate appearances isn't going to cut it, but he ripped the ball in Triple A. There's still hope for Davis because of all that power.

PREDICTION:

The Rangers did the best they could to keep Lee, but didn't have the financial werewithal to do it; as a result, after Wilson, the starting pitching is relying on youngsters and the comebacks of Webb and Feldman. In the AL West, where the starting pitching of both the Athletics and Angels is superior to that of the Rangers, will the Rangers power bats be enough? They have a deep bullpen, but so do the A's and Angels. They can really hit, but will their pitching come through?

The Young situation could get messy if they can't find a taker for him.

A solid team on the field, filled with solid citizens off of it, the Rangers have a bright future and are still loaded with prospects. I wonder about their pitching and Washington's strategic gaffes. The Rangers won their division easily in 2010 because of the fading Angels and inconsistent A's, but both teams are still threats. If Washington has to make a season-breaking decision in a series against the A's in September, will he get it right? Or will he commit a familiar gaffe?

The Rangers will score plenty of runs, but the pitching is just a bit short for them to repeat in 2011.

PREDICTED RECORD: 86-76

Oakland Athletics

2010 Record: 81-81; 2nd place, American League West.

2010 Recap:

The Athletics were again a favorite of those trying to validate Moneyball. Picked to contend, the A's hovered around .500 all year despite having an offense that could only be called atrocious.

It was their pitching that carried them through. GM Billy Beane has accumulated a lot of young arms and had there been anyone in the lineup who could hit, they might have fulfilled the hopes and dreams of those still clinging to the notion that Beane is a "genius".

Young starting pitching led by Gio Gonzalez, Trevor Cahill and Mr. 209 himself, Dallas Braden, helped the club finish at .500 for the first time since they won the AL West in 2006.

2011 ADDITIONS:

LHP Brian Fuentes signed a 2-year, $10.5 million contract.
RHP Grant Balfour signed a 2-year, $8.1 million contract with 2013 option.
OF Josh Willingham was acquired from the Washington Nationals.
OF David DeJesus was acquired from the Kansas City Royals.
DH Hideki Matsui signed a 1-year, $4.25 million contract.
RHP Rich Harden signed a 1-year, $1.5 million contract.
RHP Brandon McCarthy signed a 1-year, $1 million contract.
INF Andy LaRoche signed a minor league contract.

RHP Fernando Cabrera signed a minor league contract.
RHP Anthony Lerew signed a minor league contract.
OF Jai Miller signed a minor league contract.

2011 SUBTRACTIONS:

OF Rajai Davis was traded to the Toronto Blue Jays.
DH Jack Cust was not re-signed.
RHP Vin Mazzaro was traded to the Kansas City Royals.
RHP Ben Sheets was not re-signed.
RHP Justin Duchscherer was not re-signed.
RHP Henry Rodriguez was traded to the Washington Nationals.
3B/DH Eric Chavez was not re-signed.
OF Travis Buck was not re-signed.
OF Gabe Gross was not re-signed.
INF Akinori Iwamura was not re-signed.
INF Jeff Larish was not re-signed.
RHP Ross Wolf was not re-signed.

2011 PROJECTED STARTING ROTATION: Trevor Cahill; Dallas Braden; Gio Gonzalez; Brett Anderson; Rich Harden; Brandon McCarthy.

2011 PROJECTED BULLPEN: Andrew Bailey; Brian Fuentes; Grant Balfour; Brad Ziegler; Craig Breslow; Michael Wuertz; Joey Devine; Jerry Blevins; Tyson Ross.

2011 PROJECTED LINEUP: C-Kurt Suzuki; 1B-Daric Barton; 2B-Mark Ellis; 3B-Kevin Kouzmanoff; SS-Cliff Pennington; LF-David DeJesus; CF-Coco Crisp; RF-Josh Willingham; DH-Hideki Matsui.

2011 BENCH: 1B/OF-Conor Jackson; C-Landon Powell; INF-Adam Rosales; INF-Steve Tolleson; OF-Chris Carter; OF-Ryan Sweeney; INF-Eric Sogard.

ASSESSMENTS
MANAGEMENT:

Freedom.

Freedom from the shackles.

Freedom from the expectations.

Freedom from the constraints of a bit of creative non-fiction that was a case study in "be careful what you wish for".

Of course, I'm talking about Moneyball.

It took a few years, but the truth is slowly starting to seep out. A truth that was carefully hidden under layers of subterfuge disguised as a fly on the wall account by author Michael Lewis as to how Billy Beane created a dominant Athletics club using statistics, undervalued talent, his ruthless corporate personality and spending a fraction of what the Yankees, Red Sox and Mets did.

The problem was that the book is a farce and Beane is not a genius.

We've seen the legend come apart over the years. Fired managers; traded stars; failed deals; a bad team—all combined to remove the onus under which Beane operated for so long. I call it an "onus" because that's what it became.

The backlash against Beane was slow and deliberate. But it was there. Not a few people who saw Beane as a vainglorious attention seeker were displeased to see the Athletics downfall and annual disappointment as those invested in the story and the success of the "revolution" propped it up repeatedly with selective facts and outright fabrications.

But that's all over now.

Beane, still smart and aggressive, is able to run his team correctly without having to live up to that hype.

He's made a series of excellent maneuvers to put the Athletics into prime position to contend in the American League West.

Accumulating young starting pitching, the A's offense—supposedly the main tenet upon which Moneyball was built—was one of the worst in baseball in 2010.

That has been fixed with the acquisitions of Josh Willingham, David DeJesus and Hideki Matsui; he also bolstered the bullpen with Brian Fuentes and Grant Balfour.

It's not Moneyball, but that's a good thing. It's a winning thing. It's a thing that will make Beane something he wasn't before: respected for running his team the right way rather than being a Kim Kardashian, someone who's famous just for *being* famous and has little-to-nothing to offer aside from a media circus.

Bob Geren has survived as Athletics manager where others before him—Art Howe and Ken Macha—didn't. The implication has been that because Geren is close friends with Beane, he's been able to keep his job. The evidence of this is not to be ignored. Before 2010, Geren had never won more than 76 games and the old standby excuse of "he didn't have any talent" doesn't fit because in 2009, the A's *did* have talent and were expected to contend.

They didn't, but Geren survived.

In 2010, his club finished at 81-81.

But just as the negative perceptions surrounding Moneyball affected Beane, Howe and anyone else in its aftermath, the idea that Geren is a "yes" man who's only there because he's Beane's friend isn't accurate either. Bob Geren is an experienced minor league manager who's done a mostly good job with these Athletics. The players seem to like and respect him and he makes the correct moves. A former catcher, he handles his pitching staff well and it's not his fault that he was stuck with a load of players who couldn't hit last season.

He's got some serious talent to work with now, so we'll get a better gauge of Geren as a manager, but if the Athletics contend, Geren will be a solid pick for Manager of the Year. And he'll deserve it.

STARTING PITCHING:

At age 23, Trevor Cahill is coming into his own as a top flight starting pitcher. Cahill went 18-8 in 2010 with a sparkling 2.97 ERA; he allowed 155 hits in 196 innings; walked 63 and struck out 118. He allowed 19 homers. One of the more reliable starters in baseball last season, Cahill could be counted on to pitch at least into the seventh inning and, with a better offense, would have won 20 games.

Throughout his professional career, all the way up through the minors to the big leagues, Cahill has been consistently good with an

ERA under 3. Last season, he did it again, this time in the big leagues. He's a top of the rotation starter for the Athletics.

Were you previously aware of the etiquette of the 209?

If you weren't before you—and Alex Rodriguez—are now.

You don't tug on Superman's cape.

You don't spit into the wind.

You don't pull the mask off the old Lone Ranger.

And you don't walk across Dallas Braden's mound.

If you do, he'll show you the 209.

In case you missed it, Braden became famous for challenging the Yankees' Alex Rodriguez for running across the mound on the way back to the dugout after being retired by Braden. Braden screamed at him and went on and on about it, retribution, his old neighborhood in Arizona (the 209) and how it was unacceptable behavior on the part of A-Rod.

It got silly quickly, but Braden was right. You're not supposed to run across the mound. It's disrespectful and was par for the course in the gamesmanship and bullying which A-Rod often uses to get into his opponents' heads.

Braden became famous for his pitching antics rather than the territorial boundaries of his mound when he pitched a perfect game against the Rays on May 9th.

2010 was a breakout year for Braden. He stood up for himself (a little bit to the extreme) with A-Rod; and he showed that when he's on, he can be dominant. Braden missed time with an elbow injury and his control sometimes eludes him, but he can be a consistent winner in the big leagues if he can command his fastball.

Gio Gonzalez went 15-9 in his first full season in the big leagues. The 25-year-old righty had a fine year with 171 hits allowed in 200 innings, only 15 homers and 171 strikeouts. He walked 92 which is somewhat high, but he has excellent stuff with a searing fastball. He was consistently good in 2010.

Lefty Brett Anderson missed a large chunk of the 2010 season with elbow problems. He has a power fastball and can strike out plenty of hitters; he's a top of the rotation starter if he's healthy. Anderson went 7-6 in 19 starts and struck out 75 in 112 innings; his control was fantastic with on 22 walks; he allowed 6 homers. He's 23 and has succeeded at every level. The only question with him is if he can stay healthy.

Rich Harden has some of the best stuff in baseball. He's got a mid-90s fastball and a great slider. He could be a Cy Young Award candidate if he were ever able to make 33 starts and pitch 220 innings. That's the problem. He's never thrown more than 189 innings in his career and that was in his first go-round with the Athletics as a 22-year-old. Since then, it's been one injury after another to just about every part of his body. I think Harden should be made into a closer because he doesn't have the stamina nor the physicality to stay healthy and be a useful starter. Perhaps if he was only asked to blow people away for an inning, he'd stay off the disabled list.

Harden was traded by the Athletics to the Cubs in 2008; now he returns as a back-of-the-rotation starter. He won't stay healthy because he never does, but he's cheap and he's good when he's able to pitch.

Brandon McCarthy is another oft-injured, but talented starter the Athletics have signed to a low-cost/low-risk contract. McCarthy pitched in 11 games in the minors for the Rangers last season, but missed most of the season with shoulder problems. He's got a good fastball and curve when he's healthy, but he's never been healthy. I'd expect nothing and hope he can put it all together.

BULLPEN:

Andrew Bailey won the American League Rookie of the Year award in 2009 after taking over as the A's closer. In 2010, he was on his way to a better year than that when injuries sabotaged his season. He had a back injury and worse, an elbow injury. When he pitched, he was dominant. Bailey had a 1.47 ERA and struck of 42 in 49 innings.

Now, Bailey will start the season as the A's closer and presumably will remain there if he's healthy, but they've gotten a capable backup closer in Brian Fuentes in case Bailey gets hurt. Bailey is a top notch reliever, but the injuries are a concern.

Brian Fuentes gets by with mediocre stuff because of a funky, deceptive motion that is particulary rough on left-handed batters. His numbers against both righties and lefties are consistent and good, but he gives up a lot of homers and his strikeout rates have diminished after a terrific season with the Rockies in 2008 that led to his contract with the Angels. I don't think anyone felt comfortable with him on the hill closing, especially in the 2010 playoffs. He sometimes loses the strike zone but if he's needed to close, he'll get the job done most of the time. With the Athletics and the absence of the restrictions of the "closer's role", they'll be able to put him in more advantageous situations to utilize his stuff against lefties.

Grant Balfour signed a 2-year contract with the Athletics. Balfour has come a long way from the journeyman who every team gave a shot because of his velocity and then dumped because he had no clue where that power fastball was going. Balfour's secret to success isn't a secret. If he has his command and throws strikes, he gets people out; if he doesn't, they sit on his fastball and wait for him to either groove one or until he walks them. Balfour dominates righties and he'll do very well with the Athletics.

Brad Ziegler is a submarine throwing righty who was the closer for a brief time in 2008 and made headlines with a scoreless streak of 39 innings. Ziegler is terrific against righties and with the Athletics revamped bullpen, he'll be used in a more suitable role as a specialist rather than a crossover arm.

Veteran lefty (and former Yale student) Craig Breslow had a fine year in 2010. In 75 games, he allowed 53 hits in 74 innings and struck out 71. He did allow 9 homers. Breslow throws strikes and can get out both lefties and righties; after a career of bouncing from team-to-team, he's found a home in Oakland.

Righty Michael Wuertz missed time last season with a shoulder problem and only pitched in 48 games without his usual effectiveness. Wuertz has long been underrated and I believe he's going to be valuable to the A's this season. He's always struck out a lot of hitters and has had a strange habit of being durable (70+ games), then missing time and pitching poorly in 40 or so games the next season. It's happened for six years in a row. By that (admittedly specious logic), he's due for a 70+ game season and a solid year.

Joey Devine has missed all of the past two seasons after Tommy John surgery. Before he got hurt, he had closer stuff, a motion that reminded me of David Cone's and an array of power pitches. If he can come back, the A's bullpen will be among the best in baseball.

Jerry Blevins is a 6'6" lefty who threw 48 innings in 63 games. He pitched regularly vs righties and didn't do particularly well (.311 average), but he's more of a lefty specialist and won't be asked to do much more than that with the reinforcements the A's have brought into the fold.

Tyson Ross is a big righty with a stressful, funky motion that looks like is going to demolish his arm one day. Ross was wild (20 walks in 39 innings); allowed 4 homers and struck out 32. He's been inconsistent as a starter in the minors, but has strikeout potential.

LINEUP:

Kurt Suzuki has some pop in his bat (15 homers in 2009; 13 in 2010); hits a few doubles and is a better hitter than his .242 average; .303 on base; 18 doubles indicate. His throwing behind the plate isn't very good, but he's 27 and with a better supporting cast in the lineup, his power/on base numbers will improve.

Daric Barton was the key to the trade that sent Mark Mulder to the Cardinals and he finally began to fulfill his promise in 2010. Barton batted .273, but led the league in walks with 110 raising his on base percentage to .393. He doesn't hit for much home run power (10 last season), but he hit 33 doubles and 5 triples and if he gets on base in front of Willingham and Matsui, he'll score plenty of runs. His fielding at first base is impressive and he has a strong, accurate arm.

Veteran Mark Ellis is a fine fielding second baseman who had a good year at the plate in 2010. He batted .291 with a .358 on base and 24 doubles. His power numbers have taken a nosedive from their heights in 2007 when he hit 19 homers, but he's usually good for 10 or so. He hit 5 last year and is a good bet to return to the level of 10-15.

Kevin Kouzmanoff has never lived up to the potential he showed when he demolished Triple A in 2006 for the Indians; then he made things worse (in retrospect) for himself when he hit a grand slam on the first pitch he saw in the big leagues. He doesn't hit for average, but he does hit for 15-20 homer pop and is a good defensive third baseman. He too will benefit from the improved A's lineup.

Cliff Pennington is a good fielding shortstop who batted .250 last season. He had 26 doubles, 8 triples and 6 homers. He's a switch-hitter who can also play second, third and some outfield.

The underrated David DeJesus was acquired from the Royals for Vin Mazzaro and another propsect. He was having an excellent year before injuring his right thumb crashing into a fence; DeJesus might have been traded then had he not gotten hurt.

He's a solid all-around player. He has some power, hits around .300 and gets on base at a reasonable clip. DeJesus will steal a base here and there and play good defense in the outfield. He's a free agent at the end of the season.

Coco Crisp had his contract option exercised in what was an inexplicable move for an Athletics team that was desperate for offense and could have tried to upgrade in center field. After they acquired the bats they did, it made more sense—with their pitching—to keep Crisp. Crisp hit well after returning from injury in June and played his usual excellent defense. He's got some pop and speed and if he's healthy, it's good that the A's kept him.

Josh Willingham was acquired from the Washington Nationals. The Nationals never truly appreciated Willingham's skills at hitting the ball out of the park and doing it in important moments. I was always more concerned about Willingham coming to the plate in a game-breaking situation over anyone the Nationals had and that includes Ryan Zimmerman. Willingham has had back problems in the past, but he puts up the power numbers, walks and plays hard every day. Beane made a terrific deal getting him for a couple of minor leaguers and he'll do terrific in Oakland.

Hideki Matsui got off to a terrible start for the Angels in 2010, but as the year wore on, his production wound up where it usually does (and was nearly identical to what he did for the champion Yankees in 2009). Matsui may have his power numbers diminished slightly from the Athletics big ballpark, but the veteran hits in the clutch and is a patient hitter who's still dangerous.

BENCH:

Conor Jackson's star has fallen like a meteor in the past few years due to injury and illness. Last season for the Diamondbacks and A's, he batted .236 with 2 homers and 16 RBI in 241 plate appearances. He did get on base with a .336 on base percentage. At age 29, Jackson is still salvageable and the Athletics can keep him on the bench and use him against lefties to spell Matsui hoping he'll regain his form.

Landon Powell is a backup catcher who throws really well but doesn't hit. Powell, 29, is a .222 career hitter with no power.

Adam Rosales was acquired from the Cincinnati Reds for Aaron Miles last season. Rosales has proven he can hit in the minors and has some pop; last year, he batted .271 in 279 plate appearances and hit 7 homers. He can play all over the field defensively.

Steve Tolleson is a utility infielder and the son of former journeyman infielder Wayne Tolleson. Steve's put up good average/on base numbers in the minors and can steal some bases. He hit .286 with a .340 on base in 53 plate appearances for the A's last season.

Chris Carter was one of the keys to the trade that sent Nick Swisher to the White Sox after the 2007 season. Carter has put up huge power numbers in the minors and slumped in the big leagues last season. He's only 24 and the huge (6'5", 230 lbs) Carter won't be under as much pressure to perform this season with the acquisitions of DeJesus and Willingham. He might spend much of the season in Triple A and get another shot to win a starting job in 2012.

Ryan Sweeney is a backup outfielder who batted .294 in 331 plate appearances in 2010. He has no power, but hit 20 doubles and can play all three outfield positions.

Eric Sogard is a backup infielder who was acquired along with Kouzmaoff from the Padres for Aaron Cunningham and Scott Hairston after the 2009 season. Sogard has some pop to hit 8-10 homers and can steal a few bases. He can play second, short and third; doesn't strike out; and gets on base.

PREDICTION:

The Athletics are finally ready to contend. After many ups and downs and beliefs that were based on fantasy (see Moneyball and those who have something invested in it being proven "right), they've taken steps to fill their holes. They have young starting pitching; a deep and diverse bullpen; and a lineup that's not frightening as you look at the individuals, but solid enough to win when examined as a whole.

Willingham, Matsui and DeJesus are under-the-radar pickups; Balfour and Fuentes will assist and protect Bailey; the starting pitching is ready to blossom.

The American League West is winnable and the A's have the talent to be close to first place all season.

Geren is a good manager and Beane is always aggressive in-season to make improvements if his team is contending. And they will be.

I hesitate to think that the young pitchers are automatically going to continually improve; they've never been in a pennant race and they're in a division with two good teams.

The A's are taking the next step, but will that be enough?

No. It won't be.

They'll hang around until late in the season, but fall short in the final week.

PREDICTED RECORD: 84-78

Seattle Mariners

2010 Record: 61-101; 4th place, American League West.

2010 Recap:

The Mariners were a trendy pick to contend for a playoff spot in 2010. (I had them at 86-76 and narrowly missing the playoffs, so I'm not innocent here.) Their acquisition of Cliff Lee to go along with Felix Hernandez at the top of their rotation was meant to form a devastating1-2 punch that would counteract the lack of offense their defense-oriented lineup would provide.

Their GM, Jack Zduriencik, was called everything from an "Amazin' Exec" to a full-blown, new age genius.

It didn't work out that way.

The team was a disaster from top-to-bottom. Lee pitched well, but the other big off-season acquisitions—Chone Figgins and Milton Bradley—were disasters; Ken Griffey Jr., inexplicably brought back for another season, embarrassed the club with his "did he or didn't he" nap episode in which he was accused of sleeping in the clubhouse during a game when he was needed to hit.

Lee was traded to the Rangers after there was supposedly an agreed upon deal sending him to the Yankees.

Manager Don Wakamatsu was fired and the "genius" Zduriencik was under scrutiny for his behavior in both the way he went about his trading of Lee and for acquiring an accused sex offender, Josh Lueke, in the deal he *did* make in sending Lee to the Rangers.

The Mariners lost 101 games and were the worst team in baseball. By far.

The one bright spot was Felix Hernandez who won the Cy Young Award with a 13-12 record after pitching his guts out in many hopeless causes.

2011 ADDITIONS:

Manager Eric Wedge was hired.
DH Jack Cust signed a 1-year, $2.5 million contract.
C Miguel Olivo signed a 2-year, $7 million contract with 2013 option.
INF Brendan Ryan was acquired from the St. Louis Cardinals.
RHP Denny Bautista signed a minor league contract.
OF Jody Gerut signed a minor league contract.
C/1B Chris Gimenez signed a minor league contract.
RHP Charlie Haeger signed a minor league contract.
INF Adam Kennedy signed a minor league contract.
RHP Justin Miller signed a minor league contract.
LHP Royce Ring signed a minor league contract.
LHP Nate Robertson signed a minor league contract.
RHP Chris Smith signed a minor league contract.
RHP Chaz Roe was acquired from the Colorado Rockies.
RHP Manny Delcarmen signed a minor league contract.
OF Gabe Gross signed a minor league contract.
LHP Aaron Laffey was acquired from the Cleveland Indians.

2011 SUBTRACTIONS:

3B Jose Lopez was traded to the Colorado Rockies.
1B Russell Branyan's option was declined.
1B Casey Kotchman was not re-signed.
C Rob Johnson was traded to the San Diego Padres.
LHP Ryan Rowland-Smith was not re-signed.
C Guillermo Quiroz was not re-signed.
RHP Anthony Varvaro was not re-signed.
RHP Sean White was not re-signed.

INF/OF Chris Woodward was not re-signed.
RHP Maikel Cleto was traded to the St. Louis Cardinals.

2011 PROJECTED STARTING ROTATION: Felix Hernandez; Jason Vargas; Doug Fister; Erik Bedard; Luke French; David Pauley; Aaron Laffey.

2011 PROJECTED BULLPEN: David Aardsma; Brandon League; Garrett Olson; Dan Cortes; Justin Miller; Royce Ring; Nate Robertson; Josh Lueke.

2011 PROJECTED STARTING LINEUP: C-Miguel Olivo; 1B-Justin Smoak; 2B-Brendan Ryan; 3B-Chone Figgins; SS-Jack Wilson; LF-Milton Bradley; CF-Franklin Gutierrez; RF-Ichiro Suzuki; DH-Jack Cust.

2011 BENCH: OF-Michael Saunders; 1B-Mike Carp; INF-Josh Wilson; C-Adam Moore; INF/OF-Matt Tuiasosopo; INF-Adam Kennedy; OF-Ryan Langerhans; 2B-Dustin Ackley.

2011 POSSIBLE CONTRIBUTORS: RHP-Jose Flores; RHP-Shawn Kelley; RHP-Michael Pineda; RHP-Chaz Roe; C-Josh Bard; OF-Johermyn Chavez; OF-Greg Halman; 3B-Matt Mangini; RHP-Jamey Wright; RHP-Manny Delcarmen; OF-Gabe Gross.

ASSESSMENTS
MANAGEMENT:

I preached caution.

Remember that.

When it's all said and done, whether Mariners GM Jack Zduriencik replenishes his reputation as an executive and as a human being and turns the Mariners around, remember. Remember what I said as Zduriencik was being lauded as a new age genius with a scouting background and an affinity for new age techniques in statistical analysis.

Remember.

No one could've predicted the absolute disaster the Mariners were on and off the field last season, but you were warned.

Even as I gave Zduriencik credit for the work he did, for his aggressiveness and willingness to make bold moves, I wrote the following in my book last season:

While it's trendy to look at the flashy moves Zduriencik made, in reality, there are many questions about this Mariners team and Zduriencik recieved undue credit for a team that had everything go wrong in 2008 and turned it around in 2009 based on little more than better health and better luck. He's a smart GM and a good executive; but the "genius" label is highly premature. (Paul Lebowitz's 2010 Baseball Guide, page 137.)

On the same token of having no compunction about uttering the words, "boy did I blow *that* one", nor do I have any shame in saying "I told you so".

I told you so.

A lot can change in a year. One year ago, bandwagon jumpers the likes of Joel Sherman were writing love letters to Zduriencik and using his "success" as a hammer to continually batter the Mets. Referred to as a "Truly Amazin' Exec" by Sherman, Zduriencik was "amazin" alright. It's "amazin" he didn't get fired.

Okay, so he tried some things that made sense but didn't work. Cliff Lee was a brilliant maneuver. It didn't work. Milton Bradley wasn't a terrible idea and it got Carlos Silva's contract off the Mariners books; it didn't work.

But Chone Figgins was a bad idea in theory and it became worse in practice as Figgins's attitude—never a problem with the Angels—was miserable and contentious.

Bringing Ken Griffey Jr. back was ridiculous, but I'll give Zduriencik a pass for that because I sense it was Mariners ownership that wanted Junior back.

But the botched trade of Lee, in which a deal was apparently agreed to with the Yankees...until Zduriencik used the Yankees offer to pry exactly what he wanted from the Rangers and subsequent revelations that Zduriencik was aware of the off-field criminal allegations against Josh Lueke made him appear to be a disgusting human being.

The firing of manager Don Wakamatsu was the blame game at its height. To hold Wakamatsu responsible for the chaotic clubhouse was despicable.

On the field, after Lee and Felix Hernandez, the Mariners were atrocious. They couldn't pitch and had possibly the worst offense I've ever seen in all my years watching baseball.

From top-to-bottom the Mariners were an atrociously run, hideously behaved train wreck. Much like the "genius" label wasn't appropriate, Zduriencik isn't to blame for everything. No one could've expected this team to be so impotent offensively; presumably he didn't want to bring Griffey back; and while the behavior of Bradley was not unexpected, Figgins's poor attitude was out of character considering the player he was with the Angels.

He hired a good manager in Eric Wedge, but if the team has one more off-field catastrophe, Zduriencik is going to get fired. And he'll deserve it.

For seven seasons, Eric Wedge was a respected manager on the field and in the clubhouse for the Indians. While he's occasionally strategically challenged and does weird things by the imaginary book, it's safe to say the same nonsense that went on under Wakamatsu won't happen under Wedge because Eric Wedge doesn't tolerate crap.

Wedge oversaw the Indians rebuilding after the departure of Mike Hargrove and led them to within one game of the World Series in 2007; he was unfairly blamed for the team's demise to 97 losses two years later and was fired. Like everything else he does, Wedge handled the firing with dignity and class even as the Indians inexplicably announced he wouldn't be back with several games left in the season, leaving him to manage knowing he was fired as soon as the last out was recorded that Sunday.

It was absurd.

The players liked and respected Wedge, he's a former catcher and knows how to deal with pitchers; runs his bullpen well; and does a solid job with the lineup.

Wedge was an intelligent hire by Zduriencik and will do a good job.

STARTING PITCHING:

What is there to say about Felix Hernandez other than he's one of the top five pitchers in all of baseball?

The 25-year-old dominated in 2010 but it was hard to tell from his 13-12 record. Luckily for him, the voters looked at his other numbers and realized that he was deserving of the Cy Young Award. 2010 was the second year in a row that Hernandez pitched well enough to have won 25 games. In 2009, he won 19; in 2010, he won 13.

But his other numbers were devastating. 249 innings pitched; 194 hits allowed; 17 homers; and 232 strikeouts with a 2.27 ERA don't do justice to his dominance.

He's a superstar, plain and simple. The Mariners signed him to a contract extension worth $78 million through 2014.

It's a shame he's pitching with *this* group behind him.

Jason Vargas was one of my favorite targets for ridicule while with the Mets and after he was traded to the Mariners, but he pitched quite well last season.

It's difficult to use the term "like Hernandez" when discussing Jason Vargas, but I have to. Like Hernandez, if Vargas was given some support, he could very well have won 15 games. Vargas's motion is quirky as he throws across his body; since he's lefty, he gets away with stuff that's mediocre. He's a contact pitcher who took advantage of the dimensions of Safeco Field. In 192 innings, Vargas allowed 187 hits and struck out 116; he allowed 18 homers and walked 54. When he's not hitting his spots, he gets rocked, but he's proving to be a useful big league starter.

Apart from being Chip Carey's favorite pitcher, Doug Fister had a rough year in 2010 as he went 6-14, but his record isn't indicative of how he pitched.

Are you sensing a trend here with the Mariners pitchers?

Fister pitched respectably, but his ancillary numbers were skewered by a few games in which he got blasted and that the Mariners were so terrible offensively. In 171 innings, the righty allowed 187 hits; but only 13 homers. He could have use as a back of the rotation starter.

They can call Erik Bedard "Carl Pavano West".

When's he going to pitch? And why do the Mariners keep bringing him back? It certainly isn't for his personality as he's known to be short with his teammates and the media.

So why?

When the lefty pitches, he's very, very tough to hit. But there's a problem: Bedard has been a Mariner for three seasons and pitched in 30 games.

Yes, his numbers with the Mariners are very good. In those 30 games, he's 11-7 with 135 hits allowed and 162 strikeouts in 164 innings. But he missed all of 2010 after surgery to his labrum. If he can give the Mariners anything, perhaps they can trade him late in the season when they're hopelessly out of contention.

Or in May when they're hopelessly out of contention.

He's worth a roll of the dice as long as expectations are, well, non-existent.

Luke French is a 25-year-old lefty who went 5-7 in 16 games for the Mariners last season including 13 starts. He's a contact pitcher who allowed 88 hits in 87 innings and 13 homers. He's pitched well in the minors as a starter and if he gains stamina to go deeper into games, could have a future as a back-of-the rotation cog or perhaps a long reliever.

David Pauley is a former Red Sox prospect who pitched serviceably for the Mariners in 2010. He went 4-9, but by the last two months of the season when he was in the starting rotation to stay, he was consistently giving them six quality innings a start. He's a contact pitcher and throws strikes.

Aaron Laffey is a soft-tossing lefty who couldn't make it as a starter and could get a shot as a long man out of the bullpen. He gives up a lot of hits and walks, but not many homers.

BULLPEN:

Closer David Aardsma had surgery on his hip labrum and may or may not be ready to start the season.

Aardsma exemplifies the good and bad parts of Zduriencik. The GM got Aardsma for nothing and rejuvenated his value as Aardsma finally made use of his terrific stuff, a power fastball, a slider and changeup and because a very good closer. Aardsma's ability is no secret. The Giants drafted him in the first round and he had opportunities with the Cubs, White Sox and Red Sox before Zduriencik got him from Boston for Fabian Williamson two years ago.

But Zduriencik was looking to trade Aardsma before his hip injury and was asking for an impact bat.

For David Aardsma.

Aardsma's good and I like his stuff, but I would not surrender an impact bat for him. He strikes out over a batter per inning, but what is he? Is he a pitcher who figured it out when given the opportunity? Or will he revert back to the aggravating journeyman he was before getting to the Mariners?

If he's healthy this year, the Mariners should lower their expectations in a trade and move him for some cheap pieces.

Brandon League and his 100-mph fastball have long intrigued me. Never mind that the Mariners traded Brandon Morrow to get him. That's water over the dam. League has that slingshot fastball and is hard to hit when he throws strikes; but when he's not locating, he can be homer prone as he allowed 7 in 79 innings last season. He doesn't strike out as many hitters as someone with that kind of power fastball should which tells me he's lacking movement and secondary pitches; but he might get a chance to close if Aardsma's out to start the season.

Garrett Olson is a lefty reliever who could have some use if he threw consistent strikes and didn't allow so many homers. The Mariners used him as a multiple inning man last season and he got rocked numerous times. He's not much more effective against lefties than he is against righties, but perhaps he'd be better utilized as a lefty specialist. People suggest he could be a starter since he's been decent at it in the minors, but I don't see it in the big leagues.

Dan Cortes is a big (6'6", 230) 24-year-old right-hander who's been a mediocre and sometimes good starter in the minors and could stick with the big club this season in some capacity. His control is iffy, but he can strike people out. He pitched briefly for the Mariners last season.

Justin Miller is like the forgotten man who always goes to a big league club's camp on a minor league deal and emerges as a useful component in their bullpen. Known mostly for his tattoo-covered body, Miller has a decent fastball and good slider. He allows his hits and homers; but he throws strikes and is fearless.

Veteran journeyman lefty Royce Ring was brought in on a minor league contract. Ring is with his sixth organization for one reason and one reason only: he's lefty. And not a very good one. But with lefty relievers you never know when they're going to have one good season getting out lefties.

Lefty Nate Roberston signed a minor league contract with the Mariners after bouncing from the Tigers to the Marlins to the Phillies last season. Robertson's always struck me as a pitcher who should be a reliever. His stuff appears better suited to going once through the lineup and if he throws strikes and keeps the ball down, he can be tough. He can start if necessary, but I think the Mariners can replenish his value as a reliever.

Now we get to Josh Lueke.

The flashpoint in the horrific year had by Zduriencik occurred when the sexual assault allegations against Lueke—a 6'5" righty with a blazing fastball and lots of strikeouts—came to light.

While with Bakersfield in the Rangers minor league system, Lueke was accused of sexual assault, lied to the police and eventually pleaded no contest to lesser charges. The Rangers claimed that they told the Mariners of the Lueke situation and that they could have another player if they didn't want to keep Lueke. The Mariners went into damage control claiming they tried to get the Rangers to take Lueke back and substitute another player and the Rangers refused; Rangers GM Jon Daniels disputes this.

Former Mariners pitching coach Rick Adair, who was fired along with Wakamatsu, said he told Zduriencik of Lueke's troubles with the law. Adair had been the Rangers minor league pitching coordinator at the time of the incident.

I have no idea what happened; I have no idea who said what to whom. But I'll say this: I would not touch Josh Lueke under any circumstances in a trade or otherwise; and if Zduriencik didn't perform his due diligence on this player after being told of the incidents by Adair, traded for him anyway then lied about it, I'd have fired him.

As a pitcher, Lueke has closer stuff.

But I wouldn't want him on my team or in my organization.

LINEUP:

Miguel Olivo signed a 2-year contract to take over behind the plate. I've never understood why Olivo bounces around as much as he does. He's got a terrific arm; handles the pitching staff well; will hit his 15 homers and, even though he doesn't get on base, does enough good things that he should have a long-term job somewhere. He's a big step up from former top prospect Rob Johnson, whom the Mariners dumped on the Padres.

Justin Smoak was acquired from the Rangers in the Lee trade. The switch-hitting 24-year-old had a rough go of it as a rookie. He did hit 13 homers with the Rangers and Mariners; but he struck out 91 times in 348 plate appearances and batted only .218. He hasn't been a power hitter in the minors—his numbers are Lyle Overbay/James Loney-like—but he's got a history of getting on base and hitting for a high average; he didn't strike out much in the minors so when he gets acclimated to the big leagues, he should eventually become the contact hitter with on base skills that he was in the minors.

Brendan Ryan was acquired from the Cardinals for minor leaguer Maikel Cleto. Ryan's a good fielding utility player who slumped at the plate in 2010 after a very good year in 2009. He's got some speed and will hit a few doubles. Presumably, he'll play second base until Jack Wilson get hurt, then shift to shortstop for Dustin Ackley to take over at second base.

I didn't understand why the Mariners gave a $36 million guaranteed contract to Chone Figgins (with an option that he'll easily reach to make it worth $45 million). He was a speed player in his 30s coming off a career year. And he got off to a terrible start with the Mariners and behaved horribly. Taken out of his comfort zone with a stable organization and no-nonsense leader in Mike Scioscia, Figgins appeared to hate Seattle and couldn't deal with the rampant dysfunction.

His numbers wound up looking better than the context of his year would indicate. He batted .259 with a .340 on base and 42 stolen bases; but he was bad and the year was punctuated with a near fistfight in the dugout with then-manager Wakamatsu after being benched for not hustling—an incident that contributed to the manager's firing.

Figgins will no doubt be better this season than he was last because he can't be much worse on or off the field. That said, he's still a player who relies on his speed and is turning 33. He's, at best, going to be a moderate speed threat and get on base. That there are better hitters behind him than there were last year will help his stats. But that doesn't mean he's going to be that useful to the Mariners.

The Athletics were interested in trading for Figgins, but the Mariners held onto him and insisted they had little interest in trading him. He's a fine fielder and will hit better, but I'd try to get out from under the contract.

Jack Wilson was celebrated for his defense, but it's hard to play great defense when you're always hurt. Wilson had one terrific year for the Pirates in which he had over 200 hits, 41 doubles, 12 triples and 11 homers; but that was in 2004. Since then, he's been a mediocre bat with low on base skills and has progressively gotten worse. And he's been injury-prone. I wouldn't expect him to make it through more than half the season in good health and even then, won't hit enough to contribute much, if at all.

Milton Bradley was a nightmare off the field. Again. But this time, he asked for help with his anger issues; it was a good sign. In 73 games though, Bradley neither hit nor got on base; his mercurial nature contributed to the negativity surrounding the Mariners clubhouse. Again the Mariners were hoping to get something from Bradley this season, but he was recently arrested for making criminal threats against a woman. Bradley's owed $11 million this season and is still on the Mariners roster as of this writing, but don't be surprised to see him gone before the season starts. How much more can the Mariners take from these misanthropes before saying enough's enough?

Franklin Gutierrez is a Gold Glover in center field and is one of the best in the business defensively. Offensively, he took a fall after a breakout year in 2009. His batting average fell from .283 to .245; his on base from .339 to .303; his homers from 18 to 12. Gutierrez is 28 and I tend to think he's closer to the hitter he was in 2009 than what he posted last year. I expect a rebound season from him.

If you read me regularly, you know I'm not a fan of Ichiro Suzuki. I also endured a firestorm of attacks (which I live for) because I suggested that Ichiro could hit for more power if he chose to do so. Rather than swing for singles to bolster his batting average, collect hits and be a stat machine, if he worked the count and looked to pull some inside pitches, his average would suffer but he'd draw more walks and would be a more productive bat for the Mariners—a team who desperately needed someone to drive in runs.

If he played for the Red Sox, Phillies or Yankees and there were power bats behind him to drive him in, then it'd be fine for Ichiro to have his 220 hits, some 40 of which are for extra bases. But he's not. He's with the Mariners who needed him to be more productive.

I think he's a selfish player who's overpaid and the Mariners would be better-served, in their current state, to get rid of him; but he's popular and it's not going to happen. He's owed $34 million over the next two seasons.

Ichiro will accumulate his 220 hits for a team that's not going to contend in any way shape or form. I guess that's what's important in the world of Ichiro, isn't it?

Former Athletics slugger Jack Cust signed a 1-year contract to be the Mariners DH. After enduring Ken Griffey Jr's sad final season, the Mariners needed a power bat to DH and Cust can hit the ball out of the park. Cust was a failure as a top draft pick who'd bounced from the Diamondbacks to the Rockies to the Orioles to the Padres before winding up with the Athletics and taking advantage of what may have been his last chance. Cust strikes out 170 times a year, but he gets on base at a .370-.400 clip and will hit his homers. At any rate, he's way better than what the Mariners were using as DH last season. They'll score more runs with him in the lineup.

BENCH:

Michael Saunders is a 24-year-old outfielder who will get a chance to win the left field job if (when) Bradley is gone. The lefty-swinging Saunders has put up solid power numbers in the minors and hit 11 homers with the Mariners in 327 plate appearances. He batted .211 with a .295 on base and struck out 84 times.

Mike Carp deserved a chance to play every day last season for the Mariners to have a look and see what they have with him. Instead, with the season lost, Zduriencik inexplicably chose to re-acquire Russell Branyan from the Indians.

Why?

I dunno.

Carp is 24 and has posted good power/on base numbers in the minors. Why the Mariners decided not to give him regular playing time over the second half of the season is inexplicable.

Josh Wilson is a utility infielder who batted .227 in 388 plate appearances last season. He has no power or speed, but he has pitched a few games though.

Adam Moore is a catcher who has hit and thrown well in the minors (.303 career average; .368 on base). He didn't hit with the Mariners last season (.195 average in 218 plate appearances). Either he or veteran Josh Bard will back up Olivo this season.

Matt Tuiasosopo is a backup infielder/outfielder who batted .173 in 138 plate appearances last season. He's shown extra base power in the minors and the ability to get on base.

Adam Kennedy is with the Mariners on a minor league contract and the veteran's career has been one of ups and downs. He had a fine year with the Athletics in 2009 and signed with the Nationals and didn't hit. The veteran has shown some power in the past and can play all infield positions. Kennedy was arrested for DUI in the off-season.

Journeyman outfielder Ryan Langerhans was supposed to combine with Jeff Francoeur to be the corner outfielders for the Braves for years to come; it didn't work out that way in either case. He batted .196 last season, but he got on base at a .344 clip, so he has some use.

Dustin Ackley may get his chance to play in the big leagues regularly sooner rather than later. Ackley is 23 and was the Mariners 1st round pick in the 2009 draft. He's shown doubles power in the minors and some speed. He doesn't strike out and draws his walks. I'd think that the Mariners might keep him in the minors to start the season then bring him to the big leagues and let him play in late April/early May.

Why not?

PREDICTION:

This team is awful.

The question is whether Zduriencik can survive another 100-loss season—something that's a legitimate possibility in a rough division and league.

I honestly don't know. My hunch is he's already on thin ice after the way 2010 went. His reputation after the games of semantics he played with the Yankees in the Lee deal were bad enough, but the Lueke mess and the firing of Wakamatsu along with all the other off-field stuff does not bode well for the "Truly Amazin' Exec" and "genius".

If you think I'm gloating about being right, I'm not. I do think that Zduriencik's ethics and morals do need to be looked at a bit more closely considering his behavior last season. I can't believe that the club is going to tolerate anyone even stepping on a crack in the sidewalk this season and that's why I think Bradley will be gone by the time you're reading this.

None of that repairs the issues on the field however.

Hernandez is one of the best pitchers in baseball and he's only 25. They've improved the offense with Cust and Olivo; Figgins will be better; but they still can't hit enough to support the pitching and defense philosophy.

The Mariners are one of the worst teams in baseball and will again come close to losing 100 games. My guess is they'll be on the lookout for a new GM sometime at mid-season.

Recently elected Hall of Famer Pat Gillick still hasn't officially retired. And he lives in Seattle.

If anyone can restore credibility to this embarrassing franchise on and off the field, it's Gillick.

Don't be surprised.

PREDICTED RECORD: 65-97

American League Playoff Predictions

ALDS:

Detroit Tigers vs Boston Red Sox

Red Sox in 4.

ALDS:

Los Angeles Angels vs Chicago White Sox

White Sox in 5.

ALCS:

Chicago White Sox vs Boston Red Sox

Red Sox in 6.

AMERICAN LEAGUE CHAMPIONS:

BOSTON RED SOX

American League Award Winners:

Most Valuable Player: Carl Crawford, Boston Red Sox

Cy Young Award: Justin Verlander, Detroit Tigers

Rookie of the Year: Kyle Drabek, Toronto Blue Jays

Manager of the Year: Jim Leyland, Detroit Tigers

National League East Predicted Standings

		Wins	Losses	GB
1.	Philadelphia Phillies	106	56	---
2.	Atlanta Braves*	90	72	16
3.	Florida Marlins	82	80	24
4.	New York Mets	73	89	33
5.	Washington Nationals	66	96	40

*Denotes predicted Wild Card winner.

Philadelphia Phillies

2010 Record: 97-65; 1st place, National League East.
Defeated Cincinnati Reds in NLDS 3 games to 0.
Lost to San Francisco Giants in NLCS 4 games to 2.

2010 Recap:

Because of the ill-advised (by me anyway) attempt by Phillies GM Ruben Amaro Jr. to win while simultaneously maintaining the farm system, the Phillies season was going down the tubes at mid-season. They weren't hitting; they didn't have enough starting pitching; the bullpen was in shambles; their disabled list was a revovling door of stars; and there were rampant rumors of in-fighting and factional disputes.

Then, with the season teetering on the brink of no return, Amaro made the gutsy decision to trade for Roy Oswalt to essentially admit the mistake he made in trading Cliff Lee to get Roy Halladay.

The Phillies went on a tear not long after Oswalt's arrival, blasted their way into the playoffs, dispatched the Reds in three straight games before falling to the Giants in the NLCS.

2011 ADDITIONS:

LHP Cliff Lee signed a 5-year, $120 million contract with 2016 option.
RHP Eddie Bonine signed a minor league contract.
LHP Dan Meyer signed a minor league contract.
C Kevin Cash signed a minor league contract.

C Erik Kratz signed a minor league contract.
OF Brandon Moss signed a minor league contract.
INF Jeff Larish signed a minor league contract.
1B/3B/OF Robb Quinlan signed a minor league contract.
2B Delwyn Young signed a minor league contract.
OF Cory Sullivan signed a minor league contract.

2011 SUBTRACTIONS:

OF Jayson Werth was not re-signed.
LHP Jamie Moyer was not re-signed.
3B/OF Greg Dobbs was not re-signed.
1B Mike Sweeney was not re-signed.
RHP Chad Durbin was not re-signed.
C Paul Hoover was not re-signed.
3B Cody Ransom was not re-signed.
LHP Nate Robertson was not re-signed.

2011 PROJECTED STARTING ROTATION: Roy Halladay; Cliff Lee; Cole Hamels; Roy Oswalt; Joe Blanton; Kyle Kendrick.

2011 PROJECTED BULLPEN: Brad Lidge; Ryan Madson; Jose Contreras; J.C. Romero; Danys Baez; David Herndon; Mike Zagurski; Antonio Bastardo.

2011 PROJECTED LINEUP: C-Carlos Ruiz; 1B-Ryan Howard; 2B-Chase Utley; 3B-Placido Polanco; SS-Jimmy Rollins; LF-Raul Ibanez; CF-Shane Victorino; RF-Domonic Brown.

2011 BENCH: OF-Ben Francisco; OF/1B-Ross Gload; C-Brian Schneider; INF-Wilson Valdez; OF-John Mayberry, Jr.

2011 POSSIBLE CONTRIBUTORS: RHP-Eddie Bonine; 2B-Delwyn Young; LHP-Dan Meyer; RHP-Scott Mathieson; RHP-Vance Worley; C-Kevin Cash; INF-Brian Bocock; INF-Michael Martinez; OF-Cory Sullivan.

ASSESSMENTS
MANAGEMENT:

It takes someone confident in his station to admit a mistake.

Many GMs and baseball people wouldn't have done it due to the fear that they'd be perceived as "weak" or "wishy-washy" and lacking in decisiveness.

In fact, it's the exact opposite. It took courage for Phillies GM Ruben Amaro Jr. to look at his club and realize they needed another starting pitcher. Had he not taken the bold step and aggressively pursued Roy Oswalt, the Phillies very likely would have missed the playoffs entirely.

Laughed at though he was for the way the Cliff Lee for Roy Halladay trade turned out to be a lateral move; then for his pursuit of Lee via trade from the Mariners, Amaro didn't let that stop him. I'm sure he knew about the perception; but he accepted his mistake as the prospects he received in the Lee trade played and behaved poorly. He acquired Oswalt for far less than a pitcher of Oswalt's stature should've cost. Astros GM Ed Wade helped his old club in that vein, but Oswalt's agreeing to forgo the stipulation that his contract option for 2012 be automatically exercised so he'd waive his no trade also facilitated the trade.

Amaro was lucky in dealing with Wade; he was also lucky that the efforts to trade Jayson Werth were shelved when center fielder Shane Victorino got hurt. They couldn't trade Werth because they didn't have anyone else to play center field and without Werth, they probably wouldn't have come back and won the NL East just like they wouldn't have made it without Oswalt.

Everything clicked in for Amaro at the right time. The Phillies hit the ground running over the last two months of the season and the burgeoning disaster Amaro had cultivated with his stupid decision to trade Lee was repaired in the short term.

Then, after the season, it was repaired in the long term too as the Phillies skulked on the periphery of the Lee free agent merry-go-round and swooped in to snatch him from the Yankees.

It was masterful. And Ruben Amaro Jr. has done a total 180 in my eyes. Rather than crash the classic car into the ditch, he swerved, regained control of it, brought it home and shined it up nicely so that no one even noticed it was gone.

Charlie Manuel deserved to win Manager of the Year after everything he endured on and off the field in 2010. The injuries were one thing; the lack of hitting and firing of his hitting coach Milt Thompson was another; then there were the rumors of whatever was or wasn't going on between Jayson Werth and Chase Utley's wife.

For a manager to handle all of this in a town that's booed Santa Claus is no small feat.

Manuel makes some interesting maneuvers with his pitchers; there are times when he pushed Halladay too far because of Halladay's reputation as a "complete game pitcher"; and he makes a lot of pitching changes that are questionable—using Roy Oswalt in relief in game 4 of the NLCS made no sense whatsoever. But the players know he's in charge; that he doesn't put up with crap; and he makes mostly the right moves.

Is he a great strategic manager? No. But he has all the other attributes you want a manager to have and the players never stop playing hard for him.

Admittedly, there's not going to be much for him to do this season if everything goes according to plan. With that starting rotation, his bullpen decisions are going to be taken out of his hands for the most part. Whether Domonic Brown or Ben Francisco is the regular right fielder will be determined in spring training. Apart from that, the lineup is set and the rotation is devastating. He's got arms in the bullpen and can sit on cruise control with his veterans policing the clubhouse.

Manuel's comfortable in himself to not muck around and screw it up. This is a subtle accomplishment.

STARTING PITCHING:

Roy Halladay was the best pitcher in the National League last season. He was everything the Phillies expected and more. He was durable (250 innings with 9 complete games); he won (21-10 record); he threw strikes (a ridiculous 30 walks); struck out 219 hitters; had a 2.44 ERA; and pitched a perfect game against the Marlins.

He showed the Phillies pitchers how to comport themselves on and off the field; how to prepare and gut their way through games when he didn't have his best stuff—which was rare.

Then he turned around and, in his first post-season start ever in a remarkable 13 year career, pitched the first playoff no-hitter since Don Larsen's perfect game in 1956.

He's an old-school machine.

Cliff Lee had worn four different uniforms in the span of a year. Traded from the Indians to the Phillies and emerging on the world stage as the Stone Cold Killer in the playoffs and World Series for the Phillies, it was Lee's apparent desire to test free agency and Amaro's short-sighted stupidity that laid the foundation for Lee's trade for Halladay.

Winding up in Seattle with the Mariners in the complicated four team trade, Lee missed time early in 2010 with a strained abdominal muscle, but was excellent when he returned. Pitching for an awful Mariners team, Lee went 8-3 with a 2.34 ERA before the Mariners sorry season sent him on the move again. First it appeared as if he was destined for the Yankees, but was traded to the Rangers. Lee's back acted up late in the season and he pitched poorly, but regained his traction in the playoffs and dominated, leading the Rangers past the Rays and helping dispatch the Yankees.

After the Rangers World Series loss, Lee made the free agent rounds with the widespread expectation (fait accompli in certain circles) that he'd sign with the Yankees for a gigantic contract. But Lee had other ideas.

While it was perceived that he wanted the most dollars regardless of venue; that the Yankees fans treatment of his wife and other Rangers players wives during the ALCS gave him pause before signing there, his heart was apparently in Philadelphia, where he never wanted to leave in the first place. The appeal of joining a rotation with Halladay, Cole Hamels and Oswalt sucked him in and, for less money than the Yankees offered, Lee signed with the Phillies.

Lee's ruthless on the mound; throws inside to anyone and everyone; pounds the strike zone and his smooth, easy and repeatable motion is as good a sign for his health as there could be. He's had injuries to parts of his body other than his arm, but the motion assists his durability and he'll compete with Halladay as the best pitcher in the National League.

I'm giving the edge to Lee this year and he's my pick to win the 2011 NL Cy Young Award.

As great as Halladay and Oswalt were for the Phillies, it's unlikely they would've made their comeback without Cole Hamels. Hamels is the forgotten man as the "kid" in the big four, but Hamels has hardware in his own right having won the NLCS and World Series MVPs in the Phillies 2008 championship season.

Overshadowed, Hamels had a fantastic season despite his 12-11 record. Armed with the returning velocity he'd lacked since the 2008 season and his changeup, Hamels had a great year. In 208 innings, he struck out 211, allowed 185 hits and walked 61. He pitched deeply into games and had the Phillies not endured their team-wide hitting slump, Hamels would easily have won over 20 games.

He'll remain in the shadows surrounded by that group, but that doesn't mean he's an easy mark.

Roy Oswalt has been one of the best pitchers in baseball over the past decade for the Astros. He's accustomed to being part of star-studded rotations having pitched with Roger Clemens and Andy Pettitte and he slid in neatly with the Phillies pitching beautifully over the final two months. Oswalt posted a 7-1 record and sparkling 1.74 ERA in 12 starts as a Phillie. Oswalt's had injury problems in recent years, but like Lee, they weren't to his arm. He'd be the ace on 20 other staffs; on this one, he's either the third or fourth starter.

I'm wondering if the other pitchers let Joe Blanton sit with them at meal time or if he has to sit at the children's table.

Blanton missed a chunk of the season with an oblique injury and there were indications that the Phillies were looking to trade him to free up salary after they signed Lee. I wouldn't trade Blanton and he's still a Phillie as of this writing. With the age and wear on Halladay, Lee and Oswalt, I'd be reluctant to dump an innings-eater like Blanton to save a few bucks; what's the difference at this point?

Blanton gives up a lot of home runs, but he eats innings and throws strikes.After getting off to a slow start, Blanton had an under-the-radar, solid second half assisting the Phillies in their blazing run.

Kyle Kendrick tried to copy Halladay to middling results, but Kendrick proved that Halladay is chateubriand and Kendrick is Kendrick. He gives up a lot of hits and homers; he's a contact pitcher whose stuff is barely mediocre. But he guts his way through and can be effective at times. The stat zombies scoff at a pitcher being judged on the fact that he wins, but Kendrick wins! As a long man/spot starter, teams do worse than him.

BULLPEN:

Brad Lidge has been injury-prone and inconsistent since his all-world year in 2008. He missed the first part of the 2010 season with elbow problems and got off to a slow start. Regaining his form (as most of the Phillies did in August and September), Lidge got his slider back and pitched well.

Under contract for 2011, Lidge has an option for 2012 at $12.5 million. Given some of the odd decisions they've made contractually—the Ryan Howard contract was utter lunacy—I don't know what the Phillies are going to do with Lidge. One would assume that if he's pitching well, they'll pick up the option on the veteran closer. It would be silly to have that starting rotation and leave the bullpen in flux; then again, they can let Lidge leave after the season and go after one of the many available short relievers like Jonathan Papelbon.

I'll guess they're going to exercise Lidge's option sometime this season.

Ryan Madson injured a toe kicking a chair early in the season after a bad game and missed a portion of the season. When he was healthy, he pitched well. Madson has a good fastball and off-speed stuff. In 53 innings he allowed 42 hits and struck out 64. Madson's had trouble with the home run ball in the past, but allowed only 4 in 2010.

Madson's a free agent at the end of the season.

Jose Contreras surprised me with his smooth transition to the bullpen and the tough town of Philadelphia. His ERA was blown up to 3.34 because of a few bad outings; those aside, he was reliable. Contreras struck out 57 in 56 innings and there's never been a question about his stuff. A power fastball and great forkball are dominating pitches, but his makeup and coping skills have been the problem. After a year with the Phillies, he'll be even more comfortable and pitch better than he did last season.

J.C. Romero was mostly reliable as a lefty specialist. He had a club option for 2011 in his prior contract that would've been worth $4.5 million; the Phillies declined it and re-signed him to a 1-year, $1.35 million deal.

Romero was wild with 29 walks in 36 innings and struck out 28. His control has always been scattershot, but 29 walks in 36 innings isn't gonna cut it.

Danys Baez was inexplicably signed to a 2-year contract before last season as if there was another team that would've given him the opportunity to win the Phillies had; and if another team wanted him that badly to give him a 2-year deal, hey, lotsa luck.

Baez posted a 5.48 ERA in 47 innings. He allowed 55 hits, 6 homers, walked 23 and struck out 28. Baez had some big save seasons with the Devil Rays, but his ancillary numbers were never very good and the Phillies got exactly what Baez is: a mediocre, overpaid reliever whose reputation was bolstered by a shady stat accumulated for a bad team.

Righty David Herndon was a Rule 5 pickup from the Angels before last season and was mostly the last man out of the bullpen in blowouts and when the Phillies had no one else left. He throws hard, but doesn't strike anyone out (29 in 52 innings) and allowed 67 hits. He's closed in the minors, but I'd expect him to be in the same role as he was last season or in the minors as insurance.

Mike Zagurski is a chubby lefty with a good fastball who's had injury problems and spent much of last season in the minors. He's put up good strikeout numbers in the minors but has gotten knocked around in his chances to pitch in the big leagues. He's 28, but maybe he has a future as a lefty specialist.

Antonio Bastardo is the third mediocre lefty in the Phillies bullpen. He struck out 26 in 19 innings last season; the problem is he allowed 19 hits, but he's always tended to give up a lot of hits. His career numbers against lefties are eerily similar to those against righties. He's hittable but can strike people out.

LINEUP:

Carlos Ruiz had his career year at the plate at age 31. Ruiz, a career .260 hitter, batted .302 with a .400 on base, 28 doubles, 8 homers and 55 walks in 433 plate appearances. Ruiz has put up numbers of this kind in the minors, so maybe it's for real, but I doubt it. It's going to be hard for Ruiz to post these stats again, but he's a good clutch hitter and his main job will be handling the star pitching staff, something he's done well in his big league career.

Ryan Howard was set to be a free agent at the end of this season, but the Phillies locked him up with a deranged $125 million contract extension for which the Cardinals front office undoubtedly wanted to put a hit squad out on whoever's bright idea it was. Automatically, it made Albert Pujols a *lot* more money.

Howard missed time with an ankle injury, but still put up 31 homers and 108 RBI. He batted .276 with a .353 on base—numbers that have become par for the course for Howard. Having been awful against lefties in 2009, Howard hit well against them in 2010 raising his average against southpaws by 57 points.

He is what he is. He strikes out nearly 200 times a year; he'll hit 40 homers with 140 RBI. His on base numbers are declining but he's still a power threat at all times.

Chase Utley would never say it, but he looked like he was playing hurt early last season. He then injured his thumb at mid-season and missed 43 games. When he's healthy, Utley is one of the best if not *the* best all-around hitter in baseball. His short stroke allows him to get around on any pitcher in baseball regardless of velocity and he plays the game the right way—hard.

I found it laughable the way the Mets complained about Utley's hard slide into Ruben Tejada to break up a double play late in the season. What'd they want him to do? Hit him softly?

Utley is the hitter in the Phillies lineup I would fear most in a big spot because he hits the ball to all fields and handles both lefties and righties. He's never gotten the recognition he deserves for being as good as he is. He's a fine fielder too.

Placido Polanco was a questionable signing in my mind last season, but he played well offensively and defensively.

He batted .298 with 27 doubles and played good defense at third base. He's a better defensive second baseman, but that spot's taken in Philadelphia. Polanco's had repeated problems with his left elbow that kept him out of action; he had surgery after the season to remove a bone spur and is expected at full strength this season.

Jimmy Rollins is at a career crossroads. His production has declined every single season since his MVP year in 2007 and he still tries to do it his way. Hacking away; refusing to acknowledge that pitchers are enticing him to chase pitches he can't hit with authority; injuries; and he looked like he'd lost his aggressiveness in the playoffs. Say what you want about J-Roll, but he's never lacked in confidence; but he appeared lost.

He's in the final year of his contract now and Amaro publicly said that Rollins has to make adjustments to still be effective. Rollins sounded amenable to the idea. Whether that's the money aspect forcing him to acquiesce or that he realizes he's not the same player he was four years ago is irrelevant as long as he tries to be more patient and adjusts to the way the pitchers have adjusted to him. There was an arrogance that harmed Rollins. The "I'm gonna be J-Roll" only lasts as long as he's got a contract; now he has to change if he wants a lucrative deal somewhere after the season.

I think the contract year and alterations to his approach will lead to a resurgent year from Rollins and he's going to be an All Star again.

For all the talk that Raul Ibanez needed to be benched, traded, dumped or whatever, it's conveniently missed that he had 58 extra base hits. No, he wasn't the player who was the first half MVP of the 2009 season, but Ibanez was *never* that player at any time in his career. The National League caught up to Ibanez and he reverted to the player he was in Seattle with some concessions to the fact that he's 38-years-old. Ibanez can still hit and be productive for the Phillies and manager Manuel deserves credit for sticking with him despite the public scorn.

Shane Victorino's mid-season abdominal injury may have inadvertently had a hand in saving the Phillies season. Amaro was working on trading Jayson Werth when Victorino got hurt, but because the Phillies didn't have anyone else who could play center field, they couldn't trade Werth. They kept him and went on their tear.

Victorino is a fine defensive center fielder and had his best power year as a big leaguer with 18 homers. He may have been better off hitting his 10 homers, striking out less and getting on base more than the player he was in 2010. He'll steal his 30+ bases and provide over 50 extra base hits along with a Gold Glove in center field.

The Phillies tend to make sure their young players are absolutely, 100% ready for regular big league duty before giving them an everyday job. They did it with Utley and Howard and, I think, kept them in the minors too long; but you can't argue with the results. Whether Domonic Brown is ready to play every day will be determined this spring. My feeling is that Ben Francisco will start the season as the regular right fielder and share time with Ross Gload and by June or so, Brown will be playing every day in right field.

Brown is one of the top outfield prospects in baseball and although he struggled in 70 plate appearances last season, he's been a devastating force at the plate in the minors with five tool ability. He's only 23 and is a Rookie of the Year candidate in 2011.

BENCH:

Ben Francisco has been a serviceable everyday player before in his career with some pop and speed. The Phillies would be fine with a platoon of Francisco and Gload in right. Francisco hit 15 homers in both 2008 and 2009.

Ross Gload is a backup first baseman/outfielder and pinch hitting specialist who isn't suited to playing every day. As the lefty in a right field platoon with Francisco, he'd likely get exposed for his flaws that have kept him as a backup his whole career. Gload is a dangerous clutch hitter off the bench and can play a decent right field.

Veteran catcher Brian Schneider delivered some key hits for the Phillies in 2010. He still calls a decent game, but he can't hit or throw as well as he once did. He's a useful backup for 50 or so games.

Wilson Valdez was an invaluable utility man filling in for Rollins, Utley and Polanco. Valdez got 363 plate appearances last season with all the Phillies injuries and they don't want that to happen again; Valdez is best suited to spell the veterans once or twice a week.

John Mayberry Jr. has had some good power years with 15-20 homers in the minors and if things break a certain way, maybe he could get a chance to win the right field job.

PREDICTION:

The Phillies stand head and shoulders above the rest of the National League with that dominating starting rotation. The only concern they have is the age of Halladay, Lee and Oswalt; apart from that, they should sail into the playoffs. The bullpen is deep enough that when they're needed, they'll get the job done. They could probably use another lefty specialist, but that's something they can find in-season.

The lineup is a bit aged as well, but the Phillies are a win now team and they'll get the required production from Howard and Utley to score enough to support that pitching; it won't take much.

Lidge is a wild card. Who knows what they're going to get from him? But the Phillies will be in position to improve the bullpen on a short-term basis with a Heath Bell-type reliever who's a pending free agent. They're always aggressive during the season trying to improve and they're all in with this group. An older team, their time to win championships is over the next three years.

And that's what they're going to do in 2011 as they steamroll the National League and, led by that starting rotation, will win the World Series.

PREDICTED RECORD: 106-56

Atlanta Braves

2010 Record: 91-71; 2nd place, National League East; Won Wild Card.
Lost to San Francisco Giants in NLDS 3 games to 1.

2010 Recap:

In Bobby Cox's final season as a big league manager, the Braves got him back to the playoffs with a solid starting rotation and deep and diverse bullpen. The lineup was slightly short in the power department, but they rode their arms to win the Wild Card.

Much like the previous Braves playoff appearances save for their one World Series title under Cox, the 2010 season ended in disappointment as they were dispatched by the Giants in the NLDS in 4 games.

Chipper Jones tore the ACL in his knee making a play at third base and missed the final two months of the season and the playoffs. Jair Jurrjens had an injury-ravaged year in the season he was supposed to take the next step to stardom. Takashi Saito and Billy Wagner also got hurt—the latter being in the NLDS and possibly costing the Braves the series.

The Braves introduced Jason Heyward to the world and he became a charismatic 5 tool player with a flair for the dramatic; other youngsters Johnny Venters and Craig Kimbrel made their presence known; and Tim Hudson, Tommy Hanson and Derek Lowe had good seasons in the starting rotation.

2011 ADDITIONS:

Manager Fredi Gonzalez was hired.
2B Dan Uggla was acquired from the Florida Marlins.
RHP Scott Linebrink was acquired from the Chicago White Sox.
LHP George Sherrill signed a 1-year, $1.2 million contract.
OF/1B Joe Mather was claimed off waivers from the St. Louis Cardinals.
RHP Anthony Varvaro was claimed off waivers from the Seattle Mariners.
RHP Jay Sborz signed a minor league contract.
RHP Rodrigo Lopez signed a minor league contract.

2011 SUBTRACTIONS:

Manager Bobby Cox retired.
LHP Billy Wagner retired.
OF Matt Diaz was not re-signed.
OF Rick Ankiel was not re-signed.
OF Melky Cabrera was non-tendered.
RHP Kyle Farnsworth was not re-signed.
INF Omar Infante was traded to the Florida Marlins.
LHP Michael Dunn was traded to the Florida Marlins.
1B/3B Troy Glaus was not re-signed.
1B Derrek Lee was not re-signed.
RHP Takashi Saito was non-tendered.

2011 PROJECTED STARTING ROTATION: Tim Hudson; Derek Lowe; Tommy Hanson; Jair Jurrjens; Mike Minor; Brandon Beachy.

2011 PROJECTED BULLPEN: Craig Kimbrel; Johnny Venters; Scott Linebrink; Peter Moylan; Eric O'Flaherty; George Sherrill.

2011 PROJECTED LINEUP: C-Brian McCann; 1B-Freddie Freeman; 2B-Dan Uggla; 3B-Chipper Jones; SS-Alex Gonzalez; LF-Martin Prado; CF-Nate McLouth; RF-Jason Heyward.

2011 BENCH: 1B/OF-Eric Hinske; INF-Brooks Conrad; OF/1B-Joe Mather; C-David Ross; OF-Jordan Schafer; INF-Diory Hernandez.

2011 POSSIBLE CONTRIBUTORS: RHP-Cristhian Martinez ; RHP-Juan Abreu; RHP-Steve Marek; RHP-Kris Medlen; RHP-Anthony Vavaro; INF-Brandon Hicks; OF-Matt Young; RHP-Rodrigo Lopez; LHP-Billy Wagner.

ASSESSMENTS
MANAGEMENT:

Frank Wren acted aggressively to solve the Braves biggest need and got himself a power bat to play second base when he acquired Dan Uggla from the Marlins. That he only gave up infielder Omar Infante and lefty reliever Michael Dunn to get him made it all the more brilliant. The Marlins jumped too soon in trading Uggla; they could've gotten a lot more than Infante and Dunn had they waited.

Wren smartly jumped on Uggla and the Braves signed him to a contract extension worth $62 million through 2015 to keep him in Atlanta.

The other important matter Wren had to address was finding a replacement for legendary future Hall of Famer Bobby Cox. The process was non-existent as it was known that Fredi Gonzalez was going to be the man to replace Cox. The Braves hired him immediately and he's a good choice.

Wren added to his bullpen depth by acquiring Scott Linebrink from the White Sox and signing George Sherrill. He maintained his bench by keeping Eric Hinske and claimed Joe Mather on waivers from the Cardinals.

The Braves are taking a leap of faith that Chipper Jones will be able to return from his torn ACL. Presumably, if they needed to, they could get by with Martin Prado at third for the time being until they figured something else out, but they don't have any ready made player to step in long term at third base. Wren is aggressive in season to make trades and the Braves have the farm system to get essentially whatever they need.

Cox and Wren had a curious relationship. Not as close as the one between longtime GM John Schuerholz and Cox, the duo tolerated each other as a necessary evil more than anything else and I can't help but wonder whether Wren helped coax Cox out the door.

Cox's retirement leaves a gigantic hole for the Braves to fill. The one constant in the organization over the past 25 years has been Cox first as the GM who drafted Chipper Jones and traded for John Smoltz, then as the manager who led them to all those playoff appearances.. He's still a consultant to the club, but he's not going to know what to do with himself once spring training starts. Cox was beloved by the players and the one manager that drew widespread admiration around baseball as a manager players universally wanted to play for. He was in command of the clubhouse, fought for his players every minute of every game and all he asked was an honest effort. Players who didn't fit into the Braves way of doing things—Kenny Lofton, Yunel Escobar, John Rocker—were sent packing.

His strength was his belief in his players and this ultimately led to many of his playoff downfalls. Trusting relief pitchers who couldn't get the big outs led to so many of their disappointments, Cox could've and should've won more than one World Series in all those playoff chances. But he went with the players he had in the playoffs just as he did in the regular season; he never ripped them in the press; he was a huge reason the Braves were the dominant National League team during his tenure. And he left them in good shape for his friend and former coach Fredi Gonzalez.

Braves fans are concerned about Gonzalez's penchant for frequent pitching changes that don't make much statistical sense. Occasionally he did some odd things strategically, but like Cox, Gonzalez had control of his clubhouse. Dealing with a diva, Hanley Ramirez, Gonzalez did the best he could to rein in the mercurial and moody star. After benching him for lack of hustle, Gonzalez's fate was sealed; but while he lost his job with the Marlins, he retained his dignity and professionalism; the rest of baseball noticed and applauded him for it.

Without support from a meddling upper management, Gonzalez did a good job in navigating the clubhouse, front office and media while handling the team respectably on the field.

Gonzalez is known for the young players who developed under his stewardship which bodes well for Jason Heyward, Tommy Hanson, Craig Kimbrel, Johnny Venters and Freddie Freeman. The Marlins contended and played well above what anyone could reasonably have expected given their payroll constraints and the interference of owner Jeffrey Loria. To have the club openly flirt with Bobby Valentine couldn't have been an easy thing to deal with, but Gonzalez always had the Braves job to fall back on. He was on their short list going back to the speculation that 2010 was going to be Cox's final season. The Marlins did him a favor by firing him and letting him go to a ready-made club that's going to contend.

He's a good manager and will do very well managing the Braves. He's young enough to relate to the kids, is known and liked by the veterans. Gonzalez will be in Atlanta for a very long time and do a fine job.

STARTING PITCHING:

Tim Hudson had a fantastic year in his first full season returning from Tommy John surgery. In a Halladay-less league and had he not tired at the end of the year, Hudson might have won the Cy Young Award. As it was, he finished 4th in the voting after going 17-9 with a 2.84 ERA in 34 starts; and he allowed 189 hits in 228 innings. In his one playoff start against the Giants, he allowed 1 run in seven innings.

His pitches had their bite and he was better than he's been in years.

Hudson has been one of the best pitchers in baseball for a decade and with his newly repaired elbow, he'll be a top pitcher again. He's an ace at the top of the rotation.

Tommy Hanson was seen as the hard luck pitcher on the Braves staff. After a dominating start to his career in 2009 in which he went 11-4 with fantastic across-the-board numbers, he fell to 10-11 in 2010. He's got a moving fastball with late pop and great strikeout potential. Truth be told, his record wasn't far off from what it should've been. There were a few games in which he got blasted, but the Braves got him off the hook. Other games, he pitched 5 inning and allowed 4 runs. Then there were times he was dominant.

Hanson is only 24 and his motion is quirky with a slow windup and rapid launch to generate his velocity. I have concerns about his health with that motion, but he's big (6'6", 220); perhaps he can handle the wear.

In 202 innings, he struck out 173 and allowed 182 hits and only 14 homers. He also hit 14 batters showing he's not afraid to pitch inside. He's going to be an All Star and one of the top pitchers in baseball if he's healthy.

Derek Lowe had a resurgent season. He rediscovered his sinker and the 37-year-old gutted his way to a 16-12 record. He allowed 204 hits in 193 innings, but that was knocked out of whack by games in which he allowed 11 and 10 hits. Lowe was shaky at times, but for the most part he pitched into the sixth inning. He's always been remarkably durable and doesn't allow many homers. Gonzalez has a tendency to have a quick hook with his pitchers, so Lowe can be expected to provide his 5-6 innings and then get yanked.

Before changing my pick to Clayton Kershaw for my NL Cy Young Award pick last season (that didn't work either), I was intending to pick 24-year-old righty Jair Jurrjens to win the award.

That would've been worse.

After a 14-10 record in 2009, Jurrjens was ready to bust out, I thought. But a shoulder injury sabotaged him for spring training After he returned from the shoulder problem, he pulled a hamstring. and missed 10 starts. When he returned in July, he was solid. Jurrjens has excellent stuff—a good fastball, curve and cut fastball. He can lose his control, but is gaining poise on the mound that will improve as he matures. If healthy I still have faith that Jurrjens can be a top pitcher in the National League.

Mike Minor is a 23-year-old lefty who was a 1st round draft pick in the 2009 draft. He has excellent control and racks up the strikeouts. Minor was impressive in a two month big league stint last season striking out 43 in 40 innings, walking 11. His numbers in the minors are excellent. He's a Rookie of the Year candidate.

Brandon Beachy is a 24-year-old right handed prospect. Beachy blew people away as a reliever in the minors last season and made three big league starts late in the season. In the minors, he struck out 148 in 119 innings and only walked 28. He and Minor will vie for the 5th starter slot.

BULLPEN:

Before anything else, Billy Wagner is still on the Braves 40-man roster and despite his assertions that he was retired and that was that, I think there's a chance the could return at some point. A) Wagner isn't the type to want his career to end on the note it did with an injured oblique; B) the Braves have a legitimate shot at a championship—something that's eluded Wagner for his whole career. Plus he was excellent last season aside from the usual, Billy Wagner gacks in which he allows a big homer to blow a game. I had acutally expected him to blow a game or two down the stretch or in the playoffs to cost the Braves dearly; instead he got hurt. Don't be surprised to see Wagner in a Braves uniform on a prorated deal.

Craig Kimbrel is listed as the Braves closer, but he's a rookie. That said, he was devastating in 20 innings for the Braves last season, striking out 40, allowing 9 hits. He's wild too as he walked 16 in those 20 innings. Nobody likes a closer who can't throw strikes, but he throws so hard that he can get away with it for a time. Eventually the walks are going to cost him a few saves. He was a closer in the minors and racked up the strikeouts down there as well. If I were the Braves, I'd prefer to have a veteran closer, but they need to see what they have in Kimbrel.

Lefty Johnny Venters also has closer potential. In 83 innings, he allowed 61 hits and only 1 homer; he struck out 93 and dealt with righties and lefties equally as well. His motion is deceptive and he throws very hard with solid breaking stuff. He's mean too.

Veteran righty Scott Linebrink was acquired from the White Sox. Linebrink was once one of the most consistent set-up men in baseball when he was with the Padres. The homer ball often affected him, but he was usually reliable setting up for Trevor Hoffman. Overwork while with the Padres might have contributed to his downfall with the White Sox. Linebrink struggled last season. In 57 innings, he allowed 59 hits and *11* homers. He struck out 52 and only walked 17. Linebrink might be assisted by the vast dimensions of Turner Field, but if he gets his fastball up, he gives up the long ball. His numbers look worse than they are because of a few bad games, but he's not what he once was. Perhaps being in his free agent year will spark a renaissance for Linebrink.

Sidearming Peter Moylan is a righty specialist who appeared in 85 games in 2010, pitching 63 innings. He allowed 53 hits and struck out 52 along with surrendering 5 homers. He also walked 37, which is a lot. He's a reliable set-up man against righties.

Eric O'Flaherty is the Braves lefty specialist. O'Flaherty pitched 44 innings in 56 games, allowed 37 hits, 18 walks and struck out 36. He's actually serviceable against righities in spurts, but only sparingly.

Veteran lefty George Sherrill was signed to a 1-year contract after he was dumped by the Dodgers. Sherrill pitched wonderfully for the Orioles in 2009, was traded to the Dodgers, did well in the regular season and got blasted in the playoffs. In 2010, he still seemed shell-shocked. He was atrocious in 2010 allowing 46 hits and 24 walks in 36 innings. If the problem was due to confidence, then it might not be fixable; if it's mechanical, then Sherrill could rebound. Relief pitchers and their fluctuating performances make me think that Sherrill will return to form. This is a pitcher who emerged from the Independent Frontier League to make it to the Major League All Star Game. Don't count him out.

LINEUP:

Brian McCann returned from problems with his eyes that could severely have curtailed or ruined his career (it's hard to play baseball when you can't see) and had another fine year. His average was down slightly to .269, but he hit 21 homers, 25 doubles and had a .375 on base percentage.

Because he was the biggest threat in the Braves lineup for most of the season and had limited protection, the presence of Dan Uggla and an improved season from Nate McLouth (who could scarcely be worse) will bring McCann's numbers back up to what we've come to expect. McCann also handles the pitching staff well and had a good year throwing out would-be basestealers (30%).

Freddie Freeman will get a chance to win the first base job after the departures of Troy Glaus and Derrek Lee. The lefty-swinging Freeman's only 21 and has put up big average/on base numbers in the minors with 20 homer power. He also added 35 doubles at Triple A last season. His fielding is average. He's a Rookie of the Year candidate.

Dan Uggla was the Braves prize catch this winter. Uggla provides everything the Braves need. He hits a lot of home runs and extra base hits; he's a fiery leader who plays hard every single day. Uggla had his career year in 2010 with a .287 average; .369 on base; 33 homers (a level he reaches every single year); and 105 RBI. He also walked 78 times and cut his strikeouts to 149.

Defensively he's not great, but the Braves didn't get him for his glove; he makes most of the plays at second base. It's a bit much to ask Uggla—a career .263 hitter—to bat close to .290 again, but the power will be there as will the on base percentage. That the Braves got him for Omar Infante and Michael Dunn was highly strange on the part of the Marlins. It was a great trade for Wren and the Braves and they locked Uggla up with a contract extension.

Will Chipper Jones be able to make it back and what will the Braves do if he can't?

Jones is showing his determination and resolve with his desire and hard work in returning from knee surgery at age 39. But how much will the injury hinder him if he can come back? Jones was compromised as it was with age diminishing him to an occasional power threat with a still good command of the strike zone. Jones had 10 homers and a .381

on base in 381 plate appearances before the injury; his numbers would have ended respectably had he stayed healthy.

Is he going to repeat that production? Or is he going to come back and see that he can't do it anymore and retire early in the season as Mike Schmidt did?

I don't count out Chipper Jones, but it's hard to keep coming back from season-ending injuries especially for a player who's become notoriously injury-prone.

Alex Gonzalez received a standing ovation when he arrived in the Braves clubhouse after the trade of the reviled Yunel Escobar. Gonzalez doesn't get on base, but has 20 homer pop (he hit 23 last year for the Blue Jays and Braves); he also had 42 doubles. His defensive prowess isn't what it once was, but he's still a good fielder. One question the Braves are going to have to answer is how much the likelihood of Jones's immobility and a slowing down Gonzalez will hurt their pitching staff defensively.

Martin Prado has been predominately an infielder and occasional outfielder in his career, but with Matt Diaz gone and Uggla playing second base, he's listed on the depth chart in left field. This is all contingent on Jones's iffy comeback. If Jones can't play, one would assume that Prado will be playing third base and the Braves will either play Nate McLouth in left and Jordan Schafer in center, or use Eric Hinske.

At the plate, Prado had a great year. He finished 9th in the MVP voting with a .307 average; .350 on base; 40 doubles and 15 homers. He's proving himself to be a consistent .300 hitter and developing into an All Star player.

Nate McLouth was horrendous last season and wound up back in the minors. McLouth had a couple of good years with the Pirates in which he had 70 extra base hits in 2008; he was good in 2009 as the Pirates traded him to the Braves for a negligible return at mid-season. McLouth batted .190 last season.

McLouth isn't the star player some had him ticketed to be, but he's not a .190 hitter either. I think McLouth will have a good comeback year and at least hit his .255 and pop 15-20 homers again.

Jason Heyward made his presence felt in his first big league at bat by rocketing a pitch over the right field wall in Turner Field. Heyward lost out in the Rookie of the Year voting to Buster Posey (who I felt deserved the award), but he's going to be a star. Heyward can do it all on the field and at age 21, he's only going to get better.

He batted .277, but his on base was .393. Once he cuts down on his strikeouts, he's going to be an MVP candidate with a .400+ on base, 30 homers and 60-70 extra base hits a season.

BENCH:

Eric Hinske is a great guy to have on a team on and off the field. He's always ready to play, his teams magically end up in the playoffs and he gets big hits. Hinske hit a clutch 2-run homer in the bottom of the eigth inning of game 3 that would have turned the series in the Braves favor had their bullpen held the lead. They didn't and the Braves were eliminated in 4 games. Depending on what happens with Jones and McLouth, Hinske could see substantial playing time.

Brooks Conrad has a useful bat with pop from both sides of the plate off the bench, but his defense is horrific. He hit 8 homers (including a game winning grand slam against the Reds in a 7-run Braves ninth inning in May) and had 11 doubles. Maybe he could play a few games at third base to spell Jones, but they can't afford his defense on a regular basis.

Joe Mather was claimed off waivers from the St. Louis Cardinals. He's 28 and can play the corner infield and outfield positions. Mather has shown good power and on base skills in the minors, but he's 28-years-old. He's a backup and a pinch hitter.

David Ross is a solid backup catcher behind McCann and has some power. In 145 plate appearances, Ross batted .289 with a .392 on base,

13 doubles and 2 homers. He handles the pitching staff well and has a strong arm.

Jordan Schafer is trying to regain his big league footing after overhype and injuries to his wrist sabotaged him two years ago. Shafer batted .201 in 76 minor league games last season.

Diory Hernandez is a backup middle infielder who's hit well in the minors, but never gotten a legitimate opportunity in the majors. He's hit .319 in part time duty in Triple A in the past two seasons.

PREDICTION:

The Braves have terrific starting pitching; a young and capable bullpen with some questions at closer; and a good lineup. They do have to wonder what's going to happen with Jones and have a legitimate plan if he can't play. For right now, they'd survive with Prado at third and Hinske in left until something else can be done.

Gonzalez will slide neatly into Cox's office and run the ship in a similarly understated way. He's a good manager who will flourish in his first real opportunity to win.

Heyward is becoming a star; Uggla puts up the numbers every single year. Freeman is a rookie, so the Braves won't know whether he's ready until he proves it. They don't have many options in center field apart from McLouth, so they have to close their eyes and hope that he solved whatever the problem was last season.

McCann has better support in the lineup with Uggla, Heyward and possible return of Jones. They'll score enough to win.

Because they're in the National League East with the Phillies, the Braves will have trouble competing for the division, but they're at the top of the heap for the Wild Card and will win it.

PREDICTED RECORD: 90-72

Florida Marlins

2010 Record: 80-82; 3rd place, National League East.

2010 Recap:

The Marlins had very high—too high—expectations going into the season given their payroll constraints and flaws.

Manager Fredi Gonzalez started the season knowing he was on thin ice with those expectations and the front office's open flirting with Bobby Valentine. Gonzalez essentially sealed his own fate by chastising and benching star shortstop (and owner's pet) Hanley Ramirez for lack of hustle. The team was inconsistent through the first 70 games under Gonzalez, going 34-36 and the manager was fired. After negotiations with Valentine went back-and-forth, interim manager Edwin Rodriguez was given the job for the rest of the season.

Rodriguez was more of a conservative, play for one run type of manager than Gonzalez was, but he did a good job over the final 92 games.

Dan Uggla had his career year at the plate; Ramirez is one of the most dangerous hitters in baseball; and they established youngsters Mike Stanton, Gaby Sanchez and Logan Morrison in the majors. The starting pitching was solid; the bullpen mediocre. It was a changing of the guard for the Marlins as they dumped Cody Ross and Jorge Cantu and ended where their talent and turmoil dictated they should end up by hovering around .500 all season long.

2011 ADDITIONS:

C John Buck signed a 3-year, $18 million contract.
RHP Javier Vazquez signed a 1-year, $7 million contract.
LHP Randy Choate signed a 2-year, $2.5 million contract.
LHP Mike Dunn was acquired from the Atlanta Braves.
INF Omar Infante was acquired from the Atlanta Braves.
RHP Edward Mujica was acquired from the San Diego Padres.
RHP Ryan Webb was acquired from the San Diego Padres.
LHP Dustin Richardson was acquired from the Boston Red Sox.
OF DeWayne Wise signed a minor league contract.
3B/OF Greg Dobbs signed a minor league contract.
1B Doug Mientkiewicz signed a minor league contract.

2011 SUBTRACTIONS:

2B Dan Uggla was traded to the Atlanta Braves.
OF Cameron Maybin was traded to the San Diego Padres.
C Ronny Paulino was not re-signed.
LHP Will Ohman was not re-signed.
SS Brian Barden was not re-signed.
INF Hector Luna was not re-signed.
LHP Dan Meyer was not re-signed.
LHP Andrew Miller was traded to the Boston Red Sox.
C Mike Rivera was not re-signed.
RHP Jorge Sosa was not re-signed.
LHP Taylor Tankersley was not re-signed.
3B Chad Tracy was not re-signed.
RHP Jose Veras was not re-signed.
RHP Tim Wood was not re-signed.

2011 PROJECTED STARTING ROTATION: Josh Johnson; Ricky Nolasco; Javier Vazquez; Anibal Sanchez; Chris Volstad; Alex Sanabia.

2011 PROJECTED BULLPEN: Leo Nunez; Clay Hensley; Edward Mujica; Ryan Webb; Mike Dunn; Randy Choate; Burke Badenhop; Brian Sanches; Dustin Richardson.

2011 PROJECTED LINEUP: C-John Buck; 1B-Gaby Sanchez; 2B-Omar Infante; 3B-Wes Helms; SS-Hanley Ramirez; LF-Logan Morrison; CF-Chris Coghlan; RF-Mike Stanton.

2011 BENCH: INF-Emilio Bonifacio; C-John Baker; C-Brett Hayes; SS-Osvaldo Martinez; OF-Scott Cousins.

2011 POSSIBLE CONTRIBUTORS: INF-Donnie Murphy; RHP-Jose Ceda; RHP-Chris Hatcher; LHP-Sean West; C-Brad Davis; OF-Brian Peterson; 3B-Matt Dominguez.

ASSESSMENTS
MANAGEMENT:

The Marlins front office has an interesting dynamic of personalities. There's the petulant and reactionary owner Jeffrey Loria; there's the abrasive club president David Samson; and there are the baseball people, Larry Beinfest, Michael Hill and Dan Jennings.

It's oddly structured, but kinda works.

Despite not being the day-to-day GM, Beinfest is still running the show with the construction of the club and he's one of the most aggressive, fearless and forward thinking minds in all of baseball. Working with payroll constraints, he constantly finds players who were dispatched by other clubs and gets use from them cheaply; after they grow too expensive or are no longer productive, he dispatches them. How much Beinfest was involved with the managerial drama—the firing of Gonzalez, the negotiations with Valentine and eventual hiring of Rodriguez—is hard to tell. The Marlins keep their in-house stuff in-house. There was a known split on Valentine that complicated matters in getting a deal done.

Loria refused to allow the Mets to speak to any of his executives when they came calling; all are locked them up with long term deals. It's a clever way to do things and a case study (far better than Moneyball) in a club deciding what's more important. Is it locking up the players or locking up the talent evaluators who *find* the players?

That said, the Marlins had a strange off-season.

Given his pending free agency after 2011, that he was comng off his career year and rejected a long-term contract offer, trading Dan Uggla made sense. But for Omar Infante and Mike Dunn? That's it? I'm wondering what it is that Braves GM Frank Wren says to opposing GMs when negotiating trades. It was a similar circumstance when he got Nate McLouth from the Pirates in that the Pirates jumped on a deal before spreading the word that McLouth was available; nor did they get very much of a return for him.

It's one thing to put one over on Frank Coonelly, Neal Huntington and the Pirates, but to seemingly put one over on the Marlins?

Why did the Marlins act so capriciously in trading Uggla? Couldn't they have gotten more than *that*?

The Marlins took steps to bolster their bullpen with Ryan Webb and Edward Mujica in a trade for Cameron Maybin; they also signed journeyman Randy Choate to a 2-year contract.

Having been the club that set the standard of building a bullpen cheaply and with pitchers who'd washed out elsewhere, why would they give up Maybin to get a homer prone reliever in Mujica?

Did they have to give John Buck a 3-year contract for $18 million? What's the plan for third base?

I admire the Marlins greatly, but their winter was a head-scratcher as to the strategy.

Edwin Rodriguez did a good job in handling the turmoil of taking over for Gonzalez and waiting out the Valentine soap opera. He played little ball too much for my taste, but earned the chance to manage the team full time in 2011.

Rodriguez was caught in the middle as negotiations with Valentine came, went, came, went and finally went. Several times it was said that Valentine was going to be the Marlins next manager and then the deal fell apart again.

That he was given a contract for 2011 doesn't, by any means, suggest that Rodriguez is safe in the job. Loria has high expectations for his club and if they're floundering again; or if Ramirez acts up; or if he wants to make a change just for the sake of it, it's not difficult to fire a manager working under a 1-year deal making no money.

Rodriguez had better get the Marlins off to a quick start. The Valentine stuff isn't going to go away even though Valentine took the job as an analyst on ESPN's Sunday Night Baseball telecast, he wants to manage. And Loria wants him.

I still believe that Bobby Valentine will eventually be managing the Marlins. And if the Marlins are playing poorly in May-June, Valentine is going to get the call. It'll be at unfair and at the expense of Rodriguez, but the star manager takes precedence. It happened in Detroit as Les Moss, a baseball lifer, got his chance to manage the Tigers in 1979. He had them playing respectably at 27-26...until Sparky Anderson wanted to get back onto the field. The Tigers grabbed him. Moss was dumped.

It was cruel, but it's the business.

Rodriguez had better have eyes in the back of his head.

STARTING PITCHING:

Josh Johnson missed the last month of the season with a shoulder problem, but before that, he was one of the best pitchers in baseball. Amid all the attention paid to Ubaldo Jimenez early in the season, Johnson was actually pitching better than Jimenez as the season wore on.

With a fastball in the mid-to-upper 90s, a slider, changeup and control, Johnson can dominate. His record was 11-6, but he pitched well enough to have won 20 games. In 183 innings, he struck out 186 and walked 48; he allowed 155 hits and a minuscule 7 homers. Johnson is a Cy Young Award waiting to happen; the only question is his health. He's an ace at the top of the Marlins rotation and is locked up in a reasonable, long-term contract through 2013.

Ricky Nolasco was also signed to a long-term deal this winter. Nolasco's deal is also through 2013 and is worth $26.5 million.

Nolasco only started 26 games in 2010 because of a right knee injury, but he went 14-9 in those 26 starts. He can be homer-prone and vulnerable to the big inning, but he guts his way through games when he doesn't have his best stuff. He's got a good fastball, curve and control. In 157 innings, he allowed 169 hits, walked 33 and struck out 147. Had he not gotten hurt, he would've won 18 games. He's a solid number 2 behind Johnson.

Javier Vazquez again tries to rebuild his career after a disastrous season with the Yankees.

I thought it was a terrible idea for the Yankees to bring Vazquez back and said so, but not in my wildest dreams could I have thought that he'd be as bad as he was. The second go-round for Vazquez with the Yankees was a vicious circle. I still insist that the Yankees fans never got a chance to unleash on him for his role in the game 7 debacle in the 2004 ALCS loss to the Red Sox, so they were perfectly willing to remind him of his oderous performance in that game...six years later.

Of course it was self-defeating, but what did they care?

It didn't take long for the questions to surface again as to whether Vazquez could mentally handle New York; if the previous engagement scarred him beyond all repair; if the Ozzie Guillen assessment that Vazquez couldn't handle pitching in a big game or with pressure was accurate.

After the Cy Young caliber year he'd had in 2009 with the Braves and the powerhouse club behind him on the Yankees, all he had to do was throw his glove on the mound and be competent—nothing more—and he would've gone 16-10.

But it didn't work.

The shellacking he took from the Red Sox in 2004 still appeared to linger in his mind; the doubts, expressed daily on the radio and in print, were known.

It was important that Vazquez get off to a positive start in his second tour of duty with the Yankees. And he didn't.

Who knows how the season would've gone for him had he pitched reasonably well in his first start against the Rays on April 9th; but he didn't. He got blasted for 8 earned runs in 5 2/3 innings. Yankees manager Joe Girardi deserves some of the blame for leaving Vazquez in the game to absorb the beating he took; the damage was done in the 5-run fourth inning, but Girardi left him in. Vazquez pitched a clean fifth, then got rocked again in the sixth.

The Yankees didn't know how to judge Vazquez, nor did they know how to handle him. There were games early in the season in which he pitched well; other games he looked lost and most of those were at home. He pitched well in June and July and then the wheels came off. His diminished velocity was to blame, but he looked afraid to make a mistake for fear of being pulled from the rotation for the slightest hiccup.

No one can work that way especially someone performing under a microscope and trying to redeem himself for a bad stretch and one giant, memorable blow-up, six years previously.

Vazquez was probably thrilled to have his time as a Yankee in the rear view mirror.

Signing with the Marlins on a 1-year, $7 million deal is win-win. He'll get a chance to pitch for a talented team; there won't be the attention and pressure there was in New York; he's back in the National League East where he had his best seasons as a member of the Expos and Braves; if the Marlins fall from contention, he can be traded to a contender; and at age 35, there's still time to garner one more good multi-year contract.

I think Vazquez will pitch serviceably for the Marlins. He won't be what he was with the Braves in 2009, but a 180-190 inning season and a record in the area of 14-12 isn't out of the question.

Anibal Sanchez finally had one season in which he was able to stay 100% healthy and didn't have his recurring shoulder problems sabotage him again. Given his history, that's not something that can be too far from everyone's thoughts.

Sanchez made 32 starts in 2010 and with a little more support, could've won 16-17 games rather than the 13 he did win. Sanchez has great stuff, a fastball, curve, changeup; and all his pitches move—sometimes a bit too much; sometimes to the point where he has no idea where the ball's going. He can lose his control sometimes, but apart from that, he's a super talent. Of the 192 hits he allowed last season, only 10 were homers in 195 innings. Sanchez has the stuff to be a 15-game winner, but his health is the big obstacle in achieving that and it's never a suprise when he misses a start with an ailment, usually to his shoulder.

Chris Volstad is a 6'8", 24-year-old righty who went 12-9 last season. He's a contact pitcher who needs to have more confidence in his stuff. In 175 innings, he allowed 187 hits and 17 homers; Volstad walked 60 and struck out 102. He's got a tendency to run up high pitch counts in the middle innings and can't pitch past the sixth inning. He could be a big winner once he gains experience.

Alex Sanabia is a 22-year-old righty who was a 32nd round draft pick of the Marlins in 2006 who struggled early in his minor league career, but came into his own in 2009 and found himself in the big leagues in 2010. He showed impressive poise and control in 15 big league appearances (12 starts) last season. He walked 16 and struck out 47 while allowing 74 hits and 6 homers in 72 innings.

Sanabia tended to tire in the middle innings putting into question his future as a starting pitcher; he's only about 170 lbs, but there's something I like about a pitcher who was an afterthought as a draftee (nobody thinks they're going to get anything from a 32nd round draft pick) works his way up the ladder and has some success in the minors. It shows character. He might be better suited to be a reliever until he puts on some weight.

BULLPEN:

Leo Nunez was in and out of the role as Marlins closer. He throws very, very hard, but appears to try to throw too hard to get out of trouble, flattening his pitches and making him prone for the long ball. He strikes out over a batter per inning and is tough to hit when he's right; when he's not, he gets blasted. Nunez also tends to be streaky. He'll have a long run of clean outings, then a week where he can't get anyone out. He can be a good closer if he learns to maintain his cool.

32-year-old journeyman righty Clay Hensley was another Marlins reclamation project in the bullpen and took over as closer at the end of the season, saving 7 games. In 75 innings, Hensley allowed 54 hits and struck out 77; he has good control and only allowed 3 homers. Hensley's stuff didn't work well as a starter, but as a reliever, he can rely on his fastball and slider and not hold anything back. I'd give Nunez a chance to regain his job as the closer, but not hesitate to switch roles between he and Hensley with Hensley taking over as full time closer.

Edward Mujica and Ryan Webb were acquired from the Padres in the Maybin trade.

Mujica, a righty, had struggled in his first opportunity in the big leagues with the Indians, but found a home in the Padres bullpen. He was useful in 2009 and good in 2010. In 69 innings, he struck out 72, and allowed 59 hits. The one glaring thing is the number of homers he allowed—14!!

That's an enormous amount of homers for a reliever and should be an even bigger concern since he was pitching in the cavernous Petco Park. He only walked 6 hitters in those 69 innings, so he may have control that's *too* good. I dislike relievers who can't throw strikes, but I despise relievers who give up home runs.

I'd be worried about Mujica.

Webb was another intergral part of the Padres bullpen last season. The 25-year-old allowed 64 hits in 59 innings, walked 19 and struck out 44. On the plus side, he only allowed 1 homer. Webb got rocked by lefties at a .333 clip last season, but pitched reasonably well against them in limited action in 2009.

Mike Dunn was acquired from the Braves in the Uggla trade. He has a terrific lefty arm, can rack up the strikeouts and has closer ability. Dunn can handle both lefties and righties and his main obstacle is control. In 19 innings with the Braves last season, he walked 17 and struck out 27. He needs to throw strikes.

Veteran lefty specialist Randy Choate rejuvenated his career with his sidearm junk for the Rays and the Marlins signed him to a 2-year, $2.5 million contract. Choate is the ultimate lefty specialist. Righties, when he was allowed to pitch to them, ripped him for a .410 average in 49 plate appearances last season. I think I could hit him. Against lefties, he was very good holding them to a .202 average and .263 on base. His main job with the Marlins will be to deal with Ryan Howard,

Chase Utley and Raul Ibanez of the Phillies; and Brian McCann of the Braves.

Burke Badenhop is a useful righty long reliever. He's durable, throws strikes and pitches multiple innings in relief. He pitched 67 innings in 53 appearances and struck out 47. He induces plenty of ground balls, allowing him to get out of jams.

Brian Sanches is a 32-year-old righty who's effective against both righties and lefties. His control is sometimes lacking, but he struck out 54 in 63 innings and only allowed 43 hits with 7 homers.

Big lefty Dustin Richardson was acquired from the Red Sox for failed prospect Andrew Miller. Richardson's been good in the minors as a reliever, but had no control whatsoever in a brief trial with the Red Sox. He can strike people out, but he looks to be one of those lefties that takes a while to figure it out.

LINEUP:

John Buck was signed to a 3-year, $18 million contract that elicited eyebrow raises at best and laughter at worst. It was a strange investment for the normally frugal Marlins. Buck has power and will hit his 20 or so homers; he's serviceable defensively and is known around baseball as a tough guy; he's coming off his career year with the Blue Jays after batting .281 with 20 homers and 25 doubles. Buck is a .243 career hitter and strikes out a lot; he's never been an everyday player. It was a curious signing.

Gaby Sanchez was overshadowed by other rookies last season, but had a very good year. In 151 games, Sanchez batted .273 with 19 homers, 37 doubles and 3 triples. In the minors, he's posted better on base numbers than last season's .341 and is bound to get better as he gains big league experience.

Omar Infante was acquired along with Dunn for Uggla. Infante took advantage of his first chance to play full time last season batting

.321; but he's a singles hitter with 8-10 homer pop and no speed. He doesn't strike out much, nor does he walk. He's versatile defensively and can play anywhere adequately. But Infante for Uggla? I dunno....

Wes Helms is not an everyday player, but the Marlins are in the position where they have to start the season with him playing third base unless they make a move for an outfielder, move Logan Morrison or Chris Coghlan back to the infield or shift Gaby Sanchez over to third. Helms is a good pinch hitter with occasional pop; he's a solid defensive third baseman and a solid guy in the clubhouse. Helms is a better hitter than the .220 from last year, but the Marlins are going to have to figure something else out.

Would they be willing to give 21-year-old Matt Dominguez a shot? He's probably better than what they have now if they're intent on using Coghlan in center. Why not?

Hanley Ramirez is one of the most dangerous hitters in all of baseball but his reputation—not great to begin with after his perceived unwillingness to play through injuries down the stretch in 2009—took a drastic turn for the worse as his lackadaisical play prompted former manager Fredi Gonzalez to bench him as a disciplinary action. Ramirez refused to apologize and his relationship with owner Jeffrey Loria was held over the manager's head as if Ramirez was running the team. The widespread condemnation of Ramirez's behavior and refusal to apologize led Tony Perez and Andre Dawson to have a long talk with him about understanding and accepting the fact that his immense talent implied a great deal of responsibility. I'm convinced Perez was there to keep Dawson from beating Ramirez's face in if he said the wrong thing.

Ramirez accepted his punishment and was contrite after a few days, but eventually won the war in the Marlins clubhouse as Gonzalez was fired. Uggla was another individual who challenged Ramirez and he too is gone.

It's dangerous when an immature and gifted 27-year-old is acting the way Ramirez does. If Edwin Rodriguez tries to assert himself with Ramirez when—not if—when Ramirez pulls another of his power plays, what's going to happen?

Ramirez has MVP talent if he puts his mind to accomplishing everything he can on the field, but it's not going to happen as long as the owner enables him with coddling.

On the field, Ramirez had a season others would be jealous of. He batted .300 with a .378 on base; 21 homers; 78 RBI and 32 stolen bases. Defensively, he took a few steps back, but that may have been due to laziness more than any declining range.

Logan Morrison is one of the top hitting prospects in all of baseball. The lefty-swinging Morrison batted .283 with a .390 on base in 287 plate appearances last season. His average and on base numbers were consistently above .300/.400 in the minors and he'll hit for big power as he matures. He's got star potential and is a testament to the Marlins scouting operation as he was a 22nd round draft pick in 2005.

Chris Coghlan is apparently being shifted to center field.

Whether or not he can play it is the question. Coghlan was an infielder in the minors and was shifted to the outfield in 2009, winning Rookie of the Year. He's a good left fielder, but center is tough especially for one who's never played it.

He got off to a terrible start at the plate in 2010, but regained his footing and hit well before sustaining a ridiculous injury in which he injured his knee when he was hit in the face with a cream pie after a game winning hit.

I swear if I was a manager and that happened to one of my players in a celebration, I don't think I'd ever stop screaming. Ever.

The Marlins are going to eventually do something other than what they're planning defensively because it's not going to work.

Mike Stanton is a 21-year-old slugger who is going to hit 40 homers one day. The 6'5", 235 pound Stanton is a righty basher who hit 22 homers in 396 plate appearances last season. He's raw; is impatient and strikes out too much, but once he learns the league, he's going to be a two-fisted mauler.

BENCH:

Emilio Bonifacio is a switch-hitting utility player who will see time at every position from third base to center field. He has speed but no power whatsoever; doesn't get on base; nor does he hit for a high average.

John Baker missed most of the season with a strained flexor in his elbow. He wasn't a very good thrower before and this won't help him get any better, but he's not going to play more than 30-40 games with the signing of Buck. Baker has patience at the plate and some pop; he handles the pitchers well. He's a good backup catcher.

Brett Hayes is the other Marlins catcher and might be needed depending on the condition of Baker's elbow. He's not much of a hitter, but has shown some throwing ability. He's a pure backup.

Osvaldo Martinez is a 23-year-old infielder who had a very good year at the plate in Double A last season and showed some ability with the Marlins in a brief trial last season. He batted .302 with a .372 on base and 28 doubles in 587 plate appearances in the minors; then .326 in 14 games in the majors. Perhaps he'll get a shot at third base.

Scott Cousins is a 26-year-old, lefty-swinging outfielder and the only pure center fielder on the Marlins roster. Cousins has been a solid, all-around hitter in the minors. If Coghlan can't play center, don't be surprised to see the players shifted all over the place. Infante could move to third; Coghlan to second; or Coghlan to third or some other series of machinations to shore up an outfield defense that promises to be woeful if they follow through with their current plan.

PREDICTION:

Despite all their talent and front office intelligence, there always seems to be something haphazard going on with the Marlins. The way they pocketed revenue sharing money; Loria's constant interference with the way the team is run; the coordinated dysfunction has worked for them to a point, but as much as I respect Beinfest and the talent evaluators, I have to wonder what they're doing.

Bringing in established relief pitchers has never been the Marlins way and it's an iffy strategy to shore up what was a perceived weakness. I don't know that Mujica, Webb, Dunn and Choate are going to push the Marlins into legitimate season-long contention to improve on a club that was .500 last season. What the intent is with center field remains to be seen; I can't imagine that they think they can play Helms every day or that Coghlan will deal effectively with center field. The pitching is going to be affected negatively by a bad outfield defense.

The rush to trade Uggla and the return made no sense.

Signing John Buck? Okay. But for 3-years and $18 million? They'd have been better off with Yorvit Torrealba or by bringing Miguel Olivo back.

They can certainly hit, but a team cannot ignore defense to the degree that the Marlins clearly do.

The Marlins have good starting pitching; power; a questionable bullpen; a shoddy defense; high expectations; and a need to draw fans and attention heading into the new ballpark next season.

All of that adds up to a .500 team.

And it adds up to Bobby Valentine replacing Rodriguez as the manager in the summer.

He'll liven things up, but won't be able to alter their fate until 2012.

PREDICTED RECORD: 82-80

New York Mets

2010 Record: 79-83; 4th place, National League East.

2010 Recap:

The Mets got off to a terrible start, then had a blazing hot streak that vaulted them into surprising contention. Without Carlos Beltran due to knee surgery and Jose Reyes missing part of spring training due to a thyroid issue, the club held their own through the All Star break when a devastating West Coast swing sent them reeling back into mediocrity.

Jason Bay struggled in his transition to New York and Citi Field and a crash into the left field wall at Dodger Stadium gave him a concussion and ended his season. David Wright had a big comeback year at the plate; Reyes was up-and-down; Johan Santana again got hurt, shortening his season for the second straight year.

The season turned ugly as closer Francisco Rodriguez assaulted his father-in-law in the clubhouse family room, was arrested for assault and suspended by the club.

John Maine got hurt; Oliver Perez was horrific; Jeff Francoeur didn't listen to anyone trying to help him fulfill his potential.

Mike Pelfrey had a good, if inconsistent, year; R.A. Dickey was a discovery with his knuckleball; and Jon Niese and Ike Davis were two homegrown players to build around.

2011 ADDITIONS:

GM Sandy Alderson was hired.

Manager Terry Collins was hired.
LHP Chris Capuano signed a 1-year, $1.5 million contract.
C Ronny Paulino signed a 1-year, $1.35 million contract.
RHP D.J. Carrasco signed a 2-year, $2.4 million contract.
OF Scott Hairston signed a 1-year, $1.1 million contract.
RHP Chris Young signed a 1-year, $1.1 million contract.
RHP Taylor Buchholz signed a 1-year, $600,000 contract.
INF Brad Emaus was selected from the Toronto Blue Jays in the Rule 5 Draft.
INF Chin-lung Hu was acquired from the Los Angeles Dodgers.
RHP Boof Bonser signed a minor league contract.
LHP Tim Byrdak signed a minor league contract.
C Raul Chavez signed a minor league contract.
OF Willie Harris signed a minor league contract.
LHP Taylor Tankersley signed a minor league contract.
RHP Blaine Boyer signed a minor league contract.
C Dusty Ryan signed a minor league contract.
LHP Casey Fossum signed a minor league contract.
RHP Dale Thayer signed a minor league contract.
RHP Jason Isringhausen signed a minor league contract.

2011 SUBTRACTIONS:

GM Omar Minaya was fired.
Manager Jerry Manuel was fired.
LHP Pedro Feliciano was not re-signed.
LHP Hisanori Takahashi was not re-signed.
C Henry Blanco was not re-signed.
OF Chris Carter was not re-signed.
RHP Elmer Dessens was not re-signed.
RHP Kelvim Escobar was not re-signed.
RHP Sean Green was non-tendered.
RHP John Maine was non-tendered.
3B/1B Mike Hessman was not re-signed.
RHP Fernando Nieve was not re-signed.
INF Fernando Tatis was not re-signed.
LHP Raul Valdes was not re-signed.

OF Jesus Feliciano was not re-signed.

2011 PROJECTED STARTING ROTATION: Mike Pelfrey; R.A. Dickey; Jon Niese; Chris Young; Chris Capuano; Johan Santana.

2011 PROJECTED BULLPEN: Francisco Rodriguez; Bobby Parnell; Manny Acosta; D.J. Carrasco; Taylor Buchholz; Tim Byrdak; Taylor Tankersley; Pat Misch; Oliver Perez.

2011 PROJECTED LINEUP: C-Josh Thole; 1B-Ike Davis; 2B-Ruben Tejada; 3B-David Wright; SS-Jose Reyes; LF-Jason Bay; CF-Angel Pagan; RF-Carlos Beltran.

2011 BENCH: C-Ronny Paulino; INF-Luis Hernandez; INF/OF-Daniel Murphy; OF-Scott Hairston; OF-Willie Harris; 1B/OF-Nick Evans; INF-Brad Emaus; 2B-Luis Castillo.

2011 POSSIBLE CONTRIBUTORS: OF-Lucas Duda; INF-Chin-lung Hu; RHP-Boof Bonser; RHP-Blaine Boyer; RHP-Dillon Gee; RHP-Jenrry Mejia; C-Mike Nickeas; INF-Justin Turner; OF-Fernando Martinez; RHP-Ryota Igarashi; OF-Jason Pridie; RHP-Dale Thayer; LHP-Casey Fossum; RHP-Jason Isringhausen.

ASSESSMENTS
MANAGEMENT:

Because of the lawsuit filed against the Wilpons in the Bernie Madoff Ponzi scheme and attempted recovery of some of the money, they're in the process of seeking a minority shareholder to infuse the club with money. How this plays out will be one of the side stories of the season. Or *the* story if things go badly on the field.

After a long interview process, the Mets hired veteran baseball man Sandy Alderson to replace the fired Omar Minaya.

Alderson's career has had a fluctuating trajectory. An outsider who entered baseball as a matter of circumstance and going from lawyer to Oakland Athletics GM, he had a long and successful run working in tandem with Tony La Russa to build the best team in the American League from 1988 through 1992. When the money that was available to buy the best players was gone, so was the success. Then La Russa left and the Alderson A's fell into the netherworld of non-competitiveness.

When Billy Beane took over the A's, replacing Alderson, and became known as a "genius" because of Moneyball, Alderson's foresight in building the foundation for the stat-based "revolution" upon which Moneyball was based was credited for getting the ball rolling. Following a stint with MLB's front office, Alderson took the job as president of the San Diego Padres; his tenure was pockmarked with in-fighting, turf battles and an underlying enthusiasm on the part of the club president to encourage the varying factions—stat based and scouting—to constantly battle for control with one thing in common, fealty to Alderson.

After leaving the Padres, Alderson was given the task of cleaning up the messy disorganization and under-the-table chicanery that went on with baseball in the Dominican Republic. Then the Mets came calling.

After his hiring, he went on all the talk shows and gave as good as he got; intimidating bullies like Mike Francesa, Alderson showed he still has the passion to build a team and do it in a way that isn't designed to validate his role in Moneyball as his work with the Padres always had the aura of attempting. He's running the Mets, he's standing up to all critics and he's done things the right way in refusing to spend money for the sake of good press; instead, he's got a plan and is bringing in people with whom he's worked before and who will enact his edicts without an eye on how it can help their station.

He brought in two former GMs, both of whom failed in their stints as a boss—Paul DePodesta and J.P. Ricciardi—and are loyal to Alderson.

His actions and statements have looked good so far and instead of trying to live up to a fairy tale called Moneyball, he's doing what's best for the team.

Terry Collins was hired as the Mets manager after a process that took about as long as the GM search.

Collins has been a respected baseball man but his raging temper and known intensity cost him two jobs with the Astros and Angels. His last big league managing job was in 1999 and a mutiny amongst some of the players led to his ouster.

He's toned himself down a bit as he's aged, been a minor league director among other jobs in North America and overseas and is a stickler for detail, hustle and playing the game the right way.

The Mets need his discipline and hard charging ways.

For too long, the inmates have run the asylum for the Mets and in order for the culture to change, everyone in management has to be on the same page. That's not to suggest that Collins is going to be a "middle managing" yes-man as Moneyball implied the field manager should be, but someone who stands up for himself and what he believes while maintaining the respect of the players and his bosses.

Collins is no yes man.

He won't shy away from telling the players the way he wants things done; nor will he hesitate to bench them if they don't acquiesce. Because of the new regime, there won't be the backstabbing atmosphere of unhappy players running to assistant GMs or ownership to undermine the manager.

It won't be tolerated. Collins is in charge of the clubhouse and the players are going to play and act correctly or they won't play; nor will they be there for long.

It's a welcome change after years of dysfunction on all levels.

STARTING PITCHING:

Despite 15-9 record and solid across-the-board stats, Mike Pelfrey's season wasn't as good as it appears on paper. He got off to a great start thanks to a new split finger fastball, but once it got around the league that he was using a new pitch, he struggled.

Pelfrey's season can be divided into parts. From the beginning of the season through June, he was one of the best pitchers in baseball accumulating a 10-2 record; then he was terrible until August when he regained his form. Pelfrey is a contact pitcher, throws strikes and doesn't allow many homers. In 204 innings, he allowed 213 hits and 12 homers; he walked 68 and struck out 113. With Johan Santana expected out until the summer, Pelfrey is going to be relied on as the number one starter. It depends on which Pelfrey shows up as to whether he's going to be able to fulfill that mandate.

R.A. Dickey arrived like a bolt from the blue. It's said that it takes time for a knuckleballer to find his way in baseball, but Dickey had been a journeyman since taking up the knuckleball when injuries derailed his career as a conventional pitcher. Dickey was masterful after joining the club in late May. He went 11-9 in 27 games (26 starts), allowed 165 hits in 174 innings, 13 homers and only walked 42.

Dickey was also a leader on the staff and well-spoken representative for the club. It's always a dicey thing to expect an older pitcher who has his one big year to repeat that the next year; sometimes it's a matter of opportunity and figuring it all out; other times it's just a confluence of circumstances that comes and goes. It's different with a knuckleballer and I believe Dickey is for real.

To avoid arbitration, Dickey signed a 2-year, $7.8 million contract with a club option for 2013. He has some security for the first time in his career.

Lefty Jonathon Niese was one of the top rookie pitchers in baseball for much of the season before he tired in September. With a good fastball, curve and cutter, Niese put up some terrific performances specifically a masterpiece of a 1-hit shutout against the Padres in June. Niese wound up 9-10 on the season and his ancillary numbers don't look impressive to the naked eye, but he pitched better than his numbers. In 173 innings, he allowed 192 hits and 20 homers; he walked 62 and struck out 148. Niese has the stuff to be a 12-15 game winner in the big leagues.

6'10" righty Chris Young was signed to an incentive-laden 1-year contract. Young has pitched in 18 games in the past two years. When he's healthy, he's tough. His motion is deceptive and his height makes his fastball seem faster than it is; he has a good curve and changeup and he's willing to pitch inside. His big problems are staying healthy and late season stamina. When he was healthy and pitching well for the Padres, he had a tendency to tire out at the end of the season and couldn't be counted on for more than 150-170 innings—then in the past two years, the injuries hit his shoulder. If he's able to pitch, he's a great, low cost pickup; but after all these injuries what can the Mets reasonably expect? I'd expect very little.

Chris Capuano is a 32-year-old veteran lefty who signed a 1-year deal with the Mets. Capuano was a solid, durable starter with the Brewers for 2005 and 2006, he slumped in 2007 and underwent Tommy John surgery (for the second time) in 2008. He's a contol pitcher whose strikeout numbers—when he was healthy—were high enough that he shouldn't be considered a pure junkballer. He gives up his share of homers and hits when he's not pinpointing his spots, but he was a good mid-rotation pitcher before, maybe he can rejuvenate his career with the Mets.

Johan Santana has surgery on his shoulder and isn't expected to be able to pitch until June at the earliest. Santana wasn't as dominant as he was with the Twins last season, but he was good enough to post an 11-9 record and have an ERA under 3.00. Judging by how he actually pitched, he should've won 17 games. Santana is one of the top pitchers in baseball, but he was damaged several times by the big inning. Shoulder surgeries are tricky and it's hard to know what the Mets are going to get when Santana returns.

He'd already lost a few inches on his fastball and with him coming back from another injury that could diminish his velocity even further, it could be an issue reducing his effectiveness further. Perhaps he'll have to rely more on his changeup and locating his fastball. He can win that way, but it will take some time for him to learn to pitch differently to account for it.

BULLPEN:

Francisco Rodriguez will return as the closer. After the humiliating way his season ended as he assaulted his father-in-law in the Citi Field family room, he's going to be on his best behavior. K-Rod is a good closer but the most interesting dynamic will be if the Mets are not contending and K-Rod is approaching the 54 appearances he needs to guarantee his contract for 2012.

The provision in his contract calls for the kicker if he either finishes 55 games in 2010 or has a combined 100 games finished in 2010 and 2011. K-Rod finished 46 games last season. Will the Mets, if they're out of the race by mid-August, sit K-Rod to "unguarantee" his $17.5 million for 2012? And will the union fight it if they do?

I certainly wouldn't hesitate to sit K-Rod in order to get his contract off the books.

Another option, if he's pitching well and behaving, is to trade him while picking up some of the 2012 contract. He'd get a couple of good prospects back and I think this is the likeliest scenario, contingent on his behavior.

Bobby Parnell drew plenty of attention with his fastball after returning from the minors. Clocked at 102 mph, he has the velocity to blow people away. In 35 innings, he struck out 33 and only allowed 1 homer. He did surrender 41 hits, but that was skewered by a couple of games in which he gave up crooked numbers against the Diamondbacks and Phillies. Apart from that, he was reliable and has the potential to be a top set-up man with that power fastball.

Manny Acosta was a solid pickup from the Braves before last season. Acosta has a good fastball and struck out 42 in 39 innings. He allowed 30 hits, but his one bugaboo has always been the home run ball. His control is occasionally wanting and when he falls behind and has to throw his fastball in the strike zone, he tends to give up the long ball.

D.J. Carrasco signed a 2-year contract. A 34-year-old righty, Carrasco is a durable, multiple inning reliever who's pitched well out of the bullpen for the White Sox in 2008 and 2009 and spent last season with the Pirates and Diamondbacks. He occasionally has trouble throwing strikes, but has strikeout potential.

Taylor Buccholz is trying to regain his footing after missing 2009 with Tommy John surgery and bouncing from the Rockies to the Red Sox as he returned last season. Buchholz was an integral part of the Rockies bullpen in 2008 as a set-up man with a 2.17 ERA and 56 strikeouts in 66 innings. He has a good fastball and wicked curve;

his stuff translates better to going once through the lineup and if he's healthy, he could be a cheap find for the Mets.

Veteran lefty specialist Tim Byrdak signed a minor league contract. Byrdak has been one of the unheralded lefties in baseball since joining the Astros in 2008. He's 37, has had some trouble with the home run ball and control, but lefties have hit .202 against him in his career. He's a pure lefty specialist who should make the Mets out of spring training.

Taylor Tankersley is another lefty who, like Buchholz, is trying to regain his effectiveness. Tankersley had a good year in the Marlins bullpen in 2007, but has gotten blasted since. He didn't pitch in 2009 with a recurring stress fracture in his arm and wasn't good in 2010. For his career, he's held lefties to a .223 average so he, like Byrdak, will be a lefty specialist. The Mets will be able to use two lefties in the bullpen, so Tankersley has a good chance to make the team and get into a lot of games.

Pat Misch is a soft-tossing lefty who is short just enough on his fastball that he's unable to get inside to righties and has to rely on control and spotting his pitches. He has very good control and is a useful pitcher to have around as a long reliever/spot starter.

Oliver Perez is only still on the roster because he's making $12 million this season. Alderson has said that if Perez doesn't earn his way onto the roster, he won't be with the Mets.

I don't expect him to be with the Mets.

LINEUP:

Catching prospect Josh Thole will receive every opportunity to take over as the starter. Thole is a lefty-swinging slap hitter who's batted .300 in the minors in two of the past three seasons; his hitting style reminds me of former Pirates catcher Mike Lavalliere—a spray hitter with 25 or so doubles and maybe 8 homers. He has a strong arm behind the plate.

Ike Davis impressed in spring training 2010 and was recalled from the minors in late April. His swing was compared with John Olerud's, but after watching him over the long term, he's more of a Lyle Overbay-type with more power. He takes his walks (72 in 601 plate appearances); strikes out a lot (138 times); and has power (19 homers, 33 doubles). The 24-year-old Davis is a good fielder and will hit 25-30 homers in the big leauges with 100+ RBI and a .350+ on base percentage.

The Mets are going to give Daniel Murphy a chance to win the second base job, but I'd prefer to play Ruben Tejada there. Tejada impressed me with his fearlessness and overall solid fundamental play. Early in the season, he was overmatched, but never gave up. He puts a good move on the inside pitch and I believe will be a solid hitter and fielder at the big league level. The 21-year-old has hit above .280 in his last two minor league seasons, takes his walks and has some speed.

After a difficult 2009 season when there were questions as to whether he'd been psyched out by the vast dimensions of Citi Field, David Wright had a very good comeback year. While he's criticized for the things he doesn't do—he's never going to be a megastar player—he's still unappreciated by Mets fans.

Wright had 29 homers and 36 doubles; batted .283 and his on base percentage dropped from its usual heights of .390 or above, to .354; he struck out 161 times, but that was misleading as he was k'ing at a breakneck pace early in the season but made better contact as the season wore on.

Jose Reyes missed most of spring training with a thyroid condition and was very streaky last season. Tried in the number 3 hole in the lineup (which I thought was a great idea), Reyes went into a funk. He showed flashes of being the five tool machine he was from 2005 to 2008, but his on base percentage sank to .321 and he stole only 30 bases. Reyes is still a superstar talent and is only 27, but he's a free agent at the end of the year and with the dollars thrown around for Carl Crawford, will the Mets be willing to invest over $120 million in Reyes if he has a big year?

That's what he's going to want. At least.

If the Mets are out of contention, they have to at least listen to offers for Reyes if he's playing well. They could trade him and then pursue him again as a free agent if they so desire.

I think Reyes is going to get traded and if he's playing up to his potential, they'll get a lot for him. A lot. It may be the right move in the long run.

Jason Bay struggled through his first season in New York. I doubt it was due to fear—he handled Boston with no problem—but with some players (Carlos Beltran for example) it takes a year to get accustomed to playing in New York. Bay's defense, criticized as "poor" due to his UZR ratings, was a very good defensive left fielder for the Mets; those that are immersed in UZR explained this as the season moved along... by altering their calculations. Lo and behold, Bay wasn't as bad as they initially thought. What a shock.

A concussion sustained while crashing into the left field wall at Dodger Stadium ended Bay's season after 95 games. I believe Bay will be back to his 25 homer, 100 RBI self this season and he was a surprise with his defense, speed, solid baserunning and all-around good play.

Carlos Beltran was unfairly blamed for the Mets slide after the All Star break because that's when he came back. Of course it's possible that the continuity of the club was disrupted by Beltran's insertion into the mix, but the Mets problems went far deeper than Beltran's defense or the shifting of Pagan to right and benching of Jeff Francoeur. Beltran regained his timing as the season wore on, but he's never going to be the force he once was. His injured knee is reducing his power from the left side of the plate and it's obvious. If he plays the full season, he can still hit his 20+ homers, hit a few doubles and get on base; even stealing a few with canniness once in awhile.

His Mets career has run its course; he's a free agent at the end of the season and it would be best for all if they parted ways and the Mets got some useful pieces for him.

Angel Pagan finally stayed healthy in 2010 and showed everyone what he could do if given the chance to play regularly. In 151 games, Pagan batted .290 with a .340 on base percentage; had 11 homers; 31

doubles and 7 triples, plus 37 stolen bases. The switch hitter played hard every play and was excellent defensively in center and right field. The big issue with Pagan has always been his health. I don't think that one healthy season means he's automatically gotten over that hump, but he's the heir apparent to Beltran.

BENCH:

Catcher Ronny Paulino will begin the season suspended for using a banned substance; he'll miss the first eight games of the season. Paulino is a good part-time catcher and, batting right-handed, will see time against tough lefties to spell Thole. He has some on base ability and a little pop. Paulino is a good handler of pitchers and throws well.

Luis Hernandez is a journeyman switch-hitting utility infielder. He can play second, third and short and batted .250 in 47 plate appearances for the Mets in 2010.

Daniel Murphy is being eyed as a possible solution to second base. He blew out his knee turning a double play on a take-out slide that was said to have been dirty. Murphy can hit enough to get 300-400 at bats in the big leagues, but he's not a good enough hitter to tolerate the likelihood of inadequate range at second base. I would make Murphy a roving utility player and use him as the Athletics (under Sandy Alderson) used Tony Phillips.

Brad Emaus is a 25-year-old infielder whom the Mets selected in the Rule 5 Draft from the Toronto Blue Jays. Emaus can play second or third and has 15-20 homer power; gets on base; hits plenty of doubles; walks and doesn't strike out. He bats right-handed and can even steal a few bases.

Veteran outfielder Scott Hairston signed a 1-year contract. Hairston can play all three outfield positions, has some pop, doesn't hit for a high average or get on base. He's a fifth outfielder on a good team; a fourth outfielder on the Mets.

Mets nemesis Willie Harris was signed to a minor league contract. Harris is a versatile outfielder/third baseman who had a habit of making terrific plays defensively and getting big hits against the Mets, some of which cost them dearly in 2007-2008 as they fell out of the playoff race. Harris has speed and some pop and is a better hitter than his .183 showing last year with the Nationals.

Nick Evans has shown flashes of being a useful righty bat in the big leagues, but former manager Jerry Manuel didn't like Evans for whatever reason. He's hit for power and put up good average/on base numbers in the minors and can play first base or the corner outfield positions.

Luis Castillo is in the same boat with Perez. Alderson has said that he'll have to earn his way onto the roster. It's highly, highly, *highly* unlikely he'll play well enough to win the starting job at second base in the spring and they won't able to trade him with other teams knowing the reality of the situation. I expect him to be released early in the spring so he has a chance to hook on somewhere else. It's time for him to go.

PREDICTION:

Best case scenario in the standings, the Mets are a .500 team. In the NL East, that might get them third place.

The best case scenario in practicality is if they're around 5-10 games under .500 into the summer, Beltran is playing center field well enough to convince a few teams that he can help them in their stretch drives and there will be a moderate bidding war for his services in a trade. Alderson is savvy enough to dangle him out there and get a good return for him.

Reyes and K-Rod are different matters. Reyes, a free agent, will yield a significant return in a trade if he's healthy and playing well. The Mets circumstances financially and on the field make it a question as to whether they're going to be able to give Reyes the contract he wants at the end of the season if they want to keep him.

I expect Reyes to be traded this summer.

K-Rod's contract is a huge obstacle; it's not something that can't be worked out. If he's pitching well and behaving, someone will take him.

Alderson and his people are sifting through the muck of years of disorganization and it's not an overnight process. This season is dedicated to seeing what they have in Thole, Murphy, Pagan, Niese, Dickey, Tejada and the young players on the way. After the year, Castillo, Perez and Reyes are coming off the books. They'll have money to spend next winter (maybe) and as much as they hesitate to say it, it's known that the Mets are in a so-called "bridge" year from the Minaya regime to what Alderson, his assistants and Collins are trying to build.

They're going to have a long year, but it could be productive if they're smart, fearless and aggressive in trading.

PREDICTED RECORD: 73-89

Washington Nationals

2010 Record: 69-93; 5th place, National League East.

2010 Recap:

The Nationals made a lot of moves in the winter of 2009-2010 seemingly designed to create a veteran-laden, competitive atmosphere for their young players to learn from. Ivan Rodriguez was signed to tutor the young pitchers; Jason Marquis to give innings; Miguel Batista and Matt Capps to bolster the bullpen. Veteran baseball man Jim Riggleman had been the interim skipper after Manny Acta was fired in 2008 and was given the permanent job because of his professionalism and competence.

It was all done with Stephen Strasburg in mind. Strasburg was the centerpiece of the Nationals rebuild and it was he who would lead them out of the wilderness. The pressure on a 21-year-old was stifling, but the Nationals protected him from the media and used him cautiously; he showed devastating stuff in the face of all that hype and was the real deal...before he got hurt.

Strasburg injured his elbow in a start against the Phillies and needed Tommy John surgery.

Marquis got hurt; Capps was traded.

In an effort to win as many games as possible early, Riggleman—never known for his gentility with his pitchers—overtaxed his bullpen. By the summer, the Nationals were short in the starting rotation and had a tired bullpen. They'd played respectably for a few months, but fell into their familiar spot of last place by the time 2010 drew to a close.

2011 ADDITIONS:

OF Jayson Werth signed a 7-year, $126 million contract.
1B Adam LaRoche signed a 2-year, $16 million contract.
LHP Tom Gorzelanny was acquired from the Chicago Cubs.
INF/OF Jerry Hairston Jr. signed a 1-year, $2 million contract.
RHP Henry Rodriguez was acquired from the Oakland Athletics.
OF Rick Ankiel signed a 1-year, $1.5 million contract.
RHP Todd Coffey signed a 1 year, $1.35 million contract.
1B Michael Aubrey signed a minor league contract.
OF Jeff Frazier signed a minor league contract.
RHP Chad Gaudin signed a minor league contract.
OF/1B Matt Stairs signed a minor league contract.
OF Jonathan Van Every signed a minor league contract.
RHP Tim Wood signed a minor league contract.
INF Alex Cora signed a minor league contract.
INF Matt Antonelli signed a minor league contract.

2011 SUBTRACTIONS:

OF/1B Adam Dunn was not re-signed.
OF Josh Willingham was traded to the Oakland Athletics.
INF Adam Kennedy was not re-signed.
OF/3B Willie Harris was not re-signed.
OF Justin Maxwell was traded to the New York Yankees.
LHP Scott Olsen was not re-signed.
C Wil Nieves was not re-signed.
RHP Joel Peralta was not re-signed.
RHP Miguel Batista was not re-signed.
RHP Jason Bergmann was not re-signed.
RHP Tyler Walker was released.
LHP Jesse English was not re-signed.
RHP J.D. Martin was not re-signed.
OF Kevin Mench was not re-signed.

2011 PROJECTED STARTING ROTATION: John Lannan; Tom Gorzelanny; Jason Marquis; Livan Hernandez; Jordan Zimmerman; Luis Atilano; Stephen Strasburg.

2011 PROJECTED BULLPEN: Drew Storen; Tyler Clippard; Todd Coffey; Craig Stammen; Sean Burnett; Doug Slaten; Yunesky Maya; Ross Detwiler; Collin Balester; Henry Rodriguez.

2011 PROJECTED LINEUP: C-Ivan Rodriguez; 1B-Adam LaRoche; 2B-Danny Espinosa; 3B-Ryan Zimmerman; SS-Ian Desmond; LF-Rick Ankiel; CF-Nyjer Morgan; RF-Jayson Werth.

2011 PROJECTED BENCH: 1B/OF-Mike Morse; C-Wilson Ramos; INF/OF-Jerry Hairston, Jr.; OF-Roger Bernadina; INF-Alberto Gonzalez; C-Jesus Flores.

2011 POSSIBLE CONTRIBUTORS: RHP-Brian Broderick; RHP-Adam Carr; RHP-Cole Kimball; LHP-Atahualpa Severino; RHP-Chien-Ming Wang; OF/1B-Chris Marrero; OF-Corey Brown; RHP-Chad Gaudin; RHP-Tim Wood; 1B-Michael Aubrey; OF/1B-Matt Stairs; INF-Alex Cora; INF-Matt Antonelli.

ASSESSMENTS

MANAGEMENT:

Does GM Mike Rizzo have some diabolical scheme that he's going to spring on us at any moment to humiliate the naysayers who suggest that the Nationals decision to give Jayson Werth a 7-year, $126 million contract was an exercise in lunacy?

This is the second year in a row that the Nationals have made expansion team-style acquisitions. Last year it was Pudge, Marquis, Capps, Kennedy and Batista; this year it's Werth, Adam LaRoche, Tom Gorzelanny, Rick Ankiel and Jerry Hairston, Jr.

Why?

Why would any team give Werth that much money and *why* would a team like the Nationals pay Werth megastar money?

That contract doesn't even qualify as desperation. It's madness.

I understood what they were doing last year with the veterans; all had good repuations; all could teach the younger players to play the game correctly; but Werth?

Really?

The acquisitions Rizzo has made this winter are the kind that a team on the cusp of contention makes to fill in the missing pieces and have role players who know how to win; not to build around.

Are they waiting for Strasburg again? Waiting for Strasburg and Bryce Harper? Hoping that Werth will evolve into a centerpiece player to combine with what they already have, which isn't much to be impressed about?

With the departures of Adam Dunn and Josh Willingham (who's as good a hitter as Werth and a better guy), have the Nationals improved with Werth? Or did they make a very, very expensive lateral move with their offense?

It says something that Werth's agent, Scott Boras, didn't take the offer and call it around to see if he could do any better because if word got out, someone might've contacted Rizzo and the Nationals and talked some sense into them before Werth accepted.

Considering the way they're running the organization, they probably wouldn't have listened; therefore, the point is moot.

Jim Riggleman restored sanity to the out-of-control Nationals clubhouse. He's a competent manager who is in control of his team and does all the side things a manager has to do in today's game with handling the media and adhering to the constraints placed upon him in handling top pitching prospect Stephen Strasburg.

Riggleman had a mandate to straddle the line of babying Strasburg and trying to win. This is the only conclusion I can draw from the way he overused his bullpen to keep the Nationals respectable early in the season. He's never been one to take it easy on his pitchers and while Dusty Baker was blamed for the decline of Kerry Wood, it's conveniently forgotten that the manager of the Cubs when Wood broke in and was regularly left on the mound to throw 120+ pitches was Jim Riggleman.

The epitome of the caretaker, if and when the Nationals are contenders, they're likely to have a new manager who can "take them to the next level" and Riggleman will move on to be the bench coach of another club and possibly take over as interim manager when somene's fired.

He's a good baseball man in a tough situation.

STARTING PITCHING:

John Lannan had a very good year in 2009 that, if he were on a good team, would've netted him close to 20 wins; in 2010, he was bad enough in the first half of the season that he wound up back in the minors. He pitched much better when he was recalled in August.

His fastball's better than you'd expect and he's got a good changeup. If he's not locating his pitches or is up in the strike zone, he gets blasted; his motion is deceptive and he's more suited to be a mid-rotation, innings man who needs a good offense for support and defense to catch the ball. Last season's numbers look worse than they were because of his terrible start. He wound up with an 8-8 record, 175 hits allowed in 143 innings with 14 homers allowed; 49 walks and 71 strikeouts. That's not that far off from what he put up in 2009. I think Lannan could have a turnaround season.

Veteran lefty Tom Gorzelanny was acquired from the Cubs for three minor leaguers. Gorzelanny had a fine year for the Pirates in 2007 as he went 14-10 and pitched 200 innings; since then, he's been up and down. Gorzelanny is similar to Lannan in that he's a lefty with a deceptive motion and needs to hit his spots to be effective. His stuff is a bit better than Lannan's; he throws harder and has a good slider.

He went 7-9 for the Cubs last season, but he pitched pretty well as a starter for the most part; I'm not sure why the Cubs traded him; he's a solid starter if he's healthy.

If nothing else in his career, Jason Marquis was durable before he got to the Nationals. Marquis only made 13 starts last season because of an elbow problem and when he pitched, he was atrocious. Marquis has always been more of a "hang around in games, eat innings and win" than a pitcher who could be counted on to do the job by himself. He has a decent fastball but walks too many hitters, gives up too many hits and homers. On a good team, he'd have some use. Problem is he's on the Washington Nationals.

Veteran Livan Hernandez had a good year for the Nats in 2010. In 33 starts, he went 10-12, but he was far better than his record. He allowed 216 hits in 211 innings (very good for him); and only allowed 16 homers. Hernandez has always been an innings-gobbler and his motion is so free and easy that it's not as if he's exerting himself out on the mound. Considering he'd had an ERA of nearly five (and sometimes over six) in every season since 2006, his 3.66 ERA in 2010 was impressive.

I'd be stunned if Hernandez repeats those numbers in 2011.

Righty Jordan Zimmerman is supposedly one of the top pitching prospects in the Nationals organization. Elbow surgery cost him a calendar year, but he has the stuff to be a good starter in the big leagues. He's wild, but has a good fastball and strikeout potential. The club was cautious in his use as he returned from injury, but he pitched well in 5 of his 7 starts last season.

26-year-old righty Luis Atilano made 16 starts last season and went 6-7. He allowed 96 hits in 85 innings and 11 homers, walked 32 and struck out 40. An elbow injury knocked him out from August until the end of the season. His wildness runs up his pitch counts and his stuff translates better to going once through a lineup.

Then we get to Stephen Strasburg.

They had all sorts of rules.

They had any number of usage dictates and limits to his public and media exposure.

Nothing was left to chance.

His once in a lifetime arm would not be allowed to break down due to any overuse on the part of the manager. The club was going to keep him healthy.

Strasburg was the meal ticket.

He had some shoulder stiffness and was kept out for two weeks to make sure he was healthy enough to pitch again. Never once did he surpass 100 pitches in a start.

With a fastball clocked at over 100 mph, a vicious curveball and terrific changeup, he's a Cy Young Award waiting to happen.

Then came that fateful day in Philadelphia when his elbow blew and it was revealed that he needed Tommy John surgery.

There was no one to blame; nothing to say or do.

It puts into question what good the rules did to anyone.

Pitching coach Steve McCatty slammed his hand into the dugout wall when Strasburg threw that pitch and walked off the mound with his arm dangling uselessly by his side.

All of baseball was devastated. The experts like Rick Peterson popped out of the woodwork and gave their diagnosis and self-promoting rhetoric wondering why, why, *why* the Nationals didn't come to him and use his state-of-the-art computerized studies and techniques to repair Strasburg's mechanics to prevent such an injury from happening.

Does it matter now?

We're seeing the end result of the paranoia that is prevalent with young pitchers today. Strasburg got hurt; Joba Chamberlain is a shadow of what he could've been. There's no evidence that the lack of use contributed to the injuries/ineffectiveness any more than letting them pitch would have. It was paranoia and fear that led to the "development" techniques masquerading as guidelines.

And he blew out his elbow anyway.

I will forever be convinced—and no one will ever admit this—that there are members of the Nationals organization that are relieved that he got hurt while the club was protecting him so fiercely; since he got injured under the mandate, there was no one to blame; no one who would forever have the onus hanging over them that *they* were respnsible for the Strasburg injury.

It's human nature.

When he's back, presumably, he'll still be on the innings/pitch counts; he'll still be the focal point of the future of the Washington Nationals.

They'd better hope he stays healthy next time.

BULLPEN:

23-year-old righty Drew Storen took over as closer after Capps was traded. Storen has been a dominating strikeout pitcher in the minors with a power fastball. In 55 innings in the big leagues last season, he allowed 48 hits, walked 22 and struck out 52. His numbers were blown up by a few bad games, but he was very good for the most part. He gets out lefties and righties and has the stuff to be a very good closer.

Tyler Clippard has become a devastating set-up man with great strikeout potential. He was overused by Riggleman early in the season and slumped at mid-season before regaining his form late. Clippard's motion is deceptive and his over the top fastball is hard to lay off when it's up in the strike zone; it explodes on the hitter. In 78 games, he pitched 91 innings and struck out 112—very impressive numbers. He did allow 8 homers. Clippard needs to be used more judiciously to prevent him from running out of gas late in the season, but he can be a top reliever.

Beefy righty Todd Coffey was signed to a 1-year contract after leaving the Milwaukee Brewers. Coffey throws hard and has strikeout stuff. He allowed 65 hits in 62 innings and struck out 56; he allowed 8 homers. He'll give up a crooked number occasionally and this knocks his ERA higher than it should be, but he's a competent reliever.

Craig Stammen has been a very hittable starter over the past two season and is better suited to be a long reliever. He allows too many hits and home runs and lacks a strikeout pitch. He's been a good minor league starter, but simply doesn't have the stuff to start in the big leagues.

Sean Burnett is a lefty who can handle batters from both sides of the plate. He struck out 62 in 63 innings last season as an occasional lefty specialist/occasional crossover reliever. He has good control and only allowed 3 homers.

Doug Slaten is a veteran lefty specialist. He held lefties to a .151 average last season. He can be a little wild with 19 walks in 40 innings, but he struck out 36 and for his career has been a solid lefty reliever.

Cuban defector Yunesky Maya made 5 starts late in the season and the soft-tossing righty got away with his lollipop fastball and non-existent breaking stuff because no one had seen him before. Either he'd better come up with a great spitball or start throwing left-handed; otherwise he's not going to be in the big leagues very long. The Nationals signed him to a 4-year, $8 million deal to secure his services. In a way, this is worse than the Werth deal because at least Werth has some use.

Lefty Ross Detwiler was a 1st round pick in the 2007 draft who's shown potential as a starter in the minors. He tore his hip labrum and missed most of last season. He's a contact pitcher with a sneaky delivery and could make it as a starter once he's healthy.

Collin Balester is a 24-year-old righty who was a mediocre starter in the minors, but showed a strikeout ability as a reliever in the big leagues last season. He walked 11 and struck out 28 in 21 relief innings in 2010.

Henry Rodriguez was acquired from the Athletics in the Josh Willingham trade and has a 100-mph fastball. He walked 13 and struck out 33 in 27 innings for the A's last season. He's 24 and has closed in the minors. I wouldn't have traded Willingham, but Rodriguez may end up justifying the deal with his fastball.

LINEUP:

Last season, Ivan Rodriguez was signed to provide a veteran presence and handle Strasburg. He can't really hit anymore as he batted .266 with a .294 on base and 4 homers. He still throws well from behind the plate and calls a good game. Now his job will be to tutor young catching prospect Wilson Ramos, something for which Pudge is well-suited and willing to do.

Adam LaRoche is one of those players who is always caught on the outside looking in at free agent time. Like Orlando Hudson, he's too good to take a low-level one-year deal, but not good enough to get a 3-4 year contract. He's a decent fielder; hits 20+ homers and 40 doubles; drives in 80-100 runs; and is a well-liked professional person. Now he's got a 2-year, $16 million deal with the Nationals and is a productive, relatively inexpensive pickup.

Danny Espinosa is a 24-year-old switch-hitter who has put up excellent power speed numbers in the minors. He has a good eye and strikes out a lot. In 112 plate appearances with the Nats last season, he batted .214 with 6 homers. He'll get every opportunity to win the second base job.

Ryan Zimmerman is one of baseball's stars that no one pays much attention to. Every year the numbers go up with power, a .300 average and 70 extra base hits. He's a great fielder and has a flair for the dramatic. After the contract the Nationals gave to Werth, the right thing to do would be to tear up or extend the contract worth $45 million Zimmerman signed in early 2009.

Ian Desmond is a smooth fielding shortstop with pop. He hit 10 homers, had 27 doubles, 4 triples and 17 stolen bases last season. He's impatient at the plate and strikes out a lot, but once he learns to command the strike zone, he could be an All Star.

Rick Ankiel continues his jaunt around baseball as an outfielder who will hit for some pop and play good defense in the outfield with the great arm from his days as a pitcher. He missed a large portion of last season with a quadriceps injury and was traded from the Royals to the Braves where he hit a game-winning homer in the playoffs. He's got power, but he's a journeyman oufielder.

Nyjer Morgan was considered a top defensive outfielder and the Nats were lauded for "stealing" him from the Pirates after trading Lastings Milledge and Joel Hanrahan in the deal. Morgan's defense took several steps back in 2010 and his attitude was horrible. He started a fight with the Marlins on the field by stealing bases with the Nationals far ahead and made obscene gestures to the fans after the fight. Morgan was already appealing a suspension for throwing a ball at a fan in Philadelphia and the fight added to the controversy surrounding him. He's all over the place as a player too. He steals 35 bases a year, but has been caught stealing 34 times over the past two seasons.

Jayson Werth was signed to that ludicrous contract which will keep him on the Nats payroll until he's 39. Werth is a good player who was in a highly advantageous situation with the Phillies. He was playing for a good team that made the playoffs four straight years. He puts up good power and speed numbers, hits plenty of doubles and plays excellent defense. Werth also strikes out a lot and his reputation as a person isn't particularly positive.

Werth is not a player who should be the highest paid player on a team whether they're a contender or not. I understand having to overpay to get a player to join a non-contender; but giving Jayson Werth $126 million isn't a "slight" overpay. I am also concerned that he's going to relax and be pleased with his paycheck and not play as hard as he did before he got paid.

I expect him to play well for the Nats in the next 2-3 years, but by the time they're ready (*if* they're ready) to contend, Werth will be in his mid-30s.

This contract was deranged and has all the warning signs of a disaster.

BENCH:

Mike Morse has always been an impressive looking player, but never got a chance to play regularly in the majors. He's posted good power/on base numbers in the minors and last season, hit 15 homers, batted .289 and had a .352 on base in 98 games. With LaRoche signed to play first base, Morse will have to get his at bats in the outfield. If Morgan doesn't hit, it's a possibility that Werth could play center and Morse right. They might be a better team with that lineup.

Wilson Ramos was the Twins top prospect, but he was stuck behind Joe Mauer at catcher; it was still an interesting decision for the Twins to trade their top prospect for Matt Capps and a good use by the Nats of a pitcher they signed inexpensively and whose career they rejuvenated. Ramos is 23 and raw; defense is his strong suit; he's shown some pop in the low minors and if he listens to Rodriguez, he has a chance to be a good big league catcher.

Jerry Hairston Jr. was signed to a 1-year deal. He's a competent fielder anywhere you put him and has some pop in his bat to hit 10 homers if he's given consistent playing time.

Roger Bernadina is a 26-year-old outfielder who got a chance to play regularly last season and hit 11 homers in 461 plate appearances; he stole 16 bases and struck out 93 times. He should see regular at bats in the outfield.

Alberto Gonzalez is a utility infielder and defensive replacement who batted .247 with a .277 on base in 198 plate appearances.

Jesus Flores is a good defensive catcher who batted .301 with 4 homers and 15 RBI in 106 plate appearances last season. He's a backup.

PREDICTION:

I said it last year and I'll say it again this year: What are the Nationals doing?

Are they rebuilding? Are they trying to win now? Will the veteran players they've signed and traded for buttress a young foundation and combine to win an incrementally increasing number of games? Or are they spinning their wheels with no plan of action other than to do a lot of "stuff" to make it appear as if they're getting better when they're really not?

I have no idea what the thinking was in signing Werth to that contract; in trading Willingham; in letting Dunn leave.

I don't get it.

They did the same things last year and all it resulted in was a 69-93 season and false hopes that Strasburg was going to lead them through the wilderness.

If he does, it won't be until 2014 at the earliest.

By then Werth will be 35 and they'll have a whole new cast surround him and Strasburg; presumably Bryce Harper will be in the mix somewhere as well. But this is 2011 and the Nationals are in the exact same position as they were last season.

They'll finish in the same vicinity in the standings too.

PREDICTED RECORD: 66-96

National League Central Predicted Standings

		Wins	Losses	GB
1.	St. Louis Cardinals	88	74	---
2.	Milwaukee Brewers	84	78	4
3.	Cincinnati Reds	83	79	5
4.	Chicago Cubs	78	84	10
5.	Houston Astros	69	93	19
6.	Pittsburgh Pirates	65	97	23

St. Louis Cardinals

2010 Record: 86-76; 2nd place, National League Central.

2010 Recap:

It's hard to pinpoint exactly what went wrong with the Cardinals in 2010.

They had all the necessary components to win, but didn't.

With the best hitter in the game (Albert Pujols); an MVP candidate behind him (Matt Holliday); the best manager of his generation (Tony La Russa); a genius pitching coach (Dave Duncan); two aces at the top of the rotation (Adam Wainwright and Chris Carpenter); a top rookie pitcher (Jaime Garcia); a solid mid-season acquisition (Jake Westbrook), there was no reason for the Cardinals to be as inconsistent as they were.

After a hot start, they descended into mediocrity and while they're usually the ones pushing other teams around, they found themselves facing a team in the Cincinnati Reds that not only pushed them back, but essentially spit in their faces.

The bullpen was shaky at times; they were top-heavy in the lineup, but this doesn't explain the up-and-down nature of their season.

The Cardinals faded at the end and finished in second place behind the Reds in the NL Central despite having the talent to challenge for a championship.

2011 ADDITIONS:

OF/1B Lance Berkman signed a 1-year, $8 million contract.
INF Ryan Theriot signed a 1-year, $3.3 million contract.
C Gerald Laird signed a 1-year, $1.1 million contract.
INF Nick Punto signed a 1-year, $750,000 contract.
LHP Brian Tallet signed a 1-year, $750,000 contract.
RHP Maikel Cleto was a acquired from the Seattle Mariners.
RHP Miguel Batista signed a minor league contract.
LHP Raul Valdes signed a minor league contract.
LHP Renyel Pinto signed a minor league contract.
RHP Ian Snell signed a minor league contract.
OF Jim Edmonds signed a minor league contract.

2011 SUBTRACTIONS:

RHP Brad Penny was not re-signed.
INF Brendan Ryan was traded to the Seattle Mariners.
INF Aaron Miles was not re-signed.
LHP Dennys Reyes was not re-signed.
3B Pedro Feliz was not re-signed.
RHP Blake Hawksworth was traded to the Los Angeles Dodgers.
C Jason LaRue retired.
RHP Mike MacDougal was not re-signed.
C Matt Pagnozzi was not re-signed.
RHP Jeff Suppan was not re-signed.
OF Randy Winn was not re-signed.
OF Joe Mather was claimed off waivers by the Atlanta Braves.
LHP Evan MacLane was released to go to Japan.

2011 PROJECTED STARTING ROTATION: Chris Carpenter; Jaime Garcia; Jake Westbrook; Kyle Lohse.

2011 PROJECTED BULLPEN: Ryan Franklin; Jason Motte; Kyle McClellan; Trever Miller; Mitchell Boggs; Fernando Salas; Miguel Batista; Brian Tallet; Renyel Pinto; Raul Valdes.

2011 PROJECTED LINEUP: C-Yadier Molina; 1B-Albert Pujols; 2B-Skip Schumaker; 3B-David Freese; SS-Ryan Theriot; LF-Matt Holliday; CF-Colby Rasmus; RF-Lance Berkman.

2011 BENCH: OF-Jon Jay; INF-Nick Punto; C-Gerald Laird; INF/OF-Allen Craig; INF-Tyler Greene; C-Bryan Anderson.

2011 POSSIBLE CONTRIBUTORS: RHP-Bryan Augenstein; RHP-Maikel Cleto; RHP-Blake King; RHP-P.J. Walters; INF-Daniel Descalo; OF-Adron Chambers; OF Jim Edmonds.

ASSESSMENTS MANAGEMENT:

GM John Mozeliak's most pressing issue isn't the construction of the club itself but how the Albert Pujols contract situation is going to play itself out.

Presumably there wasn't the expectation of a big fissure between what Pujols was going to demand and what the Cardinals were willing to give him...until the Ryan Howard contract; until the Jayson Werth contract; until the Carl Crawford contract.

Pujols isn't stupid; he knows the Cardinals are limited in resources to pay him above and beyond as the Yankees and Red Sox can; that said, look at it from Pujols's point-of-view: why should he take not just less money, but drastically less money when far inferior players like Werth and Howard are making ridiculous salaries from teams in the same financial stratosphere as the Cardinals?

This is the maze Mozeliak and the Cardinals have to navigate as the spring training deadline for Pujols to sign an extension approaches. I don't blame him for it and I would think he wanted nothing more than five minutes alone with Ruben Amaro Jr. and Mike Rizzo when those contracts were announced.

Mozeliak has proven skillful at dancing between the raindrops of a front office that has acquired stat zombie leanings and the old-school manager, Tony La Russa, who has an irascible nature and is on a short-term, win-now mandate. He's put together a contending team under trying circumstances. They're top-heavy with expensive veterans and he relies on La Russa and Duncan to cobble together enough competence in the background players to support Pujols, Wainwright, Carpenter and Holliday and do it under a budget.

He does the best he can under the circumstances and isn't to blame for the ongoing Pujols drama.

With his Hall of Fame resume, Tony La Russa has the right to make demands on his upper management to try and win now. How much longer he intends to manage is the question and by now, it's doubtful he'll go elsewhere. At 66-years-old, I've long suggested that as long as he has Pujols, he'll figure he has a good chance to win; therefore, he'll be with the Cardinals as long as Pujols is. If Pujols leaves after this season, will La Russa retire? Or would he want to stay and start over again with a different core?

Carpenter isn't young; Ryan Franklin has said he's retiring after the season; there isn't a package of prospects on the way to rebuild and La Russa wouldn't have any interest in that anyway.

He signed a 1-year contract for 2011 with a mutual option for 2012.

La Russa is the best manager of this generation and his presence is worth nearly guaranteed contention. The Cardinals, with Pujols and La Russa, will be in the playoff hunt as long as there are sufficiently decent supporting cast members.

Every year we wonder if this is it for La Russa; with the Pujols situation hovering over the club like a vulture, he has to be wondering the same thing.

STARTING PITCHING:

Ace Adam Wainwright injured his elbow and underwent Tommy John surgery. He's lost for the year. The Cardinals will try Kyle McClellan, Mitchell Boggs or possibly sign Kevin Millwood as his replacement.

Chris Carpenter had his second straight predominately healthy season and led the National League in starts with 35. He went 16-9 with a 3.22 ERA, allowed 214 hits and 21 homers in 235 innings; walked

63 and struck out 179. Carpenter's injury history is a concern as he's missed nearly entire seasons three times in his career with maladies to every part of his body. That he's managed to stay healthy would lead me to believe that he's due for an injury.

Carpenter has Hall of Fame stuff with a good fastball, curve and cutter. But there are the injuries and the hovering specter of the Pujols situation. If the Cardinals fall from contention and can't sign or trade Pujols because of his no-trade clause, would they listen on Carpenter?

Carpenter is 36, is earning $15 million this season and has an option for 2012 at $15 million with a $1 million buyout. If he's healthy and pitching well, they could get a lot for him from a pitching hungry team with money like the Yankees.

It's something to watch.

Jaime Garcia is a 24-year-old lefty who finished 3rd in the Rookie of the Year voting. He went 13-8 in 28 starts with a 2.70 ERA; Garcia walked 64 and struck out 132 in 164 innings with only 9 homers allowed. A shoulder problem shortened his season.

La Russa and Duncan were judicious with Garcia's use and he rarely was used for over 100 pitches; Garcia has the potential to bust out and win 16-18 games this season, but after the shoulder issue and his age, along with still overcoming Tommy John surgery that cost him chunks of 2008 and 2009 season, he's not going to be pushed.

Jake Westbrook was acquired last summer in a three-team trade with the Padres and Indians that sent Ryan Ludwick to the Padres. A free agent at the end of the 2010 season, Westbrook signed a 2-year, $16.5 million contract to remain with the Cardinals. There's a mutual option for 2013. Westbrook had a nice recovery from Tommy John surgery and went 10-11 overall, 4-4 with the Cardinals in 12 starts. Westbrook is a professional pitcher who pounds the strike zone and, as long as he keeps the ball down, is very effective. I expect Westbrook to benefit greatly from the La Russa/Duncan tutelage and win 15 games with 200+ innings pitched.

Kyle Lohse has been awful since his breakout 2008 season that netted him a $41 million contract extension. Lohse is making $11.875

million each for 2011 and 2012. He missed substantial time last season with a forearm injury and got blasted when he did pitch. Lohse has great stuff when he's healthy, but injuries have sabotaged him repeatedly. It's about time to look at Lohse for what he is; what that is is a multi-talented righty who has the ability to dominate when he's on, but for the most part is injury-prone and, at best, inconsistent. He could come back and win 12-15 games or he could go 6-16 and miss two months with an injury.

You just don't know.

BULLPEN:

Ryan Franklin insissts he's going to retire at the end of the 2011 season. Franklin isn't a prototypical closer. He doesn't have that one dominating pitch, nor does he have an intimidating demeanor. While La Russa is known for the "name" closers he's had like Dennis Eckersley and Jason Isringhausen, he's also relied on journeymen like Dave Veres and Franklin. It's a frailty and a weakness in the Cardinals attack. Franklin gets crushed when he's not locating his pitches because he can't strike anyone out and he allows too many homers. I thought the Cardinals were going to try and find a better closer this past winter—namely Jonathan Broxton or Jonathan Papelbon—but they didn't. It's Franklin or bust.

Jason Motte has a near 100-mph fastball and deceptive short-arm motion. Motte can handle righties and lefties and strikes out a batter-per-inning; he allowed 41 hits in 52 innings and walked 18. I'd consider him as closer if Franklin struggles.

Righty Kyle McClellan might also be an option at closer. His numbers are nearly identical against righties and lefties; he throws strikes; has some strikeout ability and the stamina he lacked as a starter translates to multi-inning capabilities as a reliever.

Veteran lefty specialist Trever Miller had his ERA blown up to 4.00 by a couple of bad games, but with his ¾ lefty stuff, he's used intelligently by La Russa. Miller shouldn't be allowed to pitch to too many righties; he throws strikes, doesn't walk too many nor strike out too many.

Mitchell Boggs has been a decent right-handed starter in the minors, but he's a long man out of the bullpen in the majors. His control sometimes eludes him, but he struck out 52 in 67 innings and allowed 5 homers among the 60 hits he surrendered. Boggs is a useful long man/ spot starter.

Fernando Salas appeared in 28 games as a rookie in 2010, walked 15 and struck out 29 in 30 innings. He allowed 4 homers but can get out righties and lefties and has closed in the minors.

Veteran Miguel Batista was signed to a minor league contract and I expect him to make the club. Batista is a good guy to have on any staff because he'd mean, fearless and can pitch in any role from starter to set-up man to closer.

Brian Tallet was signed to a 1-year deal. Tallet has been a successful reliever in the past with the Blue Jays, but has struggled with the home run ball. He allowed 20 in 77 innings last season, which is ridiculous. If anyone can maximize his abilities as a lefty out of the bullpen, it's La Russa.

Renyel Pinto has also been a successful left-handed reliever with the Marlins. He has a funky, deceptive short-arm motion. He can be wild sometimes and allows his share of homers.

Raul Valdes pitched for the Mets last season and was useful out of their bullpen for stretches. He doesn't throw hard, but he throws strikes and struck out a batter per inning. Strangely, he held righties to a .216 average last season and got ripped by lefies for a .330 average and 4 homers.

LINEUP:

Yadier Molina battled a knee injury for much of the 2010 season and his production at the plate took a tumble from what he produced in 2008-2009. He batted .262 in 521 plate appearances. If he's healthy, I'd expect a bounceback year at the plate. Defensively, he's still state-of-the-art with a throwing percentage in nabbing basestealers at around 50%; a number which makes it suicidal to try and steal on him.

Molina also cemented his reputation as a player who loves the pressure and spotlight as he homered to win a fight-filled game with the Reds after Brandon Phillips made some ill-advised comments about the Cardinals, greeted Molina and the two started jawing at each other; a fistfight ensued.

He's hit some big homers before if you remember.

What's going to happen with Albert Pujols?

His contract is up after this season, he wants his extension done before spring training; he won't let the Cardinals trade him; and he wants to get paid commensurately with his abilities, production and so that he doesn't lose face by making less money than inferior players.

He has every right to make demands. But Pujols, as great as he is, has to understand that the Cardinals are not the Yankees. They can't give him $300 million and still filed a competitve club around him. He has to make a decision as to what's more important. Does he want to stay in St. Louis and wear one uniform for his whole career? Or does he want to chase the money and go elsewhere?

The talk is that Pujols wants an Alex Rodriguez-type contract. But if the Cardinals give him that, who else can they afford? It would be Pujols, Wainwright and Matt Holliday followed by a roster of players making the league minimum.

It's impossible to win that way.

Then there's the La Russa factor. If Pujols is there and La Russa isn't, Pujols is going to have significant say as to who the new manager is going to be. One of the most respected players in the game, even he can be corrupted by that power, which no player should reasonably have.

I doubt strongly that Pujols will leave the Cardinals, but he's not going to take extra-short money to stay either. Because the Phillies gave that contract to Howard, Pujols deserves his $200 million deal, but will the Cardinals find a way to make it financially feasible?

I can't imagine him in another uniform, but Wayne Gretzky was traded; Joe Montana left the 49ers; it can happen.

In the end, Pujols has to weigh his pride vs staying home vs winning.

I think he'll sign. He may already have signed by the time you're reading this.

Oh and as a player, he's still the best hitter in baseball and perhaps the best hitter I've ever seen. He's as dialed in as any hitter in history, rarely strikes out, is a great fielder and a leader in the clubhouse. He's going to win another MVP.

Skip Schumaker has made the transition into being a competent second baseman. His bat took a few steps back in 2010 after batting over .300 in each of the prior two seasons. After dipping to .265 with 24 extra base hits, I'm inclined to believe it was an off year for Schumaker and he'll be back around .300 again in 2011.

David Freese was making the most of his first opportunity to play regularly in the big leagues before an ankle injury ended his season.

Freese had been a good power hitter in the minors but didn't get his big league chance to play every day until last season at age 27. He was on his way to a respectable season with a .296 average, .361 on base and .765 OPS before he got hurt. He's an average fielder at third base.

Ryan Theriot was acquired from the Dodgers for Blake Hawksworth this winter. He's an average fielding shortstop who can also play second base. Theriot had some solid years with the Cubs in 2008-2009 batting over .280 with 20+ stolen bases. He draws a few walks and doesn't strike out.

Matt Holliday had an excellent season as Pujols's new lineup bodyguard. The Cardinals were criticized for the $120 million contract they gave to Holliday as they were supposedly bidding against themselves; whether Holliday will be worth the money in the latter stages of the contract remains to be seen, but he was fantastic last season. He hit 28 homers; drove in 103; batted .312 with a .390 on base and 45 doubles. Holliday gives everything he has on the field and is a clubhouse leader.

Colby Rasmus attracted controversy last season with his complaining about being unhappy with the Cardinals; his lack of full time player status; and that La Russa seemed to be picking on him. Rasmus has a very involved father who was his son's hitting coach and this tends to interfere with the club when they have a difference of opinion. Rasmus had supposedly asked to be traded which led to a frenzy of speculation as to what the Cardinals were going to do with him; teams started calling, but Mozeliak declared he wasn't trading him and La Russa started playing him every day.

It was made worse when Pujols called Rasmus out publicly during an angry clubhouse tirade.

Rasmus has All Star talent. He strikes out a lot, but he has power to hit 25-30 homers and steal 25 bases. He needs to stop whining.

Veteran Lance Berkman was signed to a 1-year, $8 million contract to try and play the outfield again after having not played there regularly since 2006. He's had injury problems and wasn't all that great an outfielder before. The defensive aspect could be an issue, but with the way the Cardinals pitchers induce ground balls and get strikeouts, I don't know if it's *that* much of an issue.

At the plate, Berkman still has power and on base skills and in the lineup with Pujols and Holliday—along with the motivation of free agency again next winter—I expect a big comeback year from the switch-hitting Berkman.

BENCH:

Jon Jay was given the chance to play regularly after the trade of Ludwick but he's not going to be a starter this season. Jay batted .300 with 19 doubles and 4 homers in 323 plate appearances and has shown 10 homer pop and speed in the minors. He can play all three outfield positions.

Veteran infielder Nick Punto was signed to a $750,000 contract. Punto can play the entire infield; he's a good fielder and baserunner and does little things to help his club win a few games. He batted .228 and .238 in the past two seasons, but he's a useful switch-hitter and versatile defender off the bench.

Gerald Laird was signed to a 1-year deal to backup Molina. Laird can't hit, but he's a good game-caller and throws well.

Allen Craig is a 26-year-old utility player who batted .246 in 124 plate appearances last season. Craig's shown 25 homer power in the minors and good on base skills. If Freese doesn't perform, Craig could see regular time at third base.

Tyler Greene is another utility player. He's a career .222 big league hitter in 238 plate appearances.

Bryan Anderson is a catching prospect who hit 12 homers in 82 games at Triple A Memphis last season. He's solid defensively and will probably be Triple A insurance for Molina.

PREDICTION:

The Cardinals are truly a team on the verge of drastic changes. With the Pujols situation what it is; La Russa going year-to-year; Carpenter's age; the absence of big time prospects, they're a team that has to win right now. Even if they don't come to a contract agreement with Pujols in the spring, this issue is not going to be settled by Pujols simply saying he's not going to discuss it until the end of the season; the reporters and fans are going to continually bring it up. What makes it more complicated is that Pujols has said he's not going to waive his no-trade clause if the Cardinals propose a deal.

La Russa's going to be asked about it as well and it won't take long for his irritable temper to reveal itself in a snit.

What are they going to do if they're struggling? If Carpenter gets hurt? If they can't sign Pujols?

Will they clean out other veterans? Will they aggressively take steps to make trades and improve the team immediately in the short term despite the fact that it could sentence them to five years in last place once La Russa's gone; once Pujols and Holliday get old?

They have to win now.

In the end, I believe Pujols will stay; that the club has enough talent to win the NL Central and make it to the playoffs; but that doesn't dismiss the chance that it could all go very wrong, very fast.

2011 could be the swan song for this La Russa-led Cardinals group with Pujols. I don't see it as likely, but it's possible.

Even without Wainwright, they're the best team in a moderately weak division.

PREDICTED RECORD: 88-74

Milwaukee Brewers

2010 Record: 77-85; 3rd place, National League Central.

2010 Recap:

With a power packed lineup led by Prince Fielder, Ryan Braun and Corey Hart, the Brewers were fourth in the National League in runs scored; but it was pitching that was their problem.

The starting rotation was inconsistent at best behind the superlative Yovani Gallardo; the bullpen, rife with overpaid underperformers LaTroy Hawkins and David Riske and the finished Trevor Hoffman was left to rely on young pitchers like John Axford and Zack Braddock who went through their growing pains.

Manager Ken Macha never seemed to reach the players; pitching coach Rick Peterson's supposed "guru" status couldn't work its magic with the pitchers they had.

After a bad start, they were never able to gain their footing and hovered around 10 games under .500 the entire season.

2011 ADDITIONS:

Manager Ron Roenicke was hired.
RHP Zack Greinke was acquired from the Kansas City Royals.
SS Yuniesky Betancourt was acquired from the Kansas City Royals.
RHP Shaun Marcum was acquired from the Toronto Blue Jays.
RHP Takashi Saito signed a 1-year, $1.75 million contract.
1B/OF Mark Kotsay signed a 1-year, $800,000 contract.

RHP Sean Green signed a 1-year, $875,000 contract.
C Wil Nieves signed a 1-year, $775,000 contract.
OF Brandon Boggs signed a 1-year contract.
C Mike Rivera signed a minor league contract.

2011 SUBTRACTIONS:

Manager Ken Macha was fired.
RHP Trevor Hoffman retired.
SS Alcides Escobar was traded to the Kansas City Royals.
OF Lorenzo Cain was traded to the Kansas City Royals.
RHP Jeremy Jeffress was traded to the Kansas City Royals.
RHP Jake Odorizzi was traded to the Kansas City Royals.
RHP Dave Bush was not re-signed.
LHP Chris Capuano was not re-signed.
RHP Todd Coffey was not re-signed.
LHP Doug Davis had his option declined.
OF Joe Inglett was non-tendered.
RHP David Riske was not re-signed.
RHP Chris Smith was not re-signed.
C Gregg Zaun was not re-signed.
OF Adam Stern was not re-signed.

2011 PROJECTED STARTING ROTATION: Yovani Gallardo; Zack Greinke; Shaun Marcum; Randy Wolf; Chris Narveson.

2011 PROJECTED BULLPEN: John Axford; Takashi Saito; Zack Braddock; LaTroy Hawkins; Manny Parra; Kameron Loe; Sean Green; Mike McClendon; Mitch Stetter.

2011 PROJECTED LINEUP: C-George Kottaras; 1B-Prince Fielder; 2B-Rickie Weeks; 3B-Casey McGehee; SS-Yuniesky Betancourt; LF-Ryan Braun; CF-Carlos Gomez; RF-Corey Hart.

2011 BENCH: OF-Chris Dickerson; C-Jonathon LuCroy; C-Wil Nieves; INF-Craig Counsell; 3B-Mat Gamel; OF-Brandon Boggs; 1B/OF-Mark Kotsay.

2011 POSSIBLE CONTRIBUTORS: INF-Luis Cruz; INF-Eric Farris; RHP-Pat Egan; RHP-Justin James; RHP-Brandon Kintzler; RHP-Mark Rogers; RHP-Cody Scarpetta; C-Martin Maldonado.

ASSESSMENTS
MANAGEMENT:

With the Brewers in need of starting pitching, GM Doug Melvin took steps to repair the problem by getting Shaun Marcum from the Blue Jays. To get him, he surrendered a top infield prospect in Brett Lawrie; Marcum fills a hole in the now.

Still unsatisfied with the starting rotation, Melvin pulled off a bigger score when he sent four players to the Royals for former American League Cy Young Award winner Zack Greinke. To get Greinke, he had to take the contract of Yuniesky Betancourt as well.

With the future in Milwaukee of the club's biggest (literally and figuratively) star, Prince Fielder in doubt, Melvin decided to go for it now. Time will tell if he made the right decision and you can't say he didn't acquire quality in the starting rotation.

Melvin is a competent GM who made some ghastly mistakes on relief pitchers in recent years, namely David Riske and LaTroy Hawkins. The Brewers were a mediocre club last year managed by Ken Macha, who was disliked by the players. The Macha hiring and bullpen errors are on the record of Melvin.

He's an aggressive GM when the team is in contention as evidenced by his go-for-it acquisition of C.C. Sabathia in 2008. The prospects he surrendered to the Indians in that deal haven't done anything in the big leagues yet so that softens the blow of not retaining Sabathia.

Aside from perhaps Mat Gamel, the Brewers are out of prospects to deal for a big name; with that in mind, the Brewers had better win this year; either way, they're going to have a drastically different look in 2012.

Ron Roenicke was selected as the new manager over some high profile candidates. One report had Bobby Valentine getting the Brewers job but it turned out to be a false rumor. Roenicke was a journeyman player who had to wring every ounce out of his limited ability to carve out an eight year career in the majors. He was a coach on Mike Scioscia's staff with the Angels for 11 years and managed for 5 years in the minors for the Dodgers and Giants.

With his vast experience as a big league coach and minor league manager, he's well-equipped to step right into the Brewers dugout and handle every aspect of the job.

That doesn't mean he will.

There have been many coaches and experienced minor league managers (Trey Hillman for example) who looked great on paper, but failed in practice. Roenicke is a baseball lifer and his association with Scioscia is a great start for being a competent field boss; but we won't know until he's dealing with a crisis or running a game in the spotlight. And the Brewers aren't a rebuilding team with a modest payroll; they're expected to win.

STARTING PITCHING:

Yovani Gallardo is one of the top young pitchers in baseball. The 25-year-old righty went 14-7 last season in 31 starts. He struck out 200 batters for the second straight season and had a solid hits/innings pitched ratio at 178/185 with only 12 homers allowed.

Gallardo has a live fastball and a wicked curve; he has great mound presence and confidence. The only problem he has is his control as he walked 75 last season and ran up high pitch counts that prevented him from pitching deeply into games. That said, his control and homers allowed both improved markedly in 2010 from 2009. The homers dropped from 21 to 12; the walks from 94 to 75.

One of these years, he's going put it all together and win 20 games. I don't think it's going to be this year; his improvements have come incrementally, but 16 wins is a reasonable goal with better control in 2011.

Zack Greinke was acquired from the Royals as the biggest name traded this winter.

Like Gallardo, Greinke has Cy Young-caliber stuff with a better feel for pitching. Greinke has a power fastball and control and the ability to accelerate his fastball from 92-93 to 97 when he needs it. He has a full arsenal with a curve, slider and changeup and is willing to pitch inside.

His AL Cy Young Award year in 2009 would've been difficult to match no matter what he did, but he struggled for long stretches in 2010. His ERA rose from 2.16 to 4.17; his strikeout dropped from 242 to 181 (in only 9 fewer innings); his hits allowed rose from 195 to 219; and homers allowed from 11 to 18.

While his numbers were knocked out of whack by games in which he allowed 8, 7 (twice) and 6 runs, he was nowhere near as good as he was in 2009. The move to the National League will help him improve on that performance, but if people are expecting a Roy Halladay-level of dominance, they'd better remember that Greinke has had issues with mentally handling his circumstances and has never been in a pennant race where big things are expected from him for a contending club.

I'm not prepared to say the Brewers are getting the pitcher from 2009; if they get the one from 2010, he'll win his share of games, but that's not what the Brewers are looking for; not what they need.

Shaun Marcum had a fine season for the Blue Jays after missing nearly the entire 2009 season with Tommy John surgery. In 31 starts, Marcum went 13-8 with a 3.64 ERA; he pitched 195 innings, allowed 181 hits, walked 43 and struck out 165. Marcum has a vast array of stuff led by a good fastball and slider. In 2010 he was economical and pitched deeply into games and if he repeats last season's performance for the Brewers, he'll win 18 games.

Veteran Randy Wolf was miscast as a top of the rotation starter last season and is better suited for the back end and that's where he'll be with these Brewers. Wolf was durable and pitched well in 2010 with a 13-12 record and 215 innings pitched. For years Wolf was injury prone, but this was the second straight season of 214+ innings. He allows his homers (29); walks (87) and around a hit per inning. He was a solid, durable veteran last season and that's what the Brewers need in 2011.

Chris Narveson is a 29-year-old lefty who went 12-9 in 37 appearances last season (29 starts). In 167 innings, he allowed 172 hits and 21 homers; he walked 59 and struck out 137. Narveson joined the rotation in May and evolved into a reliable starter. Interestingly, Narveson wasn't a particularly good starter in the minors. I'd be reluctant to expect him to repeat his work from last season; it was only a few months after years of inconsistency in the minors; but he won't be expected to do all that much in this rotation and it should help him relax.

BULLPEN:

John Axford took over as closer when Trevor Hoffman couldn't get anyone out. With a handlebar mustache reminiscent of Rollie Fingers, the 28-year-old Axford had a fine year. In 58 innings he struck out 76 and walked 27; he allowed 42 hits and only 1 homer. Axford was never a closer as a professional and was mired in the minors for the Yankees and Brewers before getting to the big leagues to stay last season.

The Brewers have found themselves a closer.

Veteran reliever Takashi Saito signed a 1-year contract with the Brewers after being dumped by the Braves. Saito has had injury issues, but when he's healthy he racks up the strikeouts. Saito was an underrated closer with the Dodgers but his injuries keep cropping up and shortening his season. He's 41-years-old so the Brewers are going to have to be judicious with his use; but when he *is* healthy, he's a good pitcher who gets out both lefties and righties.

23-year-old Zack Braddock is a hard-throwing lefty with a hard fastball and great strikeout ability. His control was scattershot in the big leagues with 19 walks, but he only allowed 1 homer in 33 innings with 42 strikeouts.

Braddock's control in the minors was fantastic so it's possible that he wasn't trusting his stuff and was giving the big league hitters too much credit. If he pounds the strike zone with his fastball, he's tough to hit.

LaTroy Hawkins signed a 2-year contract worth $7.5 million before last season and was a disaster. Hawkins missed most of the season with a shoulder problem and when he did pitch, he was awful. I would expect nothing from Hawkins this season and be happy if he's able to provide anything at all. If GM Melvin has a blind spot, it's for mediocre veteran relievers; first he made the mistake in giving David Riske 3-years and $13 million, then it was Hawkins. That's not the way to build an efficient bullpen.

Lefty Manny Parra had better hope he finds a home in the Brewers bullpen as a reliever because the only way he's going to get back into that starting rotation is if someone kidnaps Narveson. Parra was serviceable for a few starts but soon fell back into familiar duck and cover mode. He gives up a lot of hits and a lot of home runs, but the one thing he can do is strike people out. Parra was decent as a reliever last season and although lefties pummel him, maybe he'd be better off going once through a lineup.

6'8" righty Kameron Loe had a solid year out of the Brewers bullpen last season. In 53 games, he pitched 58 innings and allowed 54 hits; he walked 15 and struck out 46. He allowed 6 homers but his sinker and slider allow him to get plenty of ground balls.

Sean Green signed a 1-year deal after being non-tendered by the Mets. Green has adopted a sidearm delivery and increased the movement on his pitches which could make him a very useful arm against righty bats. Naturally with such a dramatic alteration in one's delivery, it's hard to maintain a release point and have control; he did strike out more than one batter an inning for the Mets last season after returning from injury, but he walked 8 in 9 innings. Green could have some use as a righty specialist.

Mike McClendon is a 26-year-old righty with closing experience in the minors. In 21 innings last season for the Brewers he allowed 15 hits and struck out 21. He walked 7 and allowed 2 homers. He's versatile and could be used as a set-up or long man.

Mitch Stetter is a lefty with a deceptive motion. Stetter had been a very good lefty specialist in 2009, but got blasted last season and wound up back in the minors and got hammered down there too. Lefty relievers tend to have nine lives and their performance fluctuates. Stetter could have a comeback year.

LINEUP:

George Kottaras is the veteran amongst the lot of Brewers catchers. Kottaras hit 9 homers last season after Gregg Zaun got hurt. Kottaras isn't a great thrower, strikes out too much and hit those 9 homers in 250 plate appearances. He'll share time with young Jonathan Lucroy.

In his final arbitration season before free agency, Prince Fielder agreed to a 1-year, $15.5 million deal for 2011. After this year, he's going to get paid by someone. The Brewers haven't come to an agreement with his agent Scott Boras and at this point, a deal is unlikely; the Brewers can't afford to pay Fielder what he wants and considering what Ryan Howard got from the Phillies, Fielder's going to want a comparable deal.

There was talk that the Brewers would consider dealing Fielder, but that was before they upgraded the starting rotation with Greinke and Marcum; they're going for it now and the best way to do that is with Fielder. Of course, if the season goes wrong, they'd be foolish not to see what the market is for Fielder and decide if an offer is superior to the draft picks they'll get when he departs.

Fielder is a pure basher at the plate who'll hit his 35 homers and have an on base percentage over .400. His numbers took a fall from 2009 as he dropped from 46 homers to 32, but he got off to a bad start in the power department with only 7 homers by June when he turned on the power. I expect a massive, MVP-quality year from Fielder as he heads into free agency.

Rickie Weeks finally lived up to the potential that made him the second pick in the 2003 draft. Weeks played in 160 games, had 175 hits, 32 doubles, 4 triples and 29 homers; he walked 76 times. He strikes out a lot with 184 last season, but if he puts up 65 extra base hits again, I'm sure the Brewers won't mind.

Finally given an everyday job, Casey McGehee built on his 16 homer season in 2009 with 23 homers, 38 doubles and 104 RBI. He batted .285 and had a .337 on base. Not bad for a player plucked off waivers from the Cubs two years ago.

Yuniesky Betancourt is reviled in stat zombie circles because he's poor defensively and never gets on base. He's owed a guaranteed $6 million in 2011 and despite his flaws, I prefer to look at the positive. They couldn't have gotten Greinke if they didn't take Betancourt; former shortstop Alcides Escobar, who went to the Royals in the trade, has more potential but didn't hit last season. Betancourt did hit 29 doubles and 16 homers last season. If he provides some pop, things could be worse.

Ryan Braun is one of the best young sluggers in baseball and is locked up in a long term contract through 2015. Every year the numbers go up: 40 doubles; 25 homers; 15 stolen bases; a .300 average; and a .360+ on base. He's a decent defensive outfielder and is an MVP candidate.

Carlos Gomez is 25 and it's time for him to fulfill his potential. He's fast and a fine defensive center fielder, but he has no patience at the plate and doesn't seem to be trying to learn to wait for a pitch to hit. He doesn't get on base and strikes out too much.

Corey Hart was on the trading block for much of the first half of the season and there were strong rumors he was heading to the San Francisco Giants, but he started hitting home runs at a rapid rate and suddenly the Brewers signed him to a 3-year, $26 million contract extension. Hart batted .283 with 31 homers, 34 doubles and 102 RBI. He's an average defensive right fielder.

BENCH:

Chris Dickerson was acquired from the Reds last August for veteran Jim Edmonds. Dickerson got a chance to play semi-regularly in the big leagues in 2009 and responded with a .275 average and .370 on base in

299 plate appearances. He's shown some speed and pop in the minors and can play center field. He struggled last season with the Reds and Brewers but if Gomez doesn't improve, Dickerson could get a chance to play.

Jonathan Lucroy will get his share of at bats behind the plate sharing time with Kottaras. Lucroy's shown power and on base ability in the minors and can really throw. I would expect him to be given every opportunity to win the everyday job, but manager Roenicke, having worked with Mike Scioscia for so long, might prefer the veteran Kottaras to handle the pitchers, at least to start the season.

Wil Nieves is a veteran backup catcher who was signed from the Washington Nationals. He's alright defensively, but can't hit.

Veteran utility player Craig Counsell returns for another season. Counsell is 40 but like Omar Vizquel, he's still savvy enough to help his team win with the opportunistic walk; a clutch hit; a timely stolen base or bunt.

Mat Gamel's time as a prospect is running out. He's put up good power/on base numbers in the minors; he has nothing left to prove down there, but hasn't hit in the big leagues and his way is blocked by McGehee and Fielder. Gamel was mediocre in a brief big league trial in 2009 and spent most of 2010 in the minors where he hit 13 homers in 82 games. It makes no sense to keep him in the big leagues if he's not going to play, but there's nowhere for him *to* play.

Brandon Boggs signed a 1-year contract coming over from the Rangers. Boggs spent most of 2010 in Triple A for the Rangers and had a fine season with a .290 average and .410 on base percentage with 10 homers. He can play all three outfield positions.

Veteran Mark Kotsay signed a 1-year contract. Kotsay was miscast as one of the White Sox rotating mediocrities at DH last season, but he's a decent defensive first baseman and has some pop off the bench.

PREDICTION:

Because of their flashy acquisitions, the Brewers are a trendy pick to contend for a playoff spot. They can hit and have excellent starting pitching.

But I have concerns.

Their defense is shaky all over the field; they're carrying black spots in their lineup in center field and at catcher; the bullpen has potential, but is untested; and Ron Roenicke is a rookie manager.

They've acquired Greinke who has some of the best stuff in baseball and also has a history of mental issues. There won't be an answer as to whether he can handle teamwide expectation until he handles them.

I don't like teams with this many questions.

I don't like them at all.

Fielder is going to have a massive season in preparation for free agency; Braun is a masher; Weeks is blossoming and McGehee and Hart are reliable.

But those questions are haunting me. What good is terrific pitching if they can't catch the ball? If the bullpen implodes? If Roenicke makes rookie managerial mistakes?

I'm not buying the Brewers this year and I think they're going to be inconsistent and fade out by season's end.

PREDICTED RECORD: 84-78

Cincinnati Reds

2010 Record: 91-71; 1st place, National League Central.
Lost to Philadelphia Phillies in NLDS 3 games to 0.

2010 Recap:

The Reds rode a powerful lineup which led the league in runs scored; a mix of young and old in their starting rotation, and a deep and diverse bullpen to their first playoff appearance since 1995. In doing so, they saved manager Dusty Baker's job.

With young, All Star talents Jay Bruce and Johnny Cueto; veteran leaders Scott Rolen and Bronson Arroyo; cogs young and old Mike Leake, Drew Stubbs, Brandon Phillips; and the exhilerating Cuban rookie with his 105 mph fastball, Aroldis Chapman; and of course, NL MVP Joey Votto, the Reds were a fun team to watch.

After getting off to a slow start, it appeared to be another customary season in the NL Central with the Cardinals winning it by default; but the Reds kicked it into high gear and fought—literally and figuratively—with the Cardinals. The turning point indeed appeared to be the bench clearing brawl started by Brandon Phillips's ill-advised negative comments about the Cardinals; the Reds were swept in the series, but subsequently went on a tear to take over first place.

The Reds took control of the division in late August and never looked back staring straight into the faces of the Cardinals, pushing them back and winning.

Overmatched against the blazing Phillies in the NLDS, the Reds were no-hit in the first game by Roy Halladay and were swept away before realizing they were even in the playoffs to begin with.

2011 ADDITIONS:

SS Edgar Renteria signed a 1-year, $2.1 million contract.
OF Fred Lewis signed a 1-year, $900,000 contract.
OF Jeremy Hermida signed a minor league contract.
LHP Dontrelle Willis signed a minor league contract.

2011 SUBTRACTIONS:

RHP Aaron Harang's option was declined.
LHP Arthur Rhodes was not re-signed.
SS Orlando Cabrera's option was declined.
RHP Russ Springer was not re-signed.
INF/OF Willie Bloomquist was not re-signed.
OF Jim Edmonds was not re-signed.
RHP Mike Lincoln was not re-signed.
OF Gary Matthews, Jr. was released.
OF Laynce Nix was not re-signed.
RHP Micah Owings was not re-signed.

2011 PROJECTED STARTING ROTATION: Bronson Arroyo; Johnny Cueto; Edinson Volquez; Mike Leake; Homer Bailey; Travis Wood.

2011 PROJECTED BULLPEN: Francisco Cordero; Aroldis Chapman; Nick Masset; Logan Ondrusek; Jordan Smith; Danny Herrera; Bill Bray; Matt Maloney.

2011 PROJECTED LINEUP: C-Ramon Hernandez; 1B-Joey Votto; 2B-Brandon Phillips; 3B-Scott Rolen; SS-Edgar Renteria; LF-Johnny Gomes; CF-Drew Stubbs; RF-Jay Bruce.

2011 BENCH: C-Ryan Hanigan; OF-Fred Lewis; INF-Paul Janish; INF-Miguel Cairo; INF-Juan Francisco.

2011 POSSIBLE CONTRIBUTORS: LHP-Dontrelle Willis; RHP-Jose Arrendondo; RHP-Jared Burton; RHP-Carlos Fisher; INF/OF-Yonder Alonso; INF-Chris Valaika; OF-Todd Frazier; OF-Chris Heisey; C-Yasmani Grandal.

ASSESSMENTS
MANAGEMENT:

Walt Jocketty again proved himself as one of the top GMs in all of baseball in turning a heretofore forgotten club into a winner.

It took a great leap of faith to believe that Scott Rolen would overcome his rampant injuries; that Mike Leake was ready to make it in the big leagues a year out of college; that Joey Votto would come back from off-field mental issues; that Aroldis Chapman would harness his devastating power into a useful component.

A similar mix of young and old that Jocketty won with as GM of the Cardinals, they were an eclectic mix, but it worked.

Many things went right for the Reds in 2010 and it's unfair—given Jocketty's history of success—to chalk it up to anything other than baseball intelligence and belief in players he knew.

Last year I felt that 2010 was the make-or-break year for both Jocketty and manager Dusty Baker; had the club not played well, I saw it as a possibility that both would be replaced.

Jocketty was right about last year's Reds and I was completely wrong.

After his final nightmarish year with the Cubs and two bad years for the Reds, Baker's reputation as a winner was taking a beating. Long reviled by the stat zombies for his unique ways of running a game and clubhouse, the one thing Baker had on his side was his record of success; with that gone, what was left?

In the final year of his contract and with his job clearly on the line, Baker turned the Reds into a winner. The players have always played hard for Baker and Baker fights for them with the umpires and opposition (Tony La Russa) if need be.

He accounted for a predominately young starting rotation by doling out their innings cautiously and relied on a deep bullpen. The lineup ran itself and when he was presented with the devastating weapon in Aroldis Chapman, he unleashed him on an unsuspecting National League without putting too much pressure on the newcomer, nor did he overuse him.

It has to be accepted that despite his faults, Baker is a successful manager who wins. He received a 2-year contract extension through 2012.

STARTING PITCHING:

Bronson Arroyo is an innings-eater who gets by with intelligence, control, durability and fearlessness. Every year, he puts up his 200+ innings and battles his way through games. Arroyo had suffered through the Reds mediocrity since arriving in probably the worst trade in Theo Epstein's Red Sox tenure (Wily Mo Pena? Really?) and used a unique motion with a straight kick leg lift like a Rockette, a sneaky fastball, a great slow curve and command.

Arroyo gives up a lot of home runs (29 in 215 innings), but he only allowed 188 hits and walked 59. It's hard to do damage with home runs when there's no one on base. He's underappreciated, but he's almost a guaranteed performer and that's why the Reds gave him a 3-year, $35 million contract extension through 2013.

25-year-old righty Johnny Cueto is developing into an All Star caliber starter. Cueto has a moving fastball, curve and change and good control. In 185 innings, Cueto allowed 181 hits, walked 56 and struck out 138; he allowed 19 homers. Cueto has been used relatively cautiously by Baker and he's slowly building his innings up to where he can be expected to reach 200 this season. He could blossom into a 15-18 game winner.

Edinson Volquez returned from Tommy John surgery and PED suspension to pitch respectably in 12 starts and help the Reds to their division title. Volquez was acquired from the Rangers for Josh Hamilton after the 2007 season and had a fantastic year in 2008 for the Reds, winning 17 games. Volquez has a good fastball and devastating changeup; he racks up high pitch counts because of his wildness and strikeouts and doesn't allow many homers. Coming off of surgery, he was limited in the number of pitches he was allowed to throw; this season the shackles should be loosened and I'd expect him to be close to what he was in 2008.

Righty Mike Leake was drafted in the first round of the 2009 draft and found himself in the Reds starting rotation in 2010. Leake reminds me of Arroyo with his control and array of pitches; he throws strikes and allows a few too many homers. He was in the rotation through August and pitched well but appeared to tire; the Reds switched him to the bullpen to limit his innings and he wound up on the disabled list in September with a shoulder issue. Leake has a chance to be a solid if not spectacular pitcher in the big leagues. I'm not sold on him; let's see how he does as he makes his way around the league in his second year; I have a feeling he may wind up in the minors in 2011.

Homer Bailey was the Reds top pitching prospect but injuries and inconsistency have made him into a question mark. He has a good fastball and a great curve, but a tendency to think he knows everything which has led to him butting heads with the organization. Bailey pitched well for the Reds last season even as a shoulder problem landed him on the disabled list for much of the summer. Overall Bailey went 4-3 in 19 starts with 109 hits allowed in 109 innings and 100 strikeouts. He could be a consistent winner if he's healthy.

24-year-old righty Travis Wood had a more impressive rookie season than Leake and looked like more of a polished, big league ready starter than Bailey.

Wood throws hard, throws strikes and strikes people out. In 102 innings, he allowed 85 hits, 9 homers, 26 walks and struck out 86. Wood's small for a pitcher (5'11", 165 lbs) so durability might be a question, but he pounds the strike zone and trusts his stuff.

BULLPEN:

Francisco Cordero is no longer the most reliable closer; nor does he strike out as many hitters as he once did. For some closers like Jonathan Papelbon, it's possible to throw out a high ERA as the result of a few bad games that bloated his numbers; for Cordero, I don't think that's accurate. He's inconsistent, loses the strike zone, doesn't throw his fastball in the upper 90s anymore, and can be homer prone. With a $12 million salary for this season and a $12 million option for 2012 (with a $1 million buyout), this is likely the last year with the Reds for the 36-year-old.

I called it with Aroldis Chapman last year. Here's the quote from last year's book: "He's raw, but could be ready as soon as this season and I think he's going to be a mega-star."

After his explosion onto the big league stage he did nothing to dissuade me from this assessment. Chapman's fastball is un...be.... lieveable. Plus he has the personality and fearlessness that comes from pitching in Cuba and making the desperation escape from that country for the opportunity to pitch in the big leagues.

I've asked repeatedly and have yet to get an answer: how did the big financial guns the Yankees, Red Sox, Mets and Dodgers miss out on this guy? Just seeing him on film, I *knew* what he was; what he could be. Chapman threw 13 big league innings last season, walked 5 and struck out 19; he allowed no homers and it's going to be nearly impossible for a left-handed hitter to do anything at all with him. In fact, they looked triumphant when they were able to hit a pop up to the second baseman against him. His slingshot motion and quirky unfolding mechanics don't help the hitter's comfort level.

He's a devastating force in the bullpen and a prime candidate for Rookie of the Year.

Nick Masset is a big, hard-throwing reliever who racks up the strikeouts. Masset's numbers were bloated by a few bad games, but he was reliable for the entire season. In 76 innings, he allowed 64 hits, walked 33 and struck out 85. 7 homers in 82 appearances isn't terrible. He's a good set-up man.

Logan Ondrusek is a 6'8", 225 pound righty who was an integral part of the Reds bullpen as a rookie. Onderusek has closed in the minors, but has control issues and isn't a strikeout guy (39 in 58 innings). He's a solid reliever.

Jordan Smith is a 25-year-old righty who appeared in 37 games in relief as a rookie in 2010. He throws strikes and is hittable allowing 45 hits and 7 homers in 42 innings.

Diminutive lefty Danny Herrera is listed at 5'6 ½" which means he's probably closer to 5'5". Herrera relies on a screwball and got knocked around at times last season with 31 hits allowed in 23 innings, but he was good for the most part as a lefty specialist.

I've long been a fan of Bill Bray's stuff, but injuries and control issues have sabotaged his career. He has a good fastball and slider and is tough on lefties. At this point in his career, he's a lefty specialist and a pretty good one if he's healthy.

Matt Maloney is a 27-year-old lefty who's been a solid starter in the minors and appeared in 7 games in relief for the Reds last season. He has good control and can strike people out; he has the chance to be a long man/spot starter in the bigs.

LINEUP:

Ramon Hernandez forms a good platoon behind the plate with Ryan Hannigan. Hernandez throws well and handles the pitchers; has some pop in his bat and gets on base. Last season he batted .297 with a .364 on base with 18 doubles and 7 homers.

Joey Votto broke into superstardom with his MVP season in 2010. After struggling off the field with anxiety and dizziness, he started bashing early in the season and carried the Reds to the division title. Votto hit 37 homers; drove in 116; batted .324 and led the league with a .424 on base. His demeanor reminds me of Don Mattingly and he has the aura of a leader in the clubhouse. Votto signed a contract extension for 3-years and $38 million. He's one of the best hitters in baseball.

Brandon Phillips has a mouth that won't quit. I'm quite convinced that a large chunk of the Reds organization wishes he would keep his opinions—such as the perception of the Cardinals around baseball—to himself. What he said about the Cardinals being despised may have been true, but it wasn't necessary to say aloud and members of his own team could've gotten hurt in the ensuing brawl that *he* started singlehandedly.

On the field, he's a Gold Glove winner; a power bat; has speed; provides extra base hits and rarely strikes out. Phillips has a contract for this season at $12 million and an option for 2012 at $12 million with a $1 million buyout. It's hard to find second baseman who do all the things that Phillips does; they won't get rid of him unless he starts behaving so ridiculously that they have no choice.

After years of injuries ruining his annually great play offensively and defensively, Scott Rolen had a memorable comeback season. He played in 133 games (a lot for him), hit 20 homers, drove in 82; batted .285 and had a .358 on base. He won another Gold Glove and is still excellent defensively. Rolen's 36 and with the litany of injuries he's had, I'd hesitate to expect him to repeat last season's durability and numbers.

Edgar Renteria won the World Series MVP and felt insulted by the Giants offer of $1 million to come back. After the regular season he had, $1 million was a fair offer. He left the Giants and signed a 1-year, $2.1 million deal with the Reds to replace Orlando Cabrera. Renteria's defense is adequate and he still hits in the clutch; he's become injury-prone and can't be counted on to play in any more than 120 games.

Johnny Gomes is a consistent slugger in left field who'll provide close to 20 homers, 25 doubles and lots of strikeouts. He's also a feisty clubhouse leader who's ready to fight and plays hard every game. He's not a good defensive outfielder.

Drew Stubbs had 22 homers, 30 stolen bases and played very good defense in center field in his first full season in the majors. He struck out 168 times. The 2006 first round pick has always struck out a lot in the minors, but never hit for that much power. I'd be worried about a drop off in the homer department in his sophomore season.

Jay Bruce is on the verge of becoming a star. The top prospect had 25 homers and batted .281 with a .353 on base in 148 games. He stayed healthy, played excellent defense in right field and his numbers against righties and lefties were almost identical. After the woeful year he had against lefties in 2009, that's a tremendous improvement.

Bruce is an All Star waiting to happen.

BENCH:

Ryan Hanigan shares time behind the plate with Hernandez and is a good hitter with a high average and on base skills. Last season, he batted .300 and had a .405 on base in 243 plate appearances; he's a slap hitter with no power, but he walks a lot. He's a fine defensive catcher as well.

Fred Lewis was signed to a 1-year contract after leaving the Blue Jays. Last season, Lewis had 31 doubles, 5 triples, 8 homers and 17 stolen bases. He's a mediocre outfielder, but can play all three positions. Lewis is a good fourth outfielder.

Paul Janish is a utility infielder who might have to play semi-regularly depending on the health and production of Renteria; he also may see time if (when) Rolen ends up on the disabled list. Janish batted .260 in 228 plate appearances with 10 doubles and 5 homers.

Veteran Miguel Cairo is still around.

Yes.

It's true. And, in fact, Cairo was quite good for the Reds last season. In 226 plate appearances, he batted .290 with a .353 on base and was used all over the field. He's a professional in every sense of the word and can hit a fastball.

Juan Francisco is a 23-year-old, lefty-swinging third baseman who's shown 20-homer power in the minors and might get a shot to play if Rolen gets injured.

PREDICTION:

I've been wrong about the Reds just about every year for the past five years.

Last season I didn't think they'd hit enough; they led the league in runs scored.

I thought Baker was going to get fired; he won the division.

I wasn't sure about the players I mentioned in the recap of the 2010 season and they all went above-and-beyond the call of duty.

They have good starting pitching, but that bullpen—while having good arms and potential—is missing something aside from the dominating Chapman. Cordero is untrustworthy.

I can't shake the feeling that everything went right for the Reds last season specifically the young pitching and Rolen staying healthy.

The lineup isn't going to be as good as it was last season; if the starting pitching doesn't perform with a short bullpen in that tough division, the Reds are going to be missing those critical components that allowed them to win 90 games last season.

The Brewers are better than last year; the Cardinals are still the Cardinals.

The Reds won't repeat their division title from a year ago; they'll have a hangover from their success and fall to mediocrity.

PREDICTED RECORD: 83-79

Chicago Cubs

2010 Record: 75-87; 5th place, National League Central.

2010 Recap:

The Cubs were a strangely constructed and expensive team that was either going to get off to a good start and the veterans would play up to their career histories, or a bad start and have to try and sell off pieces as the season went down the tubes.

It was the latter.

Manager Lou Piniella grew so frustrated with the way the Cubs were playing that first he announced that 2010 would be his final season, then he resigned altogether. Carlos Zambrano epitomized what it means to be Carlos Zambrano as he pitched poorly as a starter, was moved to the bullpen as the world's most expensive set-up man, became a starter again, nearly got into a dugout fistfight with Derrek Lee, underwent counseling, came back and was unhittable in September under new manager Mike Quade.

Lee and Ted Lilly were traded away for prospects.

There were some positives. Carlos Marmol excelled as the closer; Marlon Byrd had a good year in his first with the Cubs; Ryan Dempster was again a fine starter; Tyler Colvin was a top rookie.

Top prospect Starlin Castro was recalled and, despite Quade having to bench him for lack of hustle, showed excellent skills.

And Quade acquitted himself well as the new manager and led the Cubs to a 24-13 record after Piniella's resignation.

2011 ADDITIONS:

Manager Mike Quade was hired as full-time manager.
1B Carlos Pena signed a 1-year, $10 million contract.
RHP Matt Garza was acquired from the Tampa Bay Rays.
RHP Kerry Wood signed a 1-year, $1.5 million contract.
OF Fernando Perez was acquired from the Tampa Bay Rays.
C Max Ramirez was claimed off waivers from the Boston Red Sox.
OF Reed Johnson signed a minor league contract.
INF Augie Ojeda signed a minor league contract.
RHP Todd Wellemeyer signed a minor league contract.
INF Scott Moore signed a minor league contract.
RHP Braden Looper signed a minor league contract.

2011 SUBTRACTIONS:

OF Xavier Nady was not re-signed.
OF Sam Fuld was traded to the Tampa Bay Rays.
LHP Tom Gorzelanny was traded to the Washington Nationals.
RHP Jeff Gray was not re-signed.
RHP Bobby Howry was released.
RHP Christopher Archer was traded to the Tampa Bay Rays.

2011 PROJECTED STARTING ROTATION: Ryan Dempster; Matt Garza; Carlos Zambrano; Randy Wells; Carlos Silva.

2011 PROJECTED BULLPEN: Carlos Marmol; Kerry Wood; John Grabow; Sean Marshall; Andrew Cashner; James Russell; Justin Berg; Jeff Samardzija; Scott Maine.

2011 PROJECTED LINEUP: C-Geovany Soto; 1B-Carlos Pena; 2B-Blake DeWitt; 3B-Aramis Ramirez; SS-Starlin Castro; LF-Alfonso Soriano; CF-Marlon Byrd; RF-Kosuke Fukudome.

2011 BENCH: OF-Tyler Colvin; C-Koyie Hill; INF-Jeff Baker; C-Max Ramirez; INF-Darwin Barney; OF-Fernando Perez.

2011 POSSIBLE CONTRIBUTORS: C-Welington Castillo; RHP-Alberto Cabrera; RHP-Thomas Diamond; LHP-John Gaub; RHP-Marcus Mateo; RHP-Kyle Smit; RHP-Jeff Stevens; RHP-Casey Coleman; RHP-Braden Looper.

ASSESSMENTS
MANAGEMENT:

Jim Hendry is a survivor.

The Cubs have been an overpaid dysfunctional nightmare with onerous and immovable contracts and have thrown bad money after bad, but Hendry's still there.

The Tribune company sold the club to the Ricketts family, but Hendry's still there.

Lou Piniella resigned because he couldn't deal with the catastrophic and "only the Cubs" occurrences, but Hendry's still there.

A stat guy names Ari Kaplan was brought in to work in the front office, but Hendry's still there.

And the Cubs are starting on a different path with the new owners, new front office people, new manager, new pitching coach...and Hendry's still there.

He's under contract through 2012 and there doesn't appear to be a change in the offing.

The Cubs problems are not entirely the fault of the GM, but the contracts that he gave to Carlos Zambrano and Alfonso Soriano are impossible to move. He did some questionable things in signing Carlos Pena, trading a chunk of the farm system to get Matt Garza and then dealing the useful Tom Gorzelanny for seemingly no reason.

Patience is part of being a Cubs fan or employee, but how much patience are they going to have with Hendry if another season goes wrong and they're mired at .500 or worse? Or will they move forward with him?

I don't know if they will.

I don't know if they should.

Mike Quade took over on an interim basis for Lou Piniella in August when Piniella resigned.

A veteran baseball man with a wealth of experience, Quade knows the organization from having been Piniella's third base coach for four years. Prior to that, he was the manager of the Triple A Iowa Cubs for four years. He's managed for a total of *17* years in the minors—he deserves this opportunity for no reason other than that!

An impressive 37 game stint as the Cubs manager was highlighted by his benching of top prospect Starlin Castro after a mental gaffe (he forgot how many outs there were) in a game against the Mets in September; it set the tone that the mistake-laden and lazy Cubs of the past were not going to be tolerated because of salary or status as a hot rookie.

The Cubs went 24-13 under Quade and, most impressively, he had a positive influence on Zambrano who was brilliant over the final month.

Whether they contend or not this year, it won't be because Quade lets the inmates run the asylum. He's in charge and the players know it. That's a good start for any manager.

STARTING PITCHING:

By now it should be accepted that Ryan Dempster is a solid, durable starting pitcher in the big leagues whose contract no longer looks to be a reach and overpay for someone who had his career year entering free agency.

After returning to the starting rotation in 2008, Dempster had his third straight 200+ inning season. He has a good sinker and slider and struck out over 200 batters. He can lose the strike zone occasionally as evidenced by his 86 walks and he's susceptible to the long ball with 25 homers allowed. But he's a consistent winner who eats innings and guts his way through games. He has a player option for $14 million in 2012 so unless the Cubs sign him to an extension, there's a good chance he might want to take advantage of the weak starting pitching in baseball today and try to cash in. That equates into him having a very good 2011 season.

Matt Garza was acquired from the Rays for a package of prospects. Garza has the talent to be a Cy Young Award contender and, after years of immaturity and anger issues hindered him, has controlled his emotions to become a solid starter.

Garza has a full arsenal of pitches with a moving fastball, good curve, slider and changeup; plus he's big and durable. He gives up a lot of home runs (28 in 204 innings last season) and this might be a problem in Chicago. He's a very good acquisition for the Cubs and is primed for a breakout year in the move to the National League. His temper is always something to watch.

So which Carlos Zambrano is going to show up? Is it the dominant, Cy Young contending winner he can be? Is it the lazy, injury-prone and uninterested disabled list denizen? The raving maniac who argues with umpires, coaches, his manager, teammates and reporters? Or some combination of all of the above?

Zambrano's 2010 was as roller coaster as it gets. He was the Cubs opening day starter and got blasted by the Braves; he didn't pitch as badly as was suggested in the next three starts, but became a very expensive set-up man in the bullpen. He was serviceable as a reliever (I actually thought the idea could work); then went back into the rotation in June and was again inconsistent.

Then came the explosion.

On June 25th in his start against the crosstown White Sox, allowed 4 hits and 4 runs in the first inning and got into a screaming match with first baseman Derrek Lee in the dugout; speculation was that Zambrano was angry because he felt that Lee should've dove for one of the hits he allowed. Zambrano was suspended and the Cubs had had enough of him.

His contract, which owes him almost $36 million guaranteed through 2012 with a vesting player option in 2013, made him impossible to trade. Zambrano underwent treatment for his anger issues and came back to the Cubs at the end of July and was back on August 9th...and he pitched well for the rest of the season.

An 8-0 record in 11 starts made people again wonder whether Zambrano was ever going to fulfill that massive potential. He has a fastball, slider and cutter and can hit too. Because he's been around so long, it's easy to forget that Zambrano is still onl 29.

Can he finally break through?

Zambrano will be the difference between the Cubs being an also-ran again or making a legitimate playoff run.

Are you willing to guess which is going to show up when? Will it be one of the myriad of personalities that the mercurial Zambrano has displayed? Will it be all? Will he be good Z? Bad Z? Mediocre Z? Injured Z?

I don't know.

Righty Randy Wells came back down to to earth in 2010. Wells, a former minor league catcher who went 12-10 in 2009, fell back down to reality with an 8-14 record with 209 hits allowed in 194 innings. Truth be told, Wells pitched similarly in both years. He doesn't strike out many hitters; he throws strikes and may be better served to be a relief pitcher; but with the Cubs short in the starting rotation at the back end, they need him to start. He's a journeyman starter.

Carlos Silva had a decent comeback with the Cubs after a disastrous (and well-compensated) two years with the Mariners. Silva started the season 6-0 and looked like a lucky pickup early in the season before injuries, including a heart condition which required surgery to correct his heart rate sabotaged his year.

Silva was an innings-eater with the Twins; he got people out by relying on his defense and his sinker inducing ground balls; he'd gotten back to that early in the season with the Cubs, but after all the injuries and now a heart problem, it's hard to know what they're going to get from him. Surgery corrected his heart, but how much pounding can his body take?

BULLPEN:

I don't think people realize how dominant Carlos Marmol is.

With a quirky, whipcord motion a 95 mph fastball and a slider that should be borderline illegal, Marmol racks up a number of strikeouts that one usually sees in little league. In 77 innings, Marmol struck out 138 batters. That's not a misprint. He only allowed 40 hits and 1 homer; devastated both righties and lefties; and cut his walks to 52 (good considering he'd walked 65 in 74 innings in 2009).

The 28-year-old Marmol is one of the best closers in baseball that you may not be aware of.

Kerry Wood returns to the Cubs after spending a year-and-a-half with the Indians and a half-season with the Yankees. He took a lowball deal to come back to his baseball home, only receiving $1.5 million, but with unstated suggestions that Wood will have a job working for the Cubs long after his playing career is over. $1.5 million a fraction of what he could've gotten considering the money that was thrown around for Rafael Soriano, Brian Fuentes and Grant Balfour.

Wood rejuvenated his career after joining the Yankees and was a major reason for the Yankees strong late season run to the playoffs. He'd been injury-prone and homer-prone with the woeful Indians as their closer, but regained his strikeout stuff for the Yankees. He still throws very, very hard and has a vicious curveball. Back with the Cubs where he's comfortable, he'll have a good year setting up for Marmol.

Veteran lefty John Grabow had an ERA of over 7 last season, but he missed a large part of the season with a knee injury. In his career, he's been durable, reliable reliever with good control of a fastball, changeup and curve; he deals well with lefties and righties.

Lefty Sean Marshall has found a home in the bullpen. In 80 games and 74 innings, Marshall allowed 58 hits, walked 25 and struck out 90 with 3 homers allowed. He handles both righties and lefties with a good sinking fastball and curve.

24-year-old righty Andrew Cashner appeared in 53 games as a rookie, posted a 4.80 ERA and allowed 55 hits in 54 innings, striking out 50. Cashner throws very hard and his future may be in the starting rotation; in fact, if Wells and Silva struggle or are injured, Cashner might start this season.

Lefty James Russell appeared in 57 games as a rookie and in 47 innings struck out 42 and walked 11. He also allowed 11 homers which is a massive amount. He's a contact pitcher without a strikeout pitch and had poor results in the minors as a starter. He's best suited to be a long reliever.

Justin Berg is a 26-year-old righty who pitched in 41 games in 2010. In 40 innings, he allowed 40 hits, walked 20 and struck out 14. Pitchers who have trouble throwing strikes and don't strike anyone out are going to have trouble staying in the majors.

Maybe Jeff Samardzija should've stuck to being a wide receiver. After a promising start to his career as a rookie in 2008 in which he showed a good power fastball and strikeout ability, he's been atrocious. His control has been terrible; his strikeout rate has plummeted and he wound up back in the minors where he was mediocre as a starter.

Lefty Scott Maine was acquired from the Diamondbacks after the 2009 season for Aaron Heilman and can be a good reliever. In 13 innings, he struck out 11 and walked 5. He's closed in the minors and can strike people out.

LINEUP:

After a terrible 2009, Geovany Soto returned to form as one of the top young catcehrs in baseball. If he hadn't missed a chunk of the season with a shoulder strain, his numbers would've been MVP caliber.

In 105 games, Soto batted .280 with a .393 on base, 18 homers, 19 doubles and 53 RBI; his defense is adequate and he's an All Star waiting to happen if he stays healthy.

Carlos Pena was signed to a 1-year, $10 million contract after leaving the Rays. Pena is a fascinating case in that he had a massive all-around year with the Rays in 2007 with a .282 average, .411 on base and 46 homers after being a journeyman who was consistently dumped by one team after another. The Rays had in fact cut him that spring only to change their minds and call him back.

Pena's had degenerated into the epitome of feast or famine. He either hits a home runs, walks or strikes out and does nothing else. Last season, he batted a ridiculous .196 with 158 strikeouts; but he hit

28 homers and had a .325 on base. He's only signed to a 1-year deal, but $10 million? His production had declined precipitously since that 2007 season. I don't expect much more than what he's provided in the past two years.

Blake DeWitt was acquired from the Dodgers at mid-season for Ted Lilly and Ryan Theriot. DeWitt is an average defensive second baseman, can get on base reasonably well and has 10 home run pop.

Aramis Ramirez rebounded from a horrific start in which he batted .152 in April and .173 in May to finish with respectable numbers. He hit 25 homers, drove in 83 runs and managed to raise his average to .242. Ramirez has been one of the top power hitting third basemen in baseball for the past 10 years; 2010 was likely an anomaly. He's got a $16 million contract option for 2011. He's going to have a big year.

Starlin Castro, encountering the usual rookie struggles with discipline, had a solid first year. In 125 games, he batted .300 with a .347 on base, 31 doubles and 10 stolen bases. He was caught stealing 8 times. Defensively, he's still learning but will eventually be a fine fielder. Castro is only 21 and has All Star potential.

Alfonso Soriano is 35. The Cubs owe him $72 million. He's an indifferent defender who hustles when he's sufficiently motivated to do so. He doesn't get on base; strikes out too much; doesn't steal bases anymore; hits for intermittent power; and is going to get worse as the years pass.

That about cover it?

He'll hit his 25 homers and 40 doubles. In most cases, that wouldn't be considered all that bad, but with his ability, even at his age, he could put up massive numbers.

But he won't.

Marlon Byrd had a solid first season with the Cubs after signing a 3-year, $15 million contract after 2009. Byrd had rejuvenated his career with the Rangers and his hitting numbers were consistent on the road and at home when he was with Texas, so it should come as no surprise that he had a good year with the Cubs. Byrd's a good defensive outfielder who hit 12 homers, had 39 doubles, batted .293 and had a .346 on base. He's a positive voice in the clubhouse as well.

For some reason, Kosuke Fukudome went in and out of former manager Lou Piniella's doghouse. Fukudome is a good player. He gets on base, has some pop, hits for extra bases and steals a base here and there; he's a solid fundamental outfielder. He's in the final year of his cotract which is paying him $13.5 million. With Tyler Colvin present to take over in right field, if the Cubs fall out of contention, Fukudome could be trade bait.

BENCH:

Tyler Colvin had a fine rookie season that ended when a broken bat impaled itself in his chest as he was running the bases. The 25-year-old Colvin batted .254 with 20 homers and 18 doubles in 394 plate appearances. He needs to improve his selectivity at the plate, but he doesn't strike out much and has the ability to steal a few bases.

Koyie Hill is the backup catcher to Soto. Replacing the injured Soto for long stretches, Hill batted .217 in 231 plate appearances. He handles the pitching staff well.

Jeff Baker is a veteran utilityman who batted .272 in 224 plate appearances. He has occasional pop and can play third and second base adequately.

Well-traveled 4-A catcher Max Ramirez bounced from the Rangers to the Red Sox to the Cubs this winter. Ramirez is 26 and has shown some hitting ability in the minors. He's a backup's backup.

Darwin Barney is a 25-year-old backup infielder with a career .286 average in the minors. He's a contact hitter with a little speed.

Fernando Perez was acquired from the Rays along with Garza. A 28-year-old outfielder, Perez hit well in the minors up until 2007, but has done nothing since. I'm not sure what the Cubs wanted with him.

PREDICTION:

If everything works out right for the Cubs, they'll contend for a playoff spot; but how realistic is it to expect that?

Everything going right would include the expected seasons from Dempster and Garza; a continue in the progress Zambrano made late last season after his explosion; a repeat performance from their entire bullpen; production and health from Soriano, Pena and Soto; and growth from Castro.

The Cubs will be disciplined under Quade and the insanity that occasionally took hold of the clubhouse under Piniella won't recur; but do they have the talent to hang with the Cardinals, Brewers and Reds in a tough division?

With solid pieces in place like Soto, Garza, Castro and Marmol, the Cubs future is relatively bright, but they have a lot of questions and the key is Zambrano.

The back of the rotation is a problem and the flightiness (let's be kind) of Zambrano makes it hard to expect much more than a .500 record unless by some miracle Zambrano *finally* pitches up to his immense abilities.

It's not likely at all.

There are too many holes and a rough division for the Cubs to contend this season.

PREDICTED RECORD: 78-84

Houston Astros

2010 Record: 76-86; 4th place, National League Central.

2010 Recap:

Expected to be one of the worst teams in baseball, the Astros got off to a horrifically bad start, righted the ship to some degree thanks to the calm and impressive leadership of new manager Brad Mills. Star pitcher Roy Oswalt requested a trade and after a few months of fielding offers, he was sent to the Phillies; also, longtime Astro Lance Berkman was dealt to the Yankees as the last remnants of the championship-contending Astros were swept away.

With a resurgent Brett Myers and some good pitching from Happ and Wandy Rodriguez, the Astros went 45-38 from June through the end of the season and ended at a surprising 76-86, which wasn't bad considering they were 19 games under .500 at one point.

2011 ADDITIONS:

INF Clint Barmes was acquired from the Colorado Rockies.
INF Bill Hall signed a 1-year, $3 million contract with mutual option.
LHP Ryan Rowland-Smith signed a 1-year, $725,000 contract.
RHP Casey Fien signed a minor league contract.
RHP Ross Wolf signed a minor league contract.

2011 SUBTRACTIONS:

RHP Matt Lindstrom was traded to the Colorado Rockies.
RHP Felipe Paulino was traded to the Colorado Rockies.
LHP Tim Byrdak was not re-signed.
RHP Casey Daigle was not re-signed.
RHP Josh Banks was not re-signed.
RHP Gary Majewski was not re-signed.
RHP Brian Moehler was not re-signed.
RHP Chris Sampson was not re-signed.
OF Cory Sullivan was not re-signed.

2011 PROJECTED STARTING ROTATION: Brett Myers; Wandy Rodriguez; J.A. Happ; Bud Norris; Nelson Figueroa; Aneury Rodriguez.

2011 PROJECTED BULLPEN: Brandon Lyon; Wilton Lopez; Wesley Wright; Ryan Rowland-Smith; Jeff Fulchino; Mark Melancon; Fernando Abad.

2011 PROJECTED LINEUP: C-Jason Castro; 1B-Brett Wallace; 2B-Bill Hall; 3B-Chris Johnson; SS-Clint Barmes; LF-Carlos Lee; CF-Michael Bourn; RF-Hunter Pence.

2011 BENCH: INF-Jeff Keppinger; C-Humberto Quintero; C-J.R.Towles; SS-Tommy Manzella; OF-Jason Michaels; OF-Brian Bogusevic; INF-Angel Sanchez.

2011 POSSIBLE CONTRIBUTORS: RHP-David Carpenter; RHP-Lance Pendleton; RHP-Henry Villar; INF-Matt Downs; INF-Jimmy Paredes; INF-Anderson Hernandez.

ASSESSMENTS MANAGEMENT:

General Manager Ed Wade is so reviled in many circles that the ink Roy Oswalt trade to the Phillies wasn't complete before the blogosphere exploded with accusations from saying he was a moron to the suggestion that he was trying to help his former employers, the Phillies, at the expense of his own team. That he got a good young pitcher in J.A. Happ was ignored in the initial response.

A few hours later, there were pauses and head tilts saying, "well, that's not so bad" when he spun one of the prospects he got from the Phillies for Oswalt to the Blue Jays for a closer-to-big-league-ready Brett Wallace.

Wade is one of those baseball executives who can't do anything right even when he does do something right. A vast chunk of the Phillies championship team was acquired by the Wade regime; credit is given to former scouting director Mike Arbuckle. The failures of Phillies teams before Wade was fired? *That* was his fault.

With the Astros, his repuation—and body—took a beating when he was physically attacked by Astros pitcher Shawn Chacon; instead of repudiating Chacon completely, it was said that Wade spoke to the pitcher disrespectfully and caused the situation to spiral out of control.

As an executive, Wade's in a tough spot with the Astros. Owner Drayton McLane (who's been said to possibly be selling the team) is hands on. He's criticized for it, but in many circumstances, McLane has been right about refusing to give up on seasons and trading veterans away for youngsters.

Some of Wade's decisions have worked like Brett Myers; the trade for Michael Bourn in which he surrendered Brad Lidge is looking better now that Bourn is playing up to his potential. Time will tell how the Oswalt deal ends up; Happ is a potential 15-game winner; Wallace looks like he can hit.

He also made a good hire in manager Brad Mills.

To blame someone for the bad things and give them no credit for the good things is nonsense.

Brad Mills had extensive minor league managerial experience and came from the coaching staff of Terry Francona. Francona happened to be one of Wade's managers with the Phillies.

Mills exuded calm confidence in the introductory press conference and didn't panic when the Astros got off to a woeful 1-9 start and there was talk of them being the worst team in baseball.

They weren't.

Saddled with a weak and poorly constructed lineup, Mills did the best he could with what he had and endured the trades of the two cornerstone stars, Oswalt and Berkman; he then transitioned young players Wallace and Chris Johnson into the starting lineup.

The pitching staff enjoyed a resurgence from Myers; a solid year from Wandy Rodriguez; and the bullpen's innings and appearances were doled out reasonably.

Mills has a bright future as a big league manager if and when he gets some serious talent to work with.

STARTING PITCHING:

Brett Myers was signed to a 1-year, $5.1 million contract by the Astros before the 2010 season in a mutually advantageous deal for the Astros to get good production from a veteran starter and a veteran starter trying to rejuvenate his career.

It turned out to be a terrific deal for both.

After years of inconsistency, fluctuating roles, injuries and off-field trouble, Myers regained the form that made him one of the Phillies top starters from 2003-2006. Myers regained his good fastball, brilliant slow curve and control and went 14-8 with a 3.14 ERA; he threw 223 innings, allowed 215 hits and 20 homers. Myers was durable and consistent all season long and rather than trading him as some suggested they should, the Astros signed the 30-year-old Myers to a 2-year, $23 million extension with a club option for 2013.

Wandy Rodriguez is a fine left-handed pitcher that isn't very well known by the casual fan. Rodriguez is always seemingly just missing on becoming a top National League starter. He has a free and easy motion, a good curve and changeup. Last season, Rodriguez went 11-12 in 32 starts, but could've won 18-20 games if the Astros could score. He hovers around 200 innings for the season; can strike hitters out and get ground balls; he throws strikes.

Rodriguez signed a 3-year, $34 million contract extension to avoid arbitration and curtail his free agency.

J.A. Happ was acquired from the Phillies in the Oswalt trade and went 5-4 in 13 starts after the trade. Happ missed a chunk of the first half of the season with a forearm injury and it was a risk in trading for him as the main part of the trade. Forearms can be little injuries or they can be a precursor to something big.

Happ was durable for the Astros and, at times, brilliant. He has great stuff; a good fastball and breaking stuff; he can lose the strike zone and runs up high pitch counts which limits the depth he can give. His motion is slightly quirky as he throws across his body, but it's not otherwise stressful. Happ's not young—he's 28—and the Phillies, as they generally do, kept him in the minors longer than one would think necessary.

I like Happ and think he's got the potential to win 15-18 games for a good team.

Bud Norris is a 26-year-old righty who went 9-10 in his first full big league season in 2010. He has a good fastball, strikes people out and walks too many. In 153 innings, he allowed 151 hits, walked 77 and struck out 158. If he's ever able to throw consistent strikes, Norris could be a useful starter in the big leagues.

Veteran journeyman Nelson Figueroa will vie for the fifth spot in the rotation, but it makes little sense for a team like the Astros to start him. Figueroa has a below average fastball and has to have control with his curve or he gets hit very, very hard. His control isn't particularly good either. He's a long man/spot starter.

Aneury Rodriguez is a 23-year-old righty who was selected from the Rays in the Rule 5 Draft. Last season, at Triple A, Rodriguez went 6-5 in 27 appearances, including 17 starts. He struck out 94 in 113 innings; walked 49 and allowed 10 homers. He has to stay with the Astros all year if they want to keep him and if he shows he can start in the spring, they should give him a chance rather than waste a spot with Figueroa.

BULLPEN:

Brandon Lyon saved 20 games last season after taking over as closer from the struggling Matt Lindstrom. Lyon has a good fastball and slider and the home run ball, which has been his biggest issue, didn't hurt him as he allowed 2 in 78 innings. His ERA was bloated to 3.78 by a few bad appearances, but he was effective for most of the season. He's not who I'd choose as my closer if I were running a team, but he gets the job done most of the time.

Wilton Lopez is a 27-year-old righty who appeared in 68 games in relief in 2010. He walked 5 in 67 innings, struck out 50 and allowed 4 homers. One thing I look for in relief pitchers is that they throw strikes and for someone who's as around the plate as much as Lopez, 4 homers allowed is pretty good. He was a mediocre starter in the minors, but has found a home in the Astros bullpen.

Lefty Wesley Wright had established himself in the big leagues in 2009 but spent a chunk of 2010 in the minors. He has strikeout stuff and can get out lefties and righties. The Astros tried him as a starter briefly last season and he got rocked.

Ryan Rowland-Smith was signed as a free agent after the Mariners non-tendered him. Smith, a lefty, showed promise as a starter in 2009. Back problems and poor performance ruined his season in 2010. In 109 innings, he allowed 141 hits and 25 homers. He's a contact pitcher who loses the strike zone occasionally. It's worthwhile to try him as a starter, but he may be better used as a reliever.

Jeff Fulchino is a big (6'5", 285 pounds) righty who appeared in 50 games in relief for the Astros in 2010. In 47 innings, he struck out 46, walked 22 and allowed 7 homers. Elbow problems contributed to his fallback season after a solid 2009. If he's healthy, he's a solid set-up man.

Mark Melancon was acquired in the trade of Lance Berkman to the Yankees. Melancon throws hard but there have been times when he literally doesn't appear to know where the ball is going once he releases it. In 20 games with the Astros, however, Melancon pitched well. He only walked 8 in 18 innings and struck out 19; he gave up 12 hits and 1 homer. He's struck out a batter an inning at every level in the minors.

Fernando Abad is a 25-year-old lefty who posted a 2.84 ERA in 22 games last season. He struck out 12 in 19 innings and walked 5. He's prone to the longball and has been so at every level in the minors. Abad can get out both lefties and righties.

LINEUP:

Jason Castro is a 23-year-old former 1st round pick who throws well, but didn't hit in his first big league chance. He's been a .300 hitter with a little pop and on base skills in the minors. Last season, he batted .205 in 217 plate appearances. The Astros should give him every chance to win the starting job in 2011.

Brett Wallace is a top prospect who keeps getting traded. First he was the Cardinals top hitting prospect and was dealt to the Athletics for Matt Holliday; then the A's traded him to the Blue Jays for Michael Taylor as an ancillary note in the massive Roy Halladay for Cliff Lee machinations; then he was sent to the Astros after the Phillies acquired Anthony Gose from the Phillies, a player the Blue Jays had long coveted.

Wallace is a 24-year-old lefty swinging first baseman who batted .229 in 159 plate appearances for the Astros after he joined them. He had 6 doubles and 2 homers. Wallace has 20 home run power, has batted over .300 in his past two minor league seasons and is a patient hitter. He may not be a star, but he's going to be a productive big league bat.

Veteran Bill Hall signed a 1-year contract after contributing heavily to the injury-riddled Red Sox in 2010. Hall has had an up-and-down career. After his 35 homer season with the Brewers in 2006, he signed a $24 million contract extension and his production collapsed. Acquired by the Red Sox from the Mariners before last season, Hall played all over the place in Boston, hit 18 homers and was very useful.

As a regular player again and back in the National League, I wouldn't expect much. He didn't hit at all in his final years with the Brewers, but he does have some pop; he's adequate defensively at second base.

Chris Johnson came out of nowhere to take over the third base job and batted .308 as a rookie. The right-handed swinging Johnson had 22 doubles, 11 homers and 52 RBI in 362 plate appearances. He only walked 15 times and struck out 91, so discipline could be a problem going forward, but he's shown good extra base power in the minors. He's an average defensive third baseman at best.

Clint Barmes was acquired from the Rockies for hard-throwing Felipe Paulino. For the record, I would *not* have traded Paulino and I certainly wouldn't have traded him for Barmes.

Barmes has shown 10-20 homer power in the past and is a good defensive shortstop. He lost his starting shortstop job to Troy Tulowitzki, but played second base regularly. He batted .235 with 8 homers last season after his career year in 2009 with 23 homers.

Carlos Lee has been a historically good hitter who got off to a rotten start in 2010 and was inconsistent all year. His power numbers ended with 24 homers and 89 RBI, but Lee had been a hitter who could be counted on for 30 and 100 on an annual basis. He'd also batted over .300 in each of the previous three seasons, but his average fell to .246 and his on base to .291.

Lee is owed $37 million through 2012 and will be 35 in June. I've always liked the way Lee hits. He has great power and rarely strikes out and he's a better defender in the outfield than he's given credit for.

2010 was a bad year and I expect him to rebound in 2011.

Michael Bourn dropped off from his 2009 season in which he batted .285 with 27 doubles and 12 triples. Last season, he hit .265, stole 9 fewer bases with 52, but he missed the last two weeks of the season with an oblique strain. Bourn is a good outfielder and has speed to steal his 50+ bases.

Hunter Pence has proven that he's a 25 home run man. I know this because he's hit 25 home runs in each of the past three seasons.

Ah, stats.

Pence also hits his 30 doubles a year, steals a few bases and bats over .280. He's impatient at the plate, but has All Star potential if he can be just a bit more selective. He's a good defensive outfielder with a strong arm despite looking very awkward in everything he does.

BENCH:

Veteran infielder Jeff Keppinger wound up playing second base regularly last season and batted .288 with a .351 on base and 34 doubles. Keppinger can hit, but he's always been the type of player who's forever on the brink of being replaced. If he's needed in the starting lineup, ends up getting regular at bats and playing well.

Humberto Quintero will presumably see some time behind the plate if Castro again struggles. Quintero can't hit and has a good arm; it makes no sense for him to be playing regularly as the Astros rebuild. He batted .234 in 276 plate appearances last season.

J.R. Towles has been an absolute bust as a former top prospect who's gotten chance-after-chance to win the starting job and blown it every time. The 27-year-old Towles has hit well in the minors with a high average/on base and some pop; in the big leagues he's done absolutely nothing with a career .189 average in 319 trips to the plate.

Tommy Manzella was given a chance to win the everyday shortstop job last season, and had a finger injury that cost him a large part of the season; when he played, he didn't hit (.225, 7 doubles, 1 homer) and was mediocre defensively. If the 28-year-old makes the big league club, it'll be as a backup.

Jason Michaels is a veteran, righty batting backup outfielder with some occasional power. He can play all three outfield positions. I once thought he could've been a solid big leaguer, but at 35, he is what he is and what that is is fourth or fifth outfielder.

Brian Bogusevic is a 27-year-old, lefty swinging outfielder who had a solid season at Triple A in 2010. In 131 games, Bogusevic hit 13 homers, batted .277 and had a .364 on base with 23 stolen bases, He can play all three outfield positions.

Angel Sanchez is a utility infielder who played semi-regularly in 2010. Sanchez batted .280 with 9 doubles and 4 triples in 269 plate appearances. He has no speed and doesn't get on base.

PREDICTION:

The Astros starting pitching is serviceable with Myers, Rodriguez, Happ and Norris; the bullpen is questionable with youngsters and mediocre veterans; I've never liked Lyon as a closer.

The lineup is weak. They have black spots at catcher; journeymen with holes at second base and shortstop; youngsters at first and third base who could have trouble as the opposition adapts to them. Lee is going to rebound, Pence will chime in with his 25 homers; Bourn has speed. The bench isn't good either.

I like Mills as a manager, but a manager is limited with what he can do when a team is in the middle of a retooling as the Astros are. They're moving on completely from the glory days of 2004-2005; all the stars from those clubs are gone and it's a new era in Houston.

They're very short in key areas. Ignorant observers have compared the 2010 Astros to the 2009 Padres in that they had very good second halves. The Padres excellent play late in 2009 supposedly spurred them to their 90 wins in 2010. Equating one with the other and not examining how this was achieved is ridiculous. The Padres had a load of talent on the mound from top-to-bottom; the Astros don't. The Padres had a megastar at first base in Adrian Gonzalez; the Astros don't.

Mills is a better manager than the Padres Bud Black, but that's not going to save them this year and they're not going to approach what people irrationally expected after that spurt of good play.

PREDICTED RECORD: 69-93

Pittsburgh Pirates

2010 Record: 57-105, 6th place, National League Central.

2010 Recap:

Yurgh.

Where to begin?

This is about as bad as it gets.

The front office is inept and clueless; the manager didn't know what he was doing; the players were either young and learning their way or plainly and simply weren't very good; they couldn't hit; they couldn't pitch; and they lost, lost, lost and lost some more.

Despite the impressive youngsters Pedro Alvarez, Jose Tabata and Andrew McCutchen, this team is a disaster. Period. They were the punching bag of the entire National League and it's occurring on an annual basis now. Like the sun coming up, the one thing you've been able to count on for most of the past two decades is the Pirates finishing under .500 and, since 2005, losing 94+ games. Last year was the topper (so far) with 105.

They were rancid.

2011 ADDITIONS:

Manager Clint Hurdle was hired.
1B Lyle Overbay signed a 1-year, $5 million contract.
RHP Kevin Correia signed a 2-year, $8 million contract.
OF Matt Diaz signed a 2-year, $4.25 million contract.

LHP Scott Olsen signed a 1-year, $550,000 contract with 2012 club option.
1B/3B Garrett Atkins signed a minor league contract.
LHP Joe Beimel signed a minor league contract.
3B Josh Fields signed a minor league contract.
INF Andy Marte signed a minor league contract.
RHP Fernando Nieve signed a minor league contract.
RHP Jose Veras signed a minor league contract.
C Dusty Brown signed a minor league contract.

2011 SUBTRACTIONS:

Manager John Russell was fired.
LHP Zach Duke was traded to the Arizona Diamondbacks.
RHP Chan Ho Park was not re-signed.
OF Lastings Milledge was not re-signed.
INF Andy LaRoche was not re-signed.
2B Delwyn Young was not re-signed.
RHP Brendan Donnelly was released.
RHP Brian Bass was not re-signed.
LHP Dana Eveland was not re-signed.
OF Brandon Moss was not re-signed.
C Erik Kratz was not re-signed.
RHP Steven Jackson was not re-signed.
SS Argenis Diaz was not re-signed.

2011 PROJECTED STARTING ROTATION: Kevin Correia; James McDonald; Paul Maholm; Ross Ohlendorf; Scott Olsen; Charlie Morton.

2011 PROJECTED BULLPEN: Joel Hanrahan; Evan Meek; Daniel McCutchen; Chris Resop; Joe Beimel; Jeff Karstens; Jose Ascanio; Fernando Nieve.

2011 PROJECTED LINEUP: C-Chris Snyder; 1B-Lyle Overbay; 2B-Neil Walker; 3B-Pedro Alvarez; SS-Ronny Cedeno; LF-Jose Tabata; CF-Andrew McCutchen; RF-Garrett Jones.

2011 BENCH: OF-Matt Diaz; C/OF-Ryan Doumit; OF/1B-John Bowker; OF-Steve Pearce; INF-Josh Rodriguez; C-Jason Jaramillo.

2011 POSSIBLE CONTRIBUTORS: RHP-Kevin Hart; RHP-Ramon Aguero; RHP-Jose Veras; RHP-Brad Lincoln; OF-Alex Presley; INF-Pedro Ciriaco; RHP Chris Leroux.

ASSESSMENTS

MANAGEMENT:

On an annual basis I rail about the ineptitude of the Pirates front office.

From team president Frank Coonelly on down, there was nary a clue as to what they were doing. Whether GM Neal Huntington is truly behind some of the idiocies that have created one of the most laughably horrendous organizations I've seen in all my years of watching baseball is unknown; but he's the GM; he's the one running the team on paper and he's responsible for it whether he really is resposible for it or not.

How many more strange and inexplicable things can they do before being held accountable? Is there anyone—in MLB's front office, the Pittsburgh media, the fan base—to insist that steps are taken to repair the disaster that gets worse and worse with no end in sight?

There's a haunting absence of tone with the way this team is run.

A prime example of this was during one of the few bright spots enjoyed in a 105-loss season. On August 8th, the Pirates staged a dramatic comeback win against the Rockies as the talented rookie Pedro Alvarez hit a 3-run game winning homer off of Huston Street leading to the perception that the Pirates, as bad as they were, still had some prime talent on their roster and could stage an exciting win here and there because of that talent.

It was a nice moment to see the hapless Pirates win a game in such exciting circumstances.

Of course it was short-lived and not because reality punched them in the face on the field, but because hours after that win, the Pirates made headlines because they fired pitching coach Joe Kerrigan and bench coach Gary Varsho.

Kerrigan has a reputation as being difficult and the Pirates organization held him responsible for a mechanical change made to top pitching prospect Brad Lincoln that the club felt resulted in Lincoln getting hammered, losing velocity and winding up back in the minors.

Varsho is widely respected inside baseball and is definitely not a "yes" man. He tells it like it is and presumably, manager John Russell—in a bad situation, but a terrible manager—clearly was threatened by his bench coach. He should've been because Varsho should've replaced Russell long ago.

It's fine if the Pirates wanted to make these changes for whatever reason; in fact, they didn't have to give a reason other than "because"; but to do it when there was something good happening to them in such a woeful season?

It essentially explained the Pirates in a paragraph that started with details of their come-from-behind win and ended with the inexplicable timing of these firings.

The Pirates player personnel moves have made no sense under Huntington. From the signings of the likes of Ramon Vazquez; trades for Akinori Iwamura; the non-tendering of Matt Capps; the desperation dealing of Nate McLouth without letting the rest of baseball know that McLouth was available; the trade for the expensive Chris Snyder when they already had a catcher in Ryan Doumit—all happened within the past several years.

Nothing much changed this past winter as they signed Lyle Overbay, Matt Diaz, Joe Beimel—players whose contribution will be worthless considering the players surrounding these complementary pieces.

Huntington is said to have drafted well, but like the Royals, what difference does it make how much talent there is on the way to the big leagues if they're going to be traded or released because of cluelessness or interference from a lawyer in Coonelly acting as a baseball executive when his main qualifications for the job were that he worked in the commissioner's office and formulated the slot-money drafting system that some teams adhere to and some don't?

They're a disaster.

One smart thing the Pirates did this winter was hire a qualified manager to replace Russell. Clint Hurdle has had one season of success as a big league manager in which his Rockies rode a blazing and borderling on ridiculous hot streak all the way to the World Series. He's a competent game manager, but definitely not a difference maker in the won/lost column.

He's a disciplinarian and doesn't put up with nonsense. With those attributes and the Pirates current situation, he's a good fit. The players will play the game correctly and behave accordingly or they're not going to play. Hurdle has been a positive influence in the development of many of the young players the Rockies have brought along in recent years; that he annually accrued win totals in the mid-70s or worse during his tenure with the Rockies (apart from the 2007 pennant-winning season) may have attracted the Pirates even more. A win total in the mid-70s would represent a 20 game improvement!

Hurdle's a good choice after the customary series of endless gaffes by the Pirates.

STARTING PITCHING:

Kevin Correia was signed to a 2-year, $8 million contract.

Correia has always had excellent stuff—a good fastball, a slider and a changeup— but didn't begin to put all the pieces in place until joining the Padres in 2009. Was it that he got a chance to pitch regularly in the starting rotation after being shuttled between the majors and minors; the bullpen and rotation with the Giants? Or did he evolve?

I've always liked Correia and thought he had the potential to be a winner in the big leagues. In 2009, he went 12-11, but his record could've been much better; he threw 198 innings, allowed 194 hits and had a 3.91 ERA. He got off to a good start last season before his brother's tragic death in a rock climbing accident sent him into a tailspin. Understandably, Correia struggled for the rest of the season. His numbers from 2010 should be thrown out; if anything, he should receive credit for pitching as well as he did.

Correia can be wild and runs up high pitch counts which limits his ability to pitch deeply into the game. This is his first lucrative, multi-year contract and I expect him to pitch well even if it doesn't show up in his win total.

James McDonald was acquired in one of the few good trades that Huntington has made as he acquired McDonald from the Dodgers for Octavio Dotel. Clearly, the talented McDonald was never going to make it in Los Angeles given their expectations and lack of patience for a young pitcher who was still learning his craft; but with the Pirates and a pressureless situation, McDonald looked fantastic at times and struggled at times; but his stuff is top-notch.

A power fastball, a nice slow curve and developing changeup are the tools that turn heads and he's got a quirky, overhand motion that should be hard to gauge for both lefties and righties. I've always liked McDonald. At age 26 and with a team like the Pirates, he'll get the chance to start 30+ games and show what he can do.

28-year-old lefty Paul Maholm has been a stalwart in the Pirates rotation for the past five years, for what that's worth. Maholm has a full aresenal of pitches, a fastball, curve, slider and changeup and can win in the big leagues. His control isn't great (62 walks and high pitch counts in the middle innings); and he's a contact pitcher who needs his defense to help him. He doesn't give up a lot of homers (15 in 185 innings in 2010). He can be a winner if he's given support and improves his command. Or if he goes to another team.

Ross Ohlendorf was on and off the disabled list last season with back and arm problems. When he pitched, the results weren't good record-wise (he went 1-11), but there were times when he pitched well. Ohlendorf has a good sinking fastball and a slider; he's been a reliever in the past and can strike people out, but he was quite impressive as a starter in 2009 and he deserves at least 2011 to start and see which Ohlendorf is the one we'll see long-term.

Scott Olsen was signed to a 1-year contract after being dumped by the Nationals. If anyone is going to benefit from the strong disciplinary hand of manager Hurdle, it's Olsen. He's got a bad temper and has shown a bad attitude in the past, but when he's had a manager who's kept him in his place, he's pitched well. Specifically when he was with the Marlins and manager Joe Girardi grabbed him by the shirt collar and yanked him down the steps from the dugout to the clubhouse, it had a positive affect on Olsen. That's what he needs.

The lefty has a good fastball and changeup but hasn't pitched well in the past two seasons with the chaotic Nationals. Perhaps Hurdle can help him regain the form that made him look like he had a bright future with the Marlins his first few years in the majors. He's 27 now and it's time to grow up.

Charlie Morton was acquired from the Braves in the McLouth trade in early 2009. He has a similar motion and stuff to Carl Pavano when Pavano first broke into the majors. Morton got pounded regularly early in the season and was sent to the minors; after his return in late August, he pitched well.

Morton has strikeout potential if he commands his pitches and the 27-year-old has been an excellent starter in the minors. He can still cobble out a big league career.

BULLPEN:

Joel Hanrahan has a power fastball and the temperament to be a good closer. He handles both lefties and righties and racks up the strikeouts. In 69 innings last season, he struck out an even 100; his control is solid with only 26 walks and despite a penchant for allowing the longball, Hanrahan can be a dominant reliever.

Righty Evan Meek was one of the bright spots for the Pirates last season. In 70 games, Meek had a 2.14 ERA, allowed 53 hits in 80 innings and struck out 70. Meek can pitch multiple innings and held righties to a .199 average and lefties to a .168 average.

Daniel McCutchen is a journeyman righty who's been used as a starter and reliever and gotten ripped in both roles. McCutchen throws strikes, gives up a lot of hits and homers and simply doesn't have the stuff to be a starter or set-up man in the majors; perhaps he can be used as a long man.

Righty Chris Resop is armed with a lights out fastball and wound up with the Pirates when the Braves waived him last August. He's bounced from team-to-team without much success. The Marlins, Angels and Braves have given him shots, but his control is awful and after he falls behind, the hitters know his fastball is coming and tee off on it. He looked brilliant with the Pirates in the 22 games he appeared in late last season with improved control and a lot of strikeouts (24 in 19 innings).

Lefty specialist Joe Beimel is out on the free agent market every year and signs with someone generally in January or February. Many teams were sniffing around Beimel and he could've gone to a better team than the Pirates, but chose to sign with his hometown team. The Pirates had drafted Beimel in the 18th round of the 1998 draft and he pitched for them from 2001 to 2003. Beimel has a deliberate, across-his-body motion that's tough on lefties; he's on a minor league contract, but unless he falls flat on his face, he'll make the team.

Jeff Karstens is another journeyman righty who's been a starter and reliever in the big leagues and hasn't been particularly successful in any of his roles. He throws strikes, but gives up a lot of hits and home runs. Perhaps he, like McCutchen, can be a decent long reliever.

Jose Ascanio was acquired from the Cubs in 2009 and required surgery for a torn shoulder labrum after the season. Ascanio has a good fastball and slider and strikeout potential. His control is a bit off, but he throws hard. The labrum is a tough injury for a pitcher to regain his form.

Righty Fernando Nieve was a victim of Mets manager Jerry Manuel's frequent pitching changes and abuse. He has a 94-mph fastball and slider and pitched well early in the season out of the Mets bullpen, but that repeated use for multiple innings was his doom. He has a good arm and is a better option out of the Pirates bullpen than Karstens and McCutchen.

LINEUP:

Chris Snyder was acquired from the Diamondbacks at mid-season 2010 in a trade that made no sense whatsoever.

Snyder is solid defensively and has some pop but he's had back problems and was terrible at the plate after joining the Pirates (.169 average; .268 on base; 5 homers in 142 plate appearances); he's a better hitter than that. Snyder's owed a guaranteed $6.5 million this season.

Lyle Overbay is another pretty good veteran who signed with the Pirates because he got caught in the squeeze of having nowhere else to go to get regular playing time. Overbay is a very good defensive first baseman; has some pop; has shown the ability to get on base; and will hit his 35 or so doubles. After spending five productive, if unspectacular years with the Blue Jays, the 34-year-old Overbay wound up with the Pirates no doubt hoping he can impress another club enough for them to trade for him at mid-season as veteran insurance down the stretch.

Neil Walker is a switch-hitting Pittsburgh native who took over at second base after the disastrous trade for Akinori Iwamura was a predictable failure. Walker hit 12 homers, batted .296 and had a .349 on base with 29 doubles in 110 games. He's not a good defensive second baseman, but has shown power in the minors and can hit.

Pedro Alvarez is a raw youngster with MVP talent. The 24-year-old lefty batting third baseman can hit the ball a country mile and hit 16 homers in 386 plate appearances after his recall from Triple A. He strikes out a lot and his defense at third is weak—like Ryan Braun, he might eventually have to move to the outfield—but he can mash. Alvarez is going to be a star.

Veteran journeyman Ronny Cedeno returns as the everyday shortstop. Cedeno is a mediocre defender and career .245 hitter with a little speed. There's no justifiable reason for him to be playing regularly.

Jose Tabata had attraced controversy with his questionable attitude and off-field issues like his marriage to a much older woman, but he got a chance to play in the big leagues in 2010 and the 22-year-old was impressive. He batted .299 with a .346 on base and 19 stolen bases. He makes consistent contact and is a good defensive left fielder.

I say this every year about Andrew McCutchen: I....love....this.... kid.

There is nothing he cannot do on a baseball field and he is perhaps the smoothest and fastest runner I've ever seen in a baseball uniform. He has pop (16 homers); he hits for extra bases (35 doubles, 5 triples); he steals bases (33 in 43 attempts); he hits for average (.286); he walks (70); he doesn't strike out (89) and he gets on base (.365 OBP in each of his first two big league seasons.)

He's 24 and is going to be a megastar.

Garrett Jones had a breakout season as a part-timer for the Pirates in 2009 after spending years in Triple A with the Twins. Last season, he got the chance to play regularly and, as sometimes happens, he came down to earth with regular big league playing time. He still hit over 20 homers, but his average dropped from .293 to .247; his on base from .372 to .306. He did hit 34 doubles and will contribute to the offense with the long ball.

BENCH:

Veteran outfielder Matt Diaz was signed to a 2-year contract. Diaz hits lefties well, is a decent outfielder and has some basestealing speed. He had a subpar year after batting well over .300 in the three years in which he had the chance to play regularly with the Braves. He's pummeled lefties in his career to the tune of a .335 average.

Switch-hitting Ryan Doumit lost his starting catching job with the acquisition of Snyder and missed time with a concussion last season. His throwing behind the plate has gotten progressively worse. He's played some outfield and first base and can hit for power if he plays regularly. He makes consistent contact as well.

John Bowker is a veteran outfielder/first baseman who has occasional pop and plays solid defense.

Steve Pearce is a righty-swinging first baseman/outfielder who's posted good power/on base numbers in the minors and is a career .240 hitter with 8 homers in 416 career big league plate appearances.

Jason Jaramillo is a backup catcher with a strong arm who batted .149 in 33 games in the big leagues in 2010. He's put up some solid numbers at the plate in the minors.

PREDICTION:

The Pirates *do* have some talent in McCutchen, Alvarez, McDonald, Hanrahan and Tabata. They're loaded with journeymen and continually bring in players who are not going to be much help to them now or in the future. What possible reason do they need Beimel? Overbay? Snyder?

Until there's a competent front office that isn't led by the clueless Coonelly and the questionable Huntington, they're not going to get any better. Hurdle will be a giant step up from Russell in all aspects, but that's not going to do much good in a tough division with a shaky starting rotation, mediocre bullpen and short lineup.

I never get the idea that there's a plan in place with the Pirates aside from scouring the bargain basement bin, trading veterans for prospects and putting up the pretense that they're trying.

But trying is worthless to me unless there's a coherent strategy in place and said strategy is not forthcoming with that front office.

The Pirates will improve on last season but improving on 105 losses is similar to "only" breaking both arms and a leg in a skydiving accident—it's not *as* bad as dying, but it's still pretty bad.

Plenty bad.

If I were a competing GM, I'd call the Pirates and ask for "McCutchen" in a deal. Naturally you'd be able to get Daniel, but maybe, just maybe they'd file the wrong papers with the league and you'd wind up with Andrew.

In most cases, this would be a lottery-type move; with the Pirates, it's 50/50 that they'd screw up to that degree.

For what it's worth, I don't think they're going to lose 100 games. With the Pirates, I suppose that counts as progress.

PREDICTED RECORD: 65-97

National League West Predicted Standings

		Wins	Losses	GB
1.	Los Angeles Dodgers	89	73	---
2.	Colorado Rockies	86	76	3
3.	San Francisco Giants	81	81	8
4.	San Diego Padres	78	84	11
5.	Arizona Diamondbacks	68	94	21

Los Angeles Dodgers

2010 Record: 80-82; 4th place, National League West.

2010 Recap:

After making the playoffs in every year from 1996 through 2009, Joe Torre's managerial magic finally ran out.

The Dodgers, rife with ownership turmoil stemming from the McCourts' divorce, had a tumultuous year on the field as well. Matt Kemp was ripped for lackadaisical play; Manny Ramirez was on and off the disabled list before he was traded; their starting pitching was inconsistent and their bullpen an arson squad.

The club was streaky, but stayed within striking distance of a playoff spot into August before the lack of offense and a bad bullpen sabotaged them; they faded down the stretch and fell from contention.

Torre announced in September that he would not manage the team in 2010 and made way for Don Mattingly and Torre's managerial career ended out of the playoffs and under .500 at 80-82.

2011 ADDITIONS:

Manager Don Mattingly was hired.
RHP Jon Garland signed a 1-year, $5 million contract with 2012 club option.
INF Juan Uribe signed a 3-year, $21 million contract.
RHP Matt Guerrier signed a 3-year, $12 million contract.
C Dioner Navarro signed a 1-year, $1 million contract.

OF Marcus Thames signed a 1-year, $1 million contract.
OF Tony Gwynn, Jr. signed a 1-year, $675,000 contract.
RHP Blake Hawksworth was acquired from the St. Louis Cardinals.
LHP Ron Mahay signed a minor league contract.
LHP Dana Eveland signed a minor league contract.
OF Gabe Kapler signed a minor league contract.
OF Eugenio Velez signed a minor league contract.
RHP Tim Redding signed a minor league contract.
INF Aaron Miles signed a minor league contract.

2011 SUBTRACTIONS:

Manager Joe Torre retired.
C Russell Martin was non-tendered.
INF Ryan Theriot was traded to the St. Louis Cardinals.
C Brad Ausmus retired.
OF Reed Johnson was not re-signed.
OF Scott Podsednik was not re-signed.
INF Ronnie Belliard was released.
LHP George Sherrill was not re-signed.
RHP Justin Miller was not re-signed.
RHP Charlie Haeger was not re-signed.
INF Chin-lung Hu was traded to the New York Mets.
RHP Jeff Weaver was not re-signed.
OF Garret Anderson was released.

2011 PROJECTED STARTING ROTATION: Clayton Kershaw; Chad Billingsley; Hiroki Kuroda; Ted Lilly; Jon Garland; Vicente Padilla.

2011 PROJECTED BULLPEN: Jonathan Broxton; Hong-Chih Kuo; Matt Guerrier; Ronald Belisario; Ramon Troncoso; Carlos Monasterios; Kenley Jansen; Blake Hawksworth; John Ely; Ron Mahay.

2011 PROJECTED LINEUP: C-Rod Barajas; 1B-James Loney; 2B-Juan Uribe; 3B-Casey Blake; SS-Rafael Furcal; LF-Marcus Thames; CF-Matt Kemp; RF-Andre Ethier.

2011 BENCH: OF/1B-Jay Gibbons; C-Dioner Navarro; INF-Jamey Carroll; OF-Tony Gwynn, Jr.; OF-Xavier Paul; C-A.J. Ellis.

2011 POSSIBLE CONTRIBUTORS: INF-Ivan DeJesus; 1B-John Lindsey; OF-Jamie Hoffman; INF-Russ Mitchell; LHP-Scott Elbert; RHP-Luis Vazquez; RHP-Javy Guerra; INF-Aaron Miles.

ASSESSMENTS
MANAGEMENT:

The soap opera otherwise known as the divorce between Frank and Jamie McCourt and resulting custody battle for the Dodgers continues with no end in sight. Now it's being reported that they're in deeper financial trouble than even the Wilpons with the Mets and Frank McCourt has also been looking for investors.

Amid endless ridicule, there's no evidence that the legal battle is affecting on-field club operations. Last year, they did nothing to improve the club, but this year GM Ned Colletti has made plenty of short-term signings to make the Dodgers better.

Say what you want about the McCourts, but they've consistently put a quality, contending product on the field. So they're having a public legal fight to divvy up their assets including the Dodgers? It's their business and the team is still making maneuvers to improve.

Ned Colletti is an aggressive GM who's willing to think outside the box and trade younger players for veterans to win now. For the most part in his time with the Dodgers, they've won on the field. Some of his acquisitions have been disastrous. Andruw Jones was money thrown down the tubes; Jason Schmidt barely pitched; but there have been others like Casey Blake who've done what was expected.

Last year he traded for Ted Lilly after Lilly had been injury-prone and moderately effective with the Cubs and Lilly pitched terrific ball for the Dodgers. He kept Lilly; Hiroki Kuroda; probably overpaid for Juan Uribe; improved the bullpen with the underrated Matt Guerrier; and got Jon Garland super-cheap. You can also bet that if the Dodgers are in contention at mid-season, they're going to be looking to improve, most likely with a bat.

Don Mattingly steps right into the hot seat in his first opportunity to manage at any level as he replaces the retired Joe Torre. Mattingly was hammered for a perceived mistake he made when Torre had been ejected from a game and Mattingly went out to talk to closer Jonathan Broxton, walked off the mound, turned and said something else to Broxton and was charged with a second visit to the mound. Giants manager Bruce Bochy pointed it out and the Dodgers had to remove Broxton.

It turned out that the umpires were wrong, but that's neither here nor there. The implication was that Mattingly didn't know the rules and was not ready to be a manager.

I can't argue with the premise that it's hard for someone to go from coach to manager with no managing experience aside from some time in the Arizona Fall League; I wouldn't hire a manager with no experience. But Mattingly was a smart player; he'll have a former manager—Trey Hillman—as his bench coach. He'll make some mistakes. There's no question about that.

But his status as a former megastar player, that he's so respected throughout baseball as a man and a players' player; that he's likely to be very laid back with his rules for veteran players tells me that those players will love him so much that they won't let him fail. The thought of letting Donnie down will be so repugnant to them when he's so good to them and works so hard at his job that it will overcome the mistakes he's likely to make. As long as he relies on his instincts, listens to his coaches (Davey Lopes is on the staff too) and lets pitching coach Rick Honeycutt guide him in handling the pitchers, Mattingly will be fine. In fact, I think he's going to end up winning Manager of the Year.

STARTING PITCHING:

23-year-old lefty Clayton Kershaw is a superstar waiting to happen. I thought he was going to bust out and win the NL Cy Young Award last season, but while he pitched well, he hasn't pitched to that level...yet.

Kershaw has a great fastball and vicious curve and all the tools to be one of the best pitchers in baseball. Last season, he went 13-10 with dominant numbers across-the-board. He did pitch well enough to win over 20 games. With a 2.91 ERA; 212 strikeouts in 204 hits with 160 hits allowed and 13 homers, the only slightly black mark against him is his control. He walked 81 and runs up high pitch counts because of a lack of command and all the strikeouts.

Kershaw is going to bust out and win 18 games at some point and I say it's going to be this year with 250+ strikeouts. He might start the All Star game.

Chad Billingsley also has ace stuff. With a 95 mph fastball and devastating slider, Billingsley can dominate. His motion is pounding and he's had nagging aches and pains; his name was even bandied about in trade talks, but he's a top pitcher. Like Kershaw, Billingsley runs up high pitch counts. He went 12-11 last season, but pitched well enough to win 17-18 games. In 191 innings, he allowed 176 hits; struck out 171 and only surrendered 8 homers.

If Billingsley and Kershaw ever put it together simultaneously the Dodgers are going to put a scare into a few teams.

Hiroki Kuroda signed a far smaller deal to remain with the Dodgers than I felt he could've gotten had he pursued more money on the open market. He did get $12 million, but it's only for one year. Kuroda has wicked stuff; a good fastball and slider, a deceptive motion and he's mean. The righty went 11-13; but in 196 innings he allowed 180 hits, walked 48 and struck out 159. He only allowed 15 homers and is more efficient with his pitches than his younger rotation cohorts. Kuroda is a fine pitcher who people don't know as well as they should. He's 36-years-old.

Veteran lefty Ted Lilly has had injury problems over the past few years, he pitched very well last year for the Cubs and Dodgers. Lilly went 7-4 in 12 starts after going to LA; he allowed 61 hits in 76 innings, struck out 77 and walked 15. He tends to allow a lot of homers. Lilly was efficient and pitched deeply into games. He's always been about control and guts than stuff and after the season, he signed a 3-year. $33 million deal to stay with the Dodgers.

After a year with the Padres, Southern California native Jon Garland re-joins the Dodgers (with whom he spent the tail end of the 2009 season) on a 1-year, $5 million deal with a club option for $8 million that kicks in if he reaches 190 innings, something he's done every year since 2002.

Garland had a fine year with the Padres at 14-12 without the usual ton of hits and homers he's allowed in the past few years. Garland took advantage of the Padres big ballpark and good defense. Garland is durable and throws strikes with his sinker. He's a solid veteran.

Vicente Padilla was pitching relatively well last season before a neck injury sent him to the disabled list. He still has good stuff and he's despised around baseball (and in his own clubhouse at times) because he throws at people. He overuses a superslow curveball that looks more like an eephus pitch that I could hit. I'd tell him to cut that down to three or four times a game. Padilla can start or relieve, has good control and can strike people out.

BULLPEN:

If anything killed the Dodgers last season, it was the slump of closer Jonathan Broxton. More than anything, closing is a mental exercise and his confidence was shot after so many blown games, especially against the Phillies. Broxton lost his job as Dodgers closer and his ERA was blown out of the water by some terrible losses to the Yankees and Phillies.

Broxton has a near 100-mph fastball and can strike people out, but he loses the strike zone and let's small things enter his mind and sabotage his games. He's only 26 and can still recover. His problems are mental and not physical.

Hong-Chih Kuo saved 12 games after replacing Broxton and there's a chance he could wind up doing the job again this year if Broxton struggles. The lefty throws a near 100-mph fastball and has a brutal slider. His numbers last year were ridiculous. Lefties batted .095 against him; righties .159. He had a 1.20 ERA; allowed 29 hits and 1 homer in 60 innings and struck out 73 with only 18 walks.

I wouldn't hesitate to make a switch between Kuo and Broxton; or to start the season with Kuo closing. People will be watching closely to see what Mattingly does.

Matt Guerrier was one of the unsung keys to the Twins way of winning. With functional starting pitching and a deep and durable bullpen, Twins manager Ron Gardenhire never hesitated to make a change; Guerrier was a huge part of that. Guerrier has pitched over 73 games in each of the past four years. He throws strikes, gives up a few homers and can pitch multiple innings. He's better against righties, but handles lefties. In the Dodgers big ballpark and as Kershaw and Billingsley run up high pitch counts in the middle innings, Guerrier is going to be an imperative piece to the Dodgers hopes and he's going to do well.

Righty Ronald Belisario had a nice rookie season in 2009, but who can tell how much Joe Torre's overuse affected him? Belisario got the Scott Proctor treatment from Torre in that he was either pitching in a game or warming up to pitch in a game. Constantly.

All of Belisario's numbers took a drastic fall in 2010. I think it was due to overwork. He has a good fastball and strikes people out; hopefully for him Mattingly didn't learn that part of using a bullpen from Torre.

Ramon Troncoso's 2009-2010 mirrored Belisario's. He was used a lot in 2009, pitched well and took a tumble in 2010. He can be wild and gives up a few homers, but like Belisario, perhaps he'll rebound after a poor season. He throws hard and has a deceptive motion; he doesn't strike out as many hitters as Belisario does.

Carlos Monasterios has a good fastball and has started and relieved in the majors and minors. He's probably not suited for the bullpen because he gives up a lot of home runs, but he throws strikes. Maybe he could stick in the big leagues as a long reliever.

Kenley Jansen is a 6'6", 220 pound righty from Curacao who made the switch from being a catcher to a pitcher in 2009 and made it to the big leagues in a year.

He....throws....gas.

In 25 games, he threw 27 innings and allowed 12 hits, striking out 41. He's still learning how to pitch and can be wild as he walked 15, but hitters looked frightened of Jansen. If he throws strikes and they combine him with Kuo and a resurgent Broxton, no one is going to want to face that team in a possible playoff matchup.

Jansen is a Rookie of the Year candidate.

Righty Blake Hawksworth was acquired from the Cardinals for Ryan Theriot. Hawksworth is versatile and has good control. He was excellent as a rookie in 2009 and struggled in 2010. His numbers are comparable against lefties and righties and he can pitch multiple innings out of the bullpen or spot start. He gives up a few homers (15 in 90 innings last season).

John Ely is a 24-year-old righty who was acquired from the White Sox for Juan Pierre before the 2009 season. Ely started 18 games as a rookie last season and was impressive in May/June run, but struggled thereafter. He allowed 105 hits in 100 innings and struck out 76. He walked 40 and gave up 12 homers.

Veteran lefty Ron Mahay was signed to a minor league contract. He's still a solid lefty specialist and I expect him to make the Dodgers opening day roster.

LINEUP:

Rod Barajas hit 5 homers in 72 plate appearances after being traded to the Dodgers from the Mets. Barajas is a hacker who doesn't walk and rarely strikes out. He handles the pitching staff behind the plate, has a strong arm and will hit 20 homers with a low batting average/on base percentage.

James Loney had a down year after he looked to be a rising star in the prior three seasons. Loney's average dropped to .267; his on base to .329; and he never had much home run power to begin with; he hit 10 last season and had 41 doubles. He's a fine defensive first baseman. He'll have a rebound year in 2011.

Juan Uribe was a clutch hero for the Giants from the beginning of the season through the World Series and finally cashed in with a 3-year, $21 million contract with the rival Dodgers. Uribe is versatile, can play second, third and short; he has 20 homer power; doesn't walk; makes contact and will hit 20+ doubles. Second base is his best defensive position.

36-year-old Casey Blake had an off year in 2010. Blake is a professional all-around player with pop. His average fell to .248 last season and his on base to .320; his walks declined and his strikeouts increased. Blake is a solid veteran and good defender at third base and I expect him to have a return to his 20 homer, .275-.280 average in 2011.

Rafael Furcal only played in 97 games with hamstring and back injuries. When he played, Furcal batted .300 with a .366 on base, 23 doubles, 7 triples and 8 homers. He stole 22 bases in 26 attempts and played good defense with a howitzer arm. Furcal will be motivated to have a big year as the Dodgers have an option for 2012 at $12 million.

Marcus Thames was signed to a 1-year contract after playing in 2010 with the Yankees. Thames has power; he hit 12 homers in 82 games last season; had a .288 average and his on base was far higher than it usually is at .350. He's a terrible defensive outfielder.

Matt Kemp had a poor year in 2010. Not only did all of his numbers take a nosedive, but there were times that he didn't seem to care one way or the other as to whether the club won or lost. Kemp is overrated defensively anyway and he can't afford to be lazy in center field. This year, it can't happen with Thames and Andre Ethier flanking him and some contact pitchers on the staff.

Kemp's average dropped from .297 to .249; his on base from .352 to .310; his homers increased from 26 to 28; but he struck out 170 times, an increase of 31. His stolen bases fell from 34 to 19 and he was caught 15 times.

He had a bad year and his attitude needs an adjustment more than his swing.

Andre Ethier missed time with a finger injury. His average rose 20 points to .292, but his power numbers dropped from 42 doubles to 33; his homers from 31 to 23. A part of that can be attributed to the injury. Ethier's a burgeoning star player with power. He's not a good defensive outfielder.

BENCH:

Jay Gibbons returned to the big leagues after three years away with injuries and having been caught using PEDs. Gibbons batted .280 in 37 games and had 5 homers in 80 plate appearances. The 34-year-old has hit for good power/average/on base in the minors and he could see some substantial time in sharing left field with Thames.

Dioner Navarro was signed to a 1-year contract. Navarro's bat has disappeared. After hitting .285 as the Rays primary catcher in their pennant-winning season of 2008, he's batted .218 and .194. He's got a great arm and is insurance in case Barajas gets hurt.

Veteran infielder Jamey Carroll had a fine year playing all over the place as a utilityman. In 133 games, Carroll batted .291 with a .379 on base percentage and 12 stolen bases. I wouldn't expect him to repeat those numbers nor will he play that much barring injury.

Tony Gwynn Jr. was signed to a 1-year contract. Not only does Tony Jr. not hit like his dad, he doesn't hit like his uncle, former Dodger Chris Gwynn. His career, I think, has been bolstered by his famous name. He's a good outfielder, has speed and doesn't hit.

Xavier Paul is a 26-year-old outfielder who batted .231 in 133 plate appearances for the Dodgers in 2010. Paul has shown some pop, speed and high average/on base skills in the minors. He might see some time in left field.

A.J. Ellis is a minor league veteran catcher who's put up big batting average and on base numbers in the minors. He walks a lot and doesn't strike out; he's never shown much power, but he throws well from behind the plate; if Barajas gets hurt, he's a better option offensively and probably defensively than Navarro.

PREDICTION:

The Dodgers quietly put together a very strong off-season. They could've used another bat, but Colletti will address that need as the season moves along and if they even need it. Kemp and Blake returning to form will mitigate the need for another hitter.

Their rotation has two potential stars at the top in Kershaw and Billingsley; useful veteran cogs rounding it out. The bullpen has the potential to be devastating with Jansen, Kuo and Broxton in some combination for the seventh, eighth and ninth innings.

They'll hit enough to win games with that pitching staff.

The key to the season is Mattingly and how he handles the job of managing. I said earlier that I believe the players will love him so much that they won't let him fail no matter what he does.

With all the laughter at the expense of the owners, they spend money to win and give their GM a free hand to do what he needs to do to bring in pieces at mid-season.

Underestimate the Dodgers at your own risk.

Underestimate the Dodgers and you'll be wrong because they're going to win the NL West.

PREDICTED RECORD: 89-73

Colorado Rockies

2010 Record: 83-79; 3rd place, National League West.

2010 Recap:

The Rockies are a club that has a bizarre consistency.

I don't mean their constitution; I mean their year-in/year-out streakiness.

After spending the first five months of the season hovering around mediocrity, always hovering between .500 and six or seven games over .500, they went on their annual searing run that almost brought them to the playoffs.

On September 2nd, the Rockies were 69-64 and 7 ½ games behind the frontrunning Padres and in San Diego for a three game series. The Rockies proceeded to rip off a ten game winning streak to climb to within 1 ½ games of first place as the Padres collapsed.

They hovered around a playoff position until September 19th, battling with the Padres and Giants for the division and those clubs and the Braves for the Wild Card. In the game on that day against the Dodgers, closer Huston Street entered with a 1-run lead in the bottom of the ninth inning and he blew the save as the Dodgers tied it and eventually won it in the eleventh.

The Rockies then lost 12 of their final 13 games to fall from contention.

That they managed to make it that far with an injury-riddled and shorthanded starting rotation; a questionable bullpen; and top-heavy lineup is a testament to their hot streaks and manager Jim Tracy.

Carlos Gonzalez and Ubaldo Jimenez emerged into full-blown stars; Troy Tulowitzki catapulted himself into MVP contention with a 15-homer September.

Considering the way they played for much of the season, 83-79 was an appropriate record for them to finish with.

2011 ADDITIONS:

INF Ty Wigginton signed a 2-year, $8 million contract.
3B/2B Jose Lopez was acquired from the Seattle Mariners.
RHP Matt Lindstrom was acquired from the Houston Astros.
RHP Felipe Paulino was acquired from the Houston Astros.
C Jose Morales was acquired from the Minnesota Twins.
RHP Clayton Mortenson was acquired from the Oakland Athletics.
1B Mike Jacobs signed a minor league contract.
C Chad Moeller signed a minor league contract.
C Matt Pagnozzi signed a minor league contract.
OF Willy Taveras signed a minor league contract.
3B Joe Crede signed a minor league contract.
RHP Chris Sampson signed a minor league contract.
RHP Claudio Vargas signed a minor league contract.

2011 SUBTRACTIONS:

C Miguel Olivo was traded to the Toronto Blue Jays.
2B/SS Clint Barmes was traded to the Houston Astros.
INF/OF Melvin Mora was not re-signed.
LHP Joe Beimel was not re-signed.
RHP Octavio Dotel was not re-signed.
RHP Manny Delcarmen was non-tendered.
RHP Manny Corpas was released.
LHP Jeff Francis was not re-signed.
OF Jay Payton was not re-signed.
C Paul Phillips was not re-signed.
RHP Juan Rincon was not re-signed.
2B Kaz Matsui was not re-signed.

2011 PROJECTED STARTING ROTATION: Ubaldo Jimenez; Aaron Cook; Jorge De La Rosa; Jason Hammel; Jhoulys Chacin.

2011 PROJECTED BULLPEN: Huston Street; Matt Lindstrom; Rafael Betancourt; Matt Belisle; Franklin Morales; Felipe Paulino; Esmil Rogers; Matt Reynolds; Matt Daley.

2011 PROJECTED LINEUP: C-Chris Iannetta; 1B-Todd Helton; 2B-Jose Lopez; 3B-Ian Stewart; SS-Troy Tulowitzki; LF-Seth Smith; CF-Dexter Fowler; RF-Carlos Gonzalez.

2011 BENCH: INF-Ty Wigginton; 1B-Jason Giambi; 2B-Eric Young, Jr.; OF-Ryan Spilborghs; C-Jose Morales; INF-Jonathan Herrera; INF-Chris Nelson.

2011 POSSIBLE CONTRIBUTORS: C-Jordan Pacheco; RHP-Bruce Billings; RHP-Edgmer Escalona; RHP-Juan Nicasio; INF-Hector Gomez; C-Michael McKenry; C-Wilin Rosario; RHP-Cory Riordan; RHP-Casey Weathers; C-Chad Moeller; RHP-Clayton Mortenson; OF-Willy Taveras; 3B-Joe Crede; RHP-Chris Sampson; RHP-Claudio Vargas.

ASSESSMENTS
MANAGEMENT:

GM Dan O'Dowd has been the object of my ire before.

He's done some ridiculously stupid things; he's done some smart things. I'm still amazed that he was able to survive the relentless mediocrity over which he presided until the 2007 streak that brought the Rockies to the World Series.

O'Dowd kept his job because of that streak.

Then the club slumped in 2008, but the capital from the pennant gave him the 2009 season. Both O'Dowd and Clint Hurdle were in the final years of their contracts that season, the Rockies got off to an 18-28 start, O'Dowd fired Hurdle and replaced him with Jim Tracy and the Rockies took off, winning the Wild Card.

O'Dowd is a survivor.

This winter, he did a lot of *stuff* but I don't know if he's made the Rockies into a better team or saddled them with prohibitive contracts—some of which were completely unnecessary—for the future.

Troy Tulowitzki was locked into a long term contract through 2014; was it necessary to extend the extension until 2020?

Carlos Gonzalez has a year-and-a-half of big league service time; was it necessary to sign him to an extension through 2017?

Rafael Betancourt; Matt Lindstrom; Ty Wigginton; Jorge De La Rosa; Jose Lopez—all curious, questionable acquisitions or strange/desperate contract signings.

O'Dowd has either cemented his legacy and the future of the Rockies by ensuring these players are going to stay or he's made a mess in the future.

His past is similarly contradictory.

Whether they work or not, given his habitual ability to come crawling out of the wreckage and still have his job, O'Dowd will be the GM one way or the other.

Manager Jim Tracy collapsed at the winter meetings last December, was diagnosed with a mild heart arrhythmia and is expected to be at full strength to manage the team.

Tracy is one of the best managers in baseball not only for his strategies—which are top notch—but because he's widely respected for his straightforward manner in handling the players. Tracy trusts his players and doesn't bury them in the press. He's the type of manager the players *want* to play for and play hard for because they don't want to let him down.

His handling of young players is well-known and he doesn't adhere to the conventional wisdom of limiting pitch counts just "because". Trusting a judgment accumulated from being a baseball lifer in various capacities has given him a breadth of knowledge to be able to make the determination that a pitcher should be removed not because he's reached an arbitrary number of pitches, but because he's done.

Tracy keeps his bench players sharp by somehow finding at bats for them and doles out the innings and appearances for his starters and relievers without overusing them.

STARTING PITCHING:

27-year-old righty Ubaldo Jimenez became a full-fledged star in 2010.

Not only did he pitch a no-hitter, but he was almost unhittable from the beginning of the season through June; he slumped in the summer before regaining his form in August and struggling in September. He was definitely tired.

Jimenez has a lights out fastball in the upper 90s; a sinker and a changeup. He can be wild as he walked 92 in 221 innings, but he struck out 214 and only allowed 10 homers out of 164 hits. He's one of the best pitchers in baseball, a Cy Young Award candidate, has a personality on the mound and is locked up contractually through 2014 for a pittance ($8 million guaranteed with options for 2013-2014).

Aaron Cook is a righty sinkerballer who missed significant portions of the season with a toe problem and then a fractured leg. He gives up a lot of hits, but his sinker keeps the ball in the park. He had a bad year in 2010 and not just with injuries. In 127 innings, Cook allowed 147 hits, walked 52 and struck out 62. He *must* rely on defense and more than a little luck to get by. Cook is signed through this season with an $11.25 million mutual option for 2012.

He'd better have a good, durable year if he wants that option exercised. He might be trade bait.

What is Jorge De La Rosa?

Is he the good pitcher who's been with the Rockies in the past three seasons or is he the hittable entity he was with the Brewers and Royals early in his career?

The Rockies better hope he's the former and that he's healthy. He missed a large part of the 2010 season with a finger injury. He pitched serviceably when he was healthy. De La Rosa loses the strike zone, but he strikes people out and is willing to pitch inside; he has a superior curveball. De La Rosa was a free agent after the 2010 season, but re-signed with the Rockies for a reasonable 2-years and $21.5 million and an $11 million player option for 2013.

Jason Hammel had an identical year in 2010 as he had in 2009. In 30 starts, he won 10 and lost 8; pitched 177 innings, allowed 201 hits; 18 homers; walked 47 and struck out 141. He has a good fastball and is willing to pitch inside. He's unspectacular but solid for the back of the rotation. Hammel signed a 2-year, $7.75 million contract to avoid arbitration.

Jhoulys Chacin is a 23-year-old righty who made 21 starts last season and has terrific stuff with a power fastball and full complement of breaking pitches. He struck out 138 in 137 innings, walked 61, allowed 114 hits and 10 homers; his numbers were excellent in the minors. He has the chance to be a top of the rotation starter.

BULLPEN:

Despite his save totals, I would never, ever feel comfortable with Huston Street as my closer. He has a penchant for gacking up important games repeatedly.

On the surface, his numbers are respectable. He missed the first 2 ½ months of the season with a shoulder problem and returned to appear in 44 games and save 20. He allowed 39 hits in 47 innings with 5 homers; he walked 11 and struck out 45. Unlike other closers whose ERA was bloated by a few bad games, but were still effective, I don't trust Street.

The Rockies owe him slightly over $14 million guaranteed through 2012. Tracy is endlessly loyal to his men, but the Rockies have a former closer in Matt Lindstrom in case Street struggles.

Matt Lindstrom was acquired from the Astros for two minor leaguers. To be brutally honest, Lindstrom isn't any better than Street, but he has a 100-mph fastball and good slider. He missed time with a back problem for the Astros last season and lost his closing job to Brandon Lyon. For a pitcher with such a fastball, Lindstrom doesn't strike out enough hitters and allows too many hits. I'm love his stuff and am not sold on his perforance at all.

Veteran righty Rafael Betancourt has been excellent since coming to the Rockies from the Indians. He's pounds the strike zone, doesn't walk anyone (8 in 62 innings) and racks up the strikeouts (89). He's prone to the longball once in awhile, but he's a very good late inning reliever.

Matt Belisle had a great year for the Rockies in 2010. In 76 games, he threw 92 innings, walked 16 and struck out 91. Because he's a former starter, he's able to provide multiple innings in relief and induce groundballs with the strikeouts.

Franklin Morales is a 25-year-old lefty who handles lefties well, but gets pounded by righties. He did strike out 27 in 28 innings, but he walked 24 and allowed 5 homers. You can't trust a reliever who can't throw strikes. Morales has great stuff, but has to throw the ball over the plate.

Felipe Paulino was acquired from the Astros for Clint Barmes. Paulino has a near 100-mph fastball; his record of 1-9 looks far worse than he pitched. He allowed 95 hits in 91 innings, but much of that was due to a few bad starts. His downfall is the one bad inning; he'll be rolling along then one hit or walk will lead to another and the next thing you know, he's given up a crooked number. I think he has potential as a starter, but with that fastball and strikeout potential, he can be a useful reliever.

Esmil Rogers is a 25-year-old righty who appeared in 28 games last season including 8 starts. He allowed a lot of hits (94 in 72 innings), but struck out 66 and walked 26. He gave up 5 homers and got blasted repeatedly.

Lefty Matt Reynolds was very effective last season against lefties and righties. He walked 5 in 18 innings and struck out 17. He's been a good reliever in the minors with plenty of strikeouts.

Matt Daley is a sidearming righty who had an injury-plagued year after establishing himself in 2009. Daley allowed 27 hits in 23 innings, walked 10 and struck out 18. Sidearmers are valuable if they're used properly.

LINEUP:

For the first time in his career, catcher Chris Iannetta doesn't have a proven veteran catcher as competition for playing time. In recent years, he's had Yorvit Torrealba and Miguel Olivo sharing time with him. Now there's only Jose Morales backing him up. Iannetta has power and has shown the ability to get on base, but he batted .197 last season and wound up back in the minors. He's an average defensive catcher. I wouldn't expect much considering his struggles, but he can hit 15-20 homers.

Todd Helton had a back problem that limited him to 118 games last season. Helton's huge power numbers mysteriously disappeared in five years ago. Whether that was due to the humidor in Colorado or because of other reasons is unknown. He's 37, fields well and walks a lot. If he's healthy, he's good for 15 homers and 50 extra base hits with a high on base percentage.

Jose Lopez was acquired from the Mariners minor league pitcher Chaz Roe. Lopez can play second and third base, has pop, doesn't walk or strike out. He hits plenty of doubles and will provide 60 extra base hits if he plays regularly.

Ian Stewart is a lefty-swinging, average fielding third baseman with some power. In 121 games last season, he hit 18 homers and drove in 61; he also hit 14 doubles. He strikes out a fair amount (110 times in 441 plate apppearances); he batted .256 with a .338 on base. He and Lopez are going to share time at second and third with Eric Young, Jr. and Ty Wigginton.

Troy Tulowitzki had a month for the ages as he almost singlehandedly carried the Rockies to the playoffs before their late season stumble. Tulowitzki was having a solid if not spectacular season before a 15 homer, 40 RBI month got him into the MVP conversation.

Tulowitzki has been compared to Derek Jeter in his maturity and leadership, but he's very, very streaky. He's a fine player who hits the ball out of the park, gets on base, plays good defense and loves the spotlight. After the season, he signed a contract extension through the year 2020 that will keep him with the Rockies for the rest of his career. His deal, with the initial contract he'd signed as a rookie, is for $157.5 million.

Seth Smith is a 28-year-old lefty swinging outfielder who batted .246 with a .314 on base percentage a year after posting .293 and .378 numbers in the same categories. He has some pop with 17 homers, 19 doubles and 5 triples. He's a solid defensive outfielder.

Dexter Fowler is still finding his way in the big leagues after posting massive average/on base numbers in the minors. The 25-year-old switch hitter is an average defensive center fielder with speed. He batted .260 with a .347 on base, 20 doubles, 14 triples (leading the league) and 6 homers. He stole 13 bases and was caught 8 times. He strikes out a lot and his development is going slowly.

The same cannot be said for Carlos Gonzalez.

In 2010, Gonzalez exploded onto the scene with a near triple crown, MVP season.

The 25-year-old batted .336 with 34 homers and 117 RBI; he scored 111 runs, had 197 hits, 34 doubles, 9 triples and stole 26 bases. Gonzalez finished 3rd in the MVP voting and had the Rockies made the playoffs, he might've won it. As they did with Tulowitzki, the Rockies locked Gonzalez up early, signing him after his first full year to a 7-year, $80 million contract.

He's a star.

BENCH:

Ty Wigginton signed a 2-year, $8 million contract. Wigginton is a feisty, hard-nosed player with pop. He can play first, second and third and will see plenty of action for the Rockies. He doesn't get on base, but he'll hit 20 homers and and 25 doubles with significant at bats.

Jason Giambi may be 40; he may not be the threat he once was; but he still has a fantastic eye and power. Last season, he batted .244 in 222 plate appearances, but walked enough to get his OBP up to .378. He's on a minor league deal, but he'll make the team.

Eric Young, Jr. is a backup infielder with speed. He's a good defensive second baseman and batted .244 in 189 plate apperances last season with 17 stolen bases.

Outfielder Ryan Spilborghs batted .279 with a .360 on base and 10 homers in 133 games last season. The 31-year-old is a useful fourth outfielder.

Jose Morales is a 28-year-old backup catcher who was acquired from the Twins. He's good defensively and batted .311 in 134 at bats in 2009 backing up Joe Mauer, but fell to .194 in 19 games last season. He's been a pretty good hitter in the minors.

Jonathan Herrera is a 26-year-old, switch-hitting utilityman who batted .284 in 257 plate appearances last season. He's a slap hitter, but he's patient and doesn't strike out.

Chris Nelson is a 25-year-old backup infielder who has posted fine numbers in the minors. Last season in Triple A, he batted .313 with a .376 on base and 12 homers. He hit .280 in a brief big league stay.

PREDICTION:

The Rockies have enough talent to win the NL West and contend for the Wild Card. They have a true horse at the top of the rotation in Jimenez; De La Rosa is good if he's healthy; and Hammel is solid. Chacin has a lot of talent. Cook is a question mark and I wouldn't expect much considering how many hits he allows.

I don't like their closer options and it's highly unlikely that Tracy is going to demote Street unless he utterly implodes; even then, is Lindstrom much better? Belisle can't repeat his 2010 season and while I like Paulino, his numbers last season are what they are.

The lineup has holes behind the plate with Iannetta and no veteran insurance to take over for him if he doesn't hit. Helton is a year older and declining. Lopez, Wigginton, Smith—all have positives and negatives.

Can Gonzalez repeat his 2010 season?

The Rockies are a club that has been more than the sum of their parts for the past few years and if anyone can piece it together, it's Tracy.

That said, they have so many questions that it's hard to have them winning a tough division. With their streakiness, if they're within striking distance in September, they're a threat; but they're going to fall short in 2011.

PREDICTED RECORD: 86-76

San Francisco Giants

2010 Record: 92-70; 1st place, National League West.
Defeated Atlanta Braves in NLDS 3 games to 1.
Defeated Philadelphia Phillies in NLCS 4 games to 2.
Defeated Texas Rangers in World Series 4 games to 1.

2010 Recap:

The epitome of a club that was more than the sum of its statistical parts, the Giants won with great starting pitching; a fearless, durable closer; a scraped together bullpen; a bunch of pickups from the waiver wire and unheralded trades; youth and guts.

Tim Lincecum was a household name before last season and few outside San Francisco were aware of how good Brian Wilson and Matt Cain were; or the Giants had a star young catcher on the horizon in Buster Posey. All were major parts of the Giants championship club, but without Pat Burrell and Cody Ross, the Giants wouldn't have even made the playoffs; both were acquired by GM Brian Sabean for nothing.

Entering the playoffs against the Braves, the romantic notion was that Braves manager Bobby Cox should go out with a deep playoff run; the Giants dispatched the Braves in 4 games.

The mighty Phillies with their "big three" starting rotation of Roy Halladay, Cole Hamels and Roy Oswalt were fresh off a 3 game destruction of the Cincinnati Reds and running on all cylinders for the better part of three months. Giants manager Bruce Bochy outmaneuvered his counterpart, Charlie Manuel; the Giants pitching strangled the Phillies offense, and the club refused to be intimidated by the Phillies' bullying and took them out in six games.

The Rangers had outhustled and outplayed both the Rays and Yankees and had Cliff Lee at the top of his game and looking to bolster his free agent credentials even further with a championship. Juan Uribe had other ideas. Uribe, who in his career has murdered Lee, hit a tape measure home run in the first game of the World Series and the Giants were off and running to a 5 game domination to win a highly unlikely and well-deserved World Series.

2011 ADDITIONS:

SS Miguel Tejada signed a 1-year, $6 million contract.
RHP Jeff Suppan signed a minor league contract.
RHP Casey Daigle signed a minor league contract.
C Chris Stewart signed a minor league contract.

2011 SUBTRACTIONS:

INF Juan Uribe was not re-signed.
SS Edgar Renteria was not re-signed.
LHP Dontrelle Willis was released.
RHP Denny Bautista was not re-signed.
OF Jose Guillen was not re-signed.
RHP Brandon Medders was not re-signed.
RHP Chris Ray was not re-signed.
OF Eugenio Velez was not re-signed.
RHP Todd Wellemeyer was not re-signed.

2011 PROJECTED STARTING ROTATION: Tim Lincecum; Matt Cain; Jonathan Sanchez; Madison Bumgarner; Barry Zito.

2011 PROJECTED BULLPEN: Brian Wilson; Sergio Romo; Santiago Casilla; Jeremy Affeldt; Javier Lopez; Dan Runzler; Ramon Ramirez; Guillermo Mota.

2011 PROJECTED LINEUP: C-Buster Posey; 1B-Aubrey Huff; 2B-Freddy Sanchez; 3B-Pablo Sandoval; SS-Miguel Tejada; LF-Pat Burrell; CF-Andres Torres; RF-Cody Ross.

2011 BENCH: OF-Aaron Rowand; INF/OF-Mark DeRosa; OF-Nate Schierholtz; 1B-Travis Ishikawa; C-Eli Whiteside; INF-Emmanuel Burriss; INF-Mike Fontenot.

2011 POSSIBLE CONTRIBUTORS: OF-Darren Ford; INF-Ryan Rohlinger; RHP-Jose Casilla; LHP-Alex Hinshaw; LHP-Clayton Tanner; 3B-Conor Gillaspie; OF-Thomas Neal; C-Chris Stewart; RHP-Jeff Suppan.

ASSESSMENTS MANAGEMENT:

Because he eschews relying on stats above his own eyes and experience and isn't afraid to say so, GM Brian Sabean is routinely lambasted by stat people who consider him to be a troglodyte who's getting by on luck.

Yes, he's made some stupid free agent signings for players who are either benched (Aaron Rowand); or were relegated to cheerleader status in the post-season (Barry Zito); but he's also put together a club with a load of young pitching; a superalative closer; an emerging all-around superstar behind the plate; and fill in pieces that fit together like a puzzle.

It cost him nothing in terms of players to get Cody Ross and Pat Burrell; both contributed mightily to the Giants championship.

Sabean is a lot more savvy than he's given credit for and did a fine job in rebuilding the Giants minor league system and crafting a contender very, very quickly after the Barry Bonds era ended; and he's done it under a reasonable payroll.

Bruce Bochy has come a long way from being run out of San Diego by the dysfunction and desire of the front office to have someone who was going to listen to orders without complaint. What the Padres have gotten is Bud Black who's presided over two teams that have blown playoff spots that were essentially sewn up.

Much like Sabean, Bochy has his detractors. He's decidedly old-school with his black mustache and grabled, gruff way of talking, he does things his way and goes by his gut. He's unafraid to ask his players to give just a bit more than is customary in the way the game is played and managed today and this is part of the reason the Giants have overachieved, at least according to the numbers.

From the front office to the manager's office all the way through the clubhouse, they have a bunch of players who you have to drag out into the parking lot and kill to stop.

He rides his starting pitchers, uses his bullpen well, has a knack for making the right lineup choices and has little interest in criticism for his decisions or idiotic suggestions.

Both he and Sabean have something that no numerical projection can take away: a championship ring.

Sabean and Bochy had contract options for 2012 that the Giants have exercised. Don't be surprised to see both receive contract extensions sometime this season.

STARTING PITCHING:

Tim Lincecum was dogged by questions about his health during the season due to diminished velocity and effectiveness. In truth, the two-time National League Cy Young Award winner was due to lose some of his dominance; to go from greatness to strictly good is easy to inspire contextualized red flags.

In 2010, did Lincecum pitch "worse" than he had in his back-to-back CYA seasons from 2008 and 2009?

Of course. No pitcher can exhibit that kind of brilliance on an annual basis. But the hovering questions about Lincecum's unique motion and training regimen, along with his diminutive size, will always cast a shadow of doubt over his long term durability.

In truth, Lincecum *was* more hittable in 2010 than he was in previous years; his velocity *was* down; but it looked to me like it was due more to him trying to overuse his changeup at the expense of his fastball; and don't discount the newness of rookie catcher Buster Posey in working with the pitchers; the pitcher-relationship is something ephemeral and difficult to pinpoint. Posey was lauded for the work he did in handling the Giants pitchers, but the transition from Bengie Molina to Posey couldn't have been easy.

Lincecum struggled for stretches, but turned it on in September during the Giants frenetic run to the playoffs; and in the playoffs, he pitched one of the best games in the history of the post-season as he dismantled the Braves in game 1 of the NLDS with a 2 hit, 14 strikeout masterpiece of a complete game shutout.

Lincecum is going to return to his 2008-2009 form and again contend for the NL Cy Young Award. He's one of the best pitchers in baseball.

Matt Cain would be the ace of 20 other staffs, but with the Giants he's a superlative number 2.

Cain had a solid regular season at 13-11 with a 3.14 ERA; in 223 innings, he allowed 181 hits, walked 61, struck out 177 and gave up 22 homers. Every staff has a pitcher for whom the offense has trouble scoring—for whatever reason—and with the Giants, it's Cain. If he had better run support, he would've won 18 games. It's his lot in life to have his record diminished by a lack of scoring.

But in the playoffs and World Series, Cain took no chances on his games being ruined because his club wouldn't score. It was almost as if he decided that if the team isn't going to score for him, he'll simply not allow any runs.

In 21 post-season innings, Cain allowed 13 hits and 1 unearned run.

That's it.

He was masterful and now everyone knows that there's another young star pitcher on the Giants staff; his name is Matt Cain.

Jonathan Sanchez has some of the best stuff in baseball. He has a deceptive motion that's very hard on lefties, a good fastball, slider and changeup. At times he's unhittable; but at other times, he can't throw strikes. In 2010, he led the National League in walks with 96, but struck out 205 batters in 193 innings—both career highs. He only allowed 142 hits and had a fantastic start against the Braves in the NLDS before the Phillies and Rangers knocked him around in the NLCS and World Series.

Sanchez is an enigmatic but good mid-rotation starter who could turn the corner completely at the age of 28.

21-year-old rookie lefty Madison Bumgarner was also excellent in the post-season especially in his World Series start in which he allowed 0 runs and 3 hits in eight innings vs the Rangers.

In the regular season, he went 7-6 in 18 starts, but pitched well enough to win 13 or 14 games. He has a quirky, slingshot motion and a good fastball and control and is a worthy addition to a very good starting rotation.

Then we get to Barry Zito.

The one good thing that can be said about Zito at this point is that he makes his starts and you know what to expect from him. If he were a young pitcher making no money, he'd have use; but Zito isn't a young pitcher making no money; he's owed $64.5 million through 2013.

Zito had pitched so poorly down the stretch, was so untrustworthy that he was left off the post-season roster entirely. So lacking in confidence in their big 2007 free agent signing season that the Giants braintrust didn't even want to consider him as a long reliever in the event that one of their starters got knocked out of the box early.

On the surface and ignoring his 9-14 record, his numbers aren't bad. In 199 innings, he allowed 184 hits and 20 homers; he walked 84 and struck out 150. There are voices that say the money is gone, so it's time to accept Zito for what he is. I understand that, but cannot ignore that he's making so much money and is so consistent in his hittability and wildness that manager Bochy doesn't hesitate to yank him even if he's only allowed a hit and a walk in the middle innings.

Strangely, Zito was very good for the first half of the season, but the wheels came off in the second half. It was a false positive. He doesn't have the velocity to get inside on anyone anymore and if he's not perfect, he gets slammed.

All the Giants can do now is keep using him as an innings-eater, pull him when he gets into trouble, hope they see some of the 8-inning,

2-hit games he'll post a few times a season and accept that he's getting paid as a top rotation starter and isn't that anymore.

BULLPEN:

Brian Wilson, his black beard and post-season excellence became known to the world after the 2010 season he had.

Wilson has long been a gutty, durable and reliable closer. With a near 100 mph fastball and willingness to do the unthinkable in today's game—pitch 2 innings or more—he's a guy you want in your bullpen taking the ball with the game on the line.

In the regular season, Wilson was a horse. He saved 48 games, threw 74 innings, allowed 62 hits with only 3 homers and struck out 93. In the playoffs, he allowed 1 unearned run in 10 games.

One thing that would concern me going into 2011 is the workload and his back. Wilson's had back problems and while I generally dismiss the misapplied historical numbers of pitchers who've struggled after long post-season runs—you can't generalize with numbers designed to prove a point—it's something to watch with Wilson. He may struggle.

Righty Sergio Romo has a slinging motion from the right side and racks up the strikeouts. In 68 games and 62 innings, Romo struck out 70, walked 14 and allowed 6 homers. He surrendered a big homer to Eric Hinske in the NLDS. Romo's a solid and durable set-up man.

Righty Santiago Casilla boasts a fastball in the high-90s. In 55 innings, he struck out 56; he can get wild with 26 walks, but he's tough to hit when he's in the strike zone; he allowed 40 hits, 2 homers and had a 1.95 ERA.

Veteran lefty Jeremy Affeldt had a subpar year statistically, but that was due to a few bad games; he still throws hard and has a good curve. He handles righties and lefties, can strike people out and has good control. He's a reliable lefty out of the pen.

Lefty specialist Javier Lopez was freed from the cage of the Pittsburgh Pirates and played a key role in the Giants championship.

The sidearming Lopez pitched in 27 games and in 19 innings allowed 11 hits and struck out 16. Lefties batted .162 against him.

Dan Runzler is a 25-year-old lefty who has great strikeout numbers and control issues. In 32 innings he struck out 37, but he walked 20. He's closed in the minors, but has to gain more command to be trustworthy as anything more than an extra arm.

Ramon Ramirez was acquired from the Red Sox at mid-season and had a 0.67 ERA in 27 games for the Giants. He occasionally gives up the longball, but has pitched well and durably in the past.

Veteran Guillermo Mota signed a minor league deal with the Giants after appearing in 56 games last season. Mota still throws hard and was, for the most part, reliable last season and I expect him to make the club.

LINEUP:

Buster Posey was expected to be a big time hitter when he was taken with the 5th pick in the 2008 draft; his catching was the only thing that kept him in the minors as long as it did. Despite having a fine throwing arm and presence, the big issue for him was his ability to handle the Giants eclectic group of pitchers.

Posey wasn't recalled from the minors until May and took over as the everyday catcher. He hit from minute one and wound up with a .305 average; .357 on base; 18 homers; 23 doubles and 67 RBI in 108 games. His abilities behind the plate in the regular and post-season were most important.

It was his defense that appeared to decide the closely contested Rookie of the Year balloting with Jason Heyward of the Braves in Posey's favor.

He's already a star and will get better.

Aubrey Huff batted .290 with a .385 on base, 26 homers and 64 total extra base hits. He played a solid defensive first base. Huff had slumped with the Orioles and Tigers in 2009 and was something of a consolation choice for the Giants after Adam LaRoche rejected their contract offer, but Huff made the most of his opportunity. He's always been this type of a hitter but few paid attention to him. After the season, he signed a 2-year, $22 million contract to remain with the Giants.

Freddy Sanchez battled shoulder problems last season and only played in 111 games. He batted .292 with 22 doubles and 7 homers. He's a hacker who doesn't walk, nor does he strike out. Sanchez is an average defensive second baseman and had some big hits in the playoffs.

Pablo Sandoval had a terrible year after his breakout season in 2009. His weight was seen to be the cause, but I don't think he was much heavier in 2010 than he was in 2009. Sandoval's issue may have been pitchers exploiting his lack of patience, that he can't catch up to the high fastball and can't stop himself from chasing it.

Sandoval's average/power/on base numbers all dropped significantly in 2010. It could've been a sophomore slump or that he couldn't adjust to the new way he was being pitched. I'd expect a rebound year from Sandoval.

Over-the-hill veteran shortstop Miguel Tejada replaced over-the-hill veteran shortstop Edgar Renteria.

Tejada can still hit well enough and played surprisingly solid defense back at shortstop after he was traded from the Orioles to the Padres. He's 36, but had a fine year at the plate for the Astros in 2009 and as far as short-term veteran hole-fillers, Tejada is serviceable for 1-year at $6.5 million.

Pat Burrell's reputation was shot when he was released by the Rays after a season and a month of disinterested lack of productivity. Could it have been a return to the National League where he wasn't relegated to being a DH? It's possible. For whatever reason, some players can't adjust from the feeling that they're not playing in the game when they're DHing and must play the field to stay focused.

Either way, Burrell was a leader on and off the field for the Giants, hit 18 homers in 96 games after joining them, and was back to the player he was with the Phillies who walked and got on base frequently. His left field defense was serviceable as well.

Andres Torres took over in center field for Aaron Rowand and at the age of 32, had a fine year. Torres had never gotten the chance to play regularly and took advantage of it in 2010 with 16 homers, 43 doubles and 8 triples in 570 plate appearances. He strikes out a lot (128) and could stand to be a bit more patient, but he was a clutch player and played good defense in center field.

Cody Ross arrived as an afterthought in August after the Marlins placed him on waivers and let the Giants take him for nothing. Ross has always been unappreciated for his feisty contributions and surprising power. He didn't do much in the regular season, but in the playoffs, he ripped 2 homers off of Roy Halladay in the first game and added another one in the second game off of Roy Oswalt. Ross is tough, can play all three outfield positions and hits the ball out of the park.

BENCH:

Aaron Rowand is relegated to being a fourth outfielder unless the Giants can find a taker for his contract which still has $24 million guaranteed through 2012. Rowand got hit in the face with a pitch and it might have affected him at the plate. He's a fine outfielder and leader in the clubhouse with some power.

Mark DeRosa was signed to a 2-year, $12 million contract before last season and missed most of the season with an injured wrist. DeRosa was a fine player and leader for the Cubs in his two seasons there, but hasn't been the same since he was traded to the Indians; then the Cardinals; and last season with the Giants. Injuries have always been a hindrance to him. Not much will be expected from him this year, but if he's healthy, he can contribute as a roving utilityman.

Nate Schierholtz is a backup outfielder who was a defensive replacement and pinch hitter last season. He batted .242 with little power in 252 plate appearances.

Travis Ishikawa is a defensive-minded first baseman who batted .266 in 173 plate appearances. He's shown some pop in the past, but was used mostly for defense in 2010.

Eli Whiteside will back up Posey. The 31-year-old veteran is a solid defender who batted .238 in 140 plate appearances last season with 4 homers. He won't play much.

Emannuel Burriss was a 1st round pick of the Giants in 2006 draft and when he got to the big leagues in 2008, looked like he was going to be a good player. He's slumped since then and the switch hitter spent most of last season in the minors. He's got speed and can play second and short.

Veteran Mike Fontenot was acquired from the Cubs last August. The veteran utility infielder had a very good season in a part-time role with the Cubs in 2008, was exposed when playing regularly in 2009, and batted .283 in 261 plate appearances for the Cubs and Giants last season.

PREDICTION:

The Giants still have one of the best starting rotations in baseball and a top notch closer. The rest of the bullpen is filled with serviceable vetearns who can get the job done. My questions surround the offense and, to a degree, that pitching staff.

When a team is built around pitching and winning close games and has the success the Giants did last season, they gloss over the narrow margin for error that wound up on the positive side for them. Can they expect a repeat year from Sanchez? From Bumgarner as he goes around the league the second time? Zito is what he is; Lincecum and Cain are still great, but what if the offense can't pick up the slack for a downgrade?

Wilson was worked extremely hard all of last year; no matter how tough he is, if any pitcher is ripe for a fallback after a long season, it's him.

Tejada may not be able to handle the defensive responsibilities at shortstop all year long and Sandoval isn't Graig Nettles at third. Defense is important for a pitching-minded club and the defense on the left side of the infield is suspect.

Can Torres repeat his 2010 breakout year? Or was it a fluke?

The Giants won the World Series after a dogfight to make the playoffs, but they're in a really difficult division and with the other teams having improved and the way the Giants won last year with clutch performances from discarded veteran bats, 92 wins can fall to 81-85 very easily.

And that's where they're going to end up in 2011.

PREDICTED RECORD: 81-81

San Diego Padres

2010 Record: 90-72; 2nd place, National League West.

2010 Recap:

The Padres rode their terrific top-to-bottom pitching and good defense, along with a fair amount of Adrian Gonzalez, to the brink of a playoff spot before falling to the Giants on the final weekend.

Having spent most of the season in first place, the Padres were one of the surprises of baseball; they made some aggressive moves at mid-season in getting Ryan Ludwick and Miguel Tejada, but the hot streaks of the Rockies and Giants, along with the Braves recovering their footing after a stumble of their own, left the Padres on the outside looking in at the playoffs.

The fantastic pitching led by Clayton Richard and Mat Latos in the starting rotation and Heath Bell and Luke Gregerson in the bullpen couldn't overcome a popgun offense that was shut down too regularly to hang onto their playoff position.

2011 ADDITIONS:

SS Jason Bartlett was acquired from the Tampa Bay Rays.
2B Orlando Hudson signed a 2-year, $11.5 million contract with 2013 club option.
OF Cameron Maybin was acquired from the Florida Marlins.
RHP Aaron Harang signed a 1-year, $4 million contract with 2012 mutual option.

OF/1B Brad Hawpe signed a 1-year, $3 million contract with 2012 club option.
RHP Chad Qualls signed a 1-year, $2.55 million contract with 2012 club option.
RHP Dustin Moseley signed a 1-year, $900,000 contract.
INF Jorge Cantu signed a 1-year, $850,000 contract.
C Rob Johnson was acquired from the Seattle Mariners.
2B/OF Eric Patterson was acquired from the Boston Red Sox.
INF Jarrett Hoffpauir was claimed off waivers from the Toronto Blue Jays.
INF Kevin Frandsen signed a minor league contract.
RHP Casey Kelly was acquired from the Boston Red Sox.
1B Anthony Rizzo was acquired from the Boston Red Sox.
OF Reymond Fuentes was acquired from the Boston Red Sox.
C Gregg Zaun signed a minor league contract.
C Guillermo Quiroz signed a minor league contract.

2011 SUBTRACTIONS:

1B Adrian Gonzalez was traded to the Boston Red Sox.
C Yorvit Torrealba was not re-signed.
2B David Eckstein was not re-signed.
SS Miguel Tejada was not re-signed.
OF Scott Hairston was not re-signed.
INF/OF Jerry Hairston, Jr. was not re-signed.
OF Tony Gwynn Jr. was non-tendered.
OF/1B Matt Stairs was not re-signed.
RHP Kevin Correia was not re-signed.
RHP Jon Garland was not re-signed.
RHP Edward Mujica was traded to the Florida Marlins.
RHP Ryan Webb was traded to the Florida Marlins.
RHP Chris Young was not re-signed.
OF Jody Gerut was not re-signed.
C Chris Stewart was not re-signed.

2011 PROJECTED STARTING ROTATION: Clayton Richard; Mat Latos; Tim Stauffer; Wade LeBlanc; Aaron Harang; Cory Luebke.

2011 PROJECTED BULLPEN: Heath Bell; Luke Gregerson; Mike Adams; Joe Thatcher; Chad Qualls; Dustin Moseley; Ernesto Frieri.

2011 PROJECTED LINEUP: C-Nick Hundley; 1B-Brad Hawpe; 2B-Orlando Hudson; 3B-Chase Headley; SS-Jason Bartlett; LF-Ryan Ludwick; CF-Cameron Maybin; RF-Will Venable.

2011 BENCH: 1B/OF-Kyle Blanks; INF-Everth Cabrera; INF-Jorge Cantu; C-Rob Johnson; OF-Chris Denorfia; OF-Aaron Cunningham; 2B/OF-Eric Patterson.

2011 POSSIBLE CONTRIBUTORS: OF-Luis Durango; OF-Mike Baxter; INF-Jarret Hoffpauir; RHP-Evan Scribner; LHP-Aaron Poreda; RHP-Jeremy Hefner; C-Gregg Zaun; INF-Kevin Frandsen; RHP-Samuel Deduno.

ASSESSMENTS

MANAGEMENT:

After a year of flirtation with dealing Adrian Gonzalez, GM Jed Hoyer finally pulled the trigger with his former employers, the Boston Red Sox.

In his first months on the job, Hoyer appeared to do almost nothing significant in terms of player acquisitions, but his inexpensive signings of Yorvit Torrealba and Jon Garland paid off big in bolstering the foundation that had been left behind by Kevin Towers.

The Padres were contending and the predicted attempts (by me especially) to trade Gonzalez and Heath Bell at mid-season were placed on the backburner. Instead of subtracting, the Padres added veterans Ryan Ludwick and Miguel Tejada. They also made a move on Cliff Lee which failed.

After the Padres faltered at the end of the 2010 season, Hoyer stepped up his efforts to trade Gonzalez and got top-rated prospects from the Red Sox. It made absolute sense for him to deal Gonzalez when he did. His value was never going to be higher from then on; he was not staying in San Diego as a free agent; barring the one stupid team overspending for a rental, the Padres weren't going to get more for Gonzalez than they did; and there was always the chance for injury.

That said, the prospects are unlikely to help this Padres team.

To account for the loss of Gonzalez, Hoyer signed Orlando Hudson and traded for Cameron Maybin and Jason Bartlett. The strategy appears to be defense-minded.

I'm dubious as to whether this will work.

Bud Black won Manager of the Year and did a fantastic job handling the pitchers. I don't like the way he runs games with the lineup and think he's a hindrance offensively to a club that literally cannot afford to make mistakes to cost themselves runs.

There was the June 1st game against the Mets that was an example of this in which a struggling Francisco Rodriguez was trying to close out the game, the Padres had cut the Mets lead to 4-2 with two outs and, with Matt Stairs on the bench, Black elected to use Jerry Hairston, Jr. and Chris Denorfia. Both struck out. Whether this was a safety-first strategy due to stats (Stairs was 0 for 10 career against K-Rod, but with 4 walks), or just a bizarre decision is irrelevant. Black does weird things.

Then we get to the two collapses.

The Padres had playoff spots essentially sewn up in both 2007 and 2010.

They blew both of them on the last weekend of the season.

Is Black to blame for this? Well, if he gets credit for the success, he gets blame for the failure.

He'd better do an above-and-beyond the call of duty with the pitching staff this year because they're short in the starting rotation and have lost the centerpiece of their offense in Gonzalez.

STARTING PITCHING:

Lefty Clayton Richard was the main component in the deal that sent Jake Peavy to the White Sox in 2009. It turned out to be a great deal for the Padres as they got Richard, who provided 201 innings in 2010, plus other youngsters Aaron Poreda and Adam Russell.

Richard has a simple motion, a good fastball and slider; he loses the strike zone occasionally with 78 walks; is a decent strikeout pitcher with 153 and only allowed 16 homers. If he can cut down on the walks, he can be an 18-game winner.

Mat Latos came of age in 2010.

Always a superstar talent with a live fastball, good slider and changeup, plus a deceptive motion, his main obstacle was his penchant for losing his cool when things didn't go well. The immaturity was evident when he first arrived in the big leagues with sour faces and poor body language that will not endear anyone to their teammates nor to their old-school manager and former pitcher, Black.

In 2010, Latos controlled himself and blossomed into one of the top young pitchers in baseball. The Padres kept him on an innings count; he allowed 150 hits and 16 homers in 184 innings; he walked 50 and struck out 189. The 23-year-old righty is going to be one of the best pitchers in baseball in years to come and a Cy Young Award contender.

Tim Stauffer was a 1st round pick of the Padres in 2003 but injuries and poor performance kept him in the minors for much of the time until 2009. In 2009, he made 14 starts and was serviceable despite a 4-7 record. In 2010, Stauffer began the season in the bullpen, then shifted to the rotation full-time in September and allowed 1 run or fewer in four of his five starts. He has a good fastball, curve and cutter; allowed 65 hits in 82 innings, walked 24 and struck out 61.

Is he a late bloomer who needed time to develop and overcome injuries? Or is he the bust he was in the first few years of his career? With the departures of Jon Garland and Kevin Correia, the Padres need Stauffer to be the former. Badly. I'm reluctant to think a pitcher who's had so many rises and falls is going to automatically find his way so suddenly.

Wade LeBlanc is a soft-tossing lefty with a funky delivery. He loses the strike zone occasionally and if he doesn't hit his spots, gets hit very hard. In 146 innings in 2010, he allowed 157 hits and 24 homers; he walked 51 and struck out 110. He's a back-of-the-rotation starter.

Veteran righty Aaron Harang's career has run off the rails after several years in which he was one of the best pitchers in baseball without being recognized as such. In 2006-2007, Harang rode terrific control and durability to a 32-17 record; since then it's been injuries and ineffectiveness sabotaging him.

Last season he missed most of the summer with a back problem; when he pitched, he was effective for the most part despite a couple of terrible games in which he allowed crooked numbers of unearned runs that blew up his ERA. His fastball isn't what it was a few years ago and he can't strike people out; he's always allowed a lot of homers. Harang is from San Diego and he signed a 1-year, $4 million contract with a mutual option for 2012.

If healthy, Harang can gain some semblance of his old form; but he probably won't ever be as good as he was in his heyday.

Cory Luebke is a lefty who was the Padres 1st round pick in the 2007 draft. He's been great in the minors and showed a strikeout ability in the majors that wasn't as prevalent on the way up. He has excellent control and pitches to contact.

BULLPEN:

Heath Bell has been on and off the trade market and I still think the Padres might trade him at some point. He's a free agent at the end of the year and even though there will be many closers on the market, Bell's become dominant and will receive free agent offers that the Padres can't hope to match.

Last season, he saved 47 games and in 70 innings, struck out 86. He allowed 56 hits and walked 28 and surrended 1 homer. If the Padres are out of contention at mid-season, Bell's getting traded.

Luke Gregerson is one of the most dominant set-up men in baseball. I have no clue what the Cardinals were thinking in trading him for Khalil Greene. Gregerson has an easily repeatable motion, a good fastball and devastating slider; he'd be a terrific closer.

In 78 innings last season, he struck out 89; he did allow 8 homers, which is a lot, but it could've been due to having control that was too good and being wild in the strike zone; he'd decreased his walks from 31 in 2009 to 18 in 2010; he should pitch inside more. Apart from that, he's a force in the bullpen.

Mike Adams has found a home in the Padres bullpen after a journeyman career rife with injuries. Adams throws very hard, but he has a stressful motion. He stayed healthy last season and was great. In 70 games and 66 innings, he struck out 73, allowed 48 hits and 2 homers. He has a power fastball, a good slider and control; he's a big asset if he's healthy.

Joe Thatcher is a lefty with a wild, funky motion in which he flings the ball across his body and his arms and legs flail all over the place. He was used against both righties and lefties last season and handled both; overall he had a 1.29 ERA in 35 innings (65 appearances), with 23 hits allowed, 7 walks and 45 strikeouts.

Chad Qualls signed a short-term contract with the Padres to rejuvenate his value after pitching terribly for the Diamondbacks and Rays last season. Qualls was once a top-tier set-up man, but he was used heavily in his years with the Astros. All the overwork might have diminished his stuff just enough that he's far more hittable.

He allowed 85 hits in 59 innings last season and it would concern me that the Rays didn't try to keep him after reuniting him with his former Astros pitching coach Jim Hickey and he wasn't much more effective in Tampa than he'd been in Arizona.

Dustin Moseley was signed to a 1-year contract after being a useful swingman for the Yankees last season. He's a contact pitcher who throws strikes, doesn't strike anyone out and allows a lot of homers. As a long man, he's a good arm to have.

Ernesto Frieri is a 25-year-old righty who appeared in 33 games with a 1.71 ERA. He struck out 41 and walked 17 in 31 innings and allowed 18 hits and 2 homers. He closed in Triple A last season before being recalled, saved 17 games and had excellent across the board numbers.

LINEUP:

Nick Hundley will get a chance to be the everyday catcher with the departure of Yorvit Torrealba. Hundley is 27, not particularly good defensively and doesn't hit for average or get on base; he strikes out a lot, but has some occasional power.

With the trade of Adrian Gonzalez, Brad Hawpe will get first crack at winning the first base job; I'm sure the Padres would prefer that Kyle Blanks stakes his claim to the job, but right now, it's Hawpe.

As recently as 2009, Hawpe was an All Star with the Rockies; on an annual basis for three straight years, he had 20+ homers; a .280+ average; and a .380+ on base. Last year, he slumped and the Rockies, in a remarkable bit of strident judgment of personnel, released him. His contract was up at the end of the year and they were unlikely to re-sign him, but it was a rapid descent for Hawpe. The Rays picked him up and he didn't hit there either.

Hawpe is only 31 and last season was likely just a bad year; he wasn't a creation of Coors Field as his numbers at home and on the road are quite similar. He's not a "replacement" for Gonzalez—one of the game's best players—but he'll have a good comeback year.

Orlando Hudson joins his fourth organization in four years.

There are three ways to look at that: 1) he's a short-term, disposable stopgap; 2) he's wanted; or 3) both.

Hudson's a switch hitter; has some pop; can run; plays good defense; and is a stand-up guy. There's nothing overtly "wrong" with Hudson that he keeps moving from venue to venue armed with the knowledge that he should rent and not buy, but he's the prototypical "caught in the middle" player. He's good, but not Chase Utley/Robinson Cano good. He's been on the outside looking in at free agent riches every year since leaving the Diamondbacks. His one flaw is that he's injury-prone and the injuries have frequently been to his wrists which, to me, would be a big red flag.

Hudson wasn't great at the plate last season for the Twins with a .268 average, .338 on base, 6 homers and 10 stolen bases. He probably won't do much better in the cavernous Petco Park, but he can catch the ball. He signed a 2-year, $11.5 million contract with the Padres with an option for 2013.

With all this in mind, I wouldn't have given Hudson two years.

Chase Headley is a durable, good fielding third baseman with some pop. The Padres were expecting more in terms of power, average and on base skills given his production in the minors and his status as a 2nd round pick.

Headley hit 12 homers last season, had a .264 average and .327 on base. He struck out 139 times and stole 17 bases. He's a cog in the machine of a good lineup. Therein lies the problem the Padres have.

Jason Bartlett had his career year at the plate in 2009 and fell back into the punch-and-judy hitter he's been in every other season. Bartlett batted .254 with a .324 on base and 11 stolen bases. This is in comparison to 2009 when he hit 14 homers, batted .320, had a .389 on base and 30 stolen bases. In fairness, he had a hamstring problem last year that hindered his running.

Bartlett is an average defensive shortstop and isn't much of a solution to the Padres offenseive issues either.

Ryan Ludwick was acquired at mid-season in a three-team deal with the Cardinals and Indians in which Jake Westbrook went to the Cardinals and the Padres surrendered a couple of minor leaguers. Ludwick was intended to be lineup protection for Adrian Gonzalez, but wasn't. Not the same hitter since his breakout year in 2008 when he hit 37 homers, Ludwick has fallen into a hard mediocrity at best. With the Padres, he batted .211 with 6 homers in 59 games. He's not a good defensive outfielder and shifts from right field to left.

Cameron Maybin was acquired from the Marlins for relievers Ryan Webb and Edward Mujica. Maybin has been something of a bust since his arrival in the big leagues with the Tigers amid much fanfare and hype in 2007 at age 20. He's still only 23 and has a lot of talent; he's very raw and is like a colt learning to utilize his gifts. The routes he takes defensively are haphazard; he's still learning to run the bases; he has some pop, but strikes out too much. He's going to be a good player, but it might not be until he's in his mid-late-20s.

Will Venable is slated to take over in right field. Venable has some power (13 homers in 445 plate appearances), and speed with 29 stolen bases. He's an average defensive right fielder and batted .245 with a .324 on base last season.

BENCH:

Kyle Blanks started the season as the regular left fielder and didn't hit. Blanks has dominating size and talent. Surprisingly, the 6'6", 270 pound Blanks was a decent outfielder; but his home will be first base. Blanks got off to a slow start, but an elbow injury hindered him until he required surgery. In 120 plate appearances, he batted .157 with 3 homers, but that's too small a sample to judge him. He's put up big power/on base numbers at every level in the minors and he might wind up as the starting first baseman this year; this would move Hawpe to the outfield.

I keep saying how much I like Everth Cabrera's movements as a player, but he was horrible last year after an impressive rookie season in 2009. The 24-year-old switch-hitter batted .208 in 76 games and did nothing offensively. Defensively he's better at second base than he is at shortstop.

Veteran slugger Jorge Cantu signed a 1-year contract to backup at first and third base. Cantu has had a strange career in that he'll fall off the planet in his production as he did with the Rays who dumped him to the Reds; he was there briefly and they dispatched him as well; then he went to the Marlins on a minor league deal, won a job and had 70 extra base hits that year; the following season, he drove in 100 runs; and last year, he was providing decent pop for the Marlins when they traded him to the Rangers. He didn't hit at all for the Rangers in 105 plate appearances.

Cantu is relentless in a big spot however; he keeps fighting in his at bats until he walks, bloops a single somewhere or homers. He's a good backup for the Padres and might see significant playing time.

Former Mariners catching prospect Rob Johnson was acquired for a player to be named later. I wouldn't be surprised if the Padres get a look at Johnson and make *him* the player to be named later a la Hobie Landrith.

Johnson can catch, but he can't hit; he has a decent eye at the plate.

Chris Denorfia is a right-handed hitting outfielder who batted .271 with a .335 on base in 317 plate appearances. He has some power with 9 homers and 15 doubles and stole 8 bases in 12 tries.

Outfielder Aaron Cunningham batted .288 with a .331 on base in 147 plate appearances. He can play all three outfield positions and has shown 15 homer power and speed in the minors. He's 24.

Eric Patterson was the one big league player acquired in the Gonzalez trade. He can play second base and all three outfield positions. The 28-year-old is a .224 career hitter in parts of four seasons with the Cubs, A's and Red Sox. He has speed and has shown pop in the minors.

PREDICTION:

The team that won 90 games based on their strong top-to-bottom pitching and an offense led by Adrian Gonzalez has to face these facts: they've downgraded the rotation with the departures of Garland and Correia and are relying on the questionable Stauffer and LeBlanc and comebacking Harang; the bullpen may not be as good as it was last season with the trades of Webb and Mujica; the lineup is horrific; and the outfield defense is shaky.

Let's say hypothetically that the pitching is as strong as it was last season—a stretch—how many runs are they going to score? Bartlett can't hit; Hudson is okay, but not a hitter to be concerned about;

Ludwick has been terrible and getting worse; Maybin is a raw talent; Headley is a cog; Hawpe is a cog; Hundley doesn't hit.

Unless Blanks wins a job and mashes in the middle of the lineup, where's the power? Someone who can drive in a few runs by himself?

They don't have anyone. They're reliant on the pitching and defense and the defense is not going to be particularly good either.

They won 90 games last season because of that pitching and Gonzalez.

Gonzalez is gone and the pitching is worse.

The Padres are going to have a major fallback from their playoff near-miss to also-ran status, will trade Bell and bring up some of the youngsters they acquired in the Gonzalez deal to see what they have. It's not a rebuild, but I think even Hoyer and owner Jeff Moorad were surprised that they came so far so fast; in the long run, it might even have been a detriment because it raised expectations before the team was truly ready to take the next step.

That will be evident very quickly this season.

PREDICTED RECORD: 78-84

Arizona Diamondbacks

2010 Record: 65-97, 5th place, National League West.

2010 Recap:

For reasons I couldn't understand, the Diamondbacks were a trendy pick to contend last season.

I didn't see it that way.

And I was right.

They had hitters who hit the ball out of the park, but struck out so much that the wind power from their swinging and missing could've provided cheap power for all of Arizona. Their starting rotation was short; their bullpen horrible; their manager an inexperienced neophyte saddled with the implication that he was a stooge for the front office; and the entire team came apart not long into the season.

GM Josh Byrnes and manager A.J. Hinch were fired; pitchers Edwin Jackson and Dan Haren were traded; and Brandon Webb missed the entire season with shoulder woes.

They ended up in last place because they were awful.

2011 ADDITIONS:

GM Kevin Towers was hired.
RHP J.J. Putz signed a 2-year, $10 million contract with 2013 club option.
LHP Zach Duke was acquired from the Pittsburgh Pirates.
RHP Armando Galarraga was acquired from the Detroit Tigers.

INF/OF Melvin Mora signed a 1-year, $2 million contract.
OF/1B Xavier Nady signed a 1-year, $1.75 million contract.
INF Geoff Blum signed a 2-year, $2.7 million contract.
C Henry Blanco signed a 1-year, $1.25 million contract with 2012 mutual option.
INF Willie Bloomquist signed a 1-year, $900,000 contract with 2012 mutual option.
RHP David Hernandez was acquired from the Baltimore Orioles.
RHP Kam Mickolio was acquired from the Baltimore Orioles.
RHP Micah Owings signed a minor league contract.
INF Cody Ransom signed a minor league contract.

2011 SUBTRACTIONS:

Interim GM Jerry DiPoto was not retained.
1B Adam LaRoche was not re-signed.
3B Mark Reynolds was traded to the Baltimore Orioles.
INF Augie Ojeda was not re-signed.
RHP Rodrigo Lopez was not re-signed.
INF Bobby Crosby was released.
OF Ryan Church was non-tendered.
RHP D.J. Carrasco was not re-signed.
RHP Blaine Boyer was not re-signed.
RHP Kris Benson retired.

2011 PROJECTED STARTING ROTATION: Joe Saunders; Ian Kennedy; Daniel Hudson; Barry Enright; Zach Duke; Armando Galarraga.

2011 PROJECTED BULLPEN: J.J. Putz; Sam Demel; Juan Gutierrez; Aaron Heilman; David Hernandez; Kam Mickolio; Esmerling Vasquez; Jordan Norberto; Carlos Rosa; Micah Owings.

2011 PROJECTED LINEUP: C-Miguel Montero; 1B-Juan Miranda; 2B-Kelly Johnson; 3B-Melvin Mora; SS-Stephen Drew; LF-Xavier Nady; CF-Chris Young; RF-Justin Upton.

2011 BENCH: OF-Gerardo Parra; INF-Geoff Blum; INF-Willie Bloomquist; INF/OF-Ryan Roberts; C-Henry Blanco; INF-Tony Abreu; 1B-Brandon Allen; OF-Cole Gillespie.

2011 POSSIBLE CONTRIBUTORS: RHP-Kevin Mulvey; LHP-Zach Kroenke; C-John Hester; RHP-Yonata Ortega; INF-Cody Ransom.

ASSESSMENTS
MANAGEMENT:

For all of last season Kevin Towers was the fair-haired, newly single girl at the ball whom everyone wanted to date and/or marry.

After being surprisingly fired by the Padres after 14 years, every GM job that had even the slightest chance of coming had Towers at the top of the list of desired names to take over.

Towers spent last season as an assistant to Yankees GM Brian Cashman and waited for the right opportunity. His name popped up as a replacement for Omar Minaya with the Mets and Jerry DiPoto/ Josh Byrnes with the Diamondbacks.

Interestingly, Towers was the frontrunner for the D-Backs job when Byrnes was hired; he's been given permission by then Padres CEO Sandy Alderson to interview and presumably take the job if it were offered; it was a subtle kick out the door. The problem was that the D-Backs chose to hire Byrnes which led to Towers going back to San Diego and living under the Alderson dictatorship and go-along to get-along.

Towers is mistakenly beloved by many so-called "experts" because he's done more with less money.

Objectively, he's made some brilliant moves (getting Adrian Gonzalez and Chris Young for Adam Eaton and Akinori Otsuka is one of the best trades in baseball history); and he's done some incredibly stupid things like claiming Randy Myers on waivers in 1998 to keep him away from the Braves. Two problems: the Braves didn't want Myers and weren't going to claim him; and when Towers claimed Myers, the Blue Jays said, "here, take him" leaving the Padres on the hook for the $12 million left on Myers's contract.

He was almost fired for the transgression.

Now Towers is with the Diamondbacks and he's making his Towers-like maneuvers in signing cheap, available players to fill holes. He traded the strikeout king Mark Reynolds and signed a load of journeymen. He kept Kirk Gibson as manager and entertained offers for 23-year-old right fielder and potential star Justin Upton, ultimately deciding to keep him.

He's a pretty good GM; makes some good moves; makes some bad moves. But it's only when an executive is in the arena that he can truly be evaluated. Standing on the side and waiting for the job offers to roll in is one thing; doing the job is another. And Towers isn't as brilliant as some suggest he is.

Towers received an interestingly short 2-year guaranteed contract with club options for 2016.

Kirk Gibson took over as manager for the fired A.J. Hinch and after Towers was hired, Gibson was retained.

One of the toughest individuals I've ever seen when he was a player, Gibson brought a football mentality onto the diamond and that was to his detriment as injuries were the continuous result of that style of play. The Diamondbacks had similar records for Gibson (34-49) and Hinch (31-48), but they were managing two different teams. Gibson was dealing with the departures of Edwin Jackson and Dan Haren and a look to the future; Hinch was trying to win to save his job.

Gibson has more credibility with the players than Hinch because he's so fiery where Hinch was cerebral. That Gibson was a superstar player with the hardware (1988 NL MVP), baseball-related heroism (the big homer in the 1984 World Series off Goose Gossage; and the historic, one-legged homer off of Dennis Eckersley to win game 1 of the 1988 World Series); along with the hard as nails persona gives him cachet.

He's learning on the fly as a manager, but if one player decides not to hustle, he's not going to want to be in the vicinity of the manager who still has his temper and is still intimidating enough to make them lose control of their bowels with little more than a glare.

STARTING PITCHING:

Lefty Joe Saunders was acquired at mid-season in the trade that sent Dan Haren to the Angels.

Saunders has a decent fastball, a curve, slider and changeup. He's a pure contact pitcher who allows a lot of hits and home runs and must have a solid defense behind him to succeed. With a friendly park for hitters, Saunders is, at best a .500 pitcher. The best the Diamondbacks can hope for is around a ERA of 4 and gobbled innings. That's not what you want from the pitcher who's supposed to be your veteran anchor and for whom you traded one of the best pitchers in baseball, Haren.

The key to that trade was the youngsters the Diamondbacks got from the Angels, but they're in the low minors and what they have to show for the deal now is Saunders.

Ian Kennedy showed the results that his hype and mouth indicated was possible with the Yankees. Having washed out in the Bronx because of his inability to throw strikes; to listen; to do his talking on the field, Kennedy was traded to the Diamondbacks. He started slowly, but by May got into a groove where he was a very good pitcher for the rest of the season. Kennedy still has trouble with his command, still appears to think too much on the mound, but his body language was better and in Arizona, there are fewer reporters for him to explain the foundation of the art of pitching according to Ian Kennedy. For him to be a reliable starter, Kennedy is going to have to cut down on the number of pitches he throws; too often, he was around 100 pitches by the sixth inning, limiting how far he could be pushed. Considering how poorly he was perceived in the Yankees clubhouse by the time he was dealt, he took a gigantic step forward in 2010.

Daniel Hudson is the former top pitching prospect for the White Sox and was acquired in the trade that sent Edwin Jackson to Chicago. If the jury is out on the Saunders trade, then the Hudson trade made up for it and paid immediate dividends for interim GM Jerry DiPoto.

Hudson was brilliant after joining the Diamondbacks. The 24-year-old righty went 7-1 with a 1.69 ERA in 11 starts; he pitched 79 innings, allowed 51 hits, walked 16, struck out 70. He allowed 7 homers. He's put up huge strikeout numbers at every level with a fastball, good changeup and slider. He's going to be a top-of-the-rotation starter and an All Star.

Barry Enright is a 25-year-old righty who was a Diamondbacks 2nd round pick in 2007. He has the full arsenal with a decent fastball, curve, slider and changeup. Enright went 6-7 in 17 starts as a rookie; he allowed 20 homers in 99 innings, walked 29 and struck out 49.

If Enright's not getting his secondary pitches over or spotting his fastball, he gets hit very, very hard. He needs his defense to make plays behind him.

Zach Duke was acquired from the Pirates. The veteran lefty has had a checkered and star-crossed career with the Pirates. First he was the "next superstar" because of a hot second half in 2005; then reality (and playing for the Pirates) dragged him back into orbit and beyond. Duke has had good years; he's had bad years—all masked by the morass that is the Pirates organization. He gives up a lot of hits and doesn't strike anyone out, but he throws strikes. Duke's had some injury problems, but as a back-of-the-rotation starter, you could do worse. It will be interesting to see how he does in a different uniform with a more coherent plan. Or *a* plan.

Almost perfect Armando Galarraga was acquired from the Detroit Tigers.

The journeyman has had a strange career. He didn't make it to the big leagues to stay until he was 26, had a terrific season in 2008 for the Tigers, then fell back into the mediocrity that defined his minor league career prior to that year.

It's probably because this is what he is. He's a long reliever/spot starter/Triple A filler on a good team; a back-of-the-rotation starter on a bad team. Galarraga almost made history and my argument is that he'll be remembered *more* for umpire Jim Joyce's blown call with 2 outs in the ninth inning of his perfect game try and the resulting media frenzy.

As a swingman, he's a useful arm to have around.

BULLPEN:

Veteran reliever J.J. Putz was signed to a 2-year deal after spending 2010 as the White Sox set-up man. The oft-injured Putz missed time with a knee injury last season, but when he pitched, he was effective. He has a blow away fastball and vicious split-finger to rack up strikeouts. In 54 innings for the White Sox, he allowed 41 hits and struck out 65. He's due to have a good season for the Diamondbacks and accumulate some saves.

Sam Demel is a righty with a big fastball. In 37 innings last season, he struck out 33 and walked 12; he allowed 5 homers among the 42 hits he allowed—both numbers too high for a short reliever. The 25-year-old has closed successfully in the minors.

Juan Gutierrez receieved a chance to close as the Diamondbacks bullpen repeatedly imploded and he wasn't much better than the prior closers Chad Qualls and Aaron Heilman. He saved 15 games, but allowed 13 homers in 56 innings and walked 23 while striking out 47. He's better off as a set-up man.

Aaron Heilman would clearly prefer to be a starting pitcher after his struggles in the bullpen with the Mets, Cubs and Diamondbacks. He allows a lot of homers, loses the strike zone, doesn't strike out enough hitters and bottom-line hates being in the bullpen.

There was talk that Heilman was going to get a shot in the starting rotation, but even if he does, the Diamondbacks are deep with starting pitchers who are better than Heilman would likely be in the role, specifically Galarraga. He's going to be in the bullpen and, truth be told, he's not that bad. It's only his high profile gacks that stick in people's memories; there are relievers with worse stuff and better success than Aaron Heilman.

David Hernandez was acquired from the Orioles in the trade that sent Mark Reynolds to Baltimore. Hernandez has a good fastball and potential as a reliever, but his command is all over the place. He started 19 games as a rookie in 2009 and 8 in 2010, but his home is in the bullpen; he needs to get the ball over the plate. Striking out 72 in 79 innings? Good. Walking 42 and allowing 9 homers? Not good.

Kam Mickolio was also acquired in the Reynolds deal. Mickolio is 6'9" and weighs 255 pounds, has struggled with his control, but has piled up the strikeouts in the minors.

Esmerling Vasquez is a 27-year-old righty with a tough motion for righties, a moving fastball and changeup. He's very wild and strikes out over a batter per inning. His numbers have been far better vs lefties than righties, but if he's ever able to throw strikes consistently, he can have use against hitters from both sides of the plate.

Jordan Norberto is a lefty specialist who has trouble throwing strikes. He has a power fastball that could dominate if he could control it. He appeared in 33 games and pitched 20 innings, walked 22 and struck out 15. A reliever who can't throw strikes is worthless to me.

Carlos Rosa is a 26-year-old righty who has a good fastball and, guess what, has trouble throwing strikes. Last season, in 22 games and 20 innings, Rosa walked 12, struck out 9 and allowed 20 hits. He's shown potential as a reliever in the minors.

Micah Owings was signed to a minor league contract. Owings started his promising career with the Diamondbacks and has struggled since a solid first half of the season in 2007. He was traded to the Reds in 2008 for Adam Dunn and has been injury-prone and ineffective on the mound. He can still hit though. Owings has potential as both a pitcher and hitter and I'm hesitant to give up on him. Maybe he can make it as a reliever/pinch-hitter. I have hope.

LINEUP:

Miguel Montero missed a large portion of the season with a knee injury. He's a good defensive catcher with a strong arm and pop at the plate. He's been bad against lefties, but perhaps he should get a chance to win the everyday job once and for all. If he plays regularly, he's good for 50 extra base hits along with his good defense.

Juan Miranda is a former Yankees prospect from Cuba who will get a legitimate shot to win the first base job for the Diamondbacks. Miranda is listed at 28, but who knows how old he is? Miranda's shown good power/average/on base skills in the minors and is an adequate defensive first baseman.

Kelly Johnson had a fine offensive year after an injury-plagued 2009 with the Braves which led to him being non-tendered. Johnson had 26 homers, 36 doubles and 5 triples with a .284 average and .370 on base. He stole 13 bases and his defense was solid.

Melvin Mora was signed to a 1-year contract to replace the traded human strikeout machine Mark Reynolds. Mora is 39, but he's still a good fundamental player. He doesn't strike out; hits the occasional homer; plays adequate defense in the infield and outfield and is a good example of how to behave for the younger players.

Stephen Drew is one of the better all-around shortstops in baseball and doesn't get the recognition he deserves. He batted .278 with a .352 on base, 15 homers, 33 doubles, 12 triples and 10 stolen bases. Drew's entering his prime at age 28.

Xavier Nady is another oft-injured player trying to rejuvenate his career with the Diamondbacks. Nady has had maladies to just about every part of his body ruining what was a very productive player. Nady played semi-regularly with the Cubs last season and in 347 plate appearances batted .256 with a .306 on base, 6 homers and 13 doubles. What the 32-year-old has left is the question and the Diamondbacks have the spots in the outfield and first base to give him signifcant at bats and see if he can recover.

Chris Young had a solid year after a gradual decline from 2007-2009 left his future in question. He raised his batting average 45 points to .257; hit 27 homers, 33 doubles and stole 28 bases. He's a good center fielder and walks a fair amount. He strikes out a lot.

Justin Upton is one of the most dynamic young players in all of baseball and a potential future MVP candidate at age 23. The Diamondbacks put the word out after Towers took over that they'd listen to offers on Upton and the price was too steep for the blood of everyone to make a deal. Upton is signed through 2015, owed over $50 million.

Upton only played in 133 games because of a left shoulder injury. He hit 17 homers, 27 doubles and 3 triples; batted .273 with a .356 on base. Like most of the Diamondbacks hitters, he strikes out a lot. He stole 18 bases. He's a megastar talent.

BENCH:

Gerardo Parra is a lefty-swinging 24-year-old outfielder with good defensive skills. In 393 plate appearances in 2010, he batted .261 with a .308 on base; he had 19 doubles, 6 triples and 3 homers. He's got the speed to steal a few bases.

Veteran switch-hitting utilityman Geoff Blum signed a 2-year contract. Blum can play anywhere and has shown some pop in his bat in his career. He'll get his share of at bats at various positions.

Willie Bloomquist is essentially the same player as Blum except he doesn't hit for any power. He can steal a base or two, but doesn't do much of anything to help a team.

Ryan Roberts is also a utilityman. In 2009, Roberts played semi-regularly and had a good year at the plate with a .279 average and a .367 on base. He wound up back in the minors last season and batted .197 in 36 games for the Diamondbacks.

Henry Blanco signed a 1-year contract to backup/share the catching duties with Montero. Blanco's a good clubhouse man who still has a great arm; he's good with the pitchers. He'll play against the tough lefties.

Tony Abreu is another utility infielder who batted .233 in 201 plate appearances. He's a switch hitter and can play second, third and short; third is his best defensive position.

Brandon Allen is a power-hitting first base prospect with good average/on base skills. Allen hit 25 homers and had a .405 on base percentage at Triple A Reno last season. With the Diamondbacks, he batted .267 with a .393 on base in 56 plate appearances. He might get a chance to win the everyday job this season; he's 25 and bats left-handed.

Cole Gillespie is a 26-year-old right-handed hitting outfielder who's shown some speed and on base ability in the minors. He can play all three outfield positions.

PREDICTION:

The Diamondbacks front office has been afflicted with baseball dyslexia. They have a load of hitters who strike out a lot; and pitchers who walk a lot of hitters.

That doesn't work.

The swing for the fences style hasn't succeeded in the past few seasons because their hitters strike out a lot and simply don't hit enough home runs to make it worthwhile. One of the biggest culprits in that "strategy"—Mark Reynolds—was traded; they're retooling under Towers and looking for the similar bargains that he found while with the Padres. No reasonably intelligent baseball mind can believe they're going to get anything from Nady; the expectations for Miranda should be muted; Mora is a good veteran player, but his contribution will be negligible.

The starting pitching has great potential with Hudson, Enright and the improving Kennedy; Saunders is a cog in the machine; Duke and Galarraga are rotation filler.

The bullpen will be better only because it can't be any worse and they have a solid, veteran closer in Putz.

Towers has a long way to go in getting the Diamondbacks to respectability again and they're in a nightmarish division. There won't be the rampant chaos that surrounded the club last season with the inexperienced Hinch and the firings; Gibson is still learning on the job, but he'll teach the young players to play with intensity and a sense of urgency.

They'll be better than they were last year, but it will barely show up in the standings.

PREDICTED RECORD: 68-94

NATIONAL LEAGUE PLAYOFF PREDICTIONS

NLDS:

St. Louis Cardinals vs Philadelphia Phillies

Phillies in 3.

NLDS:

Atlanta Braves vs Los Angeles Dodgers

Dodgers in 4.

NLCS:

Los Angeles Dodgers vs Philadelphia Phillies

Phillies in 7.

NATIONAL LEAGUE CHAMPIONS:

PHILADELPHIA PHILLIES

NATIONAL LEAGUE AWARD WINNERS

Most Valuable Player: Albert Pujols, St. Louis Cardinals

Cy Young Award: Cliff Lee, Philadelphia Phillies

Rookie of the Year: Kenley Jansen, Los Angeles Dodgers.

Manager of the Year: Don Mattingly, Los Angeles Dodgers

2011 WORLD SERIES PREDICTION:

Boston Red Sox vs Philadelphia Phillies

Phillies in 6.

WORLD SERIES CHAMPIONS: PHILADELPHIA PHILLIES